LABOR

IN A GLOBAL ECONOMY

Perspectives from the U.S. and Canada

Steven Hecker
Margaret Hallock
editors

University of Oregon Books
Labor Education and Research Center
University of Oregon

D1088200

Library of Congress Catalog Card No.
91-24239

International Standard Book No.
0-87114-153-1

Labor Education and Research Center
University of Oregon
Eugene OR 97403
(503) 346-5054

Contents

Foreword and Acknowledgements

A phrase that was often heard to describe the situation of U.S. labor unions in the 1980s was "crisis and opportunity." This duality, borrowed from the Chinese, often has seemed unduly weighted to the crisis side. The U.S.-Canadian "Labor in a Global Economy" conference did not flinch from the crisis, but had as its intention the opening of a dialogue across borders on the opportunities and strategies for labor in a period of rapid global change. It has been gratifying in the months since the conference to see the rapid expansion of this dialogue, spurred both by external events such as the North American free trade negotiations and by the recognition within the union and labor relations communities of the U.S. and Canada that such discussions are essential in confronting globalization and economic restructuring.

International conferences are challenging to organize, even when the parties share a common language and a common border. There are many organizations and individuals who contributed to making the conference and this volume a reality. Our first thanks must go to the British Columbia Federation of Labour and its president, Ken Georgetti. Without their enthusiastic response to our concept of a U.S.-Canadian labor gathering, none of this would have happened. Their continued support throughout the planning process and the conference itself, especially the work of Joy MacPhail, was indispensable.

This is not to slight the contributions of the U.S. cosponsors—the Oregon AFL-CIO, Washington State Labor Council, and the University of Oregon Canadian Studies Committee—all of whom saw the value of the project and supported it with staff, advice, and funds. The University of Oregon Office of International Affairs, headed by Vice-Provost Kathleen Bowman, embraced this effort as part of the university's growing focus on international studies.

The conference and this publication received major funding from the Canadian Embassy through the Canadian Studies Conference Grant program of the Academic Relations Office and from the Canadian Labour Market and Productivity Centre (CLMPC). Consul Richard Seaborn of the Canadian Consulate in Seattle was extremely helpful in guiding us through the application process. Maryantonett Flumian, executive director of the CLMPC, made substantive as well as financial contributions to the project.

Many other groups also assisted financially. These include the Association of Western Pulp and Paper Workers, International Woodworkers of America-U.S., Oregon Education Association, Oregon Federation of Teachers, Oregon Nurses Association, Oregon Public Employees Union (SEIU), United Steelworkers of America, and the Northwest Policy Center of the University of Washington.

In addition, we could not have succeeded without the support of the organizations that contributed the time and travel expenses of many of our speakers.

Thanks are due to the members of the conference planning committee for their time, ideas, and legwork in recruiting speakers and participants. These include Ken Georgetti, Joy MacPhail, and John Weir of the BC Federation of Labour, Ross Rieder of the Pacific Northwest Labor History Association, David Rice of the Canadian Labour Congress, and Jeff Johnson of the Washington State Labor Council.

As always, we are indebted to those at the University of Oregon who did much of the detail work on the conference and this volume. Susan Reno coordinated communications with authors and kept confusion to a minimum by tracking manuscripts through their many trips across the campus and the continent. Norma Sax managed registration and the flow of materials before, during and after the conference. Barbara Oppliger took floppy disks of all descriptions and did the computer translations, typing, and revisions of manuscripts. Copy editing was performed by Lori Howard and layout and design by Connie Morehouse.

Finally, we must thank the 250 speakers and participants who turned the conference from an agenda on paper into a true learning experience. While the focus was on North America, participants came from as far away as Singapore, Taiwan, New Zealand, and Australia, reinforcing the global theme and making it real to all of us.

Steven Hecker
Margaret Hallock
April, 1991

Introduction: Labor in a Global Economy

STEVEN HECKER
Associate Professor, University of Oregon Labor Education and Research Center

MARGARET HALLOCK
Professor and Director, University of Oregon Labor Education and Research Center

"The hands that will repair the damage of recent decades must be visible ones."

—Robert Kuttner, *The End of Laissez-Faire: National Purpose and the Global Economy After the Cold War*

The economy confronting labor movements in the twenty-first century will be vastly different from the one which spawned these movements. International capital mobility, technological change, and the communications revolution have created a global economy in which individual nation states and, in turn, the labor organizations in these nations, have less influence and control over economic events. Unions in all countries know that they must understand, respond to, and shape global economic forces in order to continue to have a voice in the workplace and in public policy within their own national borders.

The U.S.-Canadian "Labor in a Global Economy" conference convened in September, 1990, in the midst of events and trends that illustrate the relationship between global economic forces and national labor movements. For example, the U.S.-Canada Free Trade Agreement (FTA) was the central issue of the 1988 Canadian federal elections. Canadian labor led the opposition, yet the agreement generated little interest in U.S. labor circles. In contrast, the announcement in June, 1990, by U.S. President George Bush and Mexican President Carlos Salinas de Gortari that they would embark on "fast track" negotiations for a similar U.S.-Mexico agreement, provoked quick and forceful reactions by both U.S. and Canadian labor unions. These negotiations now involve Canada as well as the U.S. and Mexico, and labor and other interests are mobilizing for a battle.

Meanwhile, the nations of Western Europe are quickly approaching the 1992 target for a united European market, and the European labor movements are actively negotiating the "social dimension" of that integration, including standards for the workplace, the labor market, and social programs.

The logic of a binational U.S.-Canadian conference within this larger global context is dictated by several factors. Despite the numerous international unions whose memberships span the border, contacts between Canadian and U.S. unions have been infrequent, particularly regarding strategy and strategic planning. The precipitous decline of union membership in the U.S. compared with the relative strength of Canadian unions has caused American trade unionists to pay increasing attention to the Canadian system of industrial relations. Similarly, the crisis in the U.S. health care system, manifest in the human tragedy of inadequate access to care and in collective bargaining gridlock and strife over health care benefits, also focuses attention on Canada and its system of universal health care.

Both the U.S. and Canadian economies have experienced substantial change in the past decade. The Reagan era in the U.S. brought a free market ideology and concession bargaining. Canadian unions have maintained stronger contracts and membership, but they also face market-oriented public policies and the "new industrial relations." Canadian unionists are wary about the downward pressure the FTA will exert on wages, working conditions, and labor relations practices.

The prospect of a "North American Accord" including Mexico raises anew the issue of a social charter as a central component of international trade agreements. Like the Europe 1992 document, such a charter would address questions of labor standards and conditions, environmental and health protection, and labor market policies in the context of the free flow of goods and services. Such questions are largely unexplored territory, virtually unprecedented in previous General Agreement on Tariffs and Trade (GATT) negotiations, but they are suddenly appearing on the trade negotiating table with some frequency (Farnsworth, 1991).

The articles in this volume represent an effort to address the impact of economic globalization on labor unions and labor relations in Canada and the U.S. The effects are felt internally in each nation, in relations between the countries, and in the larger global context. Some of these effects, and some of our topics, such as international labor standards and flexibility and labor market policy, are directly tied to the increasing international mobility of capital. Others, such as health care and privatization, are related in more indirect, but no less important, ways.

In the following section we briefly review the implications of globalization for the Canadian and U.S. economies. We then summarize the major themes of U.S.-Canadian comparative industrial relations research. Finally, we address the strategic options for Canadian and U.S. labor as they are presented in this volume.

THE CHALLENGES OF GLOBALIZATION

That we are living in an era of global economic integration is undeniable. Its features include the globalization of markets for products, services, and labor made possible, in part, by dramatic technological change, especially in communications and knowledge-intensive production technologies (Marshall, section one; Dorman, section three). Internationalization has led to intensified competition among firms and especially the expansion of transnational corporations, whose fortunes and interests transcend national boundaries. Export-oriented strategies predominate among both businesses and governments, and movements toward regional economic integration are a very visible part of the pattern of internationalization.

There is a powerful momentum behind economic globalization, to the point of widespread acceptance that it is an inevitable and irreversible trend, a view shared by many observers on the right, center, and left of the political spectrum. While there are dissenters from this view (Donohue, section three; Payer, 1991), even these recognize that the mobility of capital, the influence of transnational enterprises, and national governments friendly to their interests pose enormous challenges to labor movements. These movements are based on the economic climate and policies of the first half of this century, in which unions were successful to varying degrees in "taking wages out of competition," in concert with the national oligopolies with which they negotiated. Marshall (section one) details the erosion of this system and the changing "rules" for countries, enterprises, and unions.

The manifestations of globalization and competition in the U.S. and Canadian economies, public policies, and industrial relations systems are by now familiar. Both nations have experienced significant declines in manufacturing jobs and concurrent growth in service, financial, and information sectors. Increased capital mobility is reflected both in greater levels of foreign investment in the U.S. and Canada and in the relocation of corporate operations to other countries, often in the Third World. The composition of the work force in both countries is changing dramatically. Women represent an increasing percentage of the work force as do minorities and immigrant workers. The drive for increased flexibility

3

on the part of businesses and the governments of the U.S. and Canada prompts deregulation and privatization and manifests itself in an increasingly part-time and contingent work force. At the workplace, innovations in work organization and work rules, job classification systems, and traditional labor management relationships have accompanied the transition to a global economy.

INDUSTRIAL RELATIONS IN CANADA AND THE U.S.

The most often cited statistic in any comparative discussion of labor in Canada and the U.S. is the striking divergence in union density in the past twenty-five years. From a high point of about 35 percent in both countries in 1954, density began to fall. However, in 1964 a pattern of divergence began that has continued to the present. Canadian density increased, peaking above 40 percent in the early 1980s, while U.S. density has declined almost continuously to the present day. Density in Canada has begun to fall in recent years, but in 1989 it was still about 37 percent compared with 17 percent in the United States. (Meltz, 1990).

Explaining this divergence has become a major area of research in North American industrial relations. The explanations fall into the following major categories:
- Differences in public policy and labor laws;
- Different levels of employer resistance and union avoidance behavior;
- Differences in societal and cultural values and public opinion regarding unions;
- Structural changes in the economies of the U.S. and Canada; and
- Union organizing strategies.

While there is some evidence for all of these explanations, and they are by no means mutually exclusive, they are not equally plausible. Bruce (1989) makes a strong case that differences in political institutions in Canada and the U.S. have led to public policies and legislation favorable to union organization and certification in Canada. These differences include the active presence of a social democratic party, the New Democratic Party, at the federal level and in many provinces. (The Parti Quebecois, another party with strong union ties, plays a similar role in regard to labor issues in Quebec [Meltz, 1990]). There are also much smaller regional differences in legislation and union density in Canada than in the U.S., so that Canada does not have "right to work" provinces or a largely nonunion internal region like the U.S. sunbelt, where companies can escape unions.

Canadian labor law is largely provincially based, but there are a number of provisions prevalent in most jurisdictions that are particularly favorable to union organizing success. These include card check certification, found in eight of ten provinces and the federal sector, and first contract arbitration, found in five provinces. That these types of provisions have been central to (failed) U.S. labor law reform efforts over the past three decades demonstrates that their importance has not been lost on the U.S. labor movement.

However, one must be careful not to confuse cause and effect in discussing political structures, cultural values, union density, superior labor laws and enforcement, and less overt management opposition to unions in Canada. This is especially true in seeking lessons for U.S. unions from the Canadian experience. The extent to which "simple" changes in U.S. labor law, based on Canadian precedents, could significantly improve the success of union organizing, is enmeshed with these other factors. Huxley et al. (1986) ask if "Canada's experience is especially instructive" to the U.S. situation. They maintain that Canada's favorable policies are tied to the more adversarial and political nature of its unionism, and especially to the ties between unions and the New Democratic Party in English Canada and the electoral left in Quebec. They conclude:

In view of the differences between the two political cultures and institutional frameworks, and . . . in some major social values, as well, it is not clear whether the Canadian experience can be of much help to American unionists and others who are troubled by the decline of American unionism (p. 132).

Until recently the main point of these discussions has concerned the lessons U.S. unions might learn from Canada. Currently, attention is turned more to the global economic context and whether the pronounced differences of the past may disappear in a convergence that would have been unthinkable ten years ago (Morand, 1990). Globalization in general, and the U.S.-Canada Free Trade Agreement in particular, force us to examine whether the Canadian labor movement will be facing pressures of a kind and degree that U.S. unions have been dealing with since the beginning of the Reagan presidency.

That Canadian unions will face external and internal pressures from global competition, technological change, and Canadian corporations themselves is not in question. The FTA has already led to direct challenges from plant closures and job losses and pressures for harmonization and the "level playing field" which often translate into a reduced social wage for Canadian workers (Barrett, 1990). A North America free trade accord including Mexico will increase these pressures. Verma and Kochan (1990), however, argue that from the perspective of strategic choice, Canadian industrial relations need not follow the U.S. path of adjustment and turmoil. Whether it does "will ultimately depend on the strategic choices made by labor, management, and government policy makers" (p.602), all of whom retain considerable elbow room for making choices. What the U.S. lesson offers Canadians, they contend, is a suggestion of the likely consequences of alternative strategic responses. Union strength in collective bargaining and politics gives Canadian labor leaders greater influence on the process of industrial relations innovation than their American counterparts. The danger, they assert, is leaders using this strength to maintain traditional labor and management roles, resist innovation, and ultimately contribute to capital flight away from unionized firms and sectors, thereby realizing "labor's worst fears over the effects of the Free Trade Agreement" (p.604).

This formulation of the present critical juncture for labor in the U.S. and Canada is, of course, subject to debate, and many Canadian labor leaders would argue that maintaining their militant positions and opposing the innovations of the "new industrial relations" will better serve to keep Canadian labor strong. Such issues are at the center of the debate over labor strategy in the global economy, and to this strategic debate we now turn.

LABOR STRATEGIES FOR THE GLOBAL ECONOMY

Labor in industrialized countries like Canada and the U.S. is presently unable to "take wages out of competition." Its strategic options fall into three general categories:
1. Restrict the mobility of capital so that it cannot shop for cheaper labor in developing countries or lower-wage industrial nations.
2. Raise the cost of doing business in other nations through international organizing, international labor standards, and multinational bargaining campaigns.
3. Accept the mobility of capital, choose to compete in the world economy on some basis other than wages—for example, a "high-wage/high-performance" industrial policy— and deal with the adjustment side through domestic labor market policies.

These categories are not mutually exclusive, and there are examples of each approach throughout the industrialized world. Contributors to this volume offer a variety of perspectives on the feasibility and effectiveness of these strategies.

Proponents of the first approach tend to believe that the only truly effective action for labor is to restrict the freedom of capital to pursue the lowest cost of production. Other strategies, according to this school, are too reactive to globalization and accept too readily its inevitability. For example, Donohue (section three) argues convincingly that we must pay attention to plant closures and economic dislocations that affect workers where it counts—in their communities. He argues for economic analysis of the importance of domestic industries and for protecting these industries while developing an alternative economic strategy to challenge the agenda of the transnational enterprises. In a similar vein, Leo Gerard (section three) argues that unions must organize to change the terms of debate from one centered on benefits to international capital to one that focuses on the needs of workers and communities in all nations. Shirley Carr (section one) points out that labor would best be served by "managed" trade rather than free trade, and this may involve protectionist policies.

The second main strategy for labor is international cooperation in organizing and bargaining and demanding that international trade agreements include standards or conditions for the rights of workers and unions, and for social programs in the signatory nations. All of these approaches force international capital to deal with labor in both the domestic and international spheres.

Peter Dorman (section three) believes that there is no alternative to an internationalist approach, that the global economy is already highly developed and will continue to follow this path. He argues for labor standards and worker rights conditionality in trade agreements.

Larry Cohen and Fred Pomeroy (section three) present one case example of international labor cooperation in the telecommunications industry. They show how the international trade secretariats can facilitate international labor cooperation in bargaining and in community mobilization in support of bargaining. They are careful to point out, however, that such cooperation requires strong internal labor movements. Thus, organizing internally against the effects of globalization will remain a primary concern for unions. These concerns and related strategies are also discussed in section eight on organizing. The section on the forest products industry shows how global economic changes have wrought significant effects on one important regional industry. While the strategies of U.S. and Canadian unions have diverged in this industry in the past, unionists now argue that these global economic changes should be met with more coordinated labor strategies.

Several authors encourage us to focus on the link between the industrialized nations and the developing and underdeveloped nations of the Third World. Leo Gerard insists that the twin problems of debt and environmental degradation in the Third World are the problems of U.S and Canadian unionists as well. Dorman links Latin American economic performance to that of the U.S., and Donohue insists that labor in the already industrialized countries must not shift the burden of reining in multinational corporations to workers and unions in developing nations who have far fewer resources.

The third main strategy is discussed at length in this volume. There is a lively debate among unionists about shifting from a focus on the distribution of wealth to the creation of wealth. If the globalization of the economy is essentially inevitable, then it may behoove unions to make sure that their country is not in the low-wage sector. This strategy is presented by Ray Marshall (section one) and Anil Verma (section two) in the broadest sense and discussed in the papers on work flexibility and labor market training policies.

The main assumption of this strategy is that national economies and their domestic firms can compete either on the basis of wages or on the basis of product quality and responsiveness to international demand. Competing on the basis of wages inevitably leads to lower wages for everyone. The converse course is to develop high-skill, "high-performance" organizations that pay high wages. The burgeoning literature on this topic describes such an organization as one in which work requires technical skills as well as conceptual and human relations skills of design, problem solving, negotiating, and the like. The proponents of this approach argue that unions must become involved in determining the nature of work, skill acquisition, and the efficiency of production or face a future of bargaining over increasingly slim rewards.

This strategy is usually coupled with a broad domestic policy agenda that ensures that workers' interests are protected by full employment, democracy, and hearty social programs. For example, Swedish labor unions collaborate with employers at the enterprise level on issues of technological change and work design but regulate them closely at a national level. They have also established an elaborate public and universal welfare system. Max Ogden explains similar more recent developments in the Australian labor movement in section four.

This strategy is controversial among U.S. and Canadian trade unionists. Dan Marschall (section four) explains that labor-management initiatives often are fronts for antiworker and antiunion programs, and he outlines the requirements of an "authentic" flexibility or high-wage policy at the enterprise level. In section five Ted Wheelwright offers a critical view of the likely outcomes of the tripartite "Accord" through which the Australian labor movement is pursing a flexible, high-skill strategy.

Dan Swinney (section three) of the Midwest Center for Labor Research describes the evolution of that organization's program from one of reacting to plant closures and deindustrialization to a more proactive approach employing capital strategies and worker and union involvement in financial management, economic development decisions, and shop floor decision making. He argues that unions can pursue these strategies with the same integrity and the same principles as traditional labor negotiations, but this requires an educated rank and file and an organizing rather than service model of unionism.

Aspects of this debate, from strategy to tactics, run throughout the papers in this volume. However, the main debate on the broad strategic issues facing labor can be found in the first four sections.

LABOR'S ISSUES: A BATTLE WITH MANY FRONTS

The intent of the "Labor in a Global Economy" conference was to promote debate over the many strategic issues that confront labor in the 1990s in addition to the broad strategic divide described previously. The nature of the work force is changing dramatically in the industrialized world, as is the nature of work. More workers are women and minorities, and businesses increasingly rely on part-time or temporary workers, the contingent work force. Similarly, governments and businesses have used privatization as a strategy to compete and reduce costs. The challenges of representing a new work force and countering privatization are described in sections six and seven, and the challenge of organizing in a global economy is the subject of section eight. Intensified international competition, technological changes, and the ideological battle over government regulation have a clear impact on workplace conditions, including safety and health protection. These issues are discussed in articles on occupational safety and health in section nine.

Similarly, globalization has had effects on specific industries such as forest products. Articles in section ten describe the structural changes that have occurred in this industry in the past two decades and their effect on collective bargaining, particularly the erosion of the strong pattern bargaining in the Pacific Northwest United States. Unionists from the U.S. and Canada are all too keenly aware of the potentially negative effects of global economic competition in forest products and seek ways to shield workers from the most devastating of these changes.

We have also included discussions about the U.S. and Canadian health care systems (section eleven). This topic is particularly germane to U.S. and Canadian trade unionists in an era of free trade. It is well known that the U.S. health care system suffers from a dual crisis of inadequate access to care and virtually uncontrolled escalation of costs. Calls for reform are now commonplace, and many are looking to Canada's single-payer universal health care system for direction. It is critical to Canadian trade unionists that the U.S. reform its system in order to protect health care as a public good in Canada. The articles in the final section outline the crisis in the U.S. system, the principles of the Canadian system and its current controversies, and suggestions for reform.

Finally, we must elaborate at least briefly on a subject that, while mentioned by numerous authors in this collection, admittedly has not received the attention it deserves. The precarious state of the natural environment in both the industrialized and developing nations has immense implications for the world economy, for labor, and for all citizens. The search for economic growth and security in a manner that is compatible with sustaining a healthy natural environment may well be the single most important challenge facing all nations as we approach the twenty-first century. The very difficult choices and the need for creative strategies and solutions compel labor's direct and serious engagement in environmental policy making.

In this spirit the organizers of the Labor in a Global Economy conference are planning a follow-up conference on "Labor and the Global Environment," tentatively scheduled for the spring of 1992 in Vancouver, British Columbia. It is our hope that the issues and strategies presented in this volume will be expanded and pursued, and that the linkages among international trade, social and working conditions, and sustainable development will be fully explored.

REFERENCES

Barrett, Dave. "Free Trade: The Sellout." New Democratic Party, 1990.

Bruce, Peter G. "Political Parties and Labor Legislation in Canada and the U.S." *Industrial Relations*. 28(2):115–141, 1989.

Farnsworth, Clyde H. *New York Times*. "Environment Versus Freer Trade." February 11, 1991.

Huxley, Christopher, David Kettler, and James Struthers. "Is Canada's Experience 'Especially Instructive'?" In *Unions in Transition: Entering the Second Century*. Edited by S.M. Lipset. San Francisco: ICS Press, 1986.

Meltz, Noah. "Unionism in Canada, U.S.: On Parallel Treadmills." *Forum for Applied Research and Public* Policy. 5(4):46–52, 1990.

Morand, Martin J. "Convergence Yes: But At Whose Expense?" Paper presented at the Canadian Industrial Relations Association Annual Conference, Victoria, June 4, 1990.

Payer, Cheryl. "On Protectionism." *Socialism and Democracy*. 12,:105-129, 1991.

Verma, Anil, and Thomas Kochan. "Two Paths to Innovations in Industrial Relations: The Case of Canada and the United States." *Labor Law Journal*. 41(8):601–607, 1990.

Section 1

THE GLOBAL ECONOMY, FREE TRADE, AND LABOR: THE STRATEGIC CHOICES

This keynote section presents three articles that outline the broad strategic options for labor in a global economy with free trade. As discussed in the introduction, unions can adopt strategies that limit the mobility of capital, force up wages in Third-World countries, promote international labor solidarity, or focus on the nature of work and production.

Ray Marshall, former U.S. Secretary of Labor, has long stated his position that labor should have more of a voice in international trade affairs. In the following article he develops a related theme—that labor is in danger of losing its voice altogether in the U.S., and that U.S. unions should follow the example of other trade union movements by developing a concerted and explicit strategy related to global economic change. Changes in the world and domestic economies of the U.S. and Canada have destroyed the fundamental premises and conditions for traditional industrial relations systems. Labor has more difficulty in taking wages out of competition in the new economy, but it is no less important a goal. Marshall argues that labor should adopt a high-wage, high-productivity strategy in concert with advanced public policies that promote full employment, industrial democracy, worker training, and social welfare programs. Unions must make themselves indispensable in a new system of production that relies on highly skilled and trained workers and vigorous worker participation.

Shirley Carr, President of the Canadian Labour Congress (CLC), outlines three strategies that the CLC is currently following to some degree. She agrees with Marshall that unions must develop some strategy regarding productivity and competitiveness. She cautions that the autonomy of unions must be preserved in such a strategy. Second, Carr argues that there is a need for "managed" trade rather that free trade in order to preserve Canada's social programs and its domestic industries. Third, there is a need for international labor standards and international labor solidarity in organizing. As a Canadian, she is particularly concerned that standards harmonize up rather than down to the lowest common denominator as a result of free trade.

Economist Mel Watkins of the University of Toronto discusses the relationship between the Free Trade Agreement (FTA), the election victory of the New Democratic Party in Ontario in 1990, and Canada's constitutional crisis in the form of the Meech Lake Accord and Quebec separatism. His thesis is that the campaign against the FTA has united labor and other progressive movements in Canada into a new left nationalism. The stronger political emphasis on social democracy helped bring the NDP to victory in Ontario and engendered the populist struggle that defeated the Meech Lake Accord. The central lesson in Watkins' imaginative article is that labor should continue to lead popular struggles against the corporate agenda of free trade and promote coalitions of populist and progressive social movements. This theme is echoed in many other articles in this volume.

Labor in a Global Economy

RAY MARSHALL

Professor of Economics and Public Affairs, University of Texas. Ray Marshall was U.S. Secretary of Labor under President Jimmy Carter from 1977 to 1981.

INTRODUCTION

The subject of "Labor in a Global Economy" raises a number of questions: What is there about a global economy that is different from a nonglobal or mainly national economy? What are the implications of this for workers and unions? How should unions and governments respond to those new conditions?

The basic propositions developed in this paper are:

1. *Traditional labor movements were reactions to the conditions of workers in national industrial systems.* By the end of the 1930s, and certainly by the end of the 1940s, labor movements had become integral components of the economic and industrial relations systems in all of the industrialized democratic countries. These labor movements were justified by the prevailing Keynesian economic philosophies and policies of the time as essential to both speak for and protect workers' interests and to provide workers with purchasing power to keep the mass-production system going.

This combination served the industrialized democracies very well. They experienced what was probably the longest period of equitably shared prosperity in history, made possible mainly by full employment or "Keynesian" economic policies, collective bargaining, and the social safety nets. In most of the democratic industrial economies, income distribution shifted from a pyramid with a few people at the top and most at the bottom, to more of a diamond with larger proportions of income recipients in the middle.

The industrialized democracies recognized the need for economic and social justice, or equity, which means that policies should be tilted toward those who needed the most help. Equity was required to counteract the natural tendency for elitist management systems and market forces to produce inequality. Not even the staunchest defender of free markets believes they produce equity or guarantee the development of human resources. Indeed, most orthodox economists recognize the political and social need for equity, but they see an unavoidable conflict between equity and efficiency. Labor-oriented economists, by contrast, realize that from a social perspective there is no necessary conflict between equity and efficiency. Orthodox economists only examine individual welfare. They assume full employment and perfect markets, which prevents them from being able to examine social efficiency except as "market imperfections." The point is that in the real world even a perfect market will produce inequities and will not guarantee the development of human resources.

The main point, however, is that while poverty and inequities continued, the combination of Keynesian macroeconomic policies, collective bargaining, and the social safety nets produced a larger middle class of workers who strengthened the economy, as well as the polity and society.

2. *The traditional (i.e., mass-production, Keynesian economics and adversarial industrial relations) system's foundations have eroded since the 1960s—mainly because of internationalization and technological changes, which are closely interrelated.* Internationalization increased economic interdependence between countries and greatly altered the rules of the game for countries, enterprises, and unions. The initial impact of these changes has been to undermine the conditions of workers, especially in the U.S. Income distribution is now becoming more like an hourglass instead of a diamond; real wages are falling; union

power has declined; and the social "safety nets" are being shredded.

These developments have caused some analysts to argue that unions are obsolete, along with the national oligopolies to which they were closely related. The new locus of power, according to this view, is in the "high-tech" companies, which are largely unorganized, and in multinational corporations (MNCs), which are beyond the reach of most national governments and labor unions. These analysts believe changes occurred because of the mobility of capital relative to labor, and the fact that the effectiveness of unions' traditional basic operating procedures (taking labor out of competition) has been greatly reduced by intensified international competition.

The implication of this argument is that the "monopoly wage," which the unions in the industrialized democracies were able to extract, will now be lost and workers' wages and employment conditions must be set in a global economy, which implies lower wages for high-wage countries like the U.S. and Canada.

Those who advance this theory seem to have the trends on their side, especially in the U.S., but to a lesser degree in Canada, though many would argue that the "free trade" agreement between the U.S. and Canada implies that competitive market forces ultimately will produce greater convergence between conditions in the U.S. and Canada than already exist. Moreover, according to this scenario, there will be convergence between wages in the U.S.,

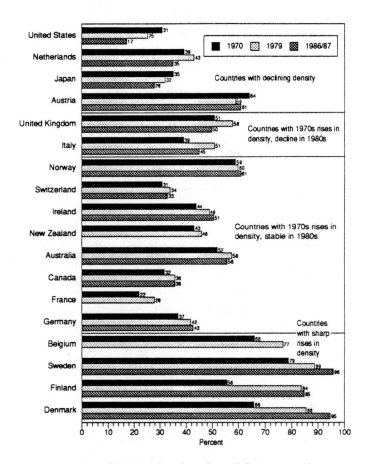

FIGURE 1. UNION MEMBERSHIP OF NONAGRICULTURAL WORKERS AS A PERCENTAGE OF NONAGRICULTURAL WAGE AND SALARY EMPLOYEES: 1970 TO 1986–87

Source: Blanchflower, David G. and Richard B. Freeman. 1990. "Going Different Ways: Unionism in the U.S. and Other Advanced OECD Countries," NBER Working Paper No. 3342. p 42.

Canada, and Mexico—especially when the U.S.-Mexico free trade agreement is consummated.

3. *What about all of this?* My view is that this scenario could come about, but it is not predetermined. Indeed, it would be wrong to generalize from the U.S. experience because unions in other countries, especially in Scandinavia and Western Europe, have generally maintained or improved their density (i.e., proportion of the work force organized) since the 1960s, and even during the 1980s (see Figure 1). In fact, the Canadian labor movement has increased its density since the 1960s, despite being subjected to some of the same environmental conditions as U.S. unions. A different set of policies and choices could therefore:

• Strengthen both workers' incomes and working conditions and labor movements and make it possible to achieve convergence by raising the wages of Third-World workers rather than lowering them in the U.S. and Canada.

- However, this scenario requires very different policies, structures, and practices, especially from those currently being pursued in the U.S.—which have put downward pressure on wages, polarized incomes, and greatly weakened unions.
- We should note, moreover, that the nonunion high-tech companies are losing competitiveness as well as the more highly unionized basic industries.

What are the forces that have produced these changes? What kinds of national policies are required? What should labor movements do?

In order to answer these questions, we must understand the economic context within which traditional industrial relations systems developed, the nature of the changes that have eroded the foundations of those traditional systems, and the kinds of adjustments that have been made by labor movements in Scandinavia and Western Europe that have continued to grow despite being subjected to the same kinds of external economic conditions that have troubled American unions. The experiences of these more successful labor movements provide some lessons for the United States, the main focus of my remarks.

THE CHANGING ECONOMY

Traditional U.S. labor-management relations are deeply rooted in the economic policies and institutions that made the United States the world's strongest economy during the first half of this century. In addition to its supportive institutions and a steady flow of highly motivated workers, the most important factors in America's economic success were abundant natural resources and the mass-production system, which made it possible to achieve relatively rapid improvements in productivity and total output through economies of scale and reinforcing interindustry shifts.

The mass-production system organized work so that most thinking, planning, and decision making was done by managerial, professional, and technical elites. Line work was simplified so that it could be done by relatively unskilled workers. The assumption was that there was "one best way" to perform a task. It was management's responsibility to discover that one best method and impose it on the system through detailed regulations, enforced by supervisors, inspectors, and administrative staffs. It was assumed that workers would "soldier" or loaf unless they were closely supervised. Management therefore sought to gain control of the work by standardizing work processes and transferring ideas, skills, and knowledge to managers and machines.

Monotonous and degrading working conditions were made more bearable by wages that were much higher than those that could be earned on the farm or in the home countries of the immigrants who flocked to America's factories, mills, and mines during the early part of this century.

The system had major weaknesses, some of which were gradually worked out by the 1940s. A serious problem for mass-production companies was to control markets and prices in order to justify the large investments required for these systems. These firms therefore worked out oligopolistic arrangements to avoid price competition and adjusted to change mainly by varying output and employment while holding prices relatively constant.

There was, however, another problem. Once they stabilized the prices of their products, the mass-production companies experienced cyclical instability because production tended to outrun consumption at administered prices. The industrialized market economy countries fixed this problem through so-called "Keynesian" monetary-fiscal policies which manipulated government spending and interest rates to generate enough total demand to keep the system operating at relatively low levels of unemployment.

Another problem was to make the system more just or equitable in order to strengthen democratic institutions and social cohesion. As noted, the mass-production system and market forces produced inequalities, which were offset only partially by public policies. And the offset was less in the United States than in most other industrial democracies, which had stronger social safety nets and better organized political and economic labor movements. Industrial relations and "welfare" or "income maintenance" policies nevertheless reinforced Keynesian macroeconomic and administered price policies. Unions, collective bargaining, unemployment compensation, and social security were all justified as ways to sustain purchasing power. Although they were brought into it reluctantly, oligopolistic companies could see the wisdom of providing purchasing power, especially when it became clear that unions and collective bargaining were not really going to challenge their control of the system—they were merely going to codify work force practices and protect workers from some of the most arbitrary company practices. The unemployment compensation system also helped companies maintain their work forces by, in effect, supplementing wages during layoffs.

Unions and their supporters had the same aversion for competition in labor markets as the oligopolists did for competitive product markets. Early unions learned that competition forced many employers to depress wages and working conditions. Workers in all industrial countries therefore organized not only to extend democracy to the work place, but also to remove labor from competition through collective bargaining and government regulations. Labor theorists, like the Webbs (1897), argued that removing labor from competition through collective bargaining and government regulations increased efficiency by preventing companies from depressing labor standards, thus forcing them to compete by becoming more efficient. The Webbs reasoned that employers who paid less than the living wage were being subsidized either by workers and their families or by society. Such subsidies therefore generated inefficiencies and made it difficult for countries to develop their human resources.

Both the mass-production system and demand-management policies were justified by the American economy's remarkable performance in World War II. After the war, the combination of economies of scale, abundant natural resources, strong global demand, and a backlog of technology (much of it, including the computer, developed by the military), ushered in the longest period of equitably-shared prosperity in U.S. history. Progressive government policies and collective bargaining counteracted the market's natural tendency to produce inequality. This whole system was reinforced by fixed exchange rates, international trade rules, and supportive financial institutions, all of which aided the expansion of America's mass-production system.

THE SYSTEM ERODES

Toward the end of the 1960s, the foundations of America's traditional economic system began to crumble. The main forces for change were technology and increased international competition, which combined to render much of the traditional mass-production system and its supporting institutions anachronistic. These changes also dramatically altered the conditions for economic viability. In a more competitive world dominated by knowledge-intensive technology, the key to economic success became human resources and a more effective organization of production systems, not natural resources and traditional economies of scale. Indeed, as the work of Theodore Schultz and other economists demonstrated, the process of substituting knowledge and skills for physical resources had been the main source of improved productivity since at least the 1920s (Carnevale, 1983; Schultz, 1981).

Technology not only contributed to the globalization of markets, but also made the mass-production system and traditional economies of scale less important. Although the traditional assembly line can be automated, that probably is not the most efficient use of the new technology. Computerized technology makes it possible to gain many of the advantages of economies of scale through flexible manufacturing systems that have enormous advantages in a more dynamic and competitive global economy. The new technology provides economies of scope as well as scale because the same technology can be used to produce different products.

Technology makes new organizations of production possible, but competition makes them necessary. This is so because a competitive internationalized information economy has very different requirements for national, enterprise, organizational, and personal success than was true of largely national goods-producing systems. One of the most important changes for public policy purposes is that national governments have less control of their economies. It therefore is no longer possible for a single country to maintain high wages and full employment through traditional combinations of monetary-fiscal policies, administered wages and prices, and fixed exchange rates. In the 1970s and 1980s, internationalization weakened the linkages between domestic consumption, investment, and output that formed the basic structure of the traditional "Keynesian" demand-management system. The weakening of these Keynesian linkages became very clear when the early 1980s U.S. tax cuts increased consumption, but also greatly stimulated imports and therefore produced much smaller increases in domestic investment than had resulted from earlier tax cuts in less globalized markets.

It would be a mistake, however, to conclude, as some have, that this more internationalized environment requires less government involvement. In an internationalized economy, national government policies must be more selective both as to function and economic sectors, but they are at least as important to successful economic performance as they were in more national goods-producing systems. In fact, careful research by David Alan Aschauer (1989a, 1989b, 1988) at the Federal Reserve Bank of Chicago has demonstrated that a major cause of the decline in productivity growth in the United States since the 1960s has been the decline in public investment for infrastructure, not, as many conservatives believe, because of a decline in private investments. These matters will be explored at greater length after a discussion of how internationalization and technological change have altered the conditions for economic viability.

THE BASIC CHOICE: LOW WAGES OR HIGHER QUALITY AND PRODUCTIVITY

These altered economic conditions do not just change the magnitude of the requirements for economic success—they fundamentally alter the necessary structures and policies. This is so because in the more competitive global information economy economic success requires greater emphasis on some factors that were much less important in traditional mass-production systems. These new factors are quality, productivity, and flexibility.

Quality, best defined as meeting customers' needs, becomes more important for two reasons. First, as the mass-production system matured and personal incomes rose, consumers became less satisfied with standardized products. Second, the more competitive environment of the 1990s is largely consumer driven; the mass-production system was more producer driven, especially after governments and oligopolies "stabilized" prices. In the more competitive environments of the 1970s and 1980s, oligopolistic pricing became anachronistic; flexible prices become more important. Furthermore, the mass-production system depended heavily on controlling national markets; with internationalization American companies have much less market control.

Productivity and flexibility are closely related to quality. The difference is that now productivity improvements are achieved by using all factors of production more efficiently, not, as in the mass-production system, mainly through economies of scale and compatible and reinforcing interindustry shifts. Indeed, in the 1970s and 1980s interindustry shifts lowered productivity growth because they were, on balance, from more productive manufacturing activities to less productive services.

Flexibility enhances productivity by facilitating the shift of resources from less to more productive outputs and improves quality through the ability to respond quickly to diverse and changing consumer needs. Moreover, flexibility in the use of workers and technology improves productivity by reducing the waste of labor and machine time. Indeed, it is probably the case that flexibility, which makes it possible to deliver a variety of automated goods in a timely manner, has more to do with competitiveness (in the sense of competing on terms that make it possible to maintain and improve incomes) than lower costs.

Firms and economies can compete in more global knowledge-intensive markets either by lowering their incomes or by becoming more productive. Since the early 1970s, American companies have been competing mainly by reducing domestic wages and shifting productive facilities to low-wage countries. This is one of the reasons that real wages are lower in the United States in 1990 than they were in 1970, and why in 1989 American wages were about tenth among the major industrialized countries (Bureau of Labor Statistics, 1990; Mishel and Frankel, 1990).

WORKER PARTICIPATION AND HIGHER-ORDER THINKING SKILLS

The fundamental issue, of course, is how to arrange production in order to achieve quality, productivity, and flexibility. The answer appears to be to restructure production systems and develop and use leading-edge technologies. Productivity is improved by work organizations that reduce waste of materials through better inventory control, promote the efficient use of labor, and develop more effective quality controls to prevent defects. High-performance systems have a high degree of employee involvement in what would have been considered "management" functions in mass-production systems. Indeed, in more productive and flexible systems, the distinctions between "managers" and "workers" become blurred.

A number of features of high-performance production systems encourage worker participation. For one thing, these systems require workers to have more knowledge and skill. And skilled, educated workers are less tolerant of monotonous, routine work and authoritarian managerial controls. Secondly, quality, productivity, and flexibility are all enhanced when production decisions are made as close to the point of production as possible. Mass-production bureaucracies were designed to achieve quantity, managerial control, and stability, not flexibility, quality, or productivity in the use of all factors of production. Mass-production systems are based on managerial information monopolies and worker controls; high-performance systems require that workers be free to make decisions. To accomplish this, information must be shared, not monopolized, because in high-performance systems, machines do more of the routine, direct work and frontline workers do more indirect work formerly done mainly by administrative staffs. One of the most important skills required for indirect work is the ability to analyze the flood of data produced by information technology. Workers who can impose order on chaotic data can use information to add value to products, improve productivity and quality, solve problems, and improve technology.

Indirect work also is more likely to be group work, requiring more communication and interpersonal skills. These skills are necessary because productivity, quality, and flexibility require close coordination between what were formerly more discrete components of the production process (e.g., research and development, design, production, inspection, distribution, sales, services). These functions were more linear in the mass-production system, but are more interactive in dynamic, consumer -oriented production systems.

Another very important skill for high-performance systems is the ability to learn. Learning not only is more important than in mass-production systems, it also is very different. The simplification of tasks and the standardization of technology and productivity in the mass-production system limits the amount of learning needed or achieved. More learning is required in a dynamic, technology-intensive work place and more of that learning must be done through the manipulation of abstract symbols. For line workers, mass-production systems stressed learning almost entirely by observation and doing.

Learning in more productive work places also is likely to be largely communal and cooperative. The mass-production system's adversarial relationships impeded the sharing of information between workers, managers, and suppliers. A high-performance system, by contrast, encourages the sharing of information and cooperative efforts to achieve common objectives. A high-performance system creates a community of interests among all of those involved in the system—managers, frontline workers, and suppliers, and is designed to improve quality, productivity, and flexibility. The mass-production system created adversarial relations designed to keep costs down. There clearly is much more learning in a community-of-interest than in an adversarial system. Communal learning, in addition, becomes more important as a means of building the consensus needed to improve the performance of more highly integrated production processes. High-performance workers are not only required to be self managers, but also must perform a greater array of tasks and adapt more readily to change. This requires a reduction of the mass-production system's detailed job classifications and work rules. Well-educated, well-trained, highly motivated workers are likely to be much more flexible and productive, especially in supportive systems that stress equity and internal cohesion. Indeed, humans are likely to be the most flexible components in a high-performance system.

Other features of high-performance work places require greater worker participation. One is the need for constant improvements in technology—or what the Japanese call "giving wisdom to the machine." Technology is best defined as how things are done. The most important fact about technology is not the physical capital itself, but the ideas, skills, and knowledge embodied in machines and structures. Technology becomes standardized when the rate at which ideas, skills, and knowledge can be transferred to a machine or structure becomes very small. Standardized technology therefore requires fewer ideas and less skill and knowledge than leading-edge technology. High-performance organizations emphasize developing and using leading-edge technologies because standardized technologies are highly mobile and therefore are likely to be employed mainly by low-paid workers. Some American companies have responded to competitive pressures by attempting to combine high technology and low-skills through automation. This combination has proved to be little, if any, more productive than standardized technology and low skilled workers. The most productive systems therefore have highly skilled workers who can develop and use leading-edge technology. And the shorter life cycle of products and technologies in a more dynamic and competitive global economy provide important advantages to continuing innovation and creativity. The more mobile technologies become, the more critical participation by highly skilled workers becomes to competitiveness.

The need to pay more attention to quality control and productivity is another reason high-performance systems work better with more worker involvement. In cases where direct contact with customers is required, flexible, highly skilled employees can provide better customer service than is true of highly specialized mass-production workers who can only provide their narrow specialized service. In manufacturing systems, moreover, even the most sophisticated machines are idiosyncratic and therefore require the close attention of skilled workers to adapt them to particular situations. With the smaller production runs permitted by information technology and required by more competitive markets, workers must control production and be able to override machines; the mass-production system usually made it impossible for people to override the equipment. The mass-production system's long production runs made it possible to amortize start-up defects over those long runs. Systems with short production runs cannot afford many start-up defects. They must therefore have workers who override the machines if the latter start producing defects. Quality-driven systems also must provide for more self-inspection by workers and this must often be on the basis of visible observation to prevent defects rather than by inspections to detect them at the end of the production process. Quality control is facilitated by just-in-time inventory and other mechanisms that make defects more visible or detectable early in production processes. Productivity and quality are enhanced by early detection; otherwise, those defective components become invisible when they enter the product, and they are discovered as the products malfunction when used by customers.

INCENTIVE SYSTEMS

The explicit or implicit incentives in any system are basic determinants of the outcomes.

High-performance organizations ordinarily stress positive-incentive systems. Mass-production incentives tend to be negative—fear of discharge or punishment; they also tend to be more individualistic and implicit. Process and time-based mass compensation systems, for example, are often unrelated to productivity or quality and may even be counterproductive, as when workers lose their jobs if productivity improves or when "incentives," especially for managers, bear no relationship to objective performance or equity and therefore create disunity within the work group. Sometimes, moreover, expressed incentives are to improve productivity, whereas the operative implicit incentives stress stability and control, or some component of the production process (e.g., reducing shipping costs or the cost of supplies), which often has negative effects on the whole system. It is easier not to pay a bonus for reasons everybody understands than it is to cut wages. High-performance incentives, by contrast, are more likely to be communal, positive, explicit, based on measurable outcomes, and directly related to the enterprise's stated objectives.

We should note that positive incentives enhance flexibility as well as productivity and quality. Group incentives and job security encourage flexibility by simultaneously overcoming the resistance to the development and use of broader skills and providing employers with greater incentives to invest in those skills. Similarly, bonus compensation systems simultaneously provide greater incentives for workers to improve productivity and quality and create a more flexible compensation system. Participative systems therefore in themselves create positive incentives.

It would be hard to overemphasize the importance of internal unity and positive incentives for high-performance, knowledge-intensive work places. This is so in part because all parties must be willing to go "all out" to achieve common objectives. In traditional mass-production systems workers are justifiably afraid to go "all out" to improve productivity for fear they will lose their jobs. This is the reason job security is one of the most important incentives a high-performance company can have. Similarly, the fragmentation of work within mass-production systems gives workers little incentive to control quality—quality is somebody else's responsibility. A high-performance system, by contrast, makes quality control everybody's responsibility. Positive incentives are required, in addition, because the effective use of information technology tends to give workers greater discretion (Zuboff, 1988). It is difficult to compel workers to think or even to tell whether or not they are doing it. It also is very hard to compel workers to go all out to improve quality and productivity.

How Do All of These Developments Affect Traditional Industrial Relations Systems?

Globalization has strengthened employers relative to unions in several important ways. As noted, unions received considerable public support during the 1930s as being necessary not only to protect workers from arbitrary treatment in Tayloristic management systems, but also to reinforce Keynesian economic policies. In advanced democratic countries, most people continue to recognize the need for unions to protect and promote workers' interests in the polity and society as well as in the work place. But they increasingly question the economic value of collective bargaining. This is due in large measure to the reduced efficacy of Keynesian policies, which created the perception that unions are no longer needed because their functions in maintaining purchasing power and stabilizing wages and prices are no longer as critical as they were in the 1930s. For the main problems confronting more competitive global economies—the control of inflation and competitiveness—unions and collective bargaining often are seen as negatives. Similarly, many employers who valued collective bargaining's stabilizing functions see less need to cooperate with unions since traditional collective bargaining processes are less effective in taking labor out of competition. On the other hand, internationalization gives employers greater market, resource, and production options, thereby strengthening companies relative to unions. The reduced public support for unions, together with the proemployer biases in American laws and policies, have enabled employers to intensify and expand their antiunion activities.

Unions also have suffered because their appeal has been mainly to skilled manual and mass-production workers and less to workers in the rapidly growing service and technical occupations. Most industrial unions have been more adept at administering contracts under largely adversarial relationships than they are at establishing cooperative relationships and improving productivity, flexibility, and quality. Exceptions include unions in the highly competitive garment and clothing industries, which always had to give greater attention to productivity in order to sustain a wage advantage over the nonunion competitors. Another exception is in areas like construction where unique customer needs made mass-production difficult, thus requiring more highly skilled workers and labor-management cooperation to meet customers' needs.

Some people interpret the relative decline of union strength in the United States to mean that unions are, like their related oligopolistic mass-production and regulated industries, anachronistic. I read it otherwise. The fact that the relative strength of American unions has declined much more than their counterparts in other countries (especially Canada, where union strength has increased since the 1960s), suggests that their problems are due to unique American factors, not to the obsolescence of trade unions per se. In fact, a case can be made that unions continue to have a vital role, though their methods, like those of mass-production companies, must be adapted to a more competitive global economy. Genuine worker participation in high-performance enterprises, for example, is unlikely unless the workers have independent sources of power to represent their interests. Indeed, unions are an integral part of high-performance companies in Sweden, Germany, and even in Japan. Independent sources of power are essential in more national high-performance economies for two major reasons. First, workers are not likely to be willing to go "all out" unless they are able to protect themselves from the adverse consequences of doing so. Second, it is very difficult to have effective participatory, cooperative arrangements between parties with greatly unequal power. This is so because the stronger party ultimately will be inclined to exert unilateral control, thus destroying cooperation and internal unity and causing the weaker party to seek countervailing power. This happened, for instance, during the 1920s and 1930s, when management's unilateral actions encouraged workers to form or seek independent unions.

Finally, more cooperative relationships between labor and management do not mean an end to adversarial relationships. Indeed, adversarial relationships between managers and workers are both functional and inevitable. What is required, of course, is to prevent conflict from becoming "function-less," to use a German term: this means conflict that makes all parties worse off. There is no necessary conflict between cooperating to make the pie bigger and bargaining to split it. However, both processes—cooperating and bargaining—require that workers have an independent source of power to represent their interests.

This is not to argue that effective nonunion systems are impossible, but it does imply that they are hard to maintain in the long run. It is especially difficult for these systems to work where management's main motives are to avoid unions or to reduce labor costs. There can be little question that the workers' ability to freely organize and bargain collectively has been an important check on arbitrary and discriminatory actions by companies or unions. I also believe that the right of self-organization has been sufficiently diluted in the United States that it no longer provides adequate safeguards to nonunion workers.

As I have argued at length elsewhere (Marshall, 1987), under modern conditions labor organizations are at least as essential for the economy, society, and polity as they were in mass-production systems. However, the methods used to protect workers must change to reflect a very different economy. For one thing, unions must play a more active role in strengthening high-performance production systems. They can do this by strengthening such noncollective bargaining participatory processes as labor management safety and health committees and joint programs to improve productivity. Unions also could encourage or force companies to develop global strategies that compel companies to take longer time perspectives, develop leading-edge technologies, and adopt more positive incentive systems. Unions should continue to challenge elitist management perquisites and unfair compensation systems that not only create disunity, but also have little or nothing to do with individual or company performance.

It is particularly important for unions to challenge management practices that maintain short-run profits, but which are contrary to the best interests of workers, communities, and the country. Examples include company policies to compete by reducing wages and employment rather than improving productivity. Other countries promote high-performance management practices through collective bargaining or regulations that require consultation with workers representatives or justifications to public bodies before plants can be closed, wages cut, or workers laid off.

Finally, unions should continue to champion public policies designed to make the United States a high-wage, equitable, full-employment economy. This will require, above all, developing more democratic institutions, effective public schools, school-to-work transition processes, and on-the-job learning systems for line workers. Worker learning systems are at least as necessary to high-performance systems as managerial training, which now consumes an inordinate share of corporate education and training resources. The joint programs in the construction, automobile, and communications industries are good beginnings, but they are only a fraction of what they should be. According to the American Society for Training and Development, 15,000 firms, less than one-half of one percent of all companies, account for over 90 percent of all work place training in the U.S. In addition, the Commission on the Skills of the American Workforce (CSAW, 1990) reported that American companies were far behind their principal Asian and European competitors in both training and organizing for high-performance.

What is required, of course, is for unions and their supporters to develop the modern intellectual equivalent of Keynesian economics to show that unions are good for the economy, as well as for the polity and society. Although unions must modernize their policies, methods, and structures to make them more responsive to their members' needs, stronger public support requires a rationale that shows unions to be essential economic institutions because they are not narrow special-interest groups since their activities strengthen the entire economy.

Despite a general understanding of the requirements for high-performance companies, it has been demonstrated that the loss of competitiveness by U.S. companies is in the largely nonunion high-tech industries, as well as in the more unionized basic industries. Moreover, the Commission on the Skills of the American Workforce also reported that most American companies were pursuing strategies that lead to lower and more unequal wages. This was in stark contrast to the companies in most other industrialized countries, a majority of which were attempting to follow high-wage, quality, and productivity strategies. Why the difference? The commission found that an overriding reason was the fact that all other countries studied had consensus goals to be competitive, world-class, high-performance countries. These countries or their labor movements therefore imposed constraints as well as positive incentives on companies that induced or compelled them to pursue the high-performance option. In addition, other countries had higher standards for students completing secondary schools and high-quality, well-organized job training programs for workers who did not complete college. In the U.S., by contrast, public schools are generally organized along mass-production principles and do not turn out many students with the requisite thinking skills for high-performance organizations. And very little is done to educate and train frontline workers. In fact, the commission found that less than 10 percent of noncollege educated frontline workers in the U.S. received any formal training. In other countries, by contrast, most noncollege workers participate in well-organized, high-quality training systems (CSAW, 1990).

ROLE OF LABOR MOVEMENTS

Public policies can help create the context within which labor movements operate, but labor movements themselves must develop the strategies, policies, and structures to strengthen their ability to protect and promote workers' interests. Labor movements can do this by being major active forces for just, democratic, full- employment, high-wage economies. Labor movements in different countries have varying degrees of power to influence national policies. While it is always possible to argue that particular national labor movements have not made the right strategic choices, it is, as a practical matter, impossible to determine the extent to which the outcomes for a particular labor movement are due to context and how much to strategic choice. Critics of U.S. unions, for example, argue that they should have become more "political" and been less wedded to collective bargaining. However, this argument is usually advanced by people who do not seem to understand either the political activities of American unions or the political structures workers face in the American context. It is highly unlikely, for example, given the political structures of the United States, that American unions could ever establish the kind of independent political labor movements that their counterparts have developed in parliamentary systems. The structure of American government makes it very difficult for third parties to get started, gives inordinate power to nonmetropolitan areas with low union densities, and makes it possible for willful minorities to block legislation. The failure of labor law reform in the 1970s, for example, had very little to do with how hard the AFL-CIO was willing to push for it or how much it was favored by labor's supporters in the Congress. The bill passed the House of Representatives by almost a 100-vote majority, and had fifty-eight of 100 votes for passing in the Senate, but the bill's supporters were unable to muster the sixty votes needed to break filibuster by a few antiunion senators at a time when a filibuster delayed other important legislation. It is, moreover, difficult to change the filibuster (or "cloture") rule because it gives great power to each senator.

It is nevertheless instructive to speculate about what those labor movements have been able to do that have maintained and improved their strength during the 1980s, relative to those like the American, that have not. My reading of the international comparison leads to the following list of factors for high-performance labor movements, most notably those in Scandinavia, which have maintained and improved their economic and political strength in the same international economic environment that has produced large losses for some unions, especially those in the United States.

1. Successful labor organizations have adopted clear goals and objectives, as well as strategies to simultaneously achieve those objectives and to gain greater support from nonlabor groups.

Strong labor movements continue to advocate full-employment policies, but they also want full employment at high and rising wages. And they advocate policies to prevent wages and incomes from polarizing as much as they have in the United States.

These labor movements realize the extent to which international competition has changed the ability to take labor out of competition and maintain full employment by traditional means. This means developing policies that permit companies to compete in international markets while maintaining full employment and equity. Labor movements have developed different strategies, but generally they recognize the need to limit wage increases to changes in productivity plus or minus the difference between changes in domestic and international prices.

All of these labor movements, in addition, recognize the need for equity, but they also are concerned with the creation of wealth, not just its distribution. The policies that flow from these objectives include measures to stimulate national investment in job and wealth-creating activities. Sources of investment funds include: private and collective pension funds, lower real interest rates, and measures to promote the development and use of leading-edge technology.

Successful labor movements give particularly high priority to public policies and collective bargaining to strengthen the education and training for all people, but especially for workers. They also have adopted high-wage strategies to force companies to become more productive, as well as adjustment policies to shift labor and other resources from low-wage to high-wage sectors.

Labor movements have always supported such human resource development activities as universal education, health care, and family support policies. Indeed, I wouldn't be surprised to find a strong correlation between union density and the degree of support for human resource development activities. There can be little doubt that in an age of multinational corporations, investing in people is the best way to strengthen a country's economy.

2. High-performance labor movements also have global strategies that are designed to support high-wage, full-employment, equity policies. Unlike groups with ideological commitments to "free markets," labor movements owe their existence to a healthy appreciation of the limitations as well as the strengths of markets. They understand that markets must operate within the framework of rules, especially those that protect basic labor standards. Such standards promote human resource development and force companies to compete by becoming more efficient, not by reducing basic labor standards. In a global economy, however, labor standards must now be part of international trade rules.

Trade-linked labor standards could, in addition, provide global purchasing power by giving Third-World workers a means to participate in the economic growth of their countries. It should be emphasized, however, that international labor standards do not imply an international minimum wage—wage differentials are too great for that to be practical. There is, however, a difference between having low wages because of a low level of economic development and suppressing wages to attract capital; the latter would violate international labor standards, the former would not. Labor standards also would allow workers to organize and bargain collectively and protect them from hazardous work places, forced labor, child labor, and discrimination because of such factors as race, ethnic origin, or union membership.

Labor movements also have a vested interest in seeing equitable solutions to the Third-World debt problem, which acts as a strong depressant on world growth, and the establishment of international financial institutions to promote an expanding world economy and avoid a recurrence of financial threats like that posed by the Third-World debt during the 1980s. A real world bank could bring discipline to international financial markets by acting as a lender of last resort, restructuring loans, and recycling funds to promote growth.

High-performance labor organizations are proactive, not merely reactive. They adopt goals and set agendas; they do not simply respond to agendas set by others. These labor movements are particularly aggressive in asserting workers' interests in international negotiations, events, policies, and institutions that affect workers. They would, for example, consider it unthinkable that activities like the U.S.-Canada free trade agreement, or the proposed Mexico-U.S. trade agreement, be consummated without active participation by labor representatives to protect workers' interests.

INTERNATIONAL COOPERATION

One of the greatest problems facing labor movements is thus to gain enough power to see to it that workers' interests are protected in international transactions and institutions. The logical development, as John R. Commons taught us, would be for labor organizations to coincide with the market—otherwise wages and working conditions can be undermined by shifting resources to areas not covered by labor standards. However, the disparities between countries and workers are too great to permit a true international labor movement, which will give international companies important advantages in whipsawing unions.

There are, however, things that unions can do, including using their economic and political leverage over MNCs in their "home" countries, promoting stronger codes of conduct for MNCs in international organizations, strengthening international cooperation through international organizations, especially at the trade secretariats, and cooperating to see to it that workers' interests are represented in international negotiations of all kinds. Workers' interests are now not very well represented in such organizations as the GATT, the International Monetary Fund, the World Bank, or the so-called "summit" economic conferences held by industrialized countries. Most of the economic experts at these meetings, especially those from the United States, consider high wages, labor standards, full employment, and equity to be negatives.

STRENGTHENING LABOR MOVEMENTS WITHIN COUNTRIES

Labor movements will have very little ability to represent workers' interests in a global economy unless they operate from strong national bases. Some of what is required to strengthen labor movements is fairly obvious, such as organizing, developing internal democracy, and being responsive to workers' concerns. There are, however, a number of factors that all strong labor movements seem to have in common; these include:

1. *Broad public support because labor movements have articulated a rationale that goes beyond narrow "special interest" concerns like higher wages and better working conditions.* Democratic countries generally accepted the idea that free and democratic labor movements are essential to democracy, but unions have not always been considered to be in the national economic interest. Unions gained support after the 1930s because they were considered to be essential to help stabilize economies and increase purchasing power, in keeping with prevailing Keynesian policies. The successful labor movements of the 1980s have articulated strategies to help their countries be just, full-employment, high-income countries—emphasizing the essential role of worker involvement in high-performance enterprises and the importance of human resource development for national welfare. These labor movements have stressed economic growth as well as the equitable distribution of income.

2. *Successful labor movements have therefore been able to develop and implement coordinated goals that attract broad support.* Because these labor movements have been led by skilled, well-informed leaders who were able to convince other groups of the importance of their role, they have been able to participate in a fairly sophisticated manner in tripartite (labor, management, government) processes.

3. *High-performance labor movements have strong local workplace entities, as well as strong national economic and political organizations.* Labor movements that are only organized around one of these dimensions (work place, national, political, or economic) have not been as strong as those that emphasize all of them.

4. *The strongest labor movements develop mechanisms for interactive communications with their members.* These labor movements therefore have extensive education and research services, both to help members advance job skills as well as for general education and strengthening labor leaders' ability to participate effectively in national organizations and political processes.

22

CONCLUSIONS

The goals, policies, and objectives of labor movements in the democratic industrial countries are rooted in mainly national, mass-production economies. This was particularly true for unions in the U.S. where the mass-production system was larger and more deeply entrenched than elsewhere. Political and economic conditions in the U.S. have made it more difficult for unions to survive, grow, and adapt. It has particularly been more difficult for unions to establish independent political movements, which is a major difference between unions in the U.S. and elsewhere. However, unions also have faced much greater opposition from employers.

A major factor in the strength of the U.S. unions has been public opinion, which was more favorable during the 1930s and 1940s than during the 1970s and 1980s. At least part of this popularity was due to the belief that unions were good for the economy because they helped maintain purchasing power, in keeping with the prevailing Keynesian policies. However, these policies became anachronistic in a more competitive internationalized information world, which also makes the oligopolistic mass-production system less effective. This leads some people to believe that unions also have become obsolete. I have argued that this is a false conclusion: high-performance organizations require much greater worker involvement, which, in turn, is most effective if workers have an independent source of power to represent their interests.

A major problem in the U.S. is the fact that unions have been so weakened since the 1960s that workers do not, in fact, have effective options to organize in the face of much stronger employer opposition. Part of the reason for intensified employer opposition is the erosion of the mass-production Keynesian safety net system that provided mutual accommodations for employers before the 1970s, when the eroding effects of technology and more competitive global markets become more apparent. These changes greatly strengthened international companies relative to unions and made it possible for almost all American companies to respond to change with cost cutting rather than quality- and productivity-improving strategies. In addition to weaker unions, American companies are not restrained in their wage-cutting strategies by public policies that create constraints and offer incentives for companies to become high-performance organizations. One of the most serious defects in the U.S. policy mix is poor public schools and the absence of high-quality comprehensive worker training systems that exist in every other major democratic industrial country.

Stronger labor movements are clearly in the national interest. The U.S. should therefore modernize its labor relations laws to make it easier for workers to organize and bargain collectively and more difficult for employers to thwart those rights by legal and illegal means.

However, unions and their supporters must strengthen their internal processes and gain greater public support if more favorable public policies are to be adopted. In achieving these objectives, unions and their supporters can learn from the experience of those labor movements that have continued to prosper despite a hostile international economic and political environment. These successful labor movements have adopted broad, popular goals for public policies to establish high wages, full employment, and economic justice. These strategies constitute the modern intellectual equivalent of Keynesian economics, which complemented and strengthened the equity, industrial relations, and labor market rationales for unions and collective bargaining. They have, in addition, developed strategies to promote international, national, and enterprise policies and institutions to achieve these objectives. These strategies require strengthening unity among workers within and between countries and promoting national policies to improve productivity, quality, flexibility, and equity. Those who believe in free, democratic, prosperous, just societies have a strong stake in how well unions and their supporters achieve these objectives.

23

REFERENCES

Aschauer, David Alan. "Is Public Expenditure Productive?" *Journal of Monetary Economics*, 23:177–200, 1989a.

———. "Public Investment and Productivity Growth in Seven Countries." *Economic Perspective.* Federal Reserve Bank of Chicago, 17–25, September/October 1989b.

———. "Rx for Productivity: Build Infrastructure." *Chicago Fed Letter.* September, 1988.

Bureau of Labor Statistics, unpublished data, May 1990.

Carnevale, Anthony. *Human Capital: A High-Yield Corporate Investment.* Washington, D.C: American Society for Training and Development, 1983.

Commission on the Skills of the American Workforce. *America's Choice: High Skills or Low Wages!* Rochester, New York: Center on Education and the Economy, 1990.

Marshall, Ray. *Unheard Voices.* New York: Basic Books, 1987.

Mishel, Larry, and David Frankel. *The State of Working America.* Washington, D.C: Economic Policy Institute, 1990.

Schultz, Theodore. *Investing in People: The Economics of Population Quality.* Berkeley, California: University of California Press, 1981.

Webb, Sidney, and Beatrice Webb. *Industrial Democracy.* London: Longman, Green and Company, 1897.

Zuboff, Shoshona. *In the Age of the Smart Machine.* New York: Basic Books, 1988.

Canadian Labor Strategies for a Global Economy

SHIRLEY G.E. CARR
President, Canadian Labour Congress

There is no doubt that we in the labor movement face enormous new challenges because of the changes in the global economy over the past decade or so. I should like to outline briefly for you how we in the Canadian labour movement understand, and have responded to, these challenges.

ECONOMIC CHANGES

From the 1950s through the mid-1970s, most of the advanced industrial countries enjoyed rapid growth, rising real incomes, near full employment, an improving array of social programs, and the steady extension of the scope of collective bargaining.

To be sure, the picture varied from country to country. Even in the 1950s and 1960s, Canada never had full employment, and our social programs—while better developed than in the U.S.—remained far from ideal when compared to those in many western European countries.

Nonetheless, the guiding assumption was that democratic governments could and should secure full employment, a comprehensive social safety net, and recognition of basic labor rights.

All that, of course, has changed significantly. Neoconservatives argue that full employment, the welfare state, and strong unions undermine growth and competitiveness. Privatization, deregulation, and promotion of so-called free markets have been the order of the day where they have taken power.

There is no firmer champion of the new orthodoxy than the current Canadian prime minister, Brian Mulroney. Any cause for self-satisfaction we in the Canadian labor movement may have had about our achievements compared to those of the U.S. labor movement must be tempered by the fact that we must now struggle hard to preserve our gains against relentless government attack.

I deeply believe that neoconservatism is no answer at all, even on its own terms. When I look around the world, I find that the most successful economies are not those most fervently committed to so-called free market economics, but rather those which remain committed to full employment, worker rights, and social justice.

The social democratic countries of northern Europe have demonstrated that it is indeed possible to reconcile the goals of economic efficiency and social equality.

Nonetheless, the political space for building a full-employment welfare state has been reduced in the new global economy. When capital is free to flow unhindered to countries where returns are higher, the bargaining power of democratic governments compared to that of international business is sharply reduced.

It is interesting to glance back to a neglected essay on "national self-sufficiency" written by the great economist Keynes just after the war. In that essay, Keynes argued full employment and the creation of a comprehensive welfare state do increase labor costs. Some kind of insulation is, therefore, necessary to prevent the lowering of wages and working conditions to the lowest common denominator in the international economy. Of course, Keynes was also a great supporter of increased economic cooperation between governments to allow for a general raising of standards.

An important reason for the rise of neoconservatism is increased competition between countries with sharply different labor standards. From at least the mid-1970s, capital has flowed increasingly to countries that have chosen to develop through low-wage, export-oriented manufacturing. A part of what used to be the industrial base of the advanced industrial countries has shifted to the low-wage developing countries. At the same time, capital itself has become vastly more mobile, capable of fleeing jurisdictions that impose too great a "burden," be it in terms of wages and working conditions, environmental standards, taxation, or other issues. Competition has been intensified by the restrictive macroeconomic policies of the major industrial countries. The governments of these countries have done little or nothing to regulate international business.

In the past year, we in Canada have become acutely aware of the flight of capital to the maquiladora export processing zone in Mexico. To take one example of literally dozens, Bendix Ltd. has shifted production of seat belts from the small town of Collingwood in Ontario to the maquiladora because it could hire workers in the maquiladora at sixty cents per hour instead of at a decent living wage, because it did not have to live up to social demands to provide pay equity for women, and so on.

LABOR STRATEGIES

How do we in the labor movement respond to these challenges? How have we in Canada responded to date?

Basically, three kinds of labor strategies are available to us. They all have some merit, and are by no means as contradictory as is often supposed to be the case.

The first strategy is for labor to become an active partner in the pursuit of competitiveness—though, I hasten to add, a partner that interprets competitiveness in a different way than does business. The second strategy is for labor to press for some degree of insulation from global market forces and unrestricted international competitive pressures. The third strategy is for labor itself to "go global" and to press for regulation of international competition in the interests of workers on an international scale.

Labor, Production, and Competition

Many advocates of the first strategy—the competitive strategy—hold that labor must drop its so-called "adversarial" stance, recognize new realities, and join with business if we are to successfully compete. They urge us to accept wage concessions or systems of so called flexible compensation like profit sharing, and to support greater workplace cooperation through quality of working life programs and "team production" approaches.

In Canada, as in the U.S., there has been a great deal of discussion in the labor movement about how to deal with demands for so-called more flexible compensation and more flexible working arrangements.

We have, as a labor movement, rejected wage concessions and insisted that workers deserve not just a decent living wage, but also the rising incomes justified by higher productivity.

We have recognized the need to renegotiate rigid job classifications and have bargained technological and job-change issues in a realistic way if—and it is a big if—the employer has bothered to consult with us in the first place. A number of unions have begun to experiment with new working arrangements.

While there has been debate over these issues, we are agreed that the first priority in any so-called cooperative arrangements must be maintenance of the independence and autonomy of the union. We know that the interests of workers are not the same as those of management, and that workers need strong unions to speak for them, not to speak for the company.

It is sometimes argued that labor has little to fear from industrial restructuring in response to international competition. Jobs which are lost in sectors vulnerable to low-wage imports can, we are told, be replaced by jobs in higher value-added, knowledge-intensive industries where labor costs account for a smaller share of total costs, and where quality and market responsiveness matter much more than price.

There is some truth to this argument. We should not mourn the loss of low wage jobs to imports if high-wage, high-productivity jobs were available to replace them. But all too often they are not.

This is particularly the case in a country like Canada that has a weakly developed manufacturing sector, and rather few advanced, high-value-added manufacturing industries that are competitive on a world scale. Even if jobs were available, we would need retraining and adjustment programs to assist workers in the transition from one sector to another.

We in the Canadian labor movement have recognized that the process of restructuring will be much less painful if governments adopt activist policies to promote the development of advanced industry. Specifically, we have recognized that a highly educated and highly trained labor force is required if we are to successfully compete in sophisticated "knowledge intensive" industries.

We have pressed strongly for major labor input into training programs, and recommendations for a national training board composed of an equal number of labor and business members have recently been presented to the federal government by a joint labor-business task force. We may well be on the threshold of the creation of a system of labor market planning and skills training in Canada in which unions will play a full and equal role with business.

The labor movement has also pressed strongly for continued government support for industrial research and development.

My central point here is that the Canadian labor movement has recognized the realities of changing international competition, and has done its best to ensure that we do not compete on the basis of low wages, but rather on the basis of skilled labor and high levels of expertise.

Insulation from Global Pressures—Labor and Trade

I turn now to the second broad labor strategy—seeking some degree of insulation form global economic forces. I start from the basic premise that—from a labor point of view—the bottom line of economic policy must be jobs and decent wages, not competitiveness.

When workers in some countries must—by force of hunger or at the point of a gun—work for starvation wages, then we cannot compete. We simply cannot, and will not, accept competition that degrades wages and working conditions to the level of the lowest cost producer in the international marketplace.

But the strategy of competing smarter by moving up the value-added ladder has its limits, particularly for a small country like Canada. With weak traditions in advanced "knowledge-intensive" manufacturing, it is difficult for us to compete with the U.S., German, and Japanese multinationals that dominate the global marketplace.

For us, the solution is not unfettered free trade, or free trade with the U.S., but rather managed trade. We must retain the instruments of national economic sovereignty to build a more diversified, stable, and productive economy.

We need the power to restrict exports of unprocessed resources if we are to break our historical pattern of exporting raw and semiprocessed resources, and importing advanced manufactured goods. We must retain the ability to tell our forest companies that they cannot export logs or pulp, but must produce newsprint and fine papers. And we must retain the ability to require such companies, particularly when they are foreign owned, to undertake research and development in Canada and to purchase Canadian-made machinery and equipment.

We are not, I stress, opposed to international trade. But we are opposed to one-sided trade arrangements that tie our hands when it comes to changing the terms on which we participate in international markets.

We want trade arrangements like the auto pact with the U.S. as it stood before the free trade deal—an arrangement that guaranteed Canada the share of jobs and production to which we were entitled because of the size of our market.

We remain strongly opposed to the free trade deal with the U.S. Over the past year, we have seen the loss of one in twelve manufacturing jobs in our country, at least partly as a result of restructuring in response to the trade deal. Many branch plants of U.S. companies have simply shifted production to the U.S.—or to Mexico—and changed their Canadian plants into warehouses.

The trade deal with the U.S. has also been at least partly responsible for a major assault on Canadian social programs. I say partly because our present federal government never liked these programs much in the first place, so it is hard to disentangle exactly what lies behind their policies.

But it is clear that recent changes to our unemployment insurance program are intended to lower benefits to match U.S. levels. It is clear that U.S. corporate tax rates have become the benchmark against which Canadian tax rates must now be set. And the standard business and government response to virtually every legislative proposal on our part—from pay equity for women to child care—is that it would raise standards compared to those in the U.S., and thus make us uncompetitive.

As a labor movement we are still trying to think our way through the economic alternatives to the free trade deal. We certainly do not contemplate policies of national self-sufficiency. Canada is and always will be heavily involved in international markets. But we need some political space in which to ensure that it is the Canadian people, and not just the large corporations, which benefit from participation in the global economy. It is our judgement that existing international arrangements through the General Agreement on Tariffs and Trade (GATT) meet our national needs much better than does the free trade deal.

International Cooperation of Labor

I turn finally to the third broad labor strategy open to us—for labor itself to organize on a global basis to regulate capital in the interests of workers.

Competition between countries is, in principle, already subject to certain international protocols such as those passed by the International Labour Organization (ILO). What is needed is effective international action to exclude from international markets goods exported by nations that refuse to recognize minimum labor rights, including firstly and most importantly the right to organize free and democratic trade unions.

In practice this might mean that ILO guidelines on minimum standards should be incorporated into the rules governing international trade promulgated and enforced by the GATT.

Going beyond minimum labor standards, we need concerted international action to prevent an erosion of wages, working conditions, and social programs to the lowest common denominator. Indeed, we should be attempting to bring about upward harmonization—a general raising of labor standards to the level in place in the most advanced countries.

The obvious example of this approach is, of course, the current attempt to develop a social charter in the European Economic Community (EEC). Trade unions in the EEC have taken the lead in developing the charter to ensure that the creation of a single market does not force standards down to the lowest common denominator within the community. We have much to learn from this process, which is as yet far from complete.

From a Canadian perspective, a word of caution must be said about social charter proposals. It is one thing to negotiate such a charter with France and Germany, which have well-developed welfare states, generally effective regulation of wages and working conditions, and measures to secure and promote worker rights. It would be quite another thing for us as Canadians—with our relatively advanced social programs—to negotiate a social charter to accompany the free trade deal.

Concerted international action to raise standards and to regulate international trade and finance is badly needed. We need a strict code of responsible corporate behavior in a wide range of areas, and we need much more effective cooperation between governments to plan international growth and development.

In the first instance we need to develop a detailed labor program for international economic cooperation. Elements of such an agenda exist—for example, in the statements periodically issued by the Trade Union Advisory Committee to the Organization for Economic Cooperation and Development (OECD), by the international confederation of free trade unions, and other international labor bodies. But it is true that much more needs to be done to develop an international economic agenda that is shared by the major trade union federations.

Of course, such an agenda would simply be a starting point. Ultimately, change at the international level will not be possible until we elect progressive national governments that are prepared to enter into international arrangements that promote the interests of workers rather than those of international big business. We need OECD and summit meetings dominated by the heads of social democratic governments, not meetings where social democrats like Francois Mitterand are isolated and forced to abandon progressive policies under international pressure.

I would finally stress that concerted international action by the labor movement—the action that is needed to build a new global economy—must be the task of the whole labor movement and not just the leadership. We need to further build the international committees that group the different national unions, bargain with international companies, discuss common objectives, and develop programs of international solidarity.

We need joint initiatives to organize those working for international companies—such as the arrangement recently entered into by the Communications Workers of Canada and the Communications Workers of America.

Finally, we need much greater emphasis on international action to assist workers in repressive countries who are struggling to build free trade unions and to secure collective bargaining rights.

Recent Developments in the Canadian Political Economy

MEL WATKINS

Professor of Economics and Political Science, University College, University of Toronto

A Canadian perspective on globalization compels a commentary on the Canada-U.S. Free Trade Agreement (FTA) and how it is working after nearly two years. But we also need to take account of two other big events in Canada.

First, there is the election of a democratic socialist government in Ontario in September 1990 and its significance for labor's response to globalization. The victory caught everyone by surprise, including the Ontario New Democratic Party and its leader Bob Rae, and the business community, which would have otherwise orchestrated a campaign against it. As it is, the new government has a clear majority, enabling it to govern for four to five years—which should be time enough to ride out the recession that is presently gathering force in Canada and particularly Ontario. Is it just possible that the miserable, mean, neoconservative decade of the 1980s is truly over?

Second, I shall comment briefly on Canada's constitutional impasse which resulted from the failure in June, 1990, of the Meech Lake Constitutional Accord. This accord attempted to accommodate Quebec's desire for more autonomy by decentralizing government generally to all the provinces. This proved unacceptable to Canada outside Quebec, but has pushed Quebec strongly toward separation. We must talk about this because Canada may very well be breaking up.

THE FREE TRADE AGREEMENT

The FTA is a comprehensive deal, covering trade—in services as well as goods—investment, and energy. Its consequences have therefore been pervasive, and for working Canadians overwhelmingly adverse. The Canadian Labour Congress has documented its impact in terms of lost jobs through layoffs and plant shutdowns.

In Ontario, job loss is running at its highest level since the recession of the early 1980s. Currently, relatively more of the job loss is from shutdowns that are permanent by their nature than from layoffs that might be temporary. We may be witnessing the assault on the Canadian manufacturing sector, which is mostly in Ontario, that some of us feared would result from a free trade agreement geared more to giving American companies access to Canadian resources than Canadian companies access to American markets. We may as well be in the midst of a wave of mergers in which, disproportionately, American companies take over Canadian companies. As head offices shift outside Canada, there are adverse effects on jobs, particularly for Toronto where so many head offices are located.

We can't be sure that all this bad news is the result of free trade, because the Canadian dollar is seriously overvalued and real interest rates absurdly high. But the simple fact is that, because of the FTA, critical decisions are being made about which side of the border to invest at a terribly bad time for Canada.

Canadian business, both foreign-owned and indigenous, supported the FTA. It saw free trade as part of a neoconservative agenda that would constrain government and limit policy. Above all, we can safely assume, it wanted to make sure there could never be a dreaded socialist government.

That is, nevertheless, what happened in Ontario. It happened in spite of the FTA. It may even have happened because of the FTA. Business, to say nothing of orthodox economists, fails to understand a fundamental point about societal response to the hammer blows of economic change. All should read Karl Polanyi's *The Great Transformation* on how workers and communities fought back against the impact of the Industrial Revolution. The economic and technological movement was matched by a social and political counter-movement. It is the means by which victory, some victory, can be snatched from the jaws of defeat.

My colleague Abraham Rotstein has argued for some time, Polanyi-like, that the movement of globalization leads to the counter-movement in countries like Canada of a defensive, interventionist, left nationalism. The FTA does indeed mean less political space for governments and for unions, but governments mostly don't use the space available. If the will is there, there is still some room for action—not necessarily enough to negate the constricting effects of the FTA, but enough to limit the damage.

As to the economic effects, is the FTA really as forward-looking as Canadian business alleged and imagined? Much was made by the proponents of how the FTA would enhance access of Canadian producers to the American market, enabling the fuller achievement of economies of scale. But that may be old-fashioned Fordist thinking in a world of customized, flexible production.

The FTA was opposed by the Canadian labor movement. The unions were opposed for straightforward but wide-ranging reasons: jobs, the assault on union rights implicit in a corporate agenda, erosion of social programs in the name of "competitiveness", harmonization with—meaning, in the nature of the asymmetry in size, harmonization to—American standards, and the loss of Canadian distinctiveness and Canadian sovereignty. It was understood that the Canadian economy was already significantly integrated into the American and becoming increasingly so; a key concern about the FTA was that it meant a quantum leap in that integration with vast political consequences.

The FTA was also opposed by an array of popular sector groups—women, environmentalists, nationalists, farmers, senior citizens, etc.—all of whom formed, along with labor, an impressive coalition. Therein lies, it seems to me, a most important point not only about politics in general but about labor politics in particular. The future lies in the commitment by labor to social movements and coalition politics, with the unions providing leadership and financial resources.

In the great free trade debate that gripped Canada before the 1988 federal election, there was, then, an interesting configuration of social and class forces. We learned much that is often obscured about the political economy of Canada. On the one hand, the right hand, was the continentalist business community. On the other, left, hand was the nationalist labor movement plus. This does not mean, of course, that Canadian unions do not, or should not, cooperate with American unions, or with American and democratic Mexican unions in opposing U.S.-Canada-Mexico free trade.

The labor coalition lost the election of 1988 and thereby lost the fight against the FTA. That is bad news. Still, the good news is that the Canadian public outside Quebec (I shall return to the matter of Quebec) opposed the agreement. There was evident in English-speaking Canada, a social democratic political culture, at least by North American standards. Having written that at the time, I can only wish that I had gone the next step and predicted the victory of the NDP in Ontario! But I can say, in retrospect, that the fear and loathing engendered by the FTA contributed to a political climate favorable to the Ontario NDP.

That means, in turn, that the NDP government in Ontario will have a mandate to act, namely, to pursue policies as if the FTA did not exist. It should contain the impact on workers and communities of plant shutdowns and layoffs. It should confront the problems created by foreign ownership. It should formulate an industrial policy, indeed an economic development strategy for the province, jointly with business and labor.

It should assert that it too stands for international competitiveness when it is properly understood to be productiveness. Ontario should trade smart, not, as business is only too tempted, trade cheap. The Ontario economy must be competitive but within the context of an economy that is high-wage by global standards with (relatively) good social programs. Workers struggled hard in the past to obtain these; they should not give them up. Nor need they give them up; after all, good social policy means a healthier and more skilled work force, which helps rather than hinders growth.

THE FTA AND THE MEECH LAKE ACCORD

A major cost of the FTA, foreseen by some, was that, by increasing north-south ties relative to east-west ties, it would weaken the glue holding Canada together as a political community. It has done that not by exacerbating regionalism overall but by advertising the difference between Quebec and the rest of Canada. Just as Quebec separatists said it would, the FTA has granted Canada sovereignty-association (political independence and economic association) vis-a-vis the United States, thereby enhancing its legitimacy for Quebec vis-a-vis the rest of Canada. It has made Quebec independence seem much more feasible.

In its folly, the Mulroney government simultaneously embraced the FTA and the Meech Lake Accord and the combination has proven deadly for the Canadian body politic. People opposed to the FTA tended to oppose Meech, seeing them as additive in their decentralizing effects. But opposition to Meech in English Canada was broader than toward the FTA. Though sometimes characterized as anti-French or anti-Quebec, most of it was a positive defense of Canada and of Canadian values. Quebec, on the other hand, with its own national project, supported Meech. The binational character of the country was unambiguously exposed.

The panCanadian elites got their way on free trade, but that only lessened their ability to get their way on Meech. The failure of Meech dramatically undermined the ability of the elites to govern Canada and unleashed powerful populist forces. In Ontario the resulting vacuum has had the commendable consequence of enabling the left to triumph.

What else will happen? Frankly, I don't know whether any accommodation is any longer possible between the two nations or whether, should Quebec leave, the rest of the country will be able to hold together. And we must now perforce factor aboriginal sovereignty into the equation.

I have two thoughts. The first is to remind ourselves that the weakening of existing nation-states, and their governing structures, is a well advertised part of the corporate agenda of globalization. Canada can be so seen as being in the vanguard of recipients of this problematic political fallout.

The second thought, growing out of the first, is that, as national state structures wither, there is a renewed case for activist subnational provincial governments. We have one in Ontario, and it should act. As it does, we will get some idea of what is possible for labor and the left in an industrialized part of North America in this age of the global economy.

Section 2

U.S. AND CANADA: COMPARATIVE POLITICAL AND INDUSTRIAL RELATIONS SYSTEMS

Although the current challenges to labor are global in nature, the labor movements of Canada and the U.S. have developed within national and state or provincial frameworks. Similarly, while union strategies must be developed and carried out in part at the international level, much will still depend on local, state or provincial, and national action. In sharing experiences and strategies across borders it is essential to understand the similarities and differences between the political, social, and industrial relations structures of Canada and the U.S. The applicability of lessons drawn from one country to the situation of the other depends on major distinctions in the systems and more subtle nuances as well.

Elaine Bernard, past president of the British Columbia New Democratic Party (NDP), provides an important starting point by comparing Canadian and U.S. political systems and, more specifically, organized labor's respective roles in these systems. The Canadian parliamentary system and the significant role of third parties in federal and provincial politics are major departures from the U.S. This is most visible in the prominence of labor's own party, the social democratic NDP, and in the concept of party discipline, which is much stronger in Canada. Bernard illustrates this distinction in the example of the failure of the U.S. Congress to enact labor law reform despite labor's alliance with the Democratic party and that party's nearly continuous control of the Congress in recent decades.

However, there are also great similarities, especially in strategic terms under current conditions. Both labor movements recognize the increasing importance of political action as a complement to collective bargaining; the need for alliances and coalitions with environmentalists, women's organizations, people of color and other progressive groups; and the importance of concrete actions to promote international solidarity.

Larry Kenney, President of the Washington State Labor Council, presents a case study of the evolution of political action strategy of the state labor federation in Washington. Within the framework of the two-party system, labor has become more active in determining the choices that voters have in general elections and in promoting labor's own candidates. Early candidate recruitment, preprimary endorsements, and substantial financial backing are central to this strategy. The conflicts and contradictions that have emerged within the Democratic party as a result of this shift in strategy provide a good illustration of the questions that face organized labor in the U.S. political system. They are not entirely different, however, from the conflicts Bernard describes between Canadian labor and the NDP, especially when the NDP moves from being the opposition to being the government.

While structural differences in the political systems are quite evident, Canadian and U.S. industrial relations systems are both based on the Wagner Act model. From this point of departure, however, they have evolved quite differently in recent decades. Anil Verma places these differences in the context of current choices facing Canadian and U.S. unions as their respective nations undergo restructuring in response to external and international pressures. He argues that Canadian and U.S. unions must take a proactive role in this restructuring process in order to preserve their essential role in the industrial relations system. Industrial relations innovations have diffused more slowly in Canada than the U.S., in part because Canada's stronger trade unions have successfully opposed the changes. This strength has bought time for Canadian labor, but such opposition will not suffice indefinitely as a strategy. Verma advocates a labor agenda for change and restructuring based on a model of joint governance characterized by procedural rather than substantive rules. Joint governance could apply to many areas including employee involvement programs, worker training, safety and health, technological change, and other workplace concerns as they arise. Despite considerable obstacles, joint governance is seen as a system compatible with collective bargaining which best balances conflict and cooperation and offers labor a path through economic transition without giving up its independence.

Labor and Politics in the U.S. and Canada

ELAINE BERNARD
Executive Director, Harvard Trade Union Program and past president of the British Columbia New Democratic Party

INTRODUCTION

In this paper I would like to do three things: make some general comments to sensitize Canadian and U.S. unionists to some of the debates and contemporary issues in both countries; briefly describe some of the significant differences between the two political systems (while attempting to avoid slipping into a Civics 101 treatise); and finally, discuss some general trends and lessons for labor from both sides of the border.

It is standard to any U.S./Canada comparative talk to start by expounding on the unique relationship between these two countries: emphasizing the peaceful nature of the relationship between our two countries for over a century, the tremendous resource wealth of the entire continent, and the shared frontier roots and immigration patterns. While Canada has the larger land territory, the U.S. population at 260 million outnumbers the Canadian by a factor of ten. The land size of Canada is impressive, but the sparse population (approximately the same as the state of California) tends to marginalize Canada's significance in U.S. consciousness. Before the recent Canadian "Meech Lake" constitutional crisis, reported in the U.S. as the possible breaking up of the nation, and the earlier Canada/U.S. Free Trade Agreement (never a major lead item in the U.S. media), Canada's main claim to fame in the U.S. media was as the source of cold weather "coming down from Canada" in the winter.

Canadians and Canada do not figure high in the consciousness of most Americans[1]—even unionists who find themselves in organizations termed "international" by virtue of their Canadian members. While Americans will readily confess to ignorance about Canadian politics and political institutions, there is an underlying feeling that overall Canadians are essentially just like Americans. Canadians are "the most domestic of foreigners," one might say. This is constantly reaffirmed by non-North Americans who insist they cannot tell the difference between Americans and Canadians.

Being constantly mistaken for Americans is something that most Canadians find annoying in the extreme. While there may be many varied and wonderful ways of describing Canadians, it frequently comes down to being simply "not Americans." No one likes being defined by what they are "not," yet, even when Canadians discuss their country, they often unconsciously accept this discourse and tend to describe Canada solely in reference to how it is different from the U.S.

Over the last few years, there has been an increased emphasis on the differences in both countries, although for very different reasons. While the labor movement has declined as a percentage of the work force in the U.S., organization has continued to increase among Canadian workers. As American working people have expressed an interest in some of Canada's more liberal labor laws, the national health care system of universal comprehensive health coverage, and the New Democratic Party (Canada's labor party), they've been told that these things are not possible within the U.S., that Canada is a very different country, and that there are profound differences in culture, institutions, and traditions that are too wide to breach. This is, of course, an argument used by conservatives and business interests who would like us to believe that unions, social programs, and even economic justice run counter to the "American" character. For many Americans, this argument may ring true in comparisons with Germany, Austria, Japan, or Sweden; but Canada is hardly seen as foreign to most Americans. In the current political climate in the U.S., unionists and progressives have been considerably bolstered by the gains made by Canadian working people. The Canadian experiences have been advocated as proven models that could be adapted to the U.S. if sufficient political pressure is mounted.

In Canada it is the progressives, rather than the conservatives, who like to emphasize the differences between the two countries. Canadian unionists and progressives want to dissociate themselves from U.S. government's international policies and interventions and the domestic attacks on working people— privatization, deregulation, and union busting—that have raged in the U.S. for many decades. Canadian progressives would like to think that the gains they have made in social programs and labor rights have become permanent features of their society. Politically, it is advantageous and popular to argue that these programs make Canada distinct from the U.S. This widely shared self-image of Canadians was summed up by a joke that was circulated shortly after U.S. President Bush coined the phrase a "kinder, gentler nation." President Bush said he wanted a kinder, gentler nation—Canada! Emphasizing the differences between Canada and the U.S., for Canadian progressives, is an attempt to defend the gains that they have made and a way of promoting further change.

It is useful for unionists on both sides of the border to be sensitive to these differences and how they are used politically by various groups. Canadians need to appreciate that although it may make good political sense at home to emphasize the differences, progressives in the U.S. are attempting to downplay the differences in order to promote important social change in their country. Similarly, Americans need to be sensitive to Canadian unionists' desires to oppose management demands for "harmonization" (at the lowest common denominator) with U.S. programs or practices.

Another important issue to highlight in this introduction is the very recent changes that have taken place in Canadian politics. The surprising results in the recent Ontario provincial elections is a clear indication of a new political consciousness.[2] In the wake of the Free Trade and the Meech Lake constitutional reform debates, there has been the rise of political awareness among English speaking Canadians[3]. These long and arduous debates have forced Canadians to carefully examine the nature of their society. I believe that in the wake of these debates, a new social democratic consciousness has been forged among English speaking Canadians, with the result being the New Democratic Party's (NDP) formation of a majority government for the first time in history in Ontario, Canada's industrial heartland and most populous province.

Finally, I would like to caution both Canadian and American unionists about overly romanticizing the rather limited gains of working people in Canada. While it may look impressive in comparison to the current situation in the U.S., Canada's social and labor policies leave much to be desired in comparison to many other advanced industrial economies. This is not an attempt to minimize these important gains, but rather to assist us in critically analyzing what factors have made it possible for us to register such gains, and what stands in the way of further achievement for working people in both countries. There have been victories and defeats on both sides of the border, and we need to share our insights into how we can promote social change and progress for working people in spite of an increasingly hostile North-American corporate environment.

POLITICS NORTH AND SOUTH

Trade unions and labor policy are greatly influenced by the political environment. The Wagner Act in the U.S., for example, is judged to be a landmark piece of legislation for trade unionists, aiding the massive growth of unionism through the 1930s and 1940s. Similarly, while not focusing on any single piece of legislation, most Canadian trade unionists would attribute at least some of their gains to a more favorable political environment. Most observers would agree that the legal framework is more sympathetic to organizing in Canada. In order to better understand why, it is important to spend some time comparing the two political systems and how labor attempts to get involved in political action.

Americans readily confess ignorance of Canadian politics and political institutions. Generally, they are very apologetic about this fact. Canadians, on the other hand, assume because of the power of the U.S. media within Canada and the international preeminence of the U.S. as the major world power, that they actually understand more than they really do about American politics. Simply put, there is a tremendous amount of confusion on both sides of the border. Although we speak the same language, the words have very different meanings.

Let me start with a simple demonstration of this last point. In both countries, we call our systems representative democracies. Both countries hold regular elections, and elect representatives at a number of levels of government to speak and legislate on our behalf. In both countries, we talk about the electoral system as being a "winner take all" system. We elect the person with the greatest number of votes, "the first past the gate." There is no proportional representation. But even the term, "winner take all" is rather confusing. In the U.S., for example, a single election does not lead to a complete clean sweep because terms of senators are staggered to institutionalize some continuity. In Canada, continuity is assured through a most undemocratic institution, an appointed upper house called the Senate.

Even the math of elections works out somewhat differently. In a U.S. primary election, the victor may not necessarily have a clear majority. But by the time of the November elections, there are generally only two choices, a Republican and a Democrat, so the successful candidate usually polls over fifty percent of the votes cast. Three-way races have not been much of a concern in the U.S. for quite a few years (although the 1990 general election saw the most successful third-party candidacies in some time), but they play a very important role in Canadian politics. In Canadian elections, the successful candidate frequently polls less than 50 percent of the total vote.

Let's examine in more detail this problem of how "the language is the same but the words have different meaning" by walking through a greatly simplified version of the election process. A first obvious question is how do you get to vote? In both countries, there is almost complete universal adult suffrage, though voters must be registered in order to vote. But here is a very significant difference. In Canada, a complete national registration is carried out by a federal government authority, imaginatively called "Elections Canada," when an election is called. In spite of the widespread registration, voter turnout in national elections in Canada is about 70 percent of the eligible voters. In the U.S., the onus is entirely on the individual citizen to get registered. Not surprisingly, in the U.S. poor people and minorities are disproportionately represented among the unregistered. In recent years only about 50 percent of those eligible to vote actually vote in presidential elections, and fewer still vote in off-year elections (Piven and Cloward, 1988, p.4).

How do we choose who will be our candidates? In the U.S. this is done through a combination of primaries, conferences, and conventions. In the state of Massachusetts, for example, in order to run for governor, you must first go to a party convention and win at least 15 percent of the vote. This allows your name to go on the ballot for the primary. Then you campaign and in September registered voters go to the polls to vote from among the primary candidates for their party candidate. Voters who have registered as Independent can vote in the primary, but they must choose either a Democrat or a Republican ballot, which re-registers them as a supporter of one of these parties. The winners of the primary for each political party then face-off in the November election.

In Canada, the political parties hold nominating conventions in each district and party members living in that district vote on who will be their candidate in the election. If you think about it, this system gives tremendous power to the political parties. Candidates may feel that they are very "electable," but if they can't win the nomination in their own party, they cannot run on the party banner. And in both Canada and the U.S., independents are very rarely elected. Party members tend to be a more focused reference group than the electorate as a whole. Various studies on the New Democratic Party (NDP) membership have shown that NDP members tend to be more pro-union, more in favor of public enterprise, and more social democratic than the Canadian electorate as a whole (Archer and Whitehorn, 1990).

Here is a massive distinction and a wonderful example of how the words are the same but the meaning totally different. A political party clearly means something very different in the two countries. Canadians are always amazed when they read U.S. labor magazines before an election and see what appears to be a political version of a "racing form," with a breakdown of the voting records of various legislators. In Canada, it is a major event when an elected official votes against his party caucus. On those rare occasions when it does happen, the individual is disciplined by being tossed out of the caucus or expelled from the party altogether. And this is not just among the left. It is true also of the Liberals and Conservatives.

In both countries labor tends to support one political party, but here again there are important distinctions behind what appears to be similar language. In the U.S., labor supports the Democrats and delivers significant votes for the Democrats. The labor movement is an important power within the Democratic party, but because of the nature of the U.S. party system, this influence within the party has not translated, for the most part, into power for labor and accountability to labor by elected legislators. To use just one illustration, in spite of a majority Democratic Congress over most of the last thirty years, labor has not been able to win any significant reforms of labor law or such significant social reforms as national health care, nor mount an effective opposition to deregulation, privatization, and government cutbacks of social programs.

In Canada, labor was a cofounder of the New Democratic Party (founded in 1961) along with the Cooperative Commonwealth Federation (a farm, labor, socialist party formed in 1932). The NDP is a social democratic labor party affiliated with the Socialist International (Archer and Whitehorn, 1990). Labor has always played a significant role in formulating party policy, and senior labor officials sit on leadership bodies of the party in most jurisdictions. Nationally for labor the problem with the NDP is that it is a third party. In national elections, it does not poll more than twenty percent of the vote, and it has never held power at this level.[4] In spite of this weakness at the national level, the party has been able to deliver some reforms for labor. In Canada, labor legislation and much social legislation is a provincial responsibility, and the party has held provincial power in some of the western provinces.[5] The Saskatchewan NDP government, for example, piloted in 1961 a system of universal comprehensive health care that became the prototype for the Canada Health Act, which extended health care to all Canadians.

The nature of the Canadian parliamentary and party systems means that once labor has convinced the party caucus to take a position, it is highly unlikely that an individual member of caucus will split ranks and vote counter to that position. There is a tendency, however, as in all social democratic parties, for disputes to take place between the caucus (the elected representatives) and the party. This becomes especially acute when the NDP is in power and party activists demand that "their" government enact key elements of party policy, such as a higher minimum wage, labor law reform, or pay equity legislation. The battle between party and caucus tends to be an ongoing struggle within the NDP. One way in which labor tries to overcome some of these conflicts is by promoting trade union activists as NDP candidates. It is felt that union activists with strong links to the labor movement would be more accountable to the labor movement, and promote labor ideas within the caucus.

Before we jump to any easy formulas about what can and should be done in the U.S., it is important to keep in mind some rather important political differences between the U.S. political system and the Canadian parliamentary system. In the U.S. there are institutionalized constitutional checks and balances. Again, this is a tricky term, because Canadians also often think of their system as having a number of "checks and balances," but the parliamentary system does not have the same power sharing concept that is found in the U.S. One simple way of illustrating the difference is that under the U.S. system there is power sharing: among the president and the executive branch, the judiciary, and the legislative branch (Congress). No one of these bodies or positions is supreme. The political system demands constant brokering and compromise, both within the legislative branch and between the executive and legislative branch. This process has been quite evident in recent decades as the Republicans have held the presidency for all but four of the last twenty-two years, while the Democrats have had a virtual lock on control of Congress.

In the Canadian system, on the other hand, parliament is, indeed, supreme. While compromise may be necessary when there is a minority government (no single party has a majority of votes in the house), majority governments have few institutionalized checks on their power. Commenting on the tremendous power of parliaments, more than one critic has labeled them as "elected dictatorships."

Many Americans have commented on what they believe to be the superiority of the parliamentary system, in that a "bad government" can be defeated in parliament and forced to go to the people before the regularly scheduled election. In practice though, this only happens in a minority government situation. The reality of Canadian parliamentary practice, where elected members always vote along party lines, means that as long as a government has a majority it can choose when it will go to the polls. Not surprisingly, this timing usually works to the government's advantage. The recent provincial election in Ontario is rather the exception that proves the rule. Here, the provincial Liberal government chose to hold a summer election while it was ahead in the polls, but the voters in Ontario used this opportunity instead to remove them from office.

LABOR POLITICAL ACTION NORTH AND SOUTH

Let's briefly look at labor's political strategy. In Canada, the main disadvantage to labor's official support for a political party is that at a federal level (and in some provinces) the NDP is not much of a "contender." There is the charge that workers are throwing away their vote on a third party rather than seeking influence through support of one of the two larger parties. Also, there are some who feel that affiliation to a political party compromises labor when it lobbies the government in power. Finally, there is some opposition within labor by union members who feel that affiliation to a political party is an attempt by the labor leadership to tell members how to vote.

However, for the most part, affiliation with the NDP has not undergone serious challenge within the labor movement in recent years. Most labor leaders argue that the advantages far outweigh the disadvantages. Both at the federal and provincial level, the NDP has played an important role in legitimating an alternative view and agenda in Canadian society. Where the NDP has held power—provincially—labor has been able to win some significant reforms with NDP governments.[6] But, even when the party is in opposition it has assisted in legitimating labor's concerns and can delay or force a government to withdraw legislation opposed by labor.

There has also been criticism of the NDP from labor for not implementing its program when in power, and/or watering down its policy formulated at convention in an attempt to curry favor with business, or position itself in the "mainstream" of public opinion. In the last federal election, for example, a number of labor leaders expressed disappointment with the NDP federal campaign's failure to make a stronger case in opposition to the Canada/U.S. Free Trade Agreement. But criticisms such as these have led to discussions not about abandoning the NDP, but rather how labor can "influence" the party more and how candidates and elected officials can be made more accountable.

In a certain sense, the NDP is more than a political party for labor. It is a political coalition, which provides a structure for labor and other progressive groups, such as the women's movement, environmentalists, students, and the peace movement, to work together. There is, of course, a constant tension within the party—expressing the very different organizational practices and beliefs of groups and individuals affiliated to the NDP. But, by and large, the party serves as a vehicle by which all of these groups can work together politically and influence each other, enhancing dialogue, while at the same time providing the cohesion to keep them together. At times, especially when compared to the U.S., the mutual influence between the popular movements and labor is readily apparent. Labor in Canada appears less separated from the popular movements and at least some of this is attributable to the NDP providing a common ground for activists to work together. The NDP gives labor a voice in politics that is not easily relegated to the charge of representing a "special-interest group."

Lastly, the NDP as a third party changes the political mathematics of elections in Canada. With three parties in the race, you do not necessarily need 50 percent to win. Most governments in Canadian jurisdictions win majorities with less than 50 percent of the vote. In the recent elections in Ontario, for example, the NDP won an impressive majority of 74 out of a possible 130 seats with only 38 percent of the popular vote.

In the U.S., labor generally supports the Democratic party, but it is not officially affiliated with the party. The Democratic party is, of course, neither a social democratic nor a labor party. In some states, where the Democratic party is strong, it is believed that labor's influence has made possible some progressive legislation and prevented antilabor legislation such as "right-to-work." But in the U.S., most labor legislation is federal and very little headway has been made in labor law reform at the national level.

In spite of their failure to win presidential elections over the last decade, the Democrats are certainly "contenders," at the federal as well as the state level. Nevertheless, there is a certain amount of frustration felt by labor with the Democrats. The nature of the U.S. congressional system and party structure means that even though labor may carry significant influence within the party, this does not necessarily translate into influence over elected officials. While labor still adheres to American Federation of Labor President Samuel Gompers' strategy of "rewarding your friends and penalizing your enemies," in practice labor has found this to be easier said than done. In a political system where it now costs at least three million dollars to run for Senate in most states (and far more in some), and where there are only two political parties, labor's rewards are small compared to business, and it has had a great deal of difficulty exacting a penalty. In recent years, labor has often been forced into a "lesser evil" strategy of voting to stop an antilabor candidate rather than working to promote a prolabor one or, indeed, supporting trade unionists as candidates. The voting records that labor publishes before an election are an attempt to help members identify "good" Democrats and legislators who should be supported because they have voted with labor's interests.

Labor does not appear to be the only group that is dissatisfied with the Democrats. The Rainbow Coalition, for example, works both inside and outside of the Democratic party to promote a progressive agenda. While at different times throughout the twentieth century labor leaders in the U.S. have called for the building of a labor or social democratic party, and even participated in third- party groupings, there are few in the labor movement today who are prepared to promote such an idea at this time. The reasons they give are mostly structural, arguing that the U.S. political system has stringent barriers to third parties, including the need for mass petitioning in order to get on the ballot. A further argument specifically in opposition to a "labor" party is labor's own relative weakness in U.S. society. Currently down to approximately 17 percent of the work force, a labor party would not be a broad enough reflection of U.S. working-class interests and diversity. Finally, it is argued that in the short term such a party could not elect anyone, therefore workers would simply be "wasting" their votes.

There are, of course, some interesting exceptions. Last year, Jackie Stump, District 28 international executive board member of the United Mine Workers of America, won a seat as an independent in the West Virginia State Legislature. In the process, Stump defeated a twenty-year incumbent Democrat. While this campaign took place during the highly politicized Pittston Coal Mine strike, it is that much more remarkable because Stump won as a "write-in" candidate in a thirty-day campaign. More recently, in last fall's election, Bernie Sanders, an independent socialist, was elected to Congress from Vermont.

But independent labor political action appears to be very much the exception to the rule in the U.S. at the moment.[7] More attention is being paid in recent years to avoiding a "scorched-earth policy" of condemning all politicians, and towards seeking an effective tool for labor to "penalize" labor's political enemies and hold elected representatives accountable. Within labor there is a growing demand that it become increasingly selective about its political support. Washington AFL/CIO President Lawrence Kenney (1991) has articulated this demand and its tactical implications.

While in both countries there is a growing dissatisfaction with incumbents and with politicians in general, in Canada this anger has tended to pay off for the NDP—which is viewed as not one of the "old line" or "establishment" parties. While some media pundits have suggested that the election of the NDP in Ontario was more a case of voting out the Liberals and Progressive Conservatives rather than voting for the NDP, two upcoming provincial elections that might prove my contention are those in Saskatchewan and British Columbia. Also, while the other two major political parties in Canada have over the last few years been dropping in popularity, the NDP appears to be growing in its "hard" vote.

GENERAL TRENDS AND LESSONS

If there is a single common trend on both sides of the border, it is a growing awareness of the need for labor to become more politically active. This has always been a debatable issue within the labor movement. Increasingly, unionists in Canada and the U.S. are seeing that issues such as free trade, deregulation, privatization, plant closures, occupational health and safety, and technological change can rarely be dealt with solely at the bargaining table. One might question whether it was ever appropriate to make a hard and fast distinction between collective bargaining and political action, but few unionists today believe that labor can leave the political arena to corporate interests.

Yet, in both countries there has been a concerted campaign to chase working people and unions out of the political arena. U.S. President Ronald Reagan performed a masterful job in placing labor further on the defensive and delegitimatizing working-class political action when he labeled labor as a "special-interest group," along with women, Afro-Americans, Hispanics, people of color, environmentalists, peace activists, the disabled, youth, elderly, etc. In short, in President Reagan's view everyone but business and corporate interests—who represent, of course, the "national interest"—are to be viewed as "special interests."

Similarly in Canada, the NDP is baited as a "captive" of special interest groups. The charge has had some effect in placing labor on the defensive in its political support. Interestingly, until very recently the NDP was reluctant to return the charge and label the Liberals and Conservatives "captives of Bay Street and Wall Street."

Aside from attempting to delegitimatize labor political participation through the charge of special interest, there are the further difficulties in the U.S. of getting working people registered. The U.S. is one of the only advanced industrial countries where the federal government takes no responsibility in assuring that the electorate is registered.

But in my assessment, the most significant factor in driving unionists from political action has been demoralization. While this is more acutely felt in the U.S. than in Canada, these are clearly tough times for organized labor. There is a widespread feeling within the movement that labor is powerless in face of deregulation, plant closures, and work reorganization. Many unionists today believe that there is nothing that labor can do to stem these international forces.

Canadian workers are not immune to this feeling of powerlessness but they are generally less demoralized than labor in the U.S. One might suggest that there is some false bravado that comes from constantly comparing the situation of Canadian unions with the U.S. Canadian labors' organizing of 36 percent of the work force and its affiliation to and building of a social democratic party which appears to be on the rise has given Canadian workers a tremendous boost. The false bravado is reflected in the fact that Canadian workers have not been significantly more successful than their U.S. counterparts in stemming the tide of deregulation, work reorganization, and plant closures, even if they have made impressive gains in union membership through the 1970s and 1980s. As well, the recent Ontario victory of the NDP has contributed to the belief that the collective strength of labor in conjunction with the NDP can still make a difference in the political arena.

While I think it is fair to say that labor in both Canada and the U.S. is relatively weak, especially compared to the massive challenges before it, it would be wrong to suggest that labor is powerless. The history of the labor movement in both countries tends to point to the fact that innovation and transformation by labor comes out of weakness, not strength. When labor is weak, it is forced for its own survival to find new sources of strength. Some of these new sources of strength include:

- Making international labor solidarity more concrete, through mutual support and organizing pacts such as the one initiated by the Communication Workers of America (CWA), the Communications and Electrical Workers of Canada, and the Canadian Auto Workers;
- organizing campaigns that draw in the whole community, such as the Century City organizing drive of custodial workers, which was part of the "Justice for Janitors" campaign, and the CWA's "Jobs With Justice" campaign; and
- reorganizing our own organizations as the B.C. Government Employees Union has done in face of massive "privatization" of provincial government services, which saw the union change from close to 100 percent public employees to a union of 60 percent public employees.

Joe Hill, the Wobbly (Industrial Workers of the World) activist and songwriter, told the American working class in his last will and testament, "Don't Mourn, Organize." One suspects that if he could return today, his advice would be slightly modified to "don't whine, organize." This is not to suggest that the problems that labor faces are not real, merely that there is a tendency within labor to reinforce the negativism and to add to the generalized feeling of powerlessness.

The period we are currently going through in both countries, indeed internationally, is one of rapid, radical change. Most institutions, from banks to schools, and from unions to management, are undergoing dramatic change. Much of labor's strengths and its strategies in the preceding years have been based upon accommodations to institutions and organizations that are today being transformed. Labor learned how to use its collective strength within the social/political environment of the time. Today, of course, this environment is changing. There were many problems with the accommodations that labor reached in the post-World War II period. While we could debate endlessly the pros and cons of such moves, few would argue that that world and those accommodations to it are rapidly disappearing. Now, we have again a chance to build anew. For labor to survive and grow, it must also change.

The challenge is to move from the defensive arena of preserving what we have to a leadership position of mobilizing working people to effect positive social change. It is clearly easier for labor in Canada to proceed with such an agenda because of the NDP. But as I hope I have shown, even with a labor party there are still major barriers and problems in effecting change in favor of working people. In the U.S., the growing dissatisfaction with the narrow political alternatives offered provides a tremendous opportunity for labor political action. American socialist labor leader Eugene V. Debs once cautioned the American workers that it was "better to vote for something you want and not get it, than to vote for something you don't want and get it." It's a good caution that still has tremendous relevance for working people today.

ENDNOTES

[1] Canadians, like most Central and South Americans, do not use the term "American" to refer to citizens of the United States of America, but in deference to U.S. readers and for brevity's sake, I have used the term unionists in the U.S. are most familiar with throughout this paper.

[2] In a victory that few predicted, on September 6, 1990, the NDP won a majority of seats in the provincial election in Ontario.

[3] Progressives in Canada generally use the term English speaking Canada in recognition that politics and culture are very different in Quebec. Most of the statements I am making about Canada are very broad strokes, even for English Canada, and they certainly do not apply to Quebec.

[4] In recent years, Canadians have tended to elect governments with majorities, which means that third parties do not have very much power in Parliament. In minority government situations, the third party's role is much more significant—it can hold the balance of power in Parliament and wrestle concessions out of the government in return for support in Parliament.

[5] Specifically, the NDP has held power in Saskatchewan, Manitoba, British Columbia and the Yukon. It currently holds power only in Yukon and Ontario.

[6] A July 20, 1989 NDP "Report of the Task Force on Labour/Party Relations," lists a variety of legislative firsts achieved by the CCF/NDP (the CCF being the NDP's predecessor). These achievements are listed under the following titles: health care, pensions, labour legislation, labour standards, (anti-scab) strikebreaking, pay equity, housing, public enterprises and review, and family support.

[7] Independent labor political action refers to a strategy by labor to engage in political action but remain independent of the parties of business.

REFERENCES

Archer, Keith, and Alan Whitehorn. "Organized Labour in the New Democratic Party." Paper presented at the Annual Meeting of the Canadian Political Science Association, University of Victoria, B.C., May 27–29, 1990.

Kenney, Lawrence,"The Political Action Strategy of the Washington State Labor Council." In *Labor in a Global Economy: Perspectives from the U.S. and Canada*, Edited by Steven Hecker and Margaret Hallock. Eugene, Oregon: U of O Books, 1991.

Piven, Frances Fox, and Richard A. Cloward. *Why Americans Don't Vote*. New York: Pantheon Books, 1988.

The Political Action Strategy of the Washington State Labor Council

LAWRENCE KENNEY

President, Washington State Labor Council, AFL-CIO

Twenty years ago when I began work with the Washington State Labor Council, our political action program was the essence of simplicity. Filing for public office began the last week of July. Our conventions were held the last week in August. The primary election was about three weeks after that. That allowed just enough time to interview most candidates and make some endorsements. Following the convention and the Labor Day holiday, we would notify those we had endorsed. And, if it was justified, we would send them some money. Our endorsements were too late to be of use in the primary election, and the money came far too late to be used effectively.

In the early 1970s, we began making congressional endorsements at the AFL-CIO Regional Conference held in the spring. Then we began taking early action in some legislative races. When State Senate majority leader Augie Mardesich was challenged in the 1978 Democratic primary, the State Labor Council Executive Board immediately endorsed his challenger, Larry Vognild, and contributed $10 thousand to the campaign—the largest legislative contribution ever made up to that time. Aided by a united labor political effort, Vognild won. He is now the Senate Democratic leader, the same job Mardesich held. That may do nothing more than give credence to the comment that "every problem was once a solution." But that's a different story.

In the late 1970s, we began regular informal meetings with some of the politically active unions and other Democratic support groups. The Round Table was made up of organizations with a commitment to political action and a willingness to pony up some bucks. What the Round Table did mostly was talk. The legislative caucuses or the party would look for candidates. Labor would discuss the campaigns and support or not support the caucus choices with varying degrees of enthusiasm.

About ten years ago we started holding an endorsing convention almost two months before filing for legislative office began. We became actively involved in primary races. Our endorsements often determined whether or not a particular candidate filed for office. Democrats who failed to get labor's endorsement sometimes would decide not to run. Although we were now exercising more influence earlier in the process, we still were mostly ratifying choices made by the Democratic legislative caucuses.

The caucuses asked only two questions of potential candidates. Question one was "Can you win?" If the answer to that was yes; the second question was "Will you run as a Democrat?" We thought there should be a third question: "What is it you believe in?" By the time we had an opportunity to ask, our options were to support the caucus choice or sit on the sidelines.

Three years ago, we changed our approach. The labor council hired a political coordinator whose job includes recruiting candidates for legislative office, advising endorsed candidates on campaign strategy, and coordinating organized labor's efforts, including fundraising, on behalf of our endorsed candidates.

Our very first year we went head-to-head with the Senate Democratic Caucus. In a conservative district in Spokane, they recruited a Democratic sheriff who was not the kind of Democrat we were willing to support. The labor council recruited a certified prolabor, ACLU liberal. We encouraged him to file and helped him plan a campaign. The Democratic caucus tried to convince us that we should support a winner, but we told them that they should support a Democrat. We won the battle when our candidate filed and theirs didn't. But we lost the war. Our candidate got about 40 percent of the vote in the general election.

That's an accurate description of the election results. But it's not a very useful analysis. We did, indeed, lose the election. It was an overwhelmingly Republican district. It was probably a poor place to take a stand, but it was the only place available. Our efforts were not in vain, however, as the Democrats learned that we are serious and that we will take chances, and as a result, the Democratic caucuses are now more selective in their recruiting.

To us, the issue is not just winning. The issue is developing credible candidates who will provide a Democratic majority that supports labor programs. That creates conflicts between us and the Democrats. It also raises concerns within organized labor. The goal of most of labor's political directors is Democratic control in the Legislature. When the Democrats are in the majority, they decide committee assignments and set the agenda. We agree that a Democratic majority is important, partly because bad legislation gets killed in committee. But the good bills that race through the committees that the Democrats control may not go any further if two or three Democratic legislators desert us when the votes are counted on the floor. Friendly committees aren't enough; we need effective majorities.

The Republican majority in the Washington Senate should be a good object lesson. With only a one-vote margin, they have effectively controlled every issue in the Senate for the last two years. The Republican caucus has shown the Democrats what it means to have true "solidarity."

I have been critical of the caucuses and I have been vocal about their shortcomings. That may not always be fair. Unlike the Republicans, neither the Democratic party nor the Democratic caucuses control enough money to be the most critical influence over Democratic candidates. For the most part, Democrats have to raise their own money and build their own campaign organizations. It may be that neither the party nor the caucuses are in a position to ask the tough questions, but someone has to ask, and perhaps we are the only ones who can. Even more likely, we may be the only ones who are willing.

This year, we were involved in a primary election battle to eliminate an incumbent Democrat, Senator Brad Owen. He's conservative and antiworker. Three years ago, when the Democrats had a one-vote majority, he voted with the Senate Republicans and gave them control on key budget issues. Despite his desertion on the budget, the Senate Democrats reappointed Owen to the Ways and Means Committee. That's like making somebody who crosses a picket line the head of the union organizing committee. The caucus didn't punish Owen for deserting them. We had to make a decision. The Democrats weren't going to hold their members accountable, and if anybody was going to, it had to be us.

We looked hard for a candidate against Owen. Our first choice was an incumbent House member, but he decided he wouldn't even run for reelection. We kept looking and we found Dan Scott, a union carpenter and an elected public utility district commissioner. Labor spent almost $100 thousand on Dan Scott's campaign. That's money that could help the Democrats win the one additional vote that they needed for a majority in the Senate. Hard work and a little luck could pick up that additional seat, but the effort is going to be $100 thousand and a lot of volunteer hours short of what it could be.

Dan Scott lost to Brad Owen. The election result was less important to us than doing the right thing—making the effort. We reminded the caucus leadership and Democratic senators at every opportunity of what we were doing. We can, and we will, hold Democratic legislators accountable to us, their largest constituency. It only makes sense. Recruiting is expensive and time-consuming. Candidates are not easy to find, and winning candidates are even harder to find. Winners who share our philosophy aren't hanging around waiting to be discovered. We spent a lot of time looking for Dan Scott. We put additional time into helping him develop a strategy and a campaign plan, and then convincing organized labor that it was a fight for all of us, and that it was worth making.

Our recruiting program has paid off with some winning campaigns. We have had some real success stories since we shifted direction. There have been some valuable additions to the Washington State

Legislature who would not be there if it had not been for our efforts. But some verities still hold. Once a candidate is elected, he or she is an officeholder and starts worrying about getting reelected. And too many other Democratic legislators try to convince them that the best way to get reelected is to avoid offending anyone, especially business.

But labor issues require legislators to take sides—with us or against us. When legislators have to choose, they consider that a "tough" vote—a situation they would prefer to avoid. "Tough votes" are an interesting phenomenon. Some of our "friends" tell us on key votes that they support our position but can't afford to vote for us and risk offending business. They are afraid they will be targeted during the next campaign if they vote for workers' rights. But in all the campaigns I've been involved in, I have never seen a political attack on any legislator because of a vote for on-the-job safety, because of a vote to help injured workers. Too many Democrats try to curry favor with business. And some of them succeed—for a while. But the minute strong probusiness candidates surface against them, business closes ranks. All the Democrats' sacrifices on the altar of business amount to naught because the business lobbyists know who their real friends are. Labor should have that same clear understanding.

What we are doing in Washington state is not a program for every state labor organization. Some critical elements must be present, and there are no guarantees. To begin with, it's a long-term project, since fundamental change does not come easily. We are doing no less than changing the basic relationships between organized labor and its political allies.

A good staff is critical, but the program must not be viewed as a staff function. There has to be involvement and commitment from the top leadership. A strong Democratic base in the Legislature is essential. It does no good to discipline a minority or a weak party. Labor's political and legislative goals have to be well defined. Support from a large majority of the Democrats for labor's programs is also necessary. Our goal is not to change the Democrats' agenda, but to rearrange their priorities.

There must be an existing cooperative relationship between organized labor and the Democrats. Change puts stress on relationships. Despite our differences, we work well with the Democratic leaders in the Legislature. We don't ignore our differences, but that doesn't mean that we have to go to the mat every time we disagree. It means that we raise the issues and we make our position clear. And when we have to go our own way, we do it!

Our political program subjects us to a lot of criticism. We have to take chances, and our judgments are not infallible. We have to make our stand in the tough races, and that means we are going uphill all the time. It makes no sense to take a stand on somebody who clearly is going to win. We have to take candidates who are behind and try to make them into winners. Our critics don't hesitate to let us know when they disagree, but that's not unexpected and it comes with the territory.

A lot of time must be spent with labor's political leaders discussing the program and talking about why it's important to take chances. Success is easy to explain and it generates support for future efforts. Losses are tougher to live with and excuses make for lousy brochures. That means we have to keep the focus on our goals and talk about how the program will get us there.

The labor coalition must be broad-based and include every union that can and will contribute to the effort. Everybody should understand the agenda, even if they don't agree with all of it. Legislators and other support groups should be invited to participate, but labor must be in control for it is, after all, a program for labor.

One of the lessons that has been driven home to me in the five years that I have been president of the Washington State Labor Council is that organized labor is a coalition. There are a lot of agendas, a lot of strong-willed people, a lot of differences among unions. There is no single source of power, no overwhelming authority figure. The president of the state labor council can exercise a lot of influence, but not much real power. Still there is a considerable willingness within the ranks of labor to work together, and when we are united, we are a formidable force.

Restructuring in Industrial Relations and the Role for Labor

ANIL VERMA

Associate Professor, Centre for Industrial Relations and Faculty of Management, University of Toronto

INTRODUCTION

The economies of Canada and the United States, like those of other industrialized nations, are under great pressure to restructure in response to a marketplace characterized by freer international trade, shifting loci of manufacturing competitiveness, and growing concern about environmental pollution. The workplace has been changing rapidly since the 1980s and some observers believe that the pace of change may accelerate further in the 1990s. Labor in both countries is besieged with demands for a flexible and adaptable workplace that can respond effectively to shifting market demands. For labor, these demands translate into pressures to lower manufacturing costs, implement new forms of work organization, introduce nontraditional compensation systems, eliminate restrictive work rules, and to assist in effective implementation of new technologies.

The challenge for free, democratic, and open economies is to make the transition to a system of industrial relations that will meet the needs of the market while preserving the pluralist tradition that provides fairness and justice on the job. Based on this premise, two themes guide the analysis and conclusions in this paper. First, industrial relations and human resource practices and policies will play a central role in any strategy to improve the performance of the U.S. and Canadian economies. Second, any industrial relations strategy that hopes to be effective in transforming the workplace must build on the pluralist foundation that recognizes the legitimacy of all parties to the system. In other words, an economic strategy that pursues the goals of productivity and quality to the exclusion of those that enhance equity and job security is not likely to be very successful in the long run. The evolving order, therefore, must be a negotiated one among all the parties. It cannot be a directed order achieved through the dominance of one party over the others.

This paper examines the often difficult and sometimes problematic role in which the labor movement finds itself in this transition. In the pluralist political system that prevails in North America, labor's role is more crucial than in jurisdictions where pluralist values are not paramount. After a brief overview of the economic situation facing the North American economy and an account of recent developments, a theoretical model of the conditions under which major change in industrial relations occurs is presented. This is followed by a discussion of the potential role of labor in organizational governance and the change process in industrial relations.

In conclusion, the paper proposes that labor should examine the merits of and adopt policies to move towards a system of joint governance of the workplace. Joint governance, it is argued, can provide flexibility and safeguard labor's interests—i.e., strengthen union security and promote worker welfare—at the same time without dramatically altering the system of collective bargaining. Joint governance offers a unique compromise between the extremes of conflict and cooperation, neither of which are likely solutions for an increasingly complex workplace.

Partial financial support from the Social Sciences and Humanities Research Council of Canada is gratefully acknowledged.

EXTERNAL PRESSURES FOR CHANGE

External pressures for change are real and present. Even as labor prepares to fight within the political process for better protection from unfair trade, there is a need to develop a workplace strategy for enhancing productivity without capitulating to management demands. In this context, it is important to understand the pressures for change and their origin.

There are several aspects of international trade today that must be assessed for their impact on industrial relations. First, there is the growth in trade in manufactured goods from the newly industrializing countries (NICs). A number of Asian countries as well as others like Brazil have emerged as exporters of goods that were traditionally traded exclusively by the industrialized countries. According to the International Monetary Fund, the Asian NICs, along with Brazil, increased their share of world exports from about 3 percent in 1965 to roughly 9 percent by the late 1980s (Farrow, 1988). Although this share is still relatively small it is expected to continue to grow at a rapid rate in the 1990s and beyond. Since labor costs are much lower in these countries (compared to those in the industrialized countries), low labor costs form a substantial part of their competitive strength.

A second development is the growing trade in technology and technology-based goods. These goods are distinguished from other goods by the fact that the cost of production is a very small fraction of its selling price. Most of its revenue goes to paying for the cost of developing the technology. Computer software is a good example of such a product. The seller must recover the investment quickly before the next generation of technology makes the product obsolete. These markets are driven by new innovations and unless a firm can bring new technologies to the market quickly, it is likely to be preempted by others.

A third development is the demand for quality in international markets. For example, in the 1950s and 1960s, most automobiles produced in North America, Europe or Japan were consumed in domestic markets. While consumers have always been conscious of quality, they did not have a chance in the past to effectively compare autos made elsewhere. In more recent years, the consumer has been exposed to a wide range of choices which in turn has brought unprecedented pressure on automakers to meet exacting quality standards.

Lastly, faced with lower cost competition from the NICs, many firms in the industrialized world have chosen to compete by adopting the differentiation strategy (Porter, 1980, 1989). A firm unable to lower costs to levels obtainable in other less-developed countries competes by differentiating its products from others. Successful differentiation, however, requires that the firm employ technological and organizational innovation to develop new products quickly. Thus, a trained and adaptable work force is indispensable to a company pursuing the differentiation route.

The preceding discussion highlights three important considerations for policy making in industrial relations. First, given these developments in international trade, our workplaces are faced with a growing demand for high quality at moderate cost. Second, technological innovation is increasingly the cornerstone for competing successfully. Third, the dynamic nature of global competition requires that workplaces be adaptive and flexible in their response to changing markets. We must be able to respond quickly in areas such as production scheduling, product lines, and design changes. In order to meet these needs and stay competitive, organizations need a work force that is skilled and well trained, involved and committed, and steeped in an environment that encourages innovation.[1]

THE EVIDENCE ON CHANGE AND INNOVATION[2] IN INDUSTRIAL RELATIONS

After a slow start in the 1970s, workplace innovations were introduced rapidly in the U.S. in the 1980s. A survey by the American Management Association showed that employee participation programs such as semiautonomous work groups and quality circles could be found in 28 percent to 36 percent of U.S.

firms (Goodmeasure, 1985). At first, it was believed that a large majority of these programs were adopted in the nonunion sector. More recent surveys, however, suggest that the adoption rate is nearly the same in the union sector. In a survey of firms' strategic business units, Ichniowski, Delaney, and Lewin (1988) found that the incidence of employee participation programs in the union sector (49 percent) compared favorably with that in the nonunion sector (44 percent).

Firm level innovations have gone considerably beyond the simple quality circles or other narrow forms of employee participation. By the late 1980s considerable use of team systems of production could be found in selected manufacturing plants (especially in the auto industry). In the steel, trucking, and airline industries employees and unions experimented with representation at the strategic level of the firm by trading wage and work rule concessions for employee stock ownership plans (ESOPs). In a small but growing number of cases worker representatives are consulted in the early stages of planning and design of new plants or processes.

In Canada, these innovations also could be observed in the 1980s but were not as broadly diffused. Although an Economic Council of Canada survey found semiautonomous work groups in 11 percent of the establishments surveyed and quality circles in 14 percent, there are some indications that these numbers may be somewhat overstated because of the higher adoption rate in the nonunion sector (Betcherman and McMullen, 1986). For example, according to Labour Canada's national file of collective agreements covering 500 or more workers, only 1.7 percent of the establishments reported a provision allowing for a joint Quality of Work Life (QWL) committee. In Ontario, a joint labor-management task force on employment and technology also found a low incidence of QWL-type programs (Kumar, Coates, and Arrowsmith, 1986).

Gain-sharing and profit-sharing plans, too, have diffused to a very limited extent in Canada. One study found that profit-sharing and gain-sharing plans, broadly defined, grew from 2 percent of direct labor costs in 1957 to a little over 3 percent "recently" (Riddell, 1987). During the same time period, fringe benefit costs rose from about 15 percent of labor costs to over 30 percent. According to Labour Canada's national file of collective agreements covering five hundred or more workers, six agreements (or 0.5 percent) provided for profit sharing in 1988 and another twenty-two (or 2 percent) contained provisions for various types of productivity bonuses (Labour Canada, 1988).

In the area of job security, the Labour Canada collective agreements file shows that 116 (or 10.4 percent) of all agreements covering 500 or more workers contained variants of employment security provisions. While this coverage is low, it strongly suggests that employment security is fast becoming a major concern on the collective bargaining agenda. This evidence suggests that overall, the pace of change has been much slower in Canada than in the United States in the 1980s.

CONDITIONS FOR MAJOR CHANGE IN INDUSTRIAL RELATIONS

If change and innovations have not diffused rapidly enough, it is possible that our pace of restructuring may be too slow to give us the competitive advantage that is needed. For labor, too often in the past restructuring issues (plant closures, wage concessions, work rule changes) have been posed with little or no time to respond. To look ahead, therefore, labor must consider its role in this process proactively. Should it have a role and if yes, what may that role be in its substance? Before examining the details of labor's policy choices, it is instructive to look at the conditions under which major change occurs in industrial relations.

The concept of strategic choice suggests that the actors in the system make choices in response to external pressures (Kochan, Katz, and McKersie, 1986). At times this implies that the 'elbow room' for making choices is large and substantial. In the context of innovations, it implies that the decision to innovate is fully within the parties' control and that lack of innovative progress is a sign of the parties' unwillingness to experiment. While this line of reasoning explains a measure of reality, it does not fully capture the constraints that are often unsurmountable, at least in the short run, by the parties to the industrial relations system.[3]

To further develop the constraints and facilitators of the change process, let us consider the interaction between factors that are relatively beyond the immediate control of the parties and those that are relatively within their control. The relative power between labor and management that is determined by market and technological conditions (also known as the Marshallian conditions) can be assumed to be relatively fixed in the short run. Thus, the parties have little control over it. On the other hand, the extent of communication between the parties, characterized *inter alia* by frequency of

FIGURE 1: CONDITIONS UNDER WHICH MAJOR CHANGE OCCURS IN INDUSTRIAL RELATIONS SYSTEMS

RELATIVE POWER	COMMUNICATION	STRATEGY
Equal	Good	Restructure: teams, socio-technical designs, etc.
	Moderate	Slow innovation
	Bad	Flight closure relocation divesture
Unequal	Good	Concessions with restructuring
	Moderate	Unilateral management initiatives
	Bad	Decertification Unilateral management initiatives

meetings and willingness to exchange information, is fully under the parties' control. Such communication does not depend on market or technological conditions. Thus, communication links lie primarily in the domain of strategic choices.

Figure 1 shows the different combinations of these two factors and the implications for the innovative and change process. For our purposes, relative power is defined in terms of management's ability to override union interests. When power is relatively unequal between the parties (i.e., management has the upper hand), management has the ability to impose changes in the short run. Widespread concessions in the 1980s in many industries in the U.S. are a good example of management's ability to impose changes. In the long run, this ability translates into union avoidance options such as relocation to green-field sites, disinvestment in old unionized plants, and decertification of existing unions. In the same way, relatively equal power would imply that management's ability to impose changes or to avoid unions through decertification or relocation is severely limited.

Concessions and union avoidance though widespread in the U.S., are far from being universal. Even under conditions of relatively unequal power, some parties appear to develop a few alternatives to total union substitution. Where the parties have developed good communication, either from an earlier time period or during the 1980s crisis years, these early concessions are followed up with a mutual desire to repair relations by engaging in innovations. The innovations do not necessarily alter the underlying relative power between the parties, but they do seem to give labor some measure of power within the overall structure in which management continues to enjoy a superior status. Thus, each side gains from the restructuring process without altering the overall power equation. As can be expected, many of these innovations are judged harshly by the critics (in labor and academe) because they have been negotiated under conditions of unequal power (Parker and Slaughter, 1988; Drago and McDonough, 1984; Rinehart, 1984).

Where the parties have little or no communication and the relative power is unequal, the joint change process comes to a grinding halt because management has little incentive to consult the union on innovations. Decertification followed by unilateral management initiatives to introduce innovations are frequent responses under these conditions. Since the union is completely neutralized under these conditions, innovations introduced under these conditions frequently lack any safeguards for workers' interests. In the long run, only a handful of these cases go on to develop a stable nonunion employment system.

In cases where communications are moderately good under conditions of relatively unequal power, management frequently takes unilateral action to introduce innovations such as employee involvement or profit-sharing plans. Much of the time, the union has little information on innovations being considered by management because managers share some things but not others. The union finds out about management plans only at the bargaining table when it is too late for the union to conduct its own study of the proposed innovation and to formulate a feasible counter-strategy.

Attempts to seek extensions or to defer the issue to the future are often unsuccessful because management has the ability to either impose the innovation unilaterally (e.g. in the case of employee involvement programs) or threaten job losses through shutdown or relocation (e.g. in the case of profit-sharing plans). Once again, innovations introduced under these conditions are not likely to be as effective because union consent is frequently obtained under duress.

Conditions of Equal Power

The change process typically has different characteristics under conditions of relatively equal power. Management does not have the ability to impose changes in the short run and it may not be able to get rid of the union in the long run because of geographical, institutional, and political factors. With relatively equal power, the worst case is that of bad communications when all innovation comes to a halt because management frequently opts for flight through closure, relocation, or divestiture. A bankruptcy closure is a loss for both sides; though, in most other cases of flight, the real losers are the workers. Such cases often serve as an illustration to others of the high costs of this option. On the other hand, if communications are good, the parties have the best chance of negotiating a series of interlinked innovations that amount to a total restructuring of the firm. Such innovations have the best chance of success in terms of being effective, stable, and becoming institutionalized.

In the in-between case where communications are only moderately good and the power is relatively equal, the change process is slowed down, considerably so in many cases. Often the union is in a position to demand advance notification of innovation proposals. Once the proposals are made known, the union can take some time to study the innovations. Lastly, the union can effectively oppose the proposed innovation or ask for changes in the original design. Even when some innovations are agreed to, any major crisis in the power relationship can lead to a revocation of the innovation agreement. Frequently, a major layoff, a closure, or a major dispute in bargaining can result in one side sharply reducing its cooperation if not completely withdrawing support of the agreement on innovations. The effect of all this is to slow down the diffusion process.

THE ROLE OF LABOR IN THE RESTRUCTURING AND CHANGE PROCESS

The previous analysis identifies the willingness and ability of unions to oppose innovations as a major factor in slowing down the introduction of innovations in Canada. Two major provincial federations of labor, in Ontario and British Columbia, as well as large unions like the Canadian Auto Workers (CAW) and the Canadian Paperworkers Union (CPU) have officially adopted policies opposing several forms of innovations. Since employers have relatively fewer options to avoid unions, the trade union policy of opposition often results in effectively blocking the introduction of innovations. Similarly, the widespread diffusion of many innovations in the U.S. appears to be related, at least in part, to the ability of management to either negotiate changes from a position of greater power or to impose them unilaterally if negotiations prove unsuccessful (Kochan and Verma, 1989).

Canadian and American unions enter the 1990s in fundamentally different positions within their respective industrial relations systems, differences which have important differential consequences for the nature and pace of innovations one can expect to see in these two countries in future years (Verma and Kochan, 1990). Canadian unions enjoy a stronger position of power first because they represent a significantly higher percentage of the labor force (roughly 36 percent compared to 16 percent in the U.S.). Second, partly because of the higher levels of union coverage and partly because of the more stringent enforcement of labor law, Canadian employers do not have the same options as their U.S. counterparts to relocate and escape unions (Verma and Thompson, 1989). Third, Canadian political institutions and the political process also results in greater say for the labor movement (Bruce, 1989). Thus, one major difference between the two countries is that the strategies adopted by Canadian labor leaders are likely to have a greater effect on the innovative process than have their counterparts in the U.S.

Having established that union power can slow down the pace of change, the big issue that faces the labor movement is the question of how labor can use the time gained from a delayed pace of change to further its interests. Labor faces two choices at this juncture. One approach would be to continue to oppose such restructuring with the objective of maintaining the status quo. This approach is likely to be effective in the short run only. Given the external pressures in the context of international markets, the price of maintaining the status quo may be large-scale flight of capital (and the resulting unemployment) or an increasingly hostile public opinion toward organized labor, or both.

The alternate approach is to use the time gained in this process to develop a proactive labor agenda for change and restructuring that can be brought to bear on the collective bargaining process. This is a complex task for many reasons. It means that labor must look at new and unfamiliar ways of doing some things at a time when it feels most comfortable with traditional collective bargaining and the contract administration that comes with it. It also means that labor leaders have to begin to educate their membership about the future and what it means for the labor-management relationship. Lastly, it requires labor to undertake joint ventures with management. In many cases, this path is politically treacherous and only those with good vision and planning can negotiate it successfully.

DEVELOPING A LABOR AGENDA FOR CHANGE AND RESTRUCTURING

An issue as complex and important as this is difficult to address adequately within the scope of a brief paper. Notwithstanding, I will try to discuss three important considerations that labor must take into account in its search for an agenda for reform. First, any future changes must judiciously mix conflict and cooperation in labor-management relations just as the Wagner Act model has proposed and achieved at least until recent years. This is crucial to maintaining a pluralist system and to ensure that one party's interests will not dominate the other's. Second, the evolving order should move the system away from substantive rules toward procedural rules. Lastly, any devolution of work rules at the shop floor must be accompanied by greater formal power for labor at higher levels of policy making.

To illustrate and develop these themes, I will use the example of worker participation or employee involvement programs. These programs have become a paradigm for the kind of changes that are arguably needed but have proved extremely problematic in most labor-management relationships. Worker participation is an ideologically charged intervention unlike some other programs such as training or pay-for-skill whose potential for disrupting labor-management relations can be much lower. Accordingly, it poses the most difficult questions for restructuring and change. A system of labor-management relations that can deal effectively with the issues of worker participation is likely to be effective with most other change initiatives.

Loyal Opposition vs. Business Partner

It is common to characterize labor-management relations in terms of conflict or cooperation. Selekman (1949) proposed a continuum of conflict and cooperation, suggesting that while conflict may characterize industrial relations, a slow trek can be (and should be) made to the other end where parties begin to work together in a spirit of cooperation. Labor's role in the two extreme situations can be likened to that of the loyal opposition in a parliamentary democracy and a business partner respectively. The loyal opposition must always oppose what the government proposes as part of its role in the system. The intent is to generate debates and set in motion a process of dialectic enquiry that will help lawmakers arrive at better decisions.

On the other hand, two partners in a business enterprise always share the same interests—financial health of the company. Dividing the proceeds of the business is normally not an issue of contention because it is determined by contract and does not have to be revised frequently. The partners can, therefore, cooperate to a large extent under the assumption that their interests are largely the same.

I will argue that both these models are inappropriate for guidance in the context of labor-management relations. The loyal opposition role requires that labor must, as a rule, oppose all management initiatives, substituting in its place a labor agenda as dictated by worker interests. In practice, unions do criticize many management decisions. However, adoption of a blanket policy of opposition may result in lost opportunities for labor to protect its interests. Introduction of new technology provides a good illustration of this dilemma. It is management that introduces new technology to the workplace, an initiative that may be opposed by unions. But unions need the new investment (to protect jobs) as much as the management needs them. If unions simply oppose every introduction of new technologies, they not only risk losing jobs for their members but may also miss the chance to negotiate terms under which the new technology will be implemented. Thus, labor may be better protected if it were to negotiate terms rather than simply oppose management decisions.

In the parliamentary system, the ruling party and the opposition do not share a common organization and their roles are not complementary in the same way as labor and management roles in an economic enterprise. Labor and management cooperation is essential in ensuring sustained economic activity; cooperation between the ruling party and the opposition is not that essential in smooth operation of the government.

Although the negative aspects of conflict are generally well understood and accepted, the implications of too much cooperation are not always that obvious. In the pluralist tradition, it is held that managers and workers do not always have the same interests. Managers seek to maximize efficiency and workers seek to improve their wages and working conditions. In this view, workers and managers can never be reconciled to the extent that they can merge their differences and identities and live in perfect harmony. If cooperation does exceed certain limits, it may be an indication that one of the parties has been co-opted to the point of abandoning its interests in favor of the interests of the other party. In other words, cooperation between labor and management can be overdone, which may lead to exploitation of one party by the other and thereby contribute to instability in the system. For example, Robertson (1989) has shown that the seemingly objective call to increase flexibility can often disguise a managerial agenda for rolling back workers' gains at the workplace. If labor were co-opted to the extent that they supported the all-embracing drive to increase flexibility, they may be hurting their own interests. Thus, the 'business partner' model is also not an appropriate one for emulation in the industrial relations context.

Employee involvement (EI) programs that seek to directly involve workers in production decisions (such as quality, productivity, etc.) illustrate this tension between conflict and cooperation well. The premise for introducing these programs in the United States and Canada is that they help improve company performance. This is in contrast to the European programs that were founded on the idea that worker participation enriches jobs and thereby increases the quality of working life. Managers have sought union support for such programs in a large number of cases. If labor-management relations are very conflictual, implementation of EI programs becomes problematic. Thus, there is an obvious need for cooperation. EI programs also require that the traditional division of labor between workers and management be modified. Workers are urged to take on some or many supervisory roles depending on the nature of the program (Verma, 1985; Walton, 1980). Thus, the old saying, "managers manage, workers grieve" is not as applicable in settings where EI programs have been introduced as in traditional settings.

For unions, full cooperation with management in implementing EI programs creates a number of complex problems. Research evidence suggests that EI programs generate stronger identification of workers with company goals (Verma and McKersie, 1987; Lischeron and Wall, 1975). This does not necessarily mean that workers will identify less with the union, but it may and it has had some implications for the union-management relationship.

First, unions are afraid that employers may be using EI programs for "ulterior" motives such as weakening or decertifying the union. The prevalence of EI programs in the nonunion sector and the emphasis that employers put on EI in a nonunion strategy suggests that EI programs do have some union avoidance potential (Kochan, McKersie, and Chalykoff, 1986; Verma and Kochan, 1985). Second, unions are concerned that workers may be co-opted into managerial interests enough to suggest changes in the collective agreement that harm worker interests. Third, while workers agree to cooperate with EI and thus contribute to company performance on the shop-floor, there is no guarantee that the increase in wealth generated will necessarily flow to the workers. Unions may have no more voice in business decisions such as new investments that affect jobs. A company could engage workers in an EI effort even as new investments are turned away from the plant into other operations elsewhere in the country and abroad.

For all of these reasons many unions and workers are not sure if cooperating with an employer-sponsored EI program is necessarily going to improve their own lot. This demonstrates one of the limits of cooperation. A number of labor groups in both the United States and Canada who have expressed strong reservations about EI programs are motivated, at least in part, by these concerns.

Shop-Floor Deregulation and Power Sharing

Although the view previously outlined explains the current reality, it does not, by itself, constitute an effective policy choice for the future. The task here is to find a modified arrangement that will ensure the success of cooperative efforts (e.g. EI programs) by combining them with arrangements that safeguard labor interests through conflict-management structures. The proposition to be examined in this analysis is that unless cooperation is combined with mechanisms to express and resolve conflict of interests, it is unlikely to succeed by itself.

Introducing EI programs is a form of deregulation of the shop-floor from a Tayloristic regime. Frequently, their effect is to dilute the numerous rules that unions have negotiated to protect workers. For example, seniority, job descriptions, and overtime rules ensure that workers are not subjected to arbitrary treatment by management. In a cooperative workplace, workers not only acquire more say in matters relating to production, but they also tend to have more influence on managerial decision making through consultative mechanisms that generally accompany implementation of EI programs. Although precise data are not available, there is anecdotal and case-study evidence to suggest that grievance rates tend to go down after the introduction of EI programs. In other words, workers find other ways of expressing their grievances and for protecting their interests. They no longer feel that contractually agreed to rules are the only way to achieve the influence and control they need over the workplace.

Many union leaders have been quick to recognize the potential of EI programs for disrupting labor-management relations. Even those leaders who agree that EI may have something to offer to both labor and management worry about the effects of the deregulation that occurs at the shop-floor on the balance of power between the two sides. They fear that the overall effect of EI may be to alter the ideological balance in favor of managerial concerns at the expense of labor. The issue for many labor leaders is to examine if this is an inherent and inevitable result of EI, or whether its potential for disruption can be reversed to advantage by using it in conjunction with other joint arrangements.

Some research studies suggest that a union's own involvement in EI may be the key to managing EI's damaging potential for labor (Verma and McKersie, 1987; Kochan, Katz, and Mower, 1984). This line of thinking will have unions participate in decisions governing EI for two reasons. First, formal union power can stall decisions that are one-sided. Second, workers will associate the gains from EI as much with the union as with management, and thus, the pro-employer sentiment that may flow from EI can be neutralized. Privately, some unionists suggest that EI may be acceptable to them if the arrangement would produce greater formal voice for the union in other matters and at other levels. For example, in a handful of cases unions have agreed to allow some restructuring in exchange for rights to information, consultation, or both (Cutcher-Gershenfeld, McKersie and Wever, 1988). From a political and behavioral standpoint, change is possible in such cases because the erosion of union power from the shop-floor is matched or exceeded by the gain in formal power at higher levels.

From Substantive to Procedural Rules

A familiar criticism of the industrial relations system in the 1980s in both Canada and the United States has been its reliance on detailed collective agreements with hundreds of substantive rules that govern the workplace. It is argued that these rules work against flexibility by restricting optimal allocation of work and labor (Katz, 1985; Kochan, Katz, and McKersie, 1986). Collective agreement provisions for activities such as subcontracting and lateral transfer across job classifications were not designed by labor, however, to restrict flexibility, but rather to restrict management's scope for making decisions that could hurt labor interests. Some observers point out that the accumulation of extensive work rules in collective agreements reflects not only labor's approach to job control in North America but also management's unilateral decision-making style.

There are problems with the substantive rule-making regime into which the current collective bargaining patterns seem to have settled down. Substantive rules can never, at least in theory, cover "all the bases." No matter how comprehensive they become over time, they cannot cover all possible future developments. Because of their inability to foresee workplace exigencies that may arise in the future, these rules tend to create unintended rigidities at the workplace. Moreover, once a rule is in place, it is difficult politically to change it without some give or take or a power struggle.

There are also some comparative arguments for moving away from substantive rules. In Japan, most workplace decisions are made in consultation with the work force to start with (Shirai, 1983) and if disputes arise they are resolved mostly through joint consultation (Matsuda, 1983). Detailed and formalized work rules do not exist in the way that they are common in North America. Similarly in (West) Germany, the Works Council resolves workplace issues through extensive consultation and dialogue and without resorting to detailed work rules (Jacobi, 1985). Although national systems vary in many other respects as well, it is not farfetched to generalize that the reliance on a set of detailed substantive work rules is mostly a North-American tradition.

Let us now consider the prospects of implementing EI in the context of substantive rule-making. Labor may want rules governing *inter alia* selection of workers, limitations on topics that EI may consider, selection and training of leaders or facilitators, etc. However, much of the EI literature points to the evolving and experimental nature of EI programs in labor-management contexts (Cutcher-Gershenfeld,

55

Kochan, and Verma, 1990). Thus, any attempt to govern EI through substantive rule making is likely to get bogged down in preliminary bargaining. Some early experiments, therefore, had the parties negotiate an agreement in principle and leave the responsibility of implementation and daily governance exclusively to management. Of course, management's exclusive control of the EI process is likely to increase the potential for adverse outcomes for labor. Thus, labor's dilemma is framed on one side by the need to find alternatives to substantive rule making and, on the other side, by the need to avoid handing over control of the EI process to management.

In summary, the discussion in the preceding sections argues that labor should proactively develop its own agenda for an active role in the change and restructuring process in the industrial relations system. To ensure that labor's interests are protected during the change process, a new system of governance must be based on three considerations. First, it must allow sufficient room for managing conflict as well as cooperation, as both are equally vital to the sustenance of a pluralist system. Second, a loosening of labor's control over the workplace (in the interest of improving productivity) must be matched by an increase in labor's power through formalized participation in decisions at higher levels of the organization. Third, as substantive rules are diluted or removed, their jurisdiction should be covered by new procedural rules that will allow labor to exercise control over decisions that affect its members.

TOWARD A NEW SYSTEM OF JOINT WORKPLACE GOVERNANCE

The Wagner Act model intended to and, indeed, does provide for joint governance of the workplace. The evolution of this model, however, has been weighed heavily in favor of substantive rules with only the grievance process as an example of a procedural rule for joint governance. Thus, much of the joint governance today is practised in the form of substantive rules that are negotiated once in two or three years. In technical terms, this may be likened to a 'batch' method of manufacturing where there is little control over the process between batches. In contrast, procedural rules are a form of 'continuous process' method of manufacturing allowing for continuous adjustment to the production process. Since industrial relations also constitute a continuous process, the argument goes, it will be better administered through procedural rules rather than through substantive rules.

The generic form for administering procedural rules is the joint labor-management committee. Joint committees predate the Wagner Act itself and, thus, are in themselves not a new idea. However, most joint committees today are strictly advisory. Few have any budgets to fund their work and fewer still have the right to requisition any information from company records to aid their investigations. Procedurally, though, joint committees do embody the principles of joint governance. To better understand the evolution of joint committees from traditional forms to more meaningful joint governance, a continuum of joint committee role and power can be created. At the bottom is a fairly weak joint committee with few powers and resources, its ability to make any impact on the workplace minuscule (see Figure 2). At the top is a joint committee with powers to implement its decisions, to requisition information from company records or commission studies from the outside, and to work with its own budget to fund its activities.

In light of our arguments above, it can now be shown that a Level 99 (meant to indicate a high level of joint governance on the continuum) joint committee is likely to meet most of the requirements of labor as well as allow change and restructuring to proceed. A joint committee with such powers and resources allows for collaboration and accommodation as well as independence for labor to oppose measures that go against its vital interests. It is assumed here that any such joint committee will also have a mechanism for resolving disputes either through a third party or through further mediation at higher levels of appeal or both. A joint committee at this level creates formal roles for the union that can make it politically feasible for the union to drop or modify many of the substantive rules of the past. Thus, it encourages reduced reliance on substantive rules and an increased role for procedural rules.

Joint Governance and EI

In the case of EI, the Level 99 joint governance form can provide effective solutions for most of the problems outlined earlier. With joint control, labor does not have to worry about the co-option of its members into a managerial agenda. For workers, EI gains are likely to be associated as much with labor as with management. Unions also do not have to worry about loss of control or any weakening of their role in the minds of the workers. Formal role and power in work-

FIGURE 2: LEVELS OF JOINT GOVERNANCE

Level 99	Joint Committee: Manages with a budget Has powers to requisition information Authority to implement decisions
Level 2	Joint Committee: No budget Right to information in some areas Advises management
Level 1	Joint Committee: No budget Receives information but no right Advises management
Level 0	No Joint Committee: Management makes decisions unilaterally Union grieves

place matters on an on-going basis (similar to the union's role in the grievance process but more potent because of the substantially larger scope) will place the union in a strong light. This should address concerns of some labor leaders who fear that EI may be a ploy to weaken unions (Verma, 1989). Unions become stronger than they presently are rather than weaker by entering into joint governance mechanisms.

While EI programs may well result in a decline in grievances filed by workers, examining the larger context suggests that declining number of grievances do not have to be a source of major concern to the union. In a traditional setting, grievances as a form of dissent are an important part of union activities. Under a joint governance regime, the union will be so busy with more weighty matters that it will hardly miss the possible decline in grievances. It may even be argued that the time freed up by declining grievances is much needed by a union that is gearing up to get involved in joint governance. Moreover, while it is realistic to assume that grievances may decline in number, there is no reason to believe that they will disappear altogether. On the contrary, if a union shares power in a meaningful way, it is likely that the grievances brought forth will be significant and well-crafted challenges to managerial decisions. It is assumed that the less significant ones will likely be settled through mutual ongoing consultations that comes with joint governance and will never go to the stage of being filed. Overall, grievances may decline in numbers but those that are filed are likely to be more substantial and significant to worker interests.

Further, unions can join management in actively encouraging workers to get involved with workplace decisions without fear that gains from higher productivity will be funnelled away from workers. Union representation on joint committees at every level can ensure that business decisions are made with labor interests in mind. Joint governance of EI alone will ensure, for example, that decisions such as subcontracting are not made with total disregard of worker interests. But as joint governance spreads to other areas, the interconnections between EI and other decisions such as subcontracting, personnel transfers, training, and introduction of new technology will increase to create a comprehensive set of checks against dominance of management interests over those of workers.

Joint Governance in Other Areas

There are not many examples of joint governance as it may apply to areas such as subcontracting and technological change. However, it is instructive to briefly review what such a system may look like. In the case of subcontracting, the traditional approach has been for the union to negotiate substantive rules limiting management's ability to subcontract. Some of the problems with this approach arise from the fact that subcontracting needs vary depending on market conditions. Thus, a subcontracting rule that may have served well in the 1970s may be inadequate in the 1980s or may prove to be excessive in the 1990s.

A system of joint governance would bring all management requests for subcontracting to a joint committee. This committee can work on a set of guidelines to process most routine requests. For example, work not traditionally performed in-house can receive quick approvals. Other types of requests may warrant more detailed investigations. Most significantly, the parties will have the flexibility to revise their guidelines as the need arises on a continuous basis. In a traditional approach, parties must wait until bargaining time in most cases and even then they must grapple with subcontracting in the context of all other issues.

Other requests that affect a large part of work performed in-house can be examined more thoroughly to see if costs can be lowered by changing work practices. Sometimes, this would result in the work remaining inside. At other times, the committee may rule in favor of subcontracting the work in exchange for guaranteed employment for affected workers. In the case of Xerox and their union, the Amalgamated Clothing and Textile Workers Union (ACTWU), a proposal to subcontract work from the wire harness department at the manufacturing plants in Rochester, New York, led to a joint study that explored ways to reduce costs and keep the work in-house (Cutcher-Gershenfeld, 1988). Although Xerox had no provision for joint governance of subcontracting, they did have one for joint governance of the EI program, which led to this unprecedented (for Xerox and ACTWU) collaboration over a traditionally divisive and explosive issue. The result of the study was that a number of changes were made in shop-floor practices and in the collective agreement to bring down manufacturing costs. Costs were reduced and much of the work remained in-house. In time, encouraged by the success of these efforts, more study teams were formed to examine other areas of potential subcontracting. Many of these teams were successful in stemming the flow of work to outside subcontractors.

One area in which more examples of joint governance can be cited is training. An illustrative example comes from the Ford-UAW agreement of 1982 which set up a Level 99 joint committee to oversee training and employee development. The committee is cochaired by labor and management representatives, has its own budget and complete authority to define and implement policy (Pascoe and Collins, 1985). Deutsch (1987) and Ferman et al. (1990) provide many other examples of joint governance in training to demonstrate the feasibility of this idea. Lastly, joint governance has also been applied quite successfully to safety and health issues (Ruttenberg, 1988). According to the Bureau of National Affairs, roughly half of all collective agreements in the U.S. contained a provision for a joint safety and health committee in 1986. Ruttenberg (1988) reported that while most committees could investigate accidents on their own authority and access information, the right to stop work and to control budgets had to be negotiated and, consequently, fewer committees at Level 99 were to be found.

Joint governance offers a way of coping with the emerging complexities of the workplace without completely turning the system of collective bargaining upside down. In that sense, it is an augmentation rather than a transformation of the industrial relations system. This is particularly important in Canada where the Wagner Act model is mostly intact despite a gentle decline in union density in the 1980s. To the examples already mentioned, one can add the Saturn plant of General Motors where all governance is joint from the plant level down to the shop-floor (Edid, 1985). Saturn's success in the marketplace will undoubtedly go a long way in validating the efficacy of joint governance of the workplace.

The Obstacles to Joint Governance

If joint governance is such a good idea what is impeding its adoption and rapid diffusion? Since joint governance is about sharing power, most managements are unlikely to be enthusiastic about it initially.

In the area of EI, management's technical expertise (relative to labor) is generally high, which leads to the belief that they can do EI on their own and that nothing is to be gained from giving the union a hand in it. Unions, on the other hand, are steeped in substantive rule making and grievance administration and any system that characteristically alters this familiar territory is threatening. Unions' own internal systems of governance and decision making may also need to be modified to adapt to participation in joint governance. These generalizations explain the slow progress of joint governance and of innovations such as EI.

What then has compelled the parties in the few examples cited to embrace joint governance? In most cases, an impending crisis or the inability to solve problems on their own appears to have made the parties more willing to work together. As shown in Figure 1, relative union power and the extent of communications were contributing factors as well. Apart from the crisis factor, most parties that agreed to joint governance had some prior experience in joint work (other than joint governance) with each other. It is tempting to hypothesize, therefore, that for many of these parties, joint governance followed as a logical step in the evolution of their relationship. For others who are hoping to embark on change and restructuring in industrial relations, it is advisable that they seek to engage in other forms of joint work before joint governance becomes a viable option (Verma, 1990). A solid foundation built on experience with joint work may be essential to the adoption and success of joint governance.

SUMMARY AND CONCLUSION

This paper has examined the potential role of labor in the change and restructuring process in industrial relations. It has been suggested that labor can either continue to press for the status quo or work proactively for change within a framework that will enhance labor security and give labor a more powerful say in the affairs of the workplace. In order to develop a strategy for the latter option, labor must carefully examine the option of joint governance, a system that is fully compatible with free collective bargaining. Joint governance, it is argued, meets the most important needs of labor as well as the demands placed by the market on the workplace. First, it permits cooperation between the parties without labor having to give up its independence or its right to grieve decisions with which it disagrees. In other words, it allows for a balance between conflict and cooperation. Second, it allows for the workplace to be free of extensive regulation through detailed work rules. Substantive rules give way to procedural rules. Third, a union's loss of control at the workplace (due to fewer substantive rules) is matched (or even exceeded) by an increase in union power at higher levels of decision making.

No doubt there are many obstacles on both sides in the path to joint governance. The purpose of this paper has been to argue that if labor has to play a proactive role in the change and restructuring process, it must carefully examine the joint governance option. Otherwise, a promising opportunity to keep our pluralist system of industrial relations healthy and prosperous would have been overlooked.

ENDNOTES

[1] For a more detailed discussion of trends in international trade and its implications for industrial relations practices see Verma and Saks (1990) and Kochan (1988).

[2] Throughout this paper I use the terms restructuring, change, and innovation somewhat interchangeably. The intent is not to modify their true meanings in English but, rather, to suggest that within the specific context of industrial relations at this time, any change for the better is best captured by arguing for restructuring through innovations in industrial relations practices and policies. In this sense, it simply reflects a normative bias on my part.

[3] This section is derived from Verma (1990).

REFERENCES

Betcherman, Gordon, and Kathryn McMullen. *Working With Technology: A Survey of Automation in Canada.* Ottawa: Ministry of Supply and Services, 1986.

Bruce, Peter. "Political Parties and Labor Legislation in Canada and the U.S." *Industrial Relations.* 28:115–41, Spring, 1989.

Cutcher-Gershenfeld, Joel. *Tracing a Transformation in Industrial Relations: The Case of Xerox Corporation and the Amalgamated Clothing and Textile Workers Union.* Washington, D.C.: U.S. Department of Labor, 1988.

Cutcher-Gershenfeld, Joel, Robert B. McKersie, and Kirsten R. Wever. *The Changing Role of Union Leaders.* Washington, D.C.: U.S. Department of Labor, 1988.

Cutcher-Gershenfeld, Joel, Thomas A. Kochan, and Anil Verma. "Recent Developments in U.S. Employee Involvement Initiatives: Erosion or Transformation." Forthcoming in *Advances in Industrial and Labor Relations* 5, JAI Press, 1990.

Deutsch, Steven. "Successful Training Programs Help Ease Impact of Technology." *Monthly Labor Review.* 14–20, November, 1987.

Drago, Robert, and Terry McDonough. "Capitalist Shopfloor Initiatives, Restructuring, and Organizing in the '80s." *Review of Radical Political Economics.* 16(4):52–57, 1984.

Edid, Marilyn. "How Power will be Balanced on Saturn's Shop Floor." *Business Week,* August 5, 1985.

Farrow, Maureen. "Globalization: Today's Business Reality." In *Business Strategies and Free Trade.* Edited by M. Farrow and A.M. Rugman, Toronto: C.D. Howe Institute, 1988.

Ferman, L., M. Hoyman, Joel Cutcher-Gershenfeld, and E. Savoie, eds. *A Union-Management Approach to Preparing Workers for the Future.* Ithaca, New York: Cornell ILR Press, 1990.

Goodmeasure & Co. *The Changing American Workplace: Work Alternatives in the 1980s.* New York: American Management Association, 1985.

Ichniowski, Casey, John T. Delaney, and David Lewin. "The New Human Resource Management in U.S. Workplaces: Is it Really New and Is It Really Nonunion?" *Relations Industrielles.* 44:97–123, Winter, 1989.

Jacobi, Otto. "World Economic Changes and Industrial Relations in the Federal Republic of Germany." In *Industrial Relations in a Decade of Economic Change.* Edited by H. Juris, M. Thompson and W. Daniels, Madison. Wisconsin: Industrial Relations Research Association, 1985.

Katz, H.C. *Shifting Gears: Changing Labor Relations in the U.S. Automobile Industry.* Cambridge, Massachusetts: MIT Press, 1985.

Kochan, Thomas A. "Looking to the Year 2000: Challenges for Industrial Relations and Human Resource Management." Presented at a conference entitled *Visions of Canada in the Year 2000.* Economic Council of Canada, Ottawa, November 30–December 2, 1988.

Kochan, Thomas A., and Anil Verma. "A Comparative View of U.S. and Canadian Industrial Relations: A Strategic Choice Perspective." *Proceedings of the Eighth World Congress.* International Industrial Relations Association, Brussels, September 4–8, 1989.

Kochan, Thomas A., and Joel Cutcher-Gershenfeld. *Institutionalizing and Diffusing Innovations in Industrial Relations.* Washington, D.C.: U.S. Department of Labor, Bureau of Labor-Management Relations and Cooperative Programs, 1988.

Kochan, Thomas A., H.C. Katz, and R.B. McKersie. *The Transformation of American Industrial Relations.* New York: Basic Books, 1986.

Kumar, P., M.L. Coates, and D. Arrowsmith. *The Current Industrial Relations Scene in Canada: 1987.* Kingston, Ontario: Queen's University Industrial Relations Centre, 1987.

Lischeron, J.A., and T.D. Wall. "Employee Participation—An Experimental Field Study." *Human Relations.* 28:863–84, 1975.

Matsuda, Yasuhiko. "Conflict Resolution in Japanese Industrial Relations." In *Contemporary Industrial Relations in Japan.* Edited by Taishiro Shirai. Madison, Wisconsin: University of Wisconsin Press, 1983.

Parker, Mike, and Jane Slaughter. *Choosing Sides: Unions and the Team Concept.* Boston: South End Press, 1988.

Pascoe, Thomas J. and Richard J. Collins. "UAW-Ford Employee Development and Training Program: Overview of Operations and Structure." *Labor Law Journal.* 36(8):519–25, 1985.

Porter, Michael E. *Competitive Strategy.* New York: Macmillan, 1980.

———. *The Competitive Advantage of Nations.* New York: Macmillan, 1989.

Riddell, Craig. "Wage Flexibility and Public Policy in Canada." Presented at the Pacific Rim Comparative Labor Policy Conference, Vancouver, B.C., June 25–26, 1987.

Rinehart, James. "Appropriating Workers' Knowledge: Quality Control Circles at a General Motors Plant." *Studies in Political Economy.* 14:75–97, Summer, 1984.

Robertson, David. "Unions and Flexibility: Conflict or Compromise?" In *Flexibility and Labour Markets in Canada and the United States.* Edited by Gilles Laflamme, Gregor Murray, Jacques Belanger and Gilles Ferland. Geneva, International Labour Organization, 1989.

Ruttenberg, Ruth. *The Role of Labor-Management Committees in Safeguarding Worker Safety and Health.* Washington, D.C.: U.S. Department of Labor, 1989.

Selekman, Benjamin M. "Varieties of Labor Relations." *Harvard Business Review.* 27(2), March, 1949.

Shirai, Taishiro. *Contemporary Industrial Relations in Japan.* Madison, Wisconsin: University of Wisconsin Press, 1983.

Verma, Anil. "Electric Cable Plant." In *Industrial Relations and Human Resource Management.* Edited by Thomas A. Kochan and Thomas A. Barocci. Boston, Massachusetts: Little Brown, 1985.

———. "Joint Participation Programs: Self-help or Suicide for Labor?" *Industrial Relations.* 28(3), Fall, 1989.

———. "The Prospects for Innovation in Canadian Industrial Relations in the 1990s." Report for Canadian Federation of Labour and World Trade Centres in Canada Joint Committee on Labour Market Adjustment, in cooperation with Employment and Immigration Canada's Industrial Adjustment Service, Ottawa, May, 1990.

Verma, Anil, and Alan M. Saks. "International Trade and Convergence in Human Resource Management Systems: Some Theoretical Propositions." Presented at *Frontiers in Global Management International Conference.* Shizuoka, Japan, June 17–20, 1990.

Verma, Anil, and Mark E. Thompson. "Managerial strategies in Industrial Relations in the 1980s: Comparing the U.S. and Canadian Experience." *Proceedings of Forty-first Annual Meeting.* Industrial Relations Research Association, Madison, Wisconsin, 1989.

Verma, Anil, and Robert B. McKersie. "Employee Involvement Programs: The Implications of Noninvolvement by Unions." *Industrial and Labor Relations Review.* 40(4), July, 1987.

Verma, Anil, and Thomas A. Kochan. "The Growth and Nature of the Nonunion Sector within a Firm." In *Challenges and Choices Facing American Labor.* Edited by Thomas A. Kochan. Cambridge, Massachusetts: M.I.T. Press, 1985.

———. "Two Paths to Innovations in Industrial Relations: The Case of Canada and the United States." *Labor Law Journal.* 41(8):601, August, 1990.

Walton, Richard E. "Establishing and Maintaining High Commitment Work Systems." In *The Organizational Life Cycle.* Edited by J.R. Kimberly and R.H. Miles. San Francisco: Jossey-Bass, 1980.

Section 3

OPTIONS FOR LABOR: LABOR STANDARDS, CAPITAL STRATEGIES, AND INTERNATIONAL LABOR SOLIDARITY

The breakdown of the postwar system of labor relations based on continued economic growth, limited competition in labor markets, and Keynesian policies to stimulate demand has been described in section one. Although U.S. trade unions have suffered the greatest losses during this process, labor in Canada and other industrial nations are all facing the pressures of deindustrialization, international competition, and flexibility.

In this chapter the authors define a number of strategies to allow labor to operate successfully in this new global environment. These include concrete instances of cooperation of unions across borders in campaigns against multinational corporations; the establishment of new mechanisms for enforcing fair labor standards in all countries that participate in international trade; and domestic capital and economic development strategies to protect workers, jobs, and communities. Many of these strategies are in their early stages of development, although considerable thought has been given to the issue. The difficult transition from local and national spheres of interest to the international stage is apparent as labor attempts to catch up to a very mobile capital adversary.

Seeing no alternative given the irreversible direction of global economic integration, Peter Dorman makes the case for an internationalist labor strategy, built around a system of international worker rights combined with measures to enhance purchasing power in the Third World. The wage gap between industrial and developing nations is real, even taking into account productivity differences. Since the suppression of worker rights leads to lower living standards and working conditions, international promotion of such rights will reduce inequalities and provide the basis for joint collective action. A variety of channels are available for promoting worker rights in trade and lending agreements. A model is presented, using Latin America as an example, of the potential impact of a combined worker rights/Third World development policy on U.S. economic growth, unemployment, and trade deficit.

Peter Donohue takes strong issue with both the feasibility and the desirability from the point of view of workers of international fair labor standards (IFLS) and worker rights conditionality (WRC) strategies. He posits in their stead a "peril point" approach to international competition as part of an alternative economic strategy to oppose the agenda of transnational enterprises. Both IFLS and WRC approaches suffer from difficulties of enforcement and definition and scope, and they fail to address trade between already industrialized nations. Furthermore, these approaches rely on labor movements and governments in developing countries to make up for the failure of those in industrialized nations to pose and implement an alternative economic strategy to that of the transnational enterprises.

Donohue is not prepared to cede the inevitability or desirability of international economic integration, but believes national self-determination must be defended for both developing and industrialized nations. The three tests for labor approaches to international competition are the ability of the strategy (1) to mobilize unionists and organize with other movements, (2) to challenge the international capitalist market's subordination of national policies and objectives to international trading performance, and (3) to overcome the power of transnational enterprises.

Canadian Steelworkers official Leo Gerard also challenges the "competitiveness ethic" and the failure of national governments to confront the rule makers of the international economic game as it is played today. The same forces that undermine living standards of workers in industrial nations are responsible for the severe environmental and developmental crises of the Third World. Unfortunately, the existing international institutions like the IMF and GATT enforce the very rules that perpetuate these problems. The creation of new international bodies to bridge the interests of the industrialized world and the Third World is essential to prevent the "lowest common denominator blackmail" that undermines solidarity. Labor alliances with environmental and other progressive forces within nations and between nations are difficult to form and maintain, but are indispensable if labor is to defend its gains.

From either side of the U.S.-Canadian border Larry Cohen and Fred Pomeroy offer concrete examples of international organizing in support of bargaining with multinational corporations. Cohen observes that it is essential to organize, educate, and mobilize members at the local and national levels in order to sustain campaigns with the multinationals. International solidarity means rejection of protectionism, support for international worker rights standards, and effective sanctions against multinationals that violate these standards. A case study of Northern Telecom, a Canadian-based telecommunications multinational, illustrates the potential power labor can exercise when U.S. and Canadian telecommunications unions worked together with members mobilized at the grassroots level.

Fred Pomeroy presents the Canadian side of the Northern Telecom story. He shows that unions that bargain with multinationals in their home country must take clear and concrete actions to show such companies that operating union in Canada is not enough if their activities undermine labor abroad. Additionally, the considerable obstacles to coordination among unions both within nations and between nations must be overcome, and labor in Canada and the U.S. appears to be recognizing this. An educated membership is essential to success because it is dangerous to assume that members will naturally take up the fight of workers in another union or country in the same way that they will fight for their own contract.

Domestically, it is critical for unions to recognize the effects of globalization and technological change and to become full participants in building a high-wage, high-employment security economy. This includes work at the political level in directing provincial and national economic development policies and at the bargaining table on issues of workplace reorganization.

Dan Swinney and his organization, the Midwest Center for Labor Research, have been engaged in just such activities in the U.S. industrial heartland. He describes the evolution of the center's strategy from one of fighting plant closures in a purely reactive mode to a more proactive labor-based economic development strategy. This strategy gives priority to long-term stability, democratic structures, and job creation and community development over the short-term interests of capital. However, it also recognizes the need for unions to develop the skills to participate in management and wealth creation, and to understand and use the strengths of the market economy, while recognizing its destructive tendencies as well.

Jim Tusler relates his experiences at ground level in working with unions using capital strategies to advance workers' interests. His humorous account of the electrician from Spokane fundraising on Wall Street to save workers' jobs from corporate raiders who aren't even sure what they own offers comic relief in a very serious situation.

Trade, Competition, and Jobs: An Internationalist Strategy

PETER DORMAN

Assistant Professor of Economics, Hamilton College

This is an epoch of global economic integration. Its causes are technical, social, and political and will not be reversed. They include the reduction in shipping and communications costs, the need to gain access to the ongoing revolution in information-based productive technology, the increasing participation of both elites and whole populations in an emerging transnational culture, and the failure of all autarchic models of development. The consequences can be seen in the widespread adoption of export-oriented strategies by both businesses and governments, the rising volume of trade relative to world output, and most dramatically in the movements toward regional economic integration.

It would be an understatement to say that these developments are not propitious for labor movements in the advanced capitalist countries. These movements are rooted in an earlier era in which class conflict was played out on a local or, at most, national level; they succeeded to varying degrees in limiting competition in labor markets, often in alliance with progressive business and political forces with an interest in bolstering domestic effective demand. This strategy is now in the process of unraveling in all of the advanced countries, since labor has not found a way to mute competition stemming from trade, while its erstwhile allies have abandoned the Keynesian view of wages and living standards in the name of "competitiveness." In practical terms, the consequences are continuing wage erosion, the deterioration of working conditions and social benefits, the loss of millions of jobs, particularly in manufacturing, the increasing difficulty in expanding or even maintaining levels of unionization, and the emergence of new pools of low-wage labor in secondary markets—the first world's Third World.

The purpose of this paper is to outline a response to this new set of conditions drawing on the principles and traditions of labor internationalism. In the following section I will take a closer look at the nature of the new competition, particularly in light of the vast international disparities in unit labor costs. This will be followed by two sections that describe and attempt to weigh the effectiveness of an internationalist program centering on the promotion of worker rights. I will conclude with a consideration of the political issues associated with this approach.

WAGES AND LABOR COSTS WORLDWIDE: THE CONTINUING GAP

It has been nearly thirty years since the term "Third World" was coined, yet, despite the reshuffling of individual countries within the hierarchy, the difference between wage rates in the advanced and developing countries has not lessened. Figure 1 provides a representative cross section for 1988. Broadly speaking, one can identify four groups: (1) the high-wage advanced countries with at least some history of social democracy, such as Sweden and West Germany[1]; (2) the United States and the other OECD countries that have caught up to it; (3) the newly industrialized countries (NICs), whose wage levels are from 10–30 percent of those of the U.S.; and (4) the rest, for whom wages have been stagnant or falling for many years. The general picture is one of great differences, far from the bold claims for factor price equalization trumpeted by Western economists in the heyday of postwar growth. The result is extraordinary pressure on higher-wage workers, both in response to the huge gap in labor costs relative to the Third World and to the smaller differences among the advanced countries, exacerbated by similarities in productivity, infrastructure, etc. At the same time, however, the implications for workers in the lower-wage countries are mixed: the wage gap offers them an opportunity to speed up the pace of industrialization and development, but at the frequent cost of hyper-exploitative wages and working conditions.

To what extent are these wage differences offset by other economic forces? There are two potential candidates, differences in productivity and the persistence of national barriers to trade.[2] Consider each:

a. *Productivity.* There are few aggregate measures of relative labor productivity, and those that exist are unreliable. Industry-specific measures are more plausible and

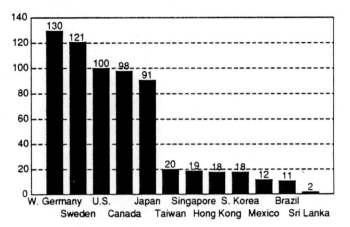

FIGURE 1. HOURLY COMPENSATION COSTS, 1988 (US = 100)

Source: U.S. Bureau of Labor Statistics, Report 771, August 1989

commonly show NIC productivity ranging from 60 to 70 percent of North-American levels.[3] The effect of this difference is to increase NIC unit labor costs, as against simple wage ratios, by approximately 50 percent. It may be, however, that these measurements fail to represent the productivity differences at the margin associated with new investment. It would be the marginal difference in productivity that would matter, for instance, to North-American workers threatened with a runaway shop. There is reason to believe that the productivity gap is substantially smaller for the most recent vintages of capital and in the most dynamic industries. This is true even though economic theory would predict more labor-intensive investment in low-wage regions.[4] Explanations include the need to integrate productive processes and intermediate outputs in worldwide, multisourced operations and the learning-by-doing benefits that are a byproduct of any technically advanced process. In Shaiken's (1988) study of engine production in Mexico, for instance, automobile companies chose to use their most sophisticated techniques with workers earning a tenth of the U.S. wage scale; the result was a level of productivity averaging approximately 80 percent of the U.S. level. (In one product Mexican productivity was actually higher.) If this is a representative result, the wage gap between countries cannot be adjusted by one-half for differences in productivity; in short, the gap is real.

b. *Trade barriers.* There are many different types of trade barriers, and they are not always easy to quantify. In addition to direct tariffs, countries apply domestic content and other regulatory laws that have the effect of raising the cost of certain imports. Recent rounds of GATT have not been successful in combatting these restrictions; nevertheless there are grounds for believing that the drift is in the direction of liberalism. First, economic integration is reducing barriers on a regional basis. While it is true that common markets often have the effect of increasing barriers to external trade, this distinction may be less salient for national labor movements. Second, the increasing use of external sourcing and export platforms of convenience weakens the effect of restrictions. Finally, much trade is now intrafirm; it is often subject to different treatment, although it has virtually the same consequences for national labor movements as interfirm trade. In short, trade barriers continue to mute the effects of differential unit labor costs, but the effects are diminishing over time.

The general conclusion is that international wage differences are nearly as consequential as they appear, and that the general trend is for their effect to sharpen over time. This fact, and the globally competitive context in which it is embedded, are at the heart of the crisis being faced by labor movements throughout the advanced capitalist world. What can be done in response? It would be reasonable to look for opportunities to expand collective action directly into the international arena through coordinated bargaining with multinational firms or across firms at the world industry level, but there are obstacles that have proved difficult to overcome. Each national labor movement is a reflection of its legal environment: the specific rights and limitations encoded in labor law dictate strategies for organization and action, and the resulting differences have hobbled efforts at international coordination.

A second problem stems directly from the wage gap itself. The effort to consolidate the struggles of workers in high- and low-wage countries faces a profound dilemma: either the objective is to equalize wages for labor of the same kind, which entails the creation of an exclusive—and probably impossible—high-wage enclave in the developing country, or workers' organizations are placed in the position of agreeing to vast internal wage differences. In the face of these difficulties the cause of international labor solidarity has languished. There are moments of real collaboration, but for the most part it continues at a low level, propelled more by disinterested virtue than pragmatic strategy, and, for all its merits, hardly seems capable of meeting the challenge posed by economic globalism. But there are other avenues of solidarity, as the following sections will argue.

WORKER RIGHTS, WAGES, AND TRADE

The strategy of promoting worker rights is straightforward: insofar as the suppression of these rights leads to lower living standards and working conditions, gaining these rights narrows the wage gap. It provides a basis for joint action, since workers in all countries have an interest in maintaining and extending these rights. In the long run, moreover, it helps create the preconditions for direct collective action on an international level. These are the same considerations that historically have underpinned the efforts of national movements to transcend narrow sectional interests. What are worker rights? As with other rights, they are simply those that workers have been able to win in particular contexts, generalized to everyone.

Two lists deserve special mention (Dorman, 1990a). The International Labour Office has proposed and its member states have, in various numbers and combinations, ratified a number of conventions governing the conditions and rights of labor. Five of these have been selected as the basis for worker rights conditionality under U.S. trade law: the right of association; the right to organize and bargain collectively; the prohibition of forced labor; a minimum age for the employment of children; and appropriate minimum conditions of work, including wages, hours, and occupational safety and health. The European Community's Social Charter (1989) provides a more comprehensive set of rights: freedom of workers' geographic and industrial mobility; general standards for living and working conditions; minimum wages; social insurance; access to training and education; the right to free association and collective bargaining; nondiscrimination in employment and compensation; rights to information and participation; restrictions on child labor; occupational health and safety; and opportunity and protection for the disabled and elderly.

Clearly these sets are diverse, and yet they do not exhaust the possible rights workers might claim. In practice, a worker rights policy must select particular rights to stress and determine the amount of shortfall to be deemed actionable. These issues are considered in greater detail elsewhere (Dorman, 1990b), but one point is especially important: it is arbitrary to restrict worker rights to the particular rights of unionization and collective bargaining, since the achievements gained by workers as citizens are no less valuable. To admit the first but not the second is particularly doubtful in the context of developing countries with a minority stratum of relatively well-paid export-sector workers.

Worker rights can be promoted through a variety of channels. The European Community has taken the road of direct regulatory harmonization; of course, this is made possible by the existence of a transnational political apparatus. (The case for transnational political mechanisms to accompany economic integration needs to be remembered as negotiations begin among the U.S., Canada, and Mexico.) U.S. trade law conditions trade benefits on worker rights performance. Programs with these provisions include the Generalized System of Preferences, which sets aside duties on selected imports from developing countries; the Overseas Private Investment Corporation, which insures direct foreign investment abroad; and Section 301 of the trade statutes, which permits complaints of "unfair trading practices" against foreign producers.[5] The ILO investigates allegations that member states are denying worker rights to which they have formally consented, but it does not possess any enforcement power. Sporadic efforts have been made to incorporate worker rights standards in GATT, but no progress has been made; developing countries fear it could be used as a justification for broad-gauged protectionism, while most of the industrialized countries have different priorities. A vigorous worker rights strategy would embrace all of these vehicles. Perhaps the most effective approach, however, would be to revise the conditionality applied by international lending institutions to include respect for worker rights: borrowers would be denied credit if they remained violators. Our inability to put this possibility on the agenda, much less see it through, reflects the tremendously undemocratic character of these ostensibly public institutions. Finally, worker rights should be incorporated into diplomacy generally, so that different policies can be coordinated for maximum effect.[6]

The ethical case for worker rights is clear enough, but the economic effects are more problematic. There are, after all, many factors that enter into the determination of wages and unit labor costs, and it is not obvious that the extent of worker rights is among the more important. This question cannot be settled speculatively; it depends on the evidence. The only direct test of the relationship between rights and wages was conducted using a small sample of developing countries and is limited by unreliable data (see Dorman, forthcoming). Nevertheless, the results were very strong and well within the realm of plausibility: a "moderate" improvement in worker rights (by, say, one point on a five-point index) is associated with approximately thirty-three percent higher wages. Future research is likely to focus on case studies, where data limitations can be more easily overcome and the influence of political and social factors can be recognized.

As an example, consider South Korea during the late 1980s. Hourly compensation costs for production workers in manufacturing rose from ten percent of the U.S. level in 1985, to eleven percent in 1986, thirteen percent in 1987 percent, and eighteen percent in 1988. What accounted for this late spurt? The other East Asian exporters also experienced wage growth during this period, but not to the same extent. The won was appreciating against the dollar, moving from 884.6 in 1986 to 734.5 in 1988, but this only displaces the problem, since the value of the won is set politically and had been purposely depressed to discourage consumption and promote exports. The answer, of course, lies to a significant extent in the upsurge of democratic and union rights that took place at the time; the magnitude of the Korean rights/ wages relationship, moreover, is consistent with the cross-sectional analysis referred to previously.[7]

Suppose that a set of aggressive worker-rights policies succeeded in bringing about a 33 percent increase in labor costs in manufacturing in the NICs. Combining the data from Figure 1, the marginal productivity difference and the rights effect, we would see the adjusted relationship portrayed in Figure 2. (Note that Sweden and West Germany have been removed; I will return to variations across advanced countries shortly.) Instead of a ratio of 1:5, the leading NICs now record 1:3; this approaches the level of wage variation commonly observed *within* countries for work of the same type. (As a rule of thumb, 1:2 may be considered the outer limit of this variation.) This is not to say that wage differences of this magnitude are not troublesome, but it does suggest that they can be brought within the range of our previous experience.

A final point should be made about the worker rights approach. It is commonly assumed that this is a policy that the advanced countries as a group might wish to apply to the developing countries, but it also has implications for economic relations between the advanced countries themselves. The wage gap between Sweden and the U.S. depicted in Figure 1, for example, suggests that U.S. workers trail their

Swedish counterparts by a unit amount in the hypothetical index of worker rights described above. It would be reasonable, then, for Sweden to apply (if they could) worker rights policies to the U.S., just as the U.S. should apply them to its lower-rights trading partners. In a sense, this process is already underway within the European Community, as northern-European labor movements press for "upward harmonization" of the community's rights standards. A comparable incentive applies to the Canadian labor movement vis-a-vis the U.S., although, having been saddled with a Free Trade Agreement without any accompanying social provisions, their options are limited.

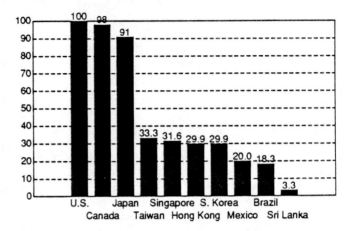

FIGURE 2. ADJUSTED COMPENSATION COSTS, 1988 (US = 100)

THE MACROECONOMIC DIMENSION

Thus far I have considered the worker-rights strategy entirely at the level of relative unit labor costs. This is often as far as the discussion goes; for instance, to demonstrate injury in the context of U.S. trade litigation, it is generally required that domestic producers (workers or firms) argue from lost market share. Yet it is likely that the macroeconomic effects of a solidaristic labor strategy are at least as significant as the market-level effects. In this section I would like to examine worker rights as a component of a more general strategy to expand purchasing power in the Third World. In broad terms, the other elements would include redistributive credit conditionality (in conjunction with worker rights conditionality), mandatory debt write-downs, coordinated transnational macropolicy (made possible by collective regulation of global financial markets), and multilateral trade management (to ensure the feasibility of the national macropolicies through which global expansion is coordinated). The common theme running through all of them is expansion and redistribution: shared growth through the acceleration of global effective demand (Mead, 1988–89; Marglin and Schor, 1990). While worker rights is only a part of this larger approach, it is nearly indispensable: without an active role for working people there can be neither the political base for these institutions on a national level nor the mechanisms to channel augmented incomes into the hands of those who want and need to spend them. By the same token, the macroeconomic effects of worker rights depend on their context, and, in particular, on whether wage increases are financed from the incomes of other workers or from the dividends of more rapid growth.

To arrive at a sense of the magnitudes involved, I will pursue the following speculation. Suppose that, instead of collapsing under the weight of debt-driven restructuring, the South and Central American economies enjoyed a modest but stable rate of growth through the 1980s, and further suppose this were translated into a plausible increase in imports from the United States. What would have been the effect on U.S. economic growth, its trade deficit, and its ability to employ its work force? Let's work through it one step at a time.[8]

1. Combined GDP for continental Latin America was $471.2B in 1986 U.S. dollars (the denomination for all future measurements), and imports from the U.S. were $46.4B. The marginal propensity to import out of GDP (the change in imports divided by the change in GDP) between 1980 and 1981 was

approximately 1/7.

2. In 1986, after four years of imposed austerity, combined GDP totaled $500.5B, while imports had fallen to $26.2B.

3. Suppose that economic growth had continued during the period at the modest rate of three percent per year. Then combined GDP would have been $567.0B.

4. Using the marginal propensity to import above, the increment to imports would have been $13.7B and total imports in 1986 would have been $60.1B.

5. The difference in imports between this scenario and the actual course of events is $33.9B. The actual trade deficit for the U.S. that year was $169.8B, so the missing exports to Latin America can be thought of as accounting for 20 percent of the total.

6. The demand multiplier for the U.S. economy is variously estimated between 2 and 2.5. Using the more conservative estimate, the missing exports would have added $67.8B, or 1.6 percent of GNP, to the U.S. economy.

7. Applying Okun's Law, which relates changes in the level of GNP to changes in the unemployment rate, the increased exports would have reduced the unemployment rate in the U.S. by .64, or over 9 percent of its actual average rate (6.9 percent) in 1986. Stated differently, the steady growth scenario would have given jobs to 754 thousand of the 8.2 million workers who, on average, were unemployed on any given day in the U.S. in 1986.

How extreme are the assumptions underlying this speculation? Three percent annual growth is quite modest for a developing country that is actually developing. As an upper bound, we might double this rate and therefore all the subsequent results. The marginal propensity to import might be criticized on the grounds that, in retrospect, spending flows were misguided and unsustainable during the early 1980s. Yet South Korea had a nearly identical propensity during the same period, and it was embarked on a spectacularly successful (in aggregate terms) growth path. Moreover, the Korean propensity to import from the United States was maintained even though Japan was assuming the key role as a provider of capital and intermediate goods. The point is that countries may import for a variety of reasons, development among them; in fact, under current conditions it is not possible for a capital-poor country to develop rapidly without massive imports of both goods and capital.[9] Finally, it is a limitation of my scenario that it abstracts from all other consequences of growth besides the increment to effective demand. It is reasonable to ask whether, on balance, the excluded effects would reinforce my hypothetical results. Among the more likely countervailing outcomes is a general rise in commodity prices, which could act as a brake on growth; on the other hand, allaying the credit crunch would permit countries to develop in a more balanced fashion, rather than engaging in headlong competition for scarce foreign exchange. And the expansion of exports from other advanced countries would enable them to grow more rapidly, thereby providing a further opportunity for U.S. export growth. In general, one would expect that the general equilibrium effects of widespread growth would be yet more growth as demand ripples through the system.

As a final observation, it is worth noting that this exercise involved only the sixteen countries of continental Latin America. Its results could be extended by adding other important trading partners, such as the Caribbean nations, the Philippines, etc. And there is no reason to write off countries that have not traded extensively with the U.S. in the past, but would do so under a growth scenario. Drawing on the widespread opportunities for progressive macropolicy throughout the Third World, it is reasonable to argue that the induced growth latent in the internationalist approach more than offsets the continuing if diminished effects of the wage gap.

POLITICAL CONSIDERATIONS

This paper has been written to show that an internationalist strategy centered on worker rights can address the crisis now confronting advanced country labor movements. The arguments have been economic and self-centered. Before closing, then, I would like to put them in a broader political context. Internationalism, of course, is the right thing. It adheres to the principle that all of us count, and that some should therefore not attempt to prosper at the expense of others. This categorical imperative should command even more support at a time of enormous poverty and hardship throughout the Third World. And there is nothing impractical about being generous; standing for principle can only enhance the position of unions and other labor-oriented institutions that are now seen as corrupt or narrowly self-interested by much of the public.

But there is more. Internationalism is necessary because all other strategies fail. Given the impetus for globalization described at the outset of this paper, it is inconceivable that a political program of generally reduced openness can succeed. Unfortunately, this has not been recognized by many in the labor movement. They win occasional rear-guard battles over particular groups of imports, unaware that they are losing the war in a rout. Even if the internationalist strategy were not good enough, we would have to try our luck with it: there is no alternative.

Finally, any strategy for a social movement—and this includes labor—must pay attention to the effect that its objectives have on its organizing process. Protectionism generally builds alliances between workers and their employers; this may even be true of domestic content legislation, since these measures protect parts suppliers. Moreover, these alliances organize workers largely along industrial lines—that is, as "special interests"—rather than along class lines. Internationalism, on the other hand, widens the circle of solidarity. Measures that promote worker rights explicitly defend *all* workers, and the pursuit of coordinated growth at the expense of other interests, such as those of creditors and runaway employers, can potentially define a global class interest. In the final analysis these considerations must be paramount, since any set of concrete objectives can be overcome by the plans of our adversaries, or simply by the random tide of events. What remains is the movement and its potential for further progress. Virtually by definition, protectionism is the path of division and atrophy, internationalism the path of coalition and growth.

ENDNOTES

[1] Of course, the reunification of Germany will temporarily depress the aggregate wage level.

[2] An additional claim is sometimes made that labor cost differences tend not to matter because of the low ratio of direct labor and total cost, but this is based on an economic misunderstanding. The appropriate ratio is direct labor to value added or vertically-integrated labor (incorporating intermediate goods) to total cost; the two are equivalent. To see this, imagine that a firm separates itself into several mini-firms that buy and sell to each other. The combined interest of the mini-firms in labor costs is exactly equal to the interest of the original enterprise.

[3] See, for example, the steel- and shirt-making studies cited by Mead (1990).

[4] I am assuming, of course, that productivity is determined primarily by technology, training and organization; there is no intrinsic reason why the workers of any country must be less productive than any other.

[5] Enforcement, of course, has been a different matter. For an assessment of the anemic GSP enforcement record see Dorman (1989).

[6] The commingling of foreign policy and worker rights concerns carries the risk that the latter may be contaminated by the former. For an example of exactly this distortion operating within the AFL-CIO, see Cantor and Schor (1987).

[7] There is plenty of room for further worker rights gains in Korea, of course. For more discussion of this interesting case, see You (1989).

[8] The following data are drawn from International Monetary Fund (various years).

[9] To a certain extent, the example of Korea belies the assertion that worker rights are needed to channel growing Third World

incomes into effective demand, since the state coordinated the acquisition of productive imports. On the other hand, precisely because it mobilized so many resources for its export drive, the Korean model *circa* 1980 is not generalizable: all developing countries cannot be Korea at once.

REFERENCES

Cantor, Daniel, and Juliet Schor. *Tunnel Vision: Labor, the World Economy, and Central America*. Boston: South End Press, 1987.

Dorman, Peter. "An Evaluation of Worker Rights Conditionality under the Generalized System of Preferences." Washington: U.S. Department of Labor, Bureau of International Labor Affairs, 1989.

————. "An Analytical Typology of Worker Rights." Unpublished, 1990a.

————. "Worker Rights and International Trade." Unpublished, 1990b.

————. "Worker Rights, Environmental Standards, and Social Tariffs: Theory and Evidence." In *Multinational Culture: Social Impact of a World Economy*. Edited by Cheryl Lehman and Russell Moore. Greenwich, Connecticut: Greenwood Press, forthcoming.

European Community. *Social Charter*. 1989.

International Monetary Fund. *Direction of Trade Statistics Yearbook*. Washington, various years.

Marglin, Stephen, and Juliet Schor. *The Golden Age of Capitalism: Reinterpreting the Postwar Experience*. Oxford: Clarendon Press, 1990.

Mead, Walter. "The United States and the World Economy." *World Policy Journal*. 6(1):1–45, 1988–89.

————. "American Economic Policy in the Antemillennial Era." *World Policy Journal*. 6(3):385–468, 1989.

————. *The Low-Wage Challenge to Global Growth: The Labor Cost-Productivity Imbalance in Newly Industrialized Countries*. Washington: Economic Policy Institute, 1990.

Shaiken, Harley. "High Tech Goes Third World: High-Tech Production Abroad May Keep American Auto Makers Competitive While Undermining the U.S. Economy." *Technology Review*. 91(1):38–47, 1988.

You, Jong-Il. "Worker Rights and Economic Development: What South Korean Experiences Tell Us." Unpublished, 1989.

Labor Alternatives to International Competition

Director of Labor Studies, Assistant Professor of Economics, San Francisco State University

INTRODUCTION

A century after the Second International Workingmen's Association called for enactment of international labor legislation regulating wages and working conditions, unionists still lack effective ways of combatting international competition.

In the name of international labor solidarity, many unionists balk at endorsing "protectionist" measures aimed at preventing international competition from forcing working and living standards to their lowest common denominator. Some instead urge that observance of international fair labor standards (IFLS) be required for governments participating in the General Agreement on Tariffs and Trade (GATT) and other international economic arrangements. Others call on their own national governments unilaterally to allow access to domestic markets to products of only those countries whose governments observe internationally recognized worker rights.

A century of fruitless efforts for IFLS, along with labor's persistent inability to influence government trade and investment policies, however, has made many other unionists skeptical about IFLS or worker rights conditionality (WRC) amounting to anything more than "good ideas," with no greater likelihood of effectiveness now than one hundred years ago. Facing destruction of lives and communities through "free trade," unionists' impatience with those counterposing abstract "international labor solidarity" to "protectionism" is understandable.

Rather than listing obstacles to implementing IFLS or worker rights conditionality, I question whether either approach is desirable from the standpoint of workers here or elsewhere. In addition, I argue that both approaches are inferior to the "peril point" approach being used in an ongoing struggle against international competition in the U.S. aircraft maintenance and repair industry.

Except as part of an alternative economic strategy, no approach can overcome the power of transnational enterprises and their political allies. The superiority of the "peril point" approach lies in its emphasis on mobilizing unionists and organizing others rather than relying on exclusively legislative and administrative measures. The "peril point" approach shows how to link isolated, defensive struggles strategically and demonstrates the possibility of an alternative set of policies, breaking with the subordination of national policies and objectives to international trading performance.

THE MESSENGER IS THE MESSAGE

Baseball, hot dogs, apple pie and . . . international fair labor standards and worker rights sounds funny, but among "internationalist" unionists in the already industrialized countries the latter have long been preferred to "protectionism" as a means of reducing "unfair competition" internationally. While some within the labor movement doubt whether IFLS and WRC approaches can be implemented politically, few have doubted their desirability.

Criticizing IFLS and WRC approaches is akin to criticizing "mom and apple pie." Doubting the conventional wisdom has often raised as many questions about which side I'm on as about IFLS and WRC themselves. For better or worse, our judgements about any message are highly colored by our understanding of who is the messenger and what is the messenger's motive. So I'd like to preface my remarks by sharing my own background and motives to help you make your own judgements about my analysis and proposals.

I grew up in Holyoke, Massachusetts, one of America's first industrial cities, whose workers have produced paper, textiles, and electrical machinery for almost a century and a half. Michael Dukakis' "Massachusetts Miracle" bypassed Holyoke and many similar communities. Since my birth almost forty years ago, workers' real wages have remained flat, contributing to Massachusetts's fall from sixth to forty-sixth place in state average real manufacturing wages. As Holyoke slowly collapsed, infant mortality rates reached those of Haiti. Heroin use among Holyokers have reached levels unequaled anywhere in North America but Canada's Maritime provinces.

I'm one of Holyoke's chief exports, native youth whose education provided a way out. Since leaving, I've lived and worked, among other places, in Gary, Indiana, which collapsed in on itself soon after I left, with unemployment exceeding Depression levels. The collapse of the Texas economy likewise preceded my moving to San Francisco, California, where, some joke, the "Big One" is a certainty after I move on.

I share this life history to show that my experience with trade liberalization isn't an abstraction but a visceral personal experience. High-minded theory aside, trade liberalization for me has meant the destruction of people's lives and communities as well as the loss of democratic control over their destiny. Rising anger and fatalism in these and other communities in the U.S., Canada, and elsewhere around the world has found expression in political quiescence as well as backward-looking localisms, with growing social fragmentation and violence.

Talk about either the "long-run" benefits of trade liberalization or, alternately, international proletarian revolution won't do. If folks aren't secure in their own neck of the woods, they will make damn poor world citizens.

THREE TESTS FOR LABOR ALTERNATIVES

The crisis unfolding over the last fifty years has demoralized national labor movements, especially in the U.S. A recent essay by the Economic Policy Institute's Jeff Faux attributes international economic integration (along with local and national economic disintegration) to a technological imperative, reflecting widespread fatalism among unionists about the possibility of reversing the destruction it has engendered (Faux, 1989).

Like Canada's Stephen Hymer, I reject "analyses" that leave little or no recourse but pursuing "competitiveness" on a "level playing field" in international competition and bandaging its victims. What we face is not the beginning, but the beginning of the end of the transnational enterprises' (TNEs) economic and political dominance of communities and nations (Hymer, 1979).

Movements opposing the TNEs and their political allies are growing among workers, farmers, and others all over the world. These movements have taken on different, often disturbing, forms in different communities and nations. But the most successful, whatever their outlook, have built on workers', farmers', and others' anger, addressing their immediate concerns while rejecting fatalistic conventional wisdom about supposedly irreversible global economic integration over which the TNEs preside (Barrett, 1989; Ritchie, 1990; Simon, 1990).

Holyokers' and others' immediate concerns must be the starting point for any labor response to international competition. Our power to shape our collective future depends on our mobilizing unionists and organizing with others moved by those concerns, rather than attempting to displace them with an abstract "international labor solidarity." Therefore, the first test for labor approaches to international competition is whether it mobilizes unionists and organizes with others in Holyoke and elsewhere.

Unionists always and everywhere ought to oppose competition. Rather than aiming at "taking wages out of competition," unionists should aim instead at "taking competition out" completely. Thus, the second test for any labor approach to international competition is whether it challenges the international capitalist market's subordination of national policies and objectives to international trading performance.

All three approaches, including the one I've been engaged with the International Association of Machinists, fail the third test for labor approaches to international competition, overcoming the power of TNEs. All three are tactics vulnerable to being outflanked by the TNEs with their superior mobility and resources internationally. Without an alternative economic strategy, all three approaches are incapable of overcoming the subordination of national policies and objectives to international trading performance.

INTERNATIONAL FAIR LABOR STANDARDS

For at least one hundred years IFLS negotiated multilaterally have been the preferred approach to international competition among unionists in already industrialized countries. The 1889 Paris convention of the Second International Workingmen's Association endorsed a Swiss government invitation to other nations for a Berne meeting to enact international legislation regulating wages and working conditions (Lorwin, 1953). Significant obstacles, however, have stood in the way of implementing international fair labor standards. Even before the international labor movement was ruptured by conflicts between national labor movements of the socialist and nonsocialist countries, other national, ideological, and political differences left IFLS little more than a gleam in its proponents' eyes (Lorwin, 1953).

After the second world war, what appeared a promising opportunity for incorporating IFLS, along with other investment and development concerns, into trade and tariff negotiations evaporated when the International Trade Organization (ITO) failed to win U.S. endorsement. The General Agreement on Tariffs and Trade (GATT), established in 1947 as an interim framework for international trade in anticipation of the ITO, excluded international disparities in wages and working conditions from negotiations (Diebold, 1956).

The labor codes of the International Labor Organization (ILO) have proven to be a wholly inadequate substitute for making enforcement of international fair labor standards a condition for governments' participation in trade liberalization as envisioned under the ill-fated ITO. This weakness was anticipated by unionists who rejected the ILO's tripartite organization and its limited powers under the 1919 Versailles Labor Convention (Lorwin, 1953).

The ILO experience suggests other obstacles to IFLS implementation. Consensually agreed upon by countries' government, labor, and business representatives, ILO codes are minimum standards for labor conditions internationally. Without the force of sanctions, observance and enforcement are left to governments' discretion. Periodic review by ILO representatives or complaints by other ILO participants may lead to censure by the ILO. But, in the absence of sanctions other than censure, national ILO delegations are often reluctant to censure another participating government.

These obstacles have led some to conclude that international fair labor standards as a means to minimize "unfair" international competition based on wages and working conditions are unlikely to be achieved in the foreseeable future (Marshall, 1987). This however begs whether, from the vantage point of workers, international fair labor standards are desirable at all.

74

A number of questions can be raised about IFLS and their desirability. The first concern their scope. A U.S. proponent of international fair labor standards recently proposed requiring that governments participating in international trade and investment agreements recognize worker rights to organize "free and independent trade unions" for purposes of collective bargaining and determination of wages, compensation, hours, safety and health, and other work standards, as well as worker rights to participate in political processes (Winpisinger, 1989). Modeled on the legal framework of U.S. labor relations, Winpisinger's proposal illustrates the problems in prescribing international fair labor standards.

Consider Winpisinger's statement that, "The right of workers to use the strike as an economic weapon would be inviolable," under international fair labor standards. What about the use of the strike by workers for noneconomic purposes? Would participating governments, including that of the U.S. itself, be expected to enforce worker rights to engage in political strikes or strikes in solidarity with workers outside their state-defined "community of interest"? Would the right to organize extend to worker self-organization for purposes other than collective bargaining, including the right to revolution?

Would the scope of international fair labor standards be limited only to workers in export industries, all wage labor, or all waged and unwaged market production? Would such standards be extended to the bulk of the world's workers outside the cash economy, whose super-exploitation, especially in unwaged household work by women, effectively subsidizes cash market and nonmarket economies alike throughout world? Would participating governments be expected to *achieve* whatever standards were established as a precondition for participating in international trade, investment and lending processes, or would they only be expected to subscribe to IFLS as a goal to retain their eligibility?

Any proposal for international fair labor standards or "internationally-recognized worker rights" implicitly presumes some concept of labor's role in national as well as international economic and social development, suggesting other questions to be considered before endorsing an international fair labor standards approach to international competition.

Don't IFLS approaches to "unfair" competition implicitly encourage governments in the newly industrializing countries (NICs) to favor export promotion over balanced growth policies linking national manufacturing, service, and agricultural sectors? IFLS approaches fatalistically presume that the subordination of national policies and objectives to international trading performance is irreversible if not, according to some IFLS proponents, preferable to alternative development paths emphasizing national over international economic and social integration.

This is ironic since every already-industrialized country (AIC) has reached that status not through "free trade" but autarky, controlling international trade and investment flows, especially late starters like South Korea. While the world market and already-industrialized countries' presence do condition national economic and social development, the "external constraint" is not immutable, but is itself conditioned by governments' choice of development strategy. The IFLS approach, by failing to counterpose an alternative strategy to that driven by the international market, combines carrots and sticks to encourage export promotion development, subordinating national policies and objectives to international trading performance.

Doesn't the IFLS approach amount to relying on labor movements and governments in the NICs to make up for the failure of those in the AICs to establish an alternative to a liberal international economic regime? While broadening labor ties internationally, the IFLS approach remains narrowly focused on remedying wage and working condition disparities as sources of "unfair" competition. The IFLS approach ducks the larger question of competition itself as national labor movements accept a subordinate role, sticking to state-defined "labor" spheres, rather than broadening its vision to pose an alternative to the economic strategy dictated by transnational enterprises and their political allies. Even its international labor solidarity amounts to little more than raising standards abroad to reduce NICs' competitive advantage in labor costs in export industries, following the failure of national labor movements in the AICs to counterpose an alternative to international capitalist competition's subordination of national policies and objectives.

This is nowhere more evident than in the troubled history of the AIC labor movements' dealings with national labor movements in the NICs. Considerable conflict has arisen over what are "free trade unions," and, relatedly, what is the proper role of other national labor movements, especially in the NICs. As a "trade-union" approach limited to "taking wages out of competition," the IFLS approach alone is silent about existing national and international regimes and labor's subordinate position within them (Garver, 1989; Kahn, 1989).

However IFLS might affect NIC wages and working conditions, how likely are they to affect them in the AICs? U.S.-NIC trade comprises only ten percent of total U.S. trade volume, while 90 percent of U.S. trade is with other AICs, some with better wages and working conditions. AIC-AIC trade that is the largest source of competition would be largely immune to IFLS arrived at consensually by participating governments. Of course, an IFLS approach, because it fails to confront competition in AIC-AIC trade, may become more relevant as AIC wages and working conditions move toward NIC levels.

In light of our "hidden agenda," the IFLS approach fails the test of mobilizing unionists and organizing others because it relies exclusively on legislative and administrative measures involving only government and national labor center officials. IFLS' dubious international labor solidarity, its bias targeting standards in the NICs without addressing them in trade across AICs' borders, and its failure to confront the subordination of national policies and objectives to international trading performance show that the IFLS approach amounts, as a U.S. critic said over thirty years ago, to a "placebo" for workers and unions in the AICs whose working and living standards, as well as national sovereignty, are being engulfed by international competition (Donohue, forthcoming).

WORKER RIGHTS CONDITIONALITY

Worker rights conditionality (WRC), an alternate approach to "taking wages out of competition" internationally, has emerged in part out of recognition of the obstacles to international fair labor standards. But many of the questions raised about IFLS approaches can also be raised about WRC approaches, particularly concerning their desirability from the standpoint of workers in both newly industrializing and already industrialized countries.

While recent U.S. trade and assistance programs have made observance of "internationally recognized worker rights" a condition for other governments to participate in the Caribbean Basin Initiative, the Generalized System of Preferences, the Overseas Private Investment Corporation, and the 1988 Omnibus Trade and Competitiveness Act, the idea goes back much further than the past decade (Cavanaugh, 1988; Dorman, 1988, 1990).

Opposing "free trade," CIO President John L. Lewis counterposed a series of bilateral agreements with other Western Hemisphere governments purchasing U.S. products and exporting raw materials to the U.S. through U.S. credits. In Lewis's proposal, crafted by economist Jett Lauck, participating governments, in addition to being expected to use U.S. credits to purchase U.S. products, were required to observe worker rights to organize and bargain collectively as well as minimum wages and working standards (Dubofsky and Van Tine, 1977).

Worker rights conditionality avoids some obstacles to IFLS approaches. Bilateral WRC approaches require only agreement between trading or credit partners, unlike IFLS, which requires a multilateral consensus about standards and enforcement. Nonetheless, many questions raised about the IFLS approach to international competition apply to worker rights conditionality too. What would be the scope of internationally recognized worker rights? Would they address only state-defined "trade-union" rights or go beyond them to workers organizing or striking for noneconomic objectives, including challenging the state and/or private property itself?

Would such "rights" be extended to workers beyond export industries, to all wage workers, to workers not working for a wage like peasants sharing crop yields, or to women, children, and others outside the cash economy subsidized by their exploitation? Would observance of such "rights" be a condition for participating in bilateral trade and credit agreements, or would they be expected to make progress toward them as goals?

Isn't the WRC approach implicitly a "big-country" approach, limited to those governments with the ability to disagree in negotiations by withholding access to their trade and/or credit? The recent Canada-U.S. Free Trade Agreement (FTA) shows that Canada, a "small country," lacks bargaining power in dealing with the U.S., whose more diversified economy is ten times the size of Canada's resource-based economy. The saying, "poor Mexico: so close to the U.S., so far from God," applies to most prospective U.S. trading partners without diverse, balanced economies. Without the "ability to disagree," which is the source of bargaining power, governments of "small countries" are unlikely to be able to resist agreement with U.S. negotiators.

As with IFLS, isn't worker rights conditionality an inducement for labor movements in U.S. trading partner countries to support export-promotion development over autarky? Doesn't WRC encourage linking national economies of "small countries" to that of the U.S., instead of linking sectors domestically in pursuit of balanced growth? Doesn't WRC encourage the subordination of national policies and objectives to international trading performance?

In light of the autarky practiced by the U.S. and other governments in industrialization, doesn't the WRC approach presume international economic integration at the expense of national economic integration? Is this a case of "do as I say, not as I do" for the NICs, not to mention the majority of nations in Africa and Asia whose economies are even more removed from the size and diversity of the U.S. and other already-industrialized countries?

What comprises a "democratically-constituted labor movement" suitable for bilateral collaboration in establishing and enforcing worker rights conditionality? Would this be limited to "trade-union" organizations accepting "the rules of the game" of existing economic, social, and political arrangements, or subscribing to U.S. or other prescriptions for "free trade unions"?

Doesn't the WRC approach, like the IFLS approach, shift the burden from labor movements in the AICs, which failed to counter international competition themselves, to those of the NICs? Like the IFLS approach, isn't targeting worker rights in the newly industrializing countries ironic if not hypocritical, since trade among already industrialized countries dwarfs NIC-AIC trade as a source of international competition?

Isn't worker rights conditionality, like IFLS, as much a symptom of AIC unionists' failure in struggling against the transnational enterprises and their political allies as it is of concern for workers in the NICs? Have AIC unionists so little regard for national self-determination or have they simply come to regard international economic integration as inevitable or even desirable? In pressuring NIC governments and national labor movements, have unionists forgotten that the transnational enterprises and their political allies in the already-industrialized countries are workers' main enemy?

Like IFLS approaches, WRC approaches fail the test of our "hidden agenda" in relying on legislative, bureaucratic, and administrative methods instead of mobilizing unionists and organizing others to challenge international capitalist competition's subordination of national policies and objectives to international trading performance.

Instead of broadening national resistance around an alternative economic strategy, national labor movements in the already-industrialized countries through the WRC approach instead urge national labor movements in the NICs to confine their struggles within the parameters bounding their own efforts in the already-industrialized countries. Given the desperate state of the labor movement in the U.S. and other already industrialized countries, this is no less ironic than AFL-CIO instruction of Soviet and Eastern European unionists on how to deal with transnational enterprises.

FAR 145 AND PERIL POINTS

Reliance on legislative and administrative means alone cannot overcome the fatalism afflicting many unionists about challenging international capitalist competition. Only approaches that mobilize unionists and organize others around an alternative economic strategy offer a direction for workers and others in the present crisis. What remains is to show, contrary to more "pragmatic" objections, how immediate struggles to protect working and living standards can be the first step toward challenging international capitalist competition's subordination of national policies and objectives to trading performance. To do so, I describe a campaign I've been involved in with Machinist aircraft maintenance and repair workers to protect existing domestic working, living, safety, and regulatory standards.

Federal Air Regulation 145 (FAR 145) is a U.S. Federal Aviation Administration (FAA) regulation that, since 1948, mandated that U.S. registered aircraft be maintained and repaired at aircraft repair stations *within* the United States. In cases where equipment failure made movement of an aircraft impossible, aircraft operators under the original rule were permitted to seek authorization for repair or maintenance work offshore at FAA-certified repair stations (DoT, 1988).

After an internal staff debate, the FAA, in 1988, lifted all restrictions on U.S.-registered aircraft maintenance and repair by foreign repair stations (DoT, 1988). Within two months, the revised FAR 145 drew over two hundred applications for certification of new foreign repair stations, and the FAA predicted another two hundred applications forthcoming (DoT, 1989a).

Behind this FAA initiative was the Reagan-Bush administrations' goal of offering access to U.S.-registered aircraft maintenance and repair markets as part of a larger deal opening the door to allowing foreign air carriers to fly domestic routes, known as "cabotage" (U.S. Special Trade Representative, 1982). Initially one of the items on the GATT agenda, civil air transport was removed at the instigation of air carriers in the AICs unwilling to provide access to NIC air carriers as mandated by GATT's requirement that trade concessions be offered to all GATT participants (Nayyar, 1988).

Subsequently, AIC carriers and their governments separately formed, in May 1989, the "Marrakesh Group," excluding the NICs, to widen access to each others' domestic civil air transport and aircraft maintenance and repair markets. As part of this larger plan for "free trade," the new FAR 145 gave the Bush administration a valuable concession to offer in exchange for access to European civil air transport markets for U.S. air carriers from other "Marrakesh Group" governments (*Aviation Daily*, 1989).

Only United Airlines and American Airlines failed to endorse the FAA action. The two largest U.S. carriers, United and American, operate huge maintenance and repair facilities in the U.S., doing as much as 30 percent of their work for other U.S.-registered aircraft operators. United's San Francisco-Oakland base is the largest aircraft maintenance and repair facility in the world, employing over twenty-six thousand workers, including thirteen thousand Machinists, over 10 percent of the industry's work force nationally (United Air Lines, 1988).

In January 1989, H.R. 145, sponsored by Congressman Norman Mineta, was introduced to reverse the FAA action. Machinist Air Transport Lodge 1781, committed itself to passage of H.R. 145 (Hitchcock, 1989). Together with Lodge 1781 officers, staff, and members, I outlined a plan to support legislative and administrative efforts with education and organizing programs by Machinists aimed at other Bay-Area residents and organizations and other groups nationally.

Showing that competition's "benefits" were the result of inducing reductions in working, living, safety, and regulatory standards, we have developed an alternative theoretical analysis of the competitive process. Using it and an independent empirical analysis showing the economic and social impact of aircraft maintenance and repair industries on local economies, we have challenged the FAA in Congressional and FAA forums, discrediting their analyses supporting the rule change (U.S. House, 1989; DoT, 1989b).

The empirical survey has also been used in outreach efforts. Alerting others in and outside the industry to the FAR 145 revisions, we have won support from a broad range of local residents and organizations, even to the extent that the chronically "free trade" local press has endorsed H.R. 145. In addition, Lodge 1781 members have contacted other locals, IAM districts, and national unions as well as community, industry, air traveler, safety, and government groups for broad-based support for H.R. 145 in different forums. At the heart of the outreach effort is "back-fence" organizing, with Machinists and others contacting acquaintances to communicate their concerns and enlist their support in any form.

Legislative progress in turn has been the result of the combined research and outreach efforts. By establishing our credibility through economic and empirical analyses, we have seized the initiative in Congress and have forced the FAA and industry representatives to demonstrate their own credibility. With over 220 members of the House, including sixty Republicans, now enrolled as H.R. 145 cosponsors, we have enough votes to pass H.R. 145 (Congressional Record, 1989).

In addition, we won a Congressional resolution directing the FAA to reconsider its December 1988 action, to which the agency has responded by holding a series of public meetings on FAR 145 around the country while suspending certification of foreign repair stations and licensing their use. In the meetings, we have forced FAA representatives to admit that the December 1988 action was based entirely on industry proponents' claims which the FAA failed to scrutinize or investigate itself (U.S. House, 1989; DoT, 1989b).

But the Bush administration's publicly stated intention to veto our bill has forced us to seek additional House support to "veto proof" H.R. 145, a necessary condition for enthusiastic Senate support of the companion bill (U.S. House, 1989).

To meet the veto threat, we have adopted a strategy of continually raising requirements for evidence and analysis in the debate. In the process, we have identified the different concerns of nonsponsors, distinguishing among those otherwise sympathetic and those committed to "free trade." Some are apprehensive that restoring forty-year prohibitions on the use of foreign repair stations would trigger foreign government retaliation against U.S. exports, particularly toward U.S. aircraft manufacturing, one of the only surplus segments of the U.S. international trade. Others are sensitive to the concerns of U.S. air carriers whose purchases of foreign aircraft have led them to seek access for maintenance and repair from foreign operations. Still others are seeking special concessions for particular countries' repair stations to maintain and repair U.S.-registered aircraft (U.S. House, 1989).

Among the former are many House members concerned about the unavailability of aircraft maintenance and repair service domestically, causing delays for U.S.-registered aircraft operators. We have met this concern by proposing an old Republican idea, called "peril points."

Introduced in 1948, the "peril point" sets limits on trade concessions in advance of negotiations. Limits on access to the U.S. domestic market would be based on prior determination of the amounts of concessions allowable without "imperiling" domestic producers' standards. By setting limits to trade concessions, these "peril points" avoided "too little, too late" inadequacies of the "escape clause" wherein an industry had to wait until actual damage occurred, then demonstrate that it was the result of specific concessions, persuade the International Trade Commission that it deserved relief, and finally have the president determine which form that relief should take (Donohue, 1986). "Peril points" preempts the difficulties and delays of after-the-fact revision of trade agreements and the combined opposition of industries and other governments to the alteration of the overall agreement.

In the case of U.S.-registered aircraft maintenance and repair, "peril points" would be determined annually in advance of certification of foreign repair stations and licensing U.S. operators to use them. "Peril points" would be based on existing domestic aircraft maintenance and repair capacity and utilization, with an eye to competitive depression of working, living, safety, and regulatory standards. Through "peril points," concerns about availability of domestic aircraft maintenance and repair service would be addressed in advance through the annual review process providing opportunity for public submissions.

At both legislative and popular levels, the "peril-point" approach to international capitalist competition succeeds by uniting allies and dividing foes over maintaining working, living, safety, and regulatory standards. In addition, the FAR 145 campaign shows the possibility of alternative policies and politics, challenging the subordination of national policies and objectives to international trading performance by mobilizing unionists and organizing others, rather than relying exclusively on legislative and administrative methods.

COMMON ENEMY, DIFFERENT STRATEGIES

By the three tests set out above, the "peril points" approach to international competition is superior to international fair labor standards and worker rights conditionality approaches. But, while meeting the requirements first, for mobilizing unionists and organizing others, and second, of challenging the international capitalist market's subordination of national policies and objectives to international trading performance, the "peril points" approach is unlikely to meet, except as part of an alternative economic strategy, the third test, overcoming the power of TNEs.

Nonetheless, by demonstrating the possibility of alternative policies and politics, the "peril points" approach shows the way to such a strategy through mobilizing unionists and organizing others to break with both fatalism about international economic integration and backward-looking localisms proclaiming "my nation, right or wrong." By connecting with national patriotic feeling and desire for national self-determination, the "peril points" approach directs unionists' efforts against the main enemy, transnational enterprises and their political allies, rather than scapegoating other workers, nations, or peoples.

REFERENCES

Aviation Daily. May 14, 1989

Barrett, Dave. *Free Trade: The Sellout.* Ottawa: NDP, 1989.

Cavanaugh, John, et al. *Trade's Hidden Costs: Worker Rights in a Changing World Economy.* Washington, D.C.: International Labor Rights and Education and Research Fund, 1988.

Congressional Record. June 27, 1989.

Diebold, William. *The End of the ITO.* Princeton, New Jersey, Princeton University, 1956.

Donohue, Peter. *From "Free Trade" to "Fair Trade": Trade Liberalization's Endorsement and Subsequent Rejection by the American Federation Of Labor and Congress of Industrial Organizations, 1934–1975.* Ph.D. Dissertation, University of Texas, Austin, August, 1986.

———. 'Free Trade' Unions and the State: Trade Liberalization's Endorsement by the AFL-CIO, 1942–1962." In *Research in Political Economy.* Edited by Paul Zarembka. Forthcoming.

———. *Statement on H.R. 145.* Subcommittee on Aviation, Committee on Public Works and Transportation, U.S. House of Representatives, June 27, 1989.

———. *Statement on FAR Parts 43, 65, Subpart E, and 145.* Federal Aviation Administration, Public Meeting, December 12–13, 1989.

Dorman, Peter. "Worker Rights and International Trade: A Case for Intervention." *Review of Radical Political Economics*. 20(2 and 3):241–6, 1988.

———. *Worker Rights and International Trade Policy*. Working paper, Smith College, February, 1990.

Dubofsky, Melvyn, and Warren Van Tyne. *John L. Lewis: A Biography*. New York: McGraw-Hill, 1977.

Faux, Jeff. *Labor in the New Global Economy*. Geneva: International Metalworkers' Federation, 1989.

Garver, Paul. "Beyond the Cold War: New Directions for Labor Internationalism." *Labor Research Review*. 8(1):61–79, 1989.

Hitchcock, Dennis. "Stop FAR 145." *Trade Winds*. Burlingame, California: Air Transport Lodge 1781, International Association of Machinists and Aerospace Workers, January, 1989.

Hymer, Stephen. "International Politics and International Economics: A Radical Approach." In *The Multinational Corporation—A Radical Approach: Papers by Stephen Herbert Hymer*. Edited by Robert Cohen, et. al. New York: Cambridge, 1979.

Kahn, Tom. "A Reply to Paul Garver." *Labor Research Review*. 8(1):61–79, 1989.

Lorwin, Lewis. *The International Labor Movement: History, Policies, and Outlook*. New York: Harper, 1953.

Marshall, F. Ray. *Unheard Voices: Labor and Economic Policy in a Competitive World*. New York: Prentice-Hall, 1987.

Nayyar, Deepak. "The Political Economy of International Trade in Services." *Cambridge Journal of Economics*. 12:279–98, n.d.

Ritchie, Mark. "Rural-Urban Cooperation: Our Populist History and Future." In *Building Bridges: The Emerging Grassroots Coalition of Labor and Community*. Edited by Jeremy Brecher and Tim Costello. New York: MR, 1990.

Simon, Joel. "Mexico's Free Trade Gamble: President Salinas' Hard-Line Economic Policies May Be Pushing the Country to the Brink of Another Revolution." *San Francisco Weekly*. September 5, 1990.

Trade Expansion Act of 1962: Law, Explanation, and Committee Reports, as Enacted October 11, 1962. Washington: Commerce Clearing House, 1962.

United Airlines. *Maintenance Operations Center Fact Sheet*. July 21, 1988.

United Nations Commission on Trade and Development (UNCTAD). *Production in Trade in Services: Policies and Their Underlying Factors Bearing on International Services Transactions*. New York: UNCTAD, 1985.

U.S. Congress. *Amendment No. 45 to the Conference Report on the Continuing Resolution H.J. Resolution 395*. December 21, 1987.

U.S. Congress. House Committee on Public Works and Transportation. Subcommittee on Aviation. *Hearings on the Use of Foreign Repair Stations by U.S. Airlines*. July, 1987.

U.S. Congress. House Committee on Public Works and Transportation. Subcommittee on Aviation. *Hearings on H.R. 145*. June 27, 1989.

U.S. Department of Transportation (DoT). Federal Aviation Administration. "Notice of Proposed Rule Making." *Federal Register*. November 24, 1987.

U.S. Department of Transportation. Federal Aviation Administration. "Foreign Repair Station Rules." *Federal Register*. November 22, 1988.

U.S. Department of Transportation. Federal Aviation Administration. *Foreign Repair Station Update*. Washington, DoT, February, 1989a.

U.S. Department of Transportation. Federal Aviation Administration. "Repair Station and Repairmen Certification Rules; Regulatory Review; Meetings." *Federal Register*. July 24, 1989b.

U.S. Special Trade Representative. *U.S. National Study on Trade in Services*. Washington, GPO, 1983.

Winpisinger, William. *Reclaiming Our Future*. San Francisco: 1989.

Challenging the Ethic of Competitiveness: What's at Stake for Labor

LEO GERARD

District Director, United Steelworks of America, Distrct 6, Ontario

INTRODUCTION

In the past twenty years, sweeping changes have taken place in the nature and structure of the world economy and in its impact on the everyday lives of working people.

- Events and developments in distant lands that twenty years ago would have been nothing more than interesting news items of little relevance to our daily lives are now primary determinants of the job security and future prospects of working men and women in North America.
- Twenty years ago, the complexity of international transactions, communications difficulties, and the restrictions faced by corporations in their offshore business activities acted as barriers to runaway plants and in effect provided workers in those plants with a measure of job security. Today, on an almost daily basis workers somewhere in North America walk into their workplace only to discover that their jobs, and sometimes even the equipment they work with, have been moved offshore to some low-wage haven for wayward capitalists.
- Twenty years ago, we still thought of international trade as a way to build the strength of individual national economies by enabling each to take advantage of the strengths of the others. Today, the international trading system is increasingly a vehicle for private enrichment.
- Technological changes that twenty years ago might have taken five years to make their way through the development process are on the shelves or on the shop floor in weeks.
- Environmental time horizons that might have been measured in centuries twenty years ago are now measured in decades or years.
- The promise of progress that captivated the Third World twenty years ago has been replaced by a reality of famine and despair for the poorest of the poor. The billions of dollars in development aid that flowed from north to south twenty years ago have been overwhelmed by more billions of dollars in debt repayments flowing from south to north.

These changes in themselves are disturbing enough. More disturbing, however, is the fact that the forces that are driving these changes are more powerful, more remote, less subject to influence, and able to move more quickly and flexibly than would have been imagined (or feared) twenty years ago. The challenge faced by the labor movement is to influence and ultimately to bring under control those powerful forces. Meeting that challenge will require working people around the world to confront directly the most basic assumptions about how the international economic system ought to work. In particular we must examine and challenge the competitiveness ethic that dominates the current discourse. The modern ethic of competitiveness—the constant search for the lowest common denominator—has transformed the trading system into an engine for private wealth creation and has turned the nations that created the system into hostages to it.

In Canada, and I suspect in the United States as well, a subtle change has taken place in recent years in the language used by the business community to describe our economic position relative to that of the rest of the world. Whereas the talk used to be about the need to continue to improve productivity to maintain Canada's standard of living, it is now about the need to improve competitiveness to maintain the job security of Canadian workers. If this were a distinction without a difference, this change could easily be ignored as an exercise in semantics driven by ideology. It is easy to understand why a business community steeped in the enthusiastic ideology of the 1980s might prefer the word "competitiveness," which speaks directly to that ideology, to "productivity" which sounds vaguely technical and unattractive. If that were all there is to it, Canadians could feel quite comfortable letting the business community use its new word, much as one might let a child continue to use a pacifier.

Unfortunately for working people, it is not an innocent exercise in semantics. The two concepts contemplate radically different economic futures and radically different economic circumstances for working people. Increased productivity, by definition, implies increases in standards of living. How those increases are distributed is up to unions, through collective bargaining, and government, through tax and other public policies, to determine. Increased competitiveness, as the concept is most often used, implies driving input costs down to the lowest common denominator and minimizing restrictions and regulations that drive costs up. The focus of efforts to minimize costs is rarely on such inputs as interest on borrowing, which would harm such deserving institutions as the banks. Rather it seems inevitably to be the wages, benefits, rights, and social entitlements of working people that are attacked.

This fixation with depressing living standards is not a phenomenon unique to the Canadian business community. Unfortunately for working people everywhere, the idea that economic success (or even survival) carries with it a price tag of public impoverishment, environmental degradation, growing inequality, and stagnant or declining living standards is not just an affliction brought on by cold weather. It is the guiding principle of international economic development and international business strategy.

It is not hard to see why the international business community finds the new ethos attractive or why the international economic system tends toward that result. The elimination of restrictions on the movement of capital has made it possible for corporations to seek the highest return available regardless of national boundaries. Advances in information technology make the control of production no more difficult on the other side of the globe than it is across the street. The enhanced mobility which these two factors afford has richly rewarded the international business elite. While these rewards to multinational corporations are obvious, it is more difficult to explain why national governments around the globe have bought so enthusiastically into this vicious, inequitable, and destructive system. Part of the explanation has its roots in a failure of democracy. The same international elites that dominate "national" business communities also dominate (directly or indirectly) national political elites. Working people are shut out of the process; those who question the unresponsiveness of their governments to the economic realities that they face lose their voice.

The key to the problem, however, can be found in a classic problem in the theory of games, the prisoners' dilemma. In the prisoners' dilemma, two prisoners are charged with the same offense. Each prisoner faces a choice: to confess, or to rat on the other guy. A confession is worth a year in jail. A conviction is worth five years in jail. Each prisoner rats on the other guy, thinking that he will get off scott free. Instead both go to jail for five years. If they had worked together and both confessed, they each would have gone to jail for one year.

National governments are playing the roles of the prisoners. The emphasis on competitiveness is justified largely on the basis that in an increasingly open world economy, production costs have to be kept down so that export markets remain open to domestic producers, and imports don't drive out production for the domestic market. Rather than confront the rule makers in the international economic game as it is being played today, national governments think they can succeed at the expense of countries that won't or can't play by lowest common denominator rules. The result is that everyone loses—except, of course, for the controllers of the game.

THE NEED FOR SOLIDARITY

The message of solidarity for working people, and for the unions that represent them around the world, couldn't be clearer. The critical question is, how do we draw some concrete meaning from the message. Part of the answer is for the labor movements of Canada and the U.S. to reinvigorate national debates and national politics on these key issues. Effective national responses to capital mobility and effective national resistance to attempts to undermine living standards and social entitlements are essential if we are to resist the tide.

The first step in building national responses is to attack the sense of inevitability, of lack of choice, that has been created about the ideology of competitiveness. Purveyors of this ideology have changed their rhetoric. There are no longer any advocates for depressed living standards and curtailed public services in Canada. The current federal government learned that lesson years ago when it tried to tamper with the key universal programs that make up Canada's "social entitlement." There is no market for unfairness in Canada. There is no audience for rabid right-wing calls for the dismantling of public services.

Instead, what we get is the crocodile tears of the corporate fat cats arguing that Canada can no longer "afford" to pay people decently; that the nation can no longer "afford" to improve workplace health and safety standards; that we can no longer "afford" to force business to clean up the environment. To do so, they argue, would damage our "competitive position" in relation to other countries. What the apostles of competitiveness do not acknowledge is that they have made a choice. They have chosen an approach to the open economy that is designed to force working people to accept lower living standards in return for a tenuous and temporary job security based on sheltering weakness; they have rejected an approach designed to raise living standards and promote employment security based on economic strength.

Both as a labor movement and as societies more generally, however, we must go beyond national responses. The new tools at the disposal of corporations that recognize no national obligations in their drive for competitive advantage demand effective international responses and institutions. The stakes are very high and go far beyond the question of maintaining the living standards of North-American or European or Japanese workers. Workers in North-American countries aren't the only victims of lowest common denominator competition. This same ideology and the international economic regime that supports it are also the major contributors to the developmental and environmental crises that pose a fundamental threat to the future of life on this planet.

The competitiveness ethic is at the root of the basic questions about society and development raised in the Brundtland Report on "Our Common Future." The same "competitive" forces that are undermining living standards in the "developed" world have further divided the Third World into the "might haves" (the so-called Newly Industrializing Countries) and the "will never haves" (including most of Africa, much of South America, and substantial parts of Asia). The effect of this division promises to be an unspeakable disaster of famine and hardship, a disaster which we must not tolerate and which they will not tolerate.

We need new and effective international institutions to counter the power of the modern stateless corporation and to make effective the national responses that are necessary to get a handle on these massive problems. The institutions we now have aren't working. Institutions like the International Monetary Fund, the General Agreement on Tariffs and Trade, and the World Bank act effectively as the enforcers of the very system that stands in the way of solutions to these problems of development and environment. Because they are dominated by the major industrialized countries and the interests of the international business community, they are totally lacking in credibility in the Third World.

Without institutions that can bridge the interests of the industrialized world with those of the Third World, there is no hope of solving these problems. We cannot expect Third-World nations and peoples to forego their attempts to improve living standards so that the industrialized world can continue to destroy the environment. And we cannot hope to build a constituency at home for environmental protection and international income redistribution as long as corporations remain free to use lowest common denominator blackmail to undermine job security and exacerbate income disparities.

All of this sounds very gloomy, I admit, and so it should. The crises we face could hardly be more daunting, and we could hardly be more poorly prepared to deal with them. We face an uphill battle against long odds even to build an effective political constituency for the changes that are needed. In much of the industrialized world, the right wing has been extremely successful in promoting the values of competitiveness and the unrestricted "free" market as common national, and indeed patriotic, values.

BUILDING PROGRESSIVE ALLIANCES

At the same time, however, the very scope of the negative effects of the lowest common denominator competitive ethic has created new potential allies who might not in the past have found anything in common with the trade union movement. The most powerful political movement on the planet today is the environmental movement. And it is gradually dawning on decision makers that the collapse of Third-World economies poses a serious long-term threat both to environmental quality and to international peace and security. Developing alliances with these important social movements is critical to the success of trade union movements everywhere in building an alternative political and economic agenda. Those alliances must be made at the domestic and the international level. Building those alliances will not be easy, either for our own constituencies in the trade union movement or for the environmental and international development movements.

We in the labor movement also must make much more effective use of our traditional lines of international communication. We have to be more concerned with the living standards and community standards of workers in other countries. Let me give you just three illustrations.

- A Canadian steel company with which the Steelworkers Union has many dealings, Ivaco, recently announced that it intended to be on the cutting edge of the invasion of Eastern Europe by Western capitalists by opening a nail mill in Poland. Shortly thereafter, it announced the closure of nail mills in North America. The company's motive is clear, as is the message to trade unionists in both Poland and North America.

- Our union in the United States, I am proud to say, has played a leading role in the effort to win a stronger Clean Air Act in the face of vociferous objections from the steel industry that tougher requirements on coke oven emissions will damage the industry and undermine job security. But if we as a union stop there, and do nothing to strengthen the international effort for environmental clean-up, the dirty industrial operations will simply be transferred to other more compliant jurisdictions, and we will have neither job security nor environmental quality.

- The Swedish company, SKF, has recently unveiled a global economic strategy that divides the world into three zones: a dollar zone, a yen zone, and a deutschmark zone. It has declared that it will move capital within and between these zones to maximize its return, without regard to national considerations. It is essential that trade unionists around the world cooperate, as we have started to do, to make sure that companies like SKF don't get away with labor and environmental practices in one part of the world that they would never dare try elsewhere.

The message to the shadowy world of international capital has to be: you can run, but you cannot hide.

Henry Ford made himself famous and his family rich with the simple observation that the economy cannot grow and ultimately cannot survive if the working people who build the products of our society cannot afford to buy them. I might add to that the observation that no economy can survive if the production process itself destroys the basis for life on the planet.

An International Mobilization Strategy

LARRY COHEN

Director of Organization, Assistant to the President, Communication Workers of America

In the United States over the last twenty years, the rate of unionization has fallen by more than half. In the private sector of this country, the rate of unionization has declined from 35 to 10 percent. By the year 2000, it may be as low as 5 percent due not so much to the failure of organizing, but to deunionization by the major unionized American employers.

In our own union, the Communications Workers of America (CWA), we face this constantly with AT&T, which is our largest employer with 15 percent of our members. AT&T revenues and profits are increasing, yet there have been massive job cuts and movement of capital from union to unorganized enterprises in the U.S., as well as to Mexico and Asia. Why invest in the United States if AT&T can invest in Mexico and pay people eighty cents per hour? We need a political movement as well as a movement in our workplaces to turn that around.

Even closer to home, in Canada in the last four or five years there's been a leveling and now a gradual decrease in the rate of unionization. But, fortunately for our Canadian brothers and sisters, the unionization rate remains at 40 percent of the work force organized, compared to our continued precipitous decline. The multinational corporations that dominate the North-American economic sphere are using the same deunionization techniques in Canada as in the United States. The decline is slower there because of the political movement that exists and the resistance of the Canadian union movement that is relatively stronger than the union movement here.

While we don't want to create an atmosphere of despair, we need to be realistic. We are in deep trouble. These trends will get worse before they get better. We need to restructure ourselves and view international cooperation as part of that restructuring. I don't think we are going to have significant cooperative efforts internationally if we don't change our own local unions and national unions in this country. We can no longer view the union solely in a traditional collective bargaining framework. Collective bargaining is still an important tool, but it's a question of emphasis or degree.

AN ORGANIZING STRATEGY FOR UNIONS

We describe CWA's priorities as a triangle—representation, organizing, and community and political action. While representation is the base of the triangle, we need resources for organizing and political action that include international cooperation. We need to mobilize our members politically and at their worksites. Then we can envision workers across national boundaries standing up for one another at their work sites and utilizing political pressure. But to get to that point on an international level, we have to better focus our resources and energy.

Our members are busy, and some work two jobs and have families to raise. But we need some of that time. The union is not an insurance company. You don't pay your dues and go home. You have to put in some of your time. Five hours a year from thirteen million union members in the United States could turn this country around. Next, think about that on a worldwide basis. What are the possibilities? I think that's the way out of this despair. We need to look at the union as an organizing vehicle, not just to organize new members but to reorganize the ones we have. In the CWA we call that mobilization and we had massive mobilization around 1989 collective bargaining involving three quarters of our members.

We are making similar attempts to mobilize beyond the workplace through Jobs with Justice and other coalitions. Jobs with Justice asks union members "to support someone else's fight as well as their own." To the extent that we reorganize ourselves around these programs and strategies, we then position ourselves to make the links we need to make with workers and their unions in other countries.

This process requires an enormous amount of work, and I don't minimize the problems. It's difficult enough to mobilize and restructure here, let alone to mobilize internationally. But we have little alternative. No matter how much we might like to, we cannot stop the worldwide movement of capital investment. We might regulate capital flight to a greater extent than we do. This country should join the rest of the world by adopting a national industrial policy. But even if we had regulation and an industrial policy, that is not going to prevent capital from moving across national boundaries.

DEALING WITH MULTINATIONAL EMPLOYERS

As we look to link up with unions in other countries both in organizing and collective bargaining, we need to consciously evaluate our international attitudes. Economic change is forcing us to reevaluate our foreign policy. Speaking in terms of our own union we've been focused for thirty years on programs in developing countries. Until recently, little of our international work has concerned our multinational employers. We are beginning by focusing on the multinationals that are eliminating jobs, cutting wages, and deunionizing.

Most of the companies that are unionized in the U.S. are multinational companies. Most CWA employers were not multinational until the last ten years. We had a few employers like ITT which, in the worst sense of the word, were multinational in the 1950s. But now AT&T is a major player in the world economy. Pacific Bell, a part of Pacific Telesis, is a major force in cable television in Europe. US West is building a cellular telephone system for Hungary. The same deregulation that is leading to an unraveling of job security for our members within those companies in the U.S. is also permitting and encouraging capital investment wherever it will get the greatest rate of return, whether it is in new subsidiaries in this country, Europe, Asia, or South America.

To summarize again, *first* we must reemphasize an organizing strategy here in the U.S. in our local and national unions. *Second*, our bargaining strategy needs to be refocused to deal with our employers as multinationals. The capital that they invest in whatever we produce can be moved somewhere else. In the CWA, our employers constantly restructure. ITT is Sheraton Hotels and Hartford Insurance Company, but their role in communications is solely through partial ownership of Alcatel, the French telecommunications giant.

PROTECTIONISM AND WORKERS' RIGHTS

Third, protectionism has got to go. This is a tough one for many of us. We are not going to build solidarity with Japanese workers if we take an inflexible position that Americans should never buy Japanese cars. As tough as that is, I think we need to reevaluate our views. We need to look at whether products are union-made, not just where they're produced. We recently reached an agreement with Zendentsu, a Japanese telecommunications union, that addresses that very point. The Japanese import very little telecommunications equipment and they export everything. We are not going to be able to turn that around unless there is some kind of mutual understanding about trade.

Fourth, international solidarity must be based on support for international standards of workers' rights. When products are produced by slaves, they should not be sold here. But where there is a labor movement, where there is protection for the right to organize, where there is a minimum or improving standard of living, we should trade with those countries and work with those unions. But, we will never build international solidarity if we always hide behind the banner of protectionism.

Fifth, cooperation on an international level requires grass-roots education as part of the mobilization. But it needs to be a two-way street. With union strength declining in this country, we need help from our European, Japanese, and Canadian brothers and sisters. But we will also have to be willing to take a stand for them when American-based multinationals are repressing workers' rights in those countries. We have to be willing to do that kind of education at the grass-roots level. Even where we have relatively good relationships with those companies in this country, we need to monitor their behavior worldwide to defend our interests here.

Finally, we need to look toward multinational sanctions against corporations that violate basic standards of workers' rights. The Organization for Economic Cooperation and Development (OECD) has guidelines that cover appropriate behavior, but they are violated every day.

We have learned a lot from the movement for divestment from South Africa. Many of us here have been involved in the efforts against Shell and other corporations. CWA, which represents 40,000 New Jersey state workers, was a leader in making New Jersey the first state to divest its state pension plan from South Africa. The Shell boycott was supported by city councils and state governments all over this country, yet much more could have been done by our union and others.

Similar international efforts might focus on several multinationals that consistently violate principles such as the right to organize. We might identify several key corporations from different industries such as food, auto and telecommunications.

INTERNATIONAL STRATEGIES

In the U.S. labor movement, we need to better recognize our increasingly difficult situation. Even though many U.S. unions are large, most industries in the U.S. are cutting union employment and limiting union influence. We need to approach our international work with more humility. We will need to ask for help more than we can give since unions in Canada and Europe are relatively stronger.

During the Pittston strike, the visit by European trade unionists to the coal fields was quite important. Japanese union help was important since Japan is a major purchaser of Pittston coal.

We also need to develop regional strategies. We need to view the United States as part of North America. We can get our inspiration from the Canadians but we must realize that we are in the middle between Canada and Mexico, not only geographically, but in terms of workers' rights. In the next century, the population of Mexico will be as great as that of the United States. The Maquiladora plants will soon employ one million workers. In our union we paid little attention until the last three years when AT&T opened manufacturing plants along the Mexican side of the Rio Grande River. Now we've been in those plants, we have seen the way those workers live, and we have publicized that to our members. The question is, "Are workers' rights in this country going up to the Canadian level where there is much better protection than here, or down to the Mexican level?"

Increasingly we need to work with European labor which hopefully will gain additional strength through European unification. Some of the resolutions enacted by the Europeans as part of the enabling legislation for unification seem amazing to us in the United States. They are discussing minimum wages on a continental basis. They are proposing no "union busting" on a continental basis. Europeans are considering guarantees in health and safety, and social security which includes free health care as well as pensions. There is great reason to believe the unification of Europe is going to actually strengthen those workers' rights. Hopefully conditions within Europe will become a model, and with our European allies we can then leverage access to that marketplace, denying participation to those corporations that violate basic principles of workers' rights. By working together North-American, European and Asian unions can drastically increase their own power. That's a proposal that will need a lot of work, with real resources.

A CASE STUDY—NORTHERN TELECOM

Finally, I present one case study from our own experience. There are examples from other unions, but I would like to examine one I've worked with myself. Northern Telecom originally was Northern Electric, the supplier for Bell Canada just as Western Electric was the supplier for AT&T in the U.S. Over the years its name changed to Northern Telecom as it became a Canadian-based multinational corporation.

The main products of Northern Telecom are central office switches, which enable telephone systems to operate. Northern also produces and markets customer premise equipment. Today, the United States is the major market for Northern Telecom and Canada is second. Northern also manufactures and markets in Asia and Europe. Northern Telecom is publicly traded on the Toronto stock exchange, but 51 percent of the stock is owned by Bell Canada. Bell Canada is nearly totally union represented. The Communications and Electrical Workers of Canada (CWC) is the principal union at Bell. In addition, about eight thousand Northern Telecom workers are organized by the Canadian Auto Workers (CAW).

In the United States, Northern employs twenty thousand workers. Fewer than one thousand are union and all of those are members of CWA. Ten years ago Northern had only a few hundred employees in the United States, installing and servicing customer premise equipment. They now have more manufacturing workers in the United States than in Canada. Northern Telecom is among the worst telecommunications companies with which we negotiate. Every negotiations is viewed by the company as an opportunity to decertify the union. They have decertified five of our bargaining units. They'll fire their best workers if they are union leaders.

As of August 1989, our largest remaining unit consisted of approximately five hundred technicians in eight eastern states. Several months prior to contract expiration, we started mobilization of our five hundred members by establishing a network in each state with "phone trees." We trained twenty-five mobilization coordinators, or one for every twenty technicians. We issued a newsletter on a regular basis detailing Northern Telecom contract news. We could not go to the Canadians for help if we didn't have our own members mobilized.

Then last summer we formed the Northern Telecom coalition with the CAW and CWC. As stated in paragraph "1" of the Agreement,

> The objective of the coalition shall be to provide a neutral atmosphere concerning labor relations in Northern Telecom workplaces in both Canada and the United States. In Canada the chief concern has been closings and layoffs. In the United States Northern Telecom has expanded employment while adopting an aggressive antiunion policy. Our ultimate goal will be to sign a pledge of neutrality with Northern Telecom agreeing not to oppose unionization and to agree to "card check" in organized units in both countries. We should also seek an agreement as to locations of new facilities and maintenance of employment in existing ones.

As we expected, we reached no agreement with Northern Telecom in bargaining and engaged in mobilization on the job, three weeks of job actions designed to "wind the company down." Then we struck the company suddenly, several weeks after the initial contract expiration date. Thanks to our coalition with the Canadians, immediate letters of support were sent from the two Canadian union presidents to the Northern Telecom chief executive officer stating that the Canadian unions would fully support the strike. Copies of the letters were distributed among the Northern technicians in the United States to boost morale.

Once we had the support of the Canadian local unions, grass-roots mobilization started in Canada to support the strike. Two leaflets were put out in the Canadian manufacturing plants signed by all three unions. The second leaflet stated "Is it a coincidence?—The history of Northern Telecom's antiworker, antiunion activities in the United States." The leaflet proposed that our unity could stop the exporting of jobs to the United States and the antiunion policy in the U.S.

This was coupled with a national boycott in the U.S. from the AFL-CIO which was important since Northern Telecom equipment is often installed on union construction jobs. There's no one component of this plan that's perfect; it's the cumulative effect.

In this case we began to get some results. CWA President Bahr received a letter from Northern Chair Paul Stern stating that the company was not antiunion. At the end of the letter, Stern said, "As you are well aware Northern Telecom and CWA are currently engaged in negotiations. Upon the conclusion of these negotiations and the return to work I will welcome the opportunity to meet with you in Washington to discuss topics of mutual concern, particularly medical care."

Our coalition at Northern Telecom applied pressure at the grass-roots level in Canada and the United States. And top officials in the unions in both Canada and the United States applied increasing pressure on the company.

Fred Pomeroy, CWC president, even attended negotiations in New York. Then we started to get press in Canada—headlines like, "Unions Team up to Fight for Jobs at High-Tech Giant"—"Unions Accuse Nortel of Union Busting in the United States." Finally, "Our Love Affair with Northern Telecom Sours."

We settled that strike favorably, largely because of the Canadian help. Without it, our technicians would probably have been replaced and the union decertified. Instead, everyone went back to work within three days of the settlement and replacement technicians were put on the bottom of the seniority list. The Canadian press summarized with headlines like, "Unions Team up to Force Nortel Strike Settlement."

Recently we received dramatic evidence of the systematic and illegal invasion of privacy by Northern Telecom in its manufacturing plant in Nashville, Tennessee. Copies of tape-recorded telephone conversations, wiretapped from pay phones in the employee cafeteria, were provided to us by a former security officer in the plant. Additional tapes were made from listening devices in the plant's sprinkler system. This surveillance was conducted from at least 1979 to 1989 as part of a broader effort in the plant to prevent unionization.

Through our Northern Telecom coalition we held a press conference in Toronto, the home of Northern Telecom, to publicize this issue in Canada. We were joined by the presidents and other officers of both the CWC and CAW. The issue received extensive coverage on television, radio, and in the newspapers.

An international Northern Telecom coalition meeting is scheduled for March 1991 in Toronto. In addition to our North-American unions, European and Japanese unions will attend along with representatives of Canadian and U.S. community, religious, and civil liberties organizations.

CONCLUSION

Our union is active in the Postal, Telegraph, and Telephone International (PTTI) an organization whose membership includes most of the telecommunication unions in the world. Recently PTTI adopted an international mobilization strategy based largely on the Northern Telecom model. Five multinational telecommunications companies were targeted (including Northern Telecom) for our initial focus.

The International Metalworkers Federation (IMF) and other international trade secretariats are pursuing similar strategies. While efforts such as these require enormous organizational commitment and education, they enable us to increase our power and rebuild our union movement in order to better the lives of our members and children.

91

Mobilizing Across Borders: Unions and Multinational Corporations

FRED POMEROY

National President, Communications and Electrical Workers of Canada

The globalization of the economy is, perhaps, the number one challenge for the labor movement in the decade ahead. The dialogue that is taking place between Canadian and U.S. unions is extremely important and long overdue. I think it is important that unions on both sides of the Canada-U.S. border work together to solve our mutual problems and build on that experience to include others around the world.

There are really two parts of the globalization issue that I will discuss in this paper. The first is techniques for bringing into line recalcitrant employers who are using the globalization of business to exploit their workers. The second is actions that we can take to build our own national economies in a way that creates the kind of high-wage jobs and protection for workers that Ray Marshall (1991) has advocated.

In this paper I will discuss the activities of the Communications and Electrical Workers of Canada (CWC) as examples of progressive activities that unions are initiating internationally. We have been fortunate to work closely with the Communications Workers of America (CWA), and our cooperation has made us more successful than would have been the case with each union working alone.

DEALING WITH MULTINATIONAL EMPLOYERS

One case study that is particularly valuable as an example of dealing with recalcitrant employers is that of Northern Telecom. Northern is probably Canada's best known and most successful high-technology company. Over a period of about seventy-five years it grew from a relatively small equipment supplier for Bell Canada to a world-class multinational. For a long time Northern accepted the idea that its employees would organize into unions and bargain collectively. The company adopted a "neutral" stance when organizing drives took place, and almost all Northern plants in Canada ended up unionized. But with deregulation of the telephone market in the United States, Northern started expanding into the U.S.

As they grew and expanded in the U.S., they adopted a stronger and stronger antiunion stance, to the point where Northern now has a policy of trying to run "union free" everywhere they can get away with it. And they go to great lengths to get away with it.

In Canada this has meant that Northern does everything possible to keep new plants union free. And plants that were already organized have become precarious operations because the work can be, and sometimes is, moved to nonunion plants in the U.S.

The movement of jobs to the southern United States has been so strong that there are now as many employees in the United States as there are in Canada (about 20,000) and the trend line is obviously in favor of the U.S. For example, when Northern won a precedent-setting contract in Japan a while ago, they sourced it from the U.S. instead of Canada, and, to add insult to injury, they now report their earnings in U.S. dollars. There's nothing wrong with U.S. dollars, but it's little wonder that Canadian workers are asking the question "what good is it to have a Canadian multinational company that is a world leader if the investment and jobs that flow from becoming a success end up somewhere else in the world?" This is a question that has increasing importance for Canadians as the full impact of the Free Trade Agreement with the United States becomes better known.

In effect, Canadian jobs are running away to the United States because the U.S. is taking on many of the attributes of a Third-World economy, with the lower wages and working conditions that go with low levels of unionization. But the U.S. is a much more dangerous proposition for Canadian workers than most Third-World countries. The close physical proximity of the U.S. to Canada and the high degree of integration between our two economies makes it much easier for companies to move Canadian operations to the sun belt than other parts of the world. I should make it very clear that this is not intended in any way to be a negative reflection on American workers or the efforts of American unions. Rather, as Shirley Carr (1991) has stated, it is a condemnation of the policies of our two governments.

Plant closures and job losses are the most obvious impact of the Free Trade Agreement. But they are not the only impact on Canadian workers. Increasingly, we are being faced with what we call "an American agenda" at the bargaining table, as employers push hard for settlements that will reflect conditions on the U.S. side of the border.

Faced with this reality, we have had no real choice but to seek new ways to fight to save our jobs and standard of living. The immediate focus has been on the United States and Canada, but we know that it will have to be expanded to include other parts of the world, and we are already working on that. We have found ourselves floundering at times because we're traveling in uncharted waters and the way ahead isn't always easy to see. But I believe we are making real, measurable progress.

For example, we used to try to coordinate the bargaining efforts of all the unions at Northern in Canada, but we didn't really have much success. Everyone wanted greater coordination, but no one was willing to give up their autonomy at the bargaining table. Consequently, coordination tended to fall apart just when it was needed most.

In 1986 CWA approached CWC and the Canadian Auto Workers (CAW), to see if we couldn't work together to strengthen our hands in both organizing and collective bargaining. A number of discussions took place over the ensuing three years, and our first real opportunity to do something concrete came in the summer of 1989, when some five hundred Northern Telecom employees in the United States ended up on strike.

A strategy meeting in Toronto led to leaflets being distributed to CAW and CWC members at Northern Telecom in Canada, explaining what the strike in the U.S. was all about. The presidents of CAW and CWC both wrote to Paul Stern, the top officer of Northern Telecom, urging him to pursue an honorable settlement at the bargaining table instead of union busting. Both CAW and CWC undertook press activities designed to put the company's activities in the public eye in Canada. Behind the scenes contact was made with the top officers of Bell Canada and BCE, which is the parent company of Northern Telecom, to urge them to use their influence to bring about an honorable settlement. Near the end of the strike I was able to go to New York and sit in on negotiations with Northern Telecom.

The thrust of the Canadian message was that the company couldn't have its cake and eat it too. It could not have a good working relationship in the plants that are organized in Canada, while busting unions in other parts of the world. Canadian workers would not sit idly by if the company tried to bust the union in the United States.

The combination of our efforts in Canada and the valiant fight that CWA members were fighting on the picket lines eventually led to a settlement of the strike. However, we don't consider the matter closed. One skirmish has been resolved, but Northern Telecom still has a policy of trying to run "union free" wherever possible. And there are many other companies like Northern Telecom who will use the global economy to threaten the job security and living standards of both Canadian and American workers. Consequently, we have been working with CWA and CAW to find new ways to meet the global challenge.

This winter we will be back in bargaining with Northern Telecom in Canada. Each of the unions involved will put a demand on the table for the company to remain neutral and honor a card check when organizing drives take place—in any country. The law is supposed to give workers the right to organize into the trade union of their choice and bargain collectively. But the spirit of that law is not being honored or upheld (Marshall, 1991), so we are going to make it an issue at the bargaining table.

To build support for our demand we will be sponsoring a conference later this year that will involve church leaders, civil rights leaders, and other progressive people from areas where the company has been actively working to discourage people from joining unions. The purpose of the conference is to expose the company's activities to the Canadian public.

We still have a lot of work to do to build the kind of international cooperation that is needed. No one strategy will be sufficient for all situations. Companies are like people. They have personalities, pressure points, and needs that are unique. Things that work with one won't work with others. But there are some common elements that we can build on and custom tailor for specific situations.

In Northern Telecom's case, the ability to sell their product around the world is very important, as it is for many businesses. But Northern is more vulnerable in some ways than other businesses. Many countries where Northern wants to do business have social democratic governments, or governments where workers have more influence than is common in North America. Northern's sales often depend on the attitude of governments toward the company, and we can have an influence on how governments see Northern, if we work through the international labor movement. Consequently, CWA and CWC have been working through the Postal, Telegraph, and Telephone International (PTTI) to develop an international alliance for dealing with multinational companies. Two Canadian companies, Northern Telecom and BCE, and four others from around the world, will come under special scrutiny by the PTTI and its affiliated unions.

As we move into the nineties we will be building an international network that is capable of assisting workers to organize, wherever the companies may go, and mobilizing support for them if they need help to obtain a satisfactory collective agreement. The efforts we are expending through the PTTI won't bring Northern Telecom or any of the selected companies to their knees overnight. But I believe we are making an important first step that will eventually pay large dividends for working people in many countries.

On another front CWA and CWC are working together to assist one another in organizing. We've been attempting to organize a particular manufacturing plant in Montreal. The company exploits its employees, many of whom are recent immigrants and fearful for their jobs. Whenever an organizing drive has been started the company has threatened to move the jobs to other plants it has established in upstate New York and Ontario. To counter this, CWA and CWC have undertaken simultaneous organizing drives in all three plants, so the employer has no place to run. Recently it looks as if our efforts are starting to pay off and there is a really good chance of an organizing breakthrough in at least one of the plants.

There are a number of other ways that we are working with CWA and other unions, both in Canada and the United States. We've had some success in building coalitions, along with the Telecommunications Workers of British Columbia, to fight off telephone deregulation. And we've participated in a number of consumer boycotts, to cite just a couple of examples.

There is one more point I should make. It is extremely important not to assume that your members are with you when you take on fights. Fighting over your own collective agreement is one thing, where the interests are clear to see, but it is quite another to involve members in a fight over someone else's contract. Consequently, it is necessary to have a well-thought-out education program to keep everyone informed and current on the issues and why they need to support them.

ECONOMIC POLICIES

A second important policy area concerns the efforts we are making to build a high-wage, high-employment security economy. We have had some experience with this on the Premier's Council in Ontario, where a number of business, labor, government, and academic leaders have worked together to develop recommendations that we believe will put Ontario on the leading edge in the next decade in terms of creating high-value-added, high-paying, secure jobs. A second part of the Premier's Council work was aimed at what the labor members call "The People's Agenda." We've just issued a report titled *People and Skills in the New Global Economy* (1990) that labor had a major role in drafting. Briefly, we now have a consensus with business, labor, academia, and government on what needs to be done to protect working people that goes well beyond anything that has been achieved thus far in North America. And our timing could not be better because we now have a government in power that will implement the recommendations in the report.

Another area of activity in CWC is what we call "workplace reorganization." Normally this is an area that unions try to stay out of and employers try to keep as their own preserve. We've decided to move into workplace reorganization and make it our issue because it has so much to do with the kinds of jobs and problems we end up with down the road and with concerns over job security and standards of living. Briefly, we are putting it on the bargaining table on the basis that we want full input into the reorganization of the workplace, and in return for our intelligent cooperation, as opposed to reluctant obedience, we want an employer to participate in a sectoral skills training council where we will have a joint say in education and training. We want a commitment that the employer will "grow the business" to make up for redundancies caused by greater efficiency. In other words, we want job security now, *and* down the road for our children.

Finally, there is a need for political action. In the recent Ontario election the NDP will form the majority NDP government. There is one important point regarding this—it's not enough to simply "get our party elected." We have to work to influence the party's agenda so it will include things like a high-wage economy, job security, day care, pay equity, affirmative action, and a long list of other priorities for working people.

If we don't make influencing the agenda a priority, we run the risk of just replacing one party of bosses with another.

In 1990 and 1991 we have a real chance of electing NDP governments in Saskatchewan and British Columbia, which means that we are becoming a national power and able to undo things like the Free Trade Agreement and turn our country right side up. There is a new ethic taking hold, and the 90s will be an exciting period of progress if we keep pushing the agenda forward.

REFERENCES

Carr, Shirley. "Canadian Labor Stratagies for a Global Economy". In *Labor in a Global Economy: Perspectives from the U.S. and Canada*. Edited by Steven Hecker and Margaret Hallock. Eugene, Oregon: U of O Books, 1991.

Marshall, Ray. "Labor in a Global Economy". In *Labor in a Global Economy: Perspectives from the U.S. and Canada*. Edited by Steven Hecker and Margaret Hallock. Eugene, Oregon: U of O Books, 1991.

People and Skills in the Global Economy. Premier's Council Report, Province of Ontario, Toronto. 1990.

Expanding Labor's Agenda: Community Coalitions, Capital Strategies, and Economic Development

DAN SWINNEY

Director, Midwest Center for Labor Research, Chicago

INTRODUCTION

The 1980s were hell for working people in general and the labor movement in particular. The hammer dropped and basic rules and assumptions about life and labor in America changed.

- I and 700 other steelworkers at Taylor Forge in Cicero, Illinois, lost their jobs because G&W had bought our company, milked it dry of cash for use in their other acquisitions, and closed its doors. Plant closings and job loss were no longer an idle bargaining threat.
- Chicago saw the loss of 3,000 of its 7,000 factories. Relatively poor but stable Chicago working-class communities saw their economies collapse while the federal government was drastically cutting social programs.
- The Air Traffic Controllers strike was crushed by Ronald Reagan, and aggressive corporate antiunion campaigns were successful in breaking unions, stalling organizing drives, breaking strikes, and further isolating the labor movement.
- Such events and trends were repeated all over the U.S. throughout the decade.

In this harsh context, new experiences, strategies, and organizations have emerged both within and allied to the labor movement. The Midwest Center for Labor Research (MCLR) is typical of this small, but developing trend. In the course of our campaigns against plant closings, we began to recognize new possibilities for the labor movement that went beyond what we previously thought was possible. The realization of these possibilities depend on solidifying labor's ties with its allies and embracing new strategic visions.

It's important to make clear that I don't formally represent the official labor movement, but rather the perspectives that emerged from these new organizations and projects. In this paper I would like to present, as a foundation for further discussion and debate: (1) some key assumptions about the current crisis and our work; (2) descriptions of particular campaigns and projects in which MCLR and similar organizations have participated; and (3) some strategic implications and requirements of this approach.

A QUALITATIVE CHANGE IN THE ECONOMY

The work of MCLR is premised on the recognition that there has been a fundamental change in the U.S. economy that has had a profound impact on all social, political, and economic questions. The U.S. enjoyed an expanding economy between World War II and the mid-1970s. This was based not only on a level of development in productive capacity, but also on U.S. international military and economic control. There were certainly sharp internal contradictions, inequalities, and injustices in the U.S., but overall there was at least the perception of an improving standard of living, increasing productive capacity, additional jobs, corporate domestic commitment, and the willingness of society to address its problems.

In the social justice and labor movements, the demands were focused on redistribution of wealth— higher wages, more benefits, more jobs, and greater access to jobs. These demands could be achieved, at least in part, because of the expanding economy. The labor-management social contract was based on the assumption that wages and benefits would increase. A requirement of this social contract was that labor keep its nose out of management issues. The left, center, and right wings of the labor movement all generally accepted the terms of this social contract, reserving their disagreements for the issue of "more or less."

In the mid-1970s, the world economic order began to change with the emergence of Third-World countries (newly industrialized countries, or NICs) as increasingly independent military and economic powers. U.S. capital was faced with increasing competition and decreasing access to markets, cheap labor, and cheap natural resources. Lulled and softened by three decades of near monopoly control, U.S. capitalists responded like most capitalists; they looked for the easiest and fastest way to maintain their rate of return.

The perceptions that major corporations cared about the standard of living of the American people or the health of their industrial sectors and companies, were challenged by the realities of:

- disinvestment and capital flight;
- a dramatic increase in financial speculation;
- the emergence of multinational corporations that flaunted their lack of national identity and commitment;
- the destruction of America's productive base and its labor pool through excessive cuts in manufacturing capacity; and
- the desertion of American communities that had for decades provided the human and physical infrastructure necessary for corporate wealth.

During the period of an expanding economy, the corporate symbol was General Motors (GM). We, who knew, cringed, but there was an element of truth to the statement that, "What was good for GM was good for the country," in that GM was investing in communities, creating well-paying jobs, developing the auto industry, paying taxes, etc. During the period of decline, new corporate symbols emerged like David Roderick, the CEO of USX. He closed steel mills and cut capacity even against the recommendations of the industry's own Iron and Steel Institute. Knowing that he could make greater profits in other markets, he claimed, "We are in this business to make money, not steel," as he oversaw the dismantling of the steel industry which resulted in wrecked communities and ruined thousands of lives.

Labor leaders, like many other leaders of the progressive social and political movement in America, were unable to respond, unable to provide vision or direction in a dramatically declining situation.

NEW EXPERIENCE AND NEW STRATEGIES: MCLR'S EXPERIENCE

In factories and in industrial communities throughout the country, labor and community leaders who represented local people on the front lines in this crisis looked for answers and direction. Finding no clear formula or guidance, they formed their own local projects and began to engage the issues of deindustrialization on a grass-roots level. These organizations took root and have grown. They have preserved a deep commitment to the labor movement and sought to strengthen those ties. They built broad-based coalitions with unions, churches, community organizations, local government, and even local business organizations to fight plant closings. They supported and assisted worker buy-outs of threatened companies. They mobilized thousands of people in these campaigns. They are still relatively small compared to the scope of the problems they address. They have small staffs and resources. But they are the seeds of something new—nothing more, nothing less.

MCLR is one of those organizations. Our experience has led us to believe that within this crisis, within this period of long-term economic decline, there is a tremendous opportunity for labor not only to successfully defend its own traditional interests but to provide leadership in restructuring and redeveloping our society.

We founded MCLR in 1982, our work almost exclusively focused on reacting to plant closings. Our targets were particular companies in particular communities, not broad "macro" studies.

Several interrelated stages in our experience have given rise to our strategic views. First, as we looked at particular companies, we found some companies where it was too late to prevent the closing or where there were insurmountable problems that could not be successfully addressed. The only course of action left was to demand justice, delay the closing, fight for just compensation, and expose the various reasons that gave rise to the closing.

But most companies we looked at were at-risk due to problems that could be addressed effectively within the framework of a market economy. Companies were at-risk or closing because of:

- mismanagement;
- failure to attain a twenty percent "hurdle rate" of profit imposed by a conglomerate owner despite being profitable companies;
- a corporate strategy that provided a high return to stockholders by "milking the cash cow;" or
- simple failure of an aging owner to plan for succession of ownership.

Deliberately short-term and near-sighted priorities within the corporate community, not the objective requirements of the market-place, were leading to plant closings.

Second, in the framework of building a movement against plant closings, the traditional "redistribution" demands simply did not provide enough depth or realism to make an organizing campaign possible. Demands simply for "jobs" or "expanded unemployment compensation and health benefits" in the context of a contracting economy provided the basis for short-term, angry rallies but were not enough to sustain long-term interest and commitment, or to win a victory.

Third, we began to understand that labor-based strategies involving ownership, partnerships, collaboration with consultants, meeting financial requirements, etc., could be handled with the same integrity as any traditional labor negotiations. As long as we were informed on the issues, knew what we wanted from advisers, and were confident that we could enter or walk away from a deal, we could act in ways that strengthened our position.

Fourth, we began to grasp the scale of the problem of plant closings on workers as well as the entire community, the city, the state, and finally the national economy. In Chicago, thousands of companies were closing, costing more than 150 thousand manufacturing jobs alone. Our standard research analysis includes a "social cost/benefit analysis" of the ripple effects of a plant closing, documenting the amount of wages, taxes, retail dollars, service sector jobs, and safety net costs for local government. The costs of deindustrialization have been so staggering that a broader coalition linking labor with community, religious, civic, development, and even local business organizations is possible.

Finally, we began to see in specific ways the cost of allowing the "free market" to determine how productive capacity should be managed. Certain powerful corporate forces were willing to wreck and abandon entire industrial sectors, companies, and communities in pursuit of their narrow objectives. Not only workers and unions, but cities and communities were at risk. No longer could labor afford a social contract that has not only reneged on increasing our standard of living but also demanded that we stay out of issues historically reserved for management. We began to understand the power and necessity of labor and the broader community going beyond demands for "redistribution" and exercising increasing control over the economy.

These perspectives led to campaigns and organizing opportunities that went way beyond the limits of traditional labor organizing. In New Bedford, Massachusetts, a campaign against Gulf&Western's plans to close Morse Cutting Tool exploded into a city-wide battle against a conglomerate by a coalition that included labor, community organizations, churches, and segments of the business community. United Electrical Workers Union organizers, when faced with a threat to close their company, documented how G&W had "milked" this company to generate cash to finance its other acquisitions. They showed how this was a profitable company that was being ruined by a narrow corporate strategy. They documented what the impact of this closing would be on a small New England industrial town. Then they organized door-to-door and patiently defined their campaign in the interests of the broader community, building a network of leadership that represented everyone but G&W. This massive base of support built on a specific analysis of corporate abuse led to the unprecedented threat by Mayor Brian Lawler to seize the company under his powers of "eminent domain" if G&W didn't invest in the company or sell it to someone who would. G&W reversed its plans to close Morse Cutting Tool, and sold the company to a local investor. The issue wasn't just jobs for union workers. It was New Bedford versus G&W. It was good business versus bad business. It was labor providing leadership for the whole community on a life and death issue.

Strategies involving major buy-out efforts and the use of eminent domain have emerged in campaigns in Chicago, Pittsburgh, Boston, St. Paul, and Syracuse. These campaigns have mobilized thousands of people and started to redefine in dramatic ways the relation of these communities to corporate raiders and corporate mismanagement and the responsibility of government in curbing corporate abuses.

BUSINESS SUCCESSION STRATEGIES

On the other hand, most plant closings don't occur in big, anchor companies in a community. Eighty-eight percent of the factories in Chicago have fewer than one hundred employees and are frequently family owned. A severe problem today is succession of ownership in these small companies. An owner who started the company in the 1940s or 1950s is now ready to retire, or is facing illness, or worse yet, suddenly dies. The company is profitable and established. The owner has made a lot of money, moved to the suburbs, sent the kids to graduate school. The son has no interest in going back into the "ghetto" or working in a dusty factory. Often this viable company closes only because there is no one who can easily take over the reins. Alone, it represents only a handful of employees. In aggregate these companies represent a significant base of manufacturing employment.

Succession problems can be simply solved through a transfer of ownership. Labor's interests can best be protected by an employee buy-out or an acquisition by a local entrepreneur committed to keeping the company in the city.

As a result of its experience, MCLR formed its own acquisition company, Chicago Focus. It specializes in succession issues, doing seminars for business owners on these problems. It is also linked to MCLR's early warning activity as a source of leads. Its priority is to identify groups of employees and minority entrepreneurs to buy a company. In Chicago, a city with a sixty percent Black and Latino population, less than one percent of the manufacturing companies are owned by Blacks or Latinos. Promoting "minority acquisitions" adds yet another dimension to our work, linking our efforts in a clear way to the broader issues of discrimination and exclusion. Chicago Focus will work only with buyers committed to keeping the company in Chicago and treating labor with respect.

Projects focusing on issues of succession, acquisition, and worker ownership have emerged in a number of cities, and given rise to a number of organizations with technical, development, and financial capacity. Additionally there are legal firms and investment banking companies that are directly connected with the labor movement. In the fall of 1990 there was a conference organized by the National AFL-CIO which brought many of these groups together with top union leadership to further explore coordination in this field.

ECONOMIC DEVELOPMENT

As I have discussed, the problems that emerge in particular companies are widely felt in the broader community. Each stage of our work has included the building of a coalition that has included segments of the development and business community who have a self-interest in the maintenance of viable local companies and who come into conflict with corporate raiders and mis-managers of various stripes.

In this contact, we have become familiar with the issues of economic development. Through plant closing campaigns that exposed abuse of government industrial revenue bonds, we became familiar with some of the economic development financing mechanisms. Through campaigns involving eminent domain and plant closing legislation, we became familiar with how far government would or wouldn't go in its interventions into the economy. Through buy-out strategies, we have had to know all the aspects of business development. We have also learned about traditional economic development practices, their possibilities, and their limits.

Labor is at the heart of business and economic development. It is labor's collective work and skill that makes it all possible. Labor is in the key strategic position to determine whether a business succeeds or fails. Going beyond the demands of redistribution to the issues of control and management has enhanced our sense of the kind of leadership labor can provide in economic development.

And as with other sectors of traditional leadership, the local business and development community is generally unprepared to deal with the scale and character of the economic problems that haunt our cities. There is a void of leadership, and therefore an opening for the labor movement to provide leadership in development issues that represent its interests. A labor movement guided by new visions and closely linked with its allies can build an economy that has long-term stability, places job creation and development as the first priority, utilizes more broadly democratic structures, and incorporates the real interest of the community in development.

The possibilities for ownership, control, and setting the agenda for economic development give us unique opportunities not just to do a better job managing what has been built before, but to restructure companies, methods of production, and community coordination in new ways that reflect labor and popular interests in the economy, rather than traditional corporate culture, values, and priorities.

AN EFFECTIVE STRATEGY FOR CONTROL

There are several key points that must be underscored in using these strategic approaches. First, we must acknowledge that the "market economy" exists as an objective fact. We must understand its features. It can be used legitimately and constructively as a measure of success and efficiency. Its force can create positive incentives for productivity and performance. Development can take place within this framework. It can be used to facilitate and strengthen economic democracy.

Clearly, accepting and using the strengths of the market economy does not mean embracing "free market ideology." "Free market ideology" allows the most destructive and retrograde trends of the corporate world to run amok and destroy what has taken decades to build. Understanding the positive potential of the marketplace does not mean the market economy can solve all of labor's or the community's problems. By exhausting what's possible in the marketplace, we can also expose its limits in concrete, particular ways—indicating problems that must be addressed through planning and coordination. Our approach to economic planning is premised on a "social cost/benefit analysis" which allows us to place the needs of workers, communities, and the society as a whole over the value of a maximum return to shareholders. There must be a return to shareholders, there must be profits, there must be wealth. But these are achieved in ways that must be linked to meeting the needs of the whole community.

Second, a strategy for control requires the ability and willingness to produce efficiently. It requires knowledge of the company, of markets, productivity, and management rather than just the skills necessary to do one particular job. Unions must develop the internal talent to grapple with all aspects of production. We must look at programs designed to increase labor participation, not only as a possible antilabor move by management (which they may be!), but because they are one way to gain critical knowledge and the training essential to a labor campaign for control of production. To understand and address the issues of management is not the same as cooperation with "management" and its traditionally narrow antilabor objectives.

Third, all of this requires the honing and appropriate use of the skills that made labor strong in the first place—the picket line, mass rallies, the strike, direct action, the boycott, in-plant actions, and corporate campaigns. Without a labor movement that can act militantly with collective discipline, and risk great sacrifice, no victory, even at a particular plant, may be possible. Without this militant capacity as a foundation, capital strategies and community coalitions can destabilize and demoralize our ranks. On the other hand, the labor movement cannot "go it alone" in its campaigns. It must weave its leadership together with leadership from the broader community and pursue an agenda that includes its interests as part of building a stable economy and just society.

Each aspect of this work must be guided by an organizing model of unionism rather than a service model. We look for opportunities for in-depth education of the rank and file to undergird our mass campaigns and rallies. We look for and promote every opportunity for rank and file involvement and for ways that extend and build internal union democracy.

CONCLUSION

Finally, the territory for this work has and will frequently be on a local level at a particular company within a particular community. It must be seen as a step toward creating national industrial and economic policies that correspond to the needs of labor and the broader public. We must take the lessons of these experiences and generalize them in ways that allow their convertibility to national legislation, policy, and programs. Many of the local plant closing projects have joined together within a national Federation for Industrial Retention and Renewal (FIRR) to advocate policy options collectively. On the other hand, this work serves to create the constituency and leadership that is necessary for the passage and implementation of national policy. These national objectives will only be achieved if there is a determined fight plant by plant and community by community.

In conclusion, the possibilities that exist today would have been inconceivable ten years ago. But the conditions have changed and the starkness of the social, economic, and moral crisis in our countries has created the space for new leadership to emerge. If armed with effective programs that correspond to these new conditions, labor leadership can quickly go from the defensive to the offensive, and expect broad public support. On the other hand, we don't have the luxury of a lot of time. The destruction that is occurring to the productive capacity in our countries and to the human infrastructure demands quick attention and action. Ten years from now, we may not have the opportunities we have today, and the terms for our work will be completely different and more difficult.

The situation is challenging and holds great promise. Our society is at a critical turning point. It is up to us to act with new visions and new allies.

Labor Has No Choice But to Play the Capital Strategies Game

JIM TUSLER

Job Training and Partnership Act Liaison, Washington State Labor Council, AFL-CIO

At labor gatherings held four or five years ago the issue of capital strategies for labor was rarely discussed. It simply wasn't on labor's menu of options. Today, with the demise of the capital/labor "social contract," labor has no choice but to engage in sophisticated capital strategies.

By some measures the U.S. economy has been booming over the last six to eight years. Economists tell us that we are in the longest period of postwar prosperity. We are also told that the U.S. has been a veritable job-generating machine. By these same accounts the Washington state economy is said to be booming—the Boeing Corporation is doing great, therefore all workers should be doing fine. But those of us who operate in the real world know that this is not so! That's not the economy that union representatives and their members deal with on a daily basis. Let's look at some of the numbers.

Although eight million jobs have been created in the U.S. economy over the last few years, three-fifths of those jobs pay less than $8,000 a year. These are minimum wage and part time jobs. These jobs have increased the number of working poor in our economy and have served as a drag on wages and living standards for all workers.

According to the U.S. Department of Labor, Washington state, during the mid-1980s, had the third-highest rate of plant closures on a per capita basis. Historically, the per capita income of Washington workers had always been about 10 percent above the national average, but today we are at or below the national average in compensation.

I recently heard a news report that King County, the most populous and wealthy county in my state, had an infant mortality rate higher than the country of Indonesia. King County is the home of the dynamic and extremely profitable Boeing Corporation. This is a disgrace.

But supposedly we have a social safety net, and what about the "thousand points of light?" What seemed like a great victory on plant closure prenotification four years ago turns out to affect about 4 percent of the employers in Washington state. Moreover, there are loopholes in the law big enough to drive a whole business through.

We have also heard a great deal about worker retraining programs. However, there has been lots of talk and little action. Only 3 to 5 percent of the workers who lose their jobs through a plant closure actually receive any kind of retraining assistance.

The Department of Labor's Work Force 2000 opus is being quoted everywhere these days. A literal interpretation reads that workers of the future will change their careers five to seven times throughout their working lives. What they don't tell you is that only about one in nine workers are going to change their careers because they will be moving to a better job, with better rates of pay and working conditions. Our system does not currently train workers to prepare them for making these upward moves. This whole discussion of the future work force, and all of its abundant assumptions, is virtually worthless outside the context of a discussion of a comprehensive industrial policy.

To make matters worse the "unemployment gap" problem is growing ever wider in Washington state. Currently only two out of every five jobless workers are eligible for unemployment benefits. Over the last few years I have gone to at least one funeral per month for fallen brothers and sisters, people who our economy chewed up and spit out.

All of these failings, and others, require that labor become involved in capital strategies. Our future as workers and the fate of our communities depends on it. In the remainder of this paper I will discuss two capital strategies we have used in Washington state over the past couple of years.

Three years ago we had ten thousand shipyard workers out of work. The industry was in desperate shape. To boot, the Lockheed Corporation had locked out an additional 1,200 workers. We had nine major shipyards and seven were in bankruptcy.

One company in particular was family-owned and had a very checkered business history. Labor had been in and out of a lot of scrapes with this company. The company was $210 million in debt and in bankruptcy. The company was represented by nine unions in the metal trades, and health and welfare benefits for its workers had not been paid for about three weeks. All of the unions were represented at the bankruptcy hearing and were told that the company's asset base was at best $35 million.

The unions were in a bind. We had five hundred workers who couldn't afford to lose their jobs. We needed a capital strategy that would save their jobs and in some way help resurrect the shipyard from bankruptcy and serve as a model to build the industry back up.

Against these long odds we accomplished this goal without one dollar changing hands. We sat down with the creditors and talked turkey. The creditors understood that if the company went down they would have received about thirteen cents on the dollar. Instead, we worked out a deal where most of the workers kept their jobs—the president of one of the unions became the new CEO—and the creditors would receive an adequate rate of return over a number of years.

What we sold was the skill level, commitment to work, and integrity of the work force. We may have been lucky but we saved jobs, brought the company back up, and gained an enormous amount of credibility in the investment community.

The second example comes from a sawmill in rural Okanagon County in north-central Washington. The mill was the largest employer in a county that traditionally had the highest unemployment rates in the state. The mill, Omak Wood Products, was owned by Sir James Goldsmith, a British corporate raider extraordinaire.

When pattern bargaining came up for the industry, Goldsmith's representative sat quietly through the contract negotiations. When the industry got up and walked out, Goldsmith's man said "Gee, we can come to an agreement." His proposal was for a three-year contract with "no wage increases the first year, a 20 percent increase the second year, and you dial in the number for the third year—you want say 30 percent?" He was the most congenial guy in the world. Meanwhile everyone on both sides knew that Goldsmith was ready to dump the mill.

Soon after who should arrive in the small rural town but Louisiana Pacific fresh from a string of union-busting operations at its western facilities. They were smart enough not to have the name of the company on their cars but everyone knew who they were. We knew we had to do something and quickly.

We formed a workers' committee and the local union president and I took a trip to Wall Street. Not the one in Seattle, but the other one—in New York City. The plan was to convince an investment banker that the workers could buy and run the mill.

Probably the finest moment in my life came when I was physically thrown out of Salomon Brothers. They didn't like our proposal and we didn't talk right, so off we went to Drexel Burnham.

While we were at Drexel's palatial offices watching all kinds of sharks wheel and deal, the federal marshals came in to serve the first of many subpoenas on Drexel Burnham. (I learned that those marshals actually do pack guns and they make it a point to let you know that they do. And we thought that just happened out west.)

To start our discussions with Drexel Burnham we wrote two things on the board. Rather than talking about labor management cooperation we said, "we are going to preserve family wage jobs and the collective bargaining relationship with the workers." These were our bottom lines, and we would rather that the mill go down if those two conditions were not met.

Drexel said they could raise $80 million for this facility and we said we could pay $30 million for it. There was a lot of compromising going on. We made a direct personal appeal to Sir James Goldsmith, who as it turned out didn't even know he owned the mill, and he agreed to sell it to us for $30 million. The mill is standing and operating today, and it is still the largest employer in the county. Best of all Lousianna Pacific does not own it—but the workers do.

I hope that these two examples give some sense of what can be done if we do a little brainstorming and have the moxie to get involved in capital strategies. It's not that hard to do. If an electrician from Spokane can do it, so can a lot of other trade unionists. Capital strategies are just another type of organizing; another tool we need to put in our tool kits to help represent our members.

Section 4

FLEXIBILITY, THE NATURE OF WORK, AND LABOR MARKET POLICY

The nature of work and production are undergoing rapid change as a result of new technology and global economic change. How labor should respond to this restructuring is perhaps the key strategic debate in this volume. In Section 1, Ray Marshall presented the general case that labor should develop an explicit strategy that would move enterprises and nations toward a high-skill, high-wage economy. While others would not argue against high wages or high skills, labor's specific tactics in this arena are the subject of legitimate debate. In many cases, corporate demands for flexibility have swamped union efforts to maintain union autonomy and preserve workers' rights and jobs. Quality of work life, employee involvement, and team-concept programs remain extremely controversial even as they continue to diffuse through many industries and unions.

Dan Marschall of the AFL-CIO's Human Resources Development Institute (HRDI) has studied a number of union and joint labor-management efforts to develop a flexible work environment. He usefully outlines criteria for an "authentic" flexibility policy at the enterprise level, one that does not undermine workers or their union. These criteria have been put to the test in two demonstration projects in HRDI's Upgrading and Career Ladder Program. Lessons from these programs include the need for a true commitment to continuous learning and skill upgrading, the value of "practice-based" learning and on-the-job training, and the critical aspect of true worker-centered and participatory schemes.

Max Ogden of the Australian Council of Trade Unions (ACTU) presents an example of a union high-wage strategy in the context of national economic policy. Australian unions entered into an historic "Accord" with the Australian Labor Party in 1983, a comprehensive policy covering wages, jobs, health care and industrial policy. The Australian unions followed Ray Marshall's advice to shift from a focus on the distribution of wealth to the creation of wealth by developing a long-term strategy regarding worker training, production efficiency, job design, and worker participation. Ogden also follows on Dan Marschall's article by describing tactics and principles at the enterprise level. See also Section five for additional perspectives on unions and economic restructuring in Australia and New Zealand.

Steven Deutsch presents an analytical article focusing on state initiatives in the U.S. and legislative and union initiatives in industrialized countries. He is particularly knowledgeable about European and Scandinavian countries. His analysis points up the divergent experience and strategies of governments and unions in Europe and the U.S. and, to some extent, Canada. For example, the U.S. is the only country that does not have an independent work research institute.

Maryantonett Flumian heads up a new Canadian enterprise, the Canadian Labour Market and Productivity Center. This Centre is funded by the government to facilitate consultation and programs between management and labor on economic issues, particularly work and training. The Centre has initiated discussions and programs emphasizing workplace learning and the need for skill enhancement in the global economy. It has now established a National Training Board to oversee the development of national standards and certification and undertake initiatives in particular industries.

These articles together present a detailed description of the training and job design aspects of the high-wage, high-skill strategy that runs throughout this volume.

Achieving Authentic Labor Market Flexibility: A North-American Union Perspective

DANIEL MARSCHALL

Deputy Assistant Director, Human Resources Development Institute, AFL-CIO

Since it emerged full force more than a decade ago, the subject of "labor market flexibility" has continued to evoke controversy worldwide. The Organization for Economic Cooperation and Development (OECD) recently completed a "Conference on Labor Market Flexibility and Work Organization" in Paris. Participants discussed the issue and current developments in a number of countries. In an expert report prepared on the United States, flexibility is framed in terms of labor-management dynamics, especially in reference to a "dualism model" in which some employers advocate cooperative policies that benefit the interests of both parties, while others maintain an "adversarial" stance that undermines unions and lowers workers' living standards (Lewin, 1990).

Mention "flexibility" to U.S. trade unionists and you're certain to get a skeptical, if not outright hostile, response. This is because so many employers and policy makers play fast and loose with the term, using it as an umbrella for all manner of antiworker, antiunion, and low-wage policies that destabilize the lives of working people. Too often, when employers call for flexibility they really mean more concessions from union members, greater unilateral management control over the work process, and opposition to legislation such as the minimum wage.

"The national labor law of the United States is supposed to guarantee workers' rights to organize and bargain collectively. But, in practice, these rights are not secure," Markley Roberts of the AFL-CIO Economic Research Department commented at the OECD conference. "Some 95 percent of employers resist unionization of their workers. About 75 percent hire labor-management consultants who are really union-busters who guide employers within the letter of the labor law to violate the spirit of the law. In recent years, the National Labor Relations Board has found some ten thousand discriminatory discharges a year of workers fired for union activity" (Roberts, 1990).

As Meulders and Wilkin (1987) have pointed out, flexibility measures often disguise efforts by the powerful in society to enhance their discretion and freedom of action at the expense of the weak. For conservative ideologues, of course, the mere existence of trade unions is a barely tolerable "labor market rigidity." In the political climate of the 1980s, the quest to eliminate rigidities was expressed in the wholesale deregulation of industries in the U.S. and Britain, (Rosenberg, 1990) along with concerted antiunion campaigns by many employers.

Assuming that positive connotations of flexibility merit continued usage of the term, it remains for unions and community-based organizations to take up the challenge and define flexibility in a distinctively proworker and people-oriented manner. In this paper I will elaborate on some leading characteristics of "authentic flexibility," dealing only with the microeconomic level of the firm. For flexibility policies to be authentic, they must:

- be oriented towards the long-term;
- foster career mobility and skill formation among workers;

- facilitate product quality and innovation, and;
- contribute to the continuing vitality and adaptability of the company.

The European Trade Union Institute (ETUI) has documented how unions in many countries have taken the lead in developing alternative approaches to employer manipulation of flexibility. My characterization of authentic flexibility is similar to their advocacy of policies that "achieve flexibility and structural change by giving working people security in the change process and an ability to influence change in their interests" (European Trade, 1985).

The following three characteristics flow from the experience of the Human Resources Development Institute (HRDI), the employment and training arm of the AFL-CIO, in our operation of demonstration projects as part of the Upgrading and Career Ladder Program (UCLP). The existence of the UCLP, in the context of changing government policies towards continuous learning at the state and federal levels, provides some reason for optimism about the capacity of the the U.S. economy to adapt to the pressures of global competition.

THE ESSENTIAL STARTING POINT

My central proposition is that authentic labor market flexibility requires that U.S. companies devote more resources to training, retraining, skill upgrading, and continuous learning for the segments of their work forces most intimately associated with the production process. In turn, the human resource practices of "enlightened" companies must be nurtured by compatible government policies, especially at the federal level. An important goal is the creation of comprehensive "high-performance work and learning systems" that are thoroughly integrated into corporate strategy and, ultimately, become pervasive in the firm's culture and its prevailing management philosophy.

The starting point for authentic flexibility is therefore a significant commitment by management to continuous learning. In organized workplaces, of course, unions must share in this outlook. This point may seem self-evident. I make it because there now exists a yawning gap between rhetoric and reality when it comes to continuous learning. If you read corporate publications such as *Business Week*, you could easily gain the impression that those segments of business that advocate enlightened human resource policies have triumphed over those who rely upon union avoidance schemes or what Cornell University researchers have called the "flight response" of outsourcing production to the lowest bidder (Klingel and Martin, 1988). The rhetoric of enhanced human resource investment—"our people are our greatest asset"—is ubiquitous, prompted by the fact that forward-looking companies are notably assertive and prolific in promoting what they have accomplished.

Reality is quite different when you assess business practices across the board. One study after another has noted that U.S. companies woefully underinvest in the skills of their workers, especially blue-collar technical workers and lower-level service workers (Carnevale and Gainer, 1989; Dertouzos, 1989; Mangum, 1989). With funding from the State of New York and the Carnegie Foundation, the National Center on Education and the Economy tackled this question in 1989–90 by interviewing more than two thousand people at 550 agencies and companies in the U.S. and six other countries. Out of the firms surveyed, 95 percent cling to authoritarian supervisory techniques, rely on wage cuts and layoffs rather than retraining during slack periods, and readily move production to low-wage areas (Commission, 1990).

In September 1990, the Office of Technology Assessment (OTA) of the U.S. Congress released its comprehensive two-year study, *Worker Training: Competing in the New International Economy.* It concludes that most American companies place a low value on training, slash corporate training budgets during economic downturns, focus training efforts on higher-level managers and professional staff, and overemphasize narrow, job-specific training rather than gaining transferable skills. The report presents a wide variety of options for expanding the federal role in skill formation, including a "national training levy" that would allow employers to choose whether to spend a certain percentage of payroll costs on training or pay an equivalent amount to a publicly administered training fund (U.S. Congress, 1990).

At the company level, significant commitment is the essential starting point. Contract provisions represent the most tangible expression of that commitment in unionized firms. Collectively-bargained, joint training programs have existed for many years in the building and construction industry, where the mechanisms stretch from local Joint Apprenticeship and Training Committees to national training trusts that promote uniform curriculum and skill upgrading for journey-level workers. In the last decade aspects of this model have been utilized in the creation of joint training programs in the auto, communications, and steel industries, among others. Researchers Michelle Hoyman and Louis Ferman estimate that some one million bargaining unit members are covered by such joint training programs (Hoyman, 1989).

Through the Upgrading and Career Ladder Program (UCLP), an effort to develop prototypes of workplace-based training for currently employed workers, HRDI has witnessed several levels of commitment. One of our demonstration projects involves the Boeing Company and the Machinists' Union (IAM). In the Puget Sound Region of Washington state, Boeing employs about 106 thousand workers, some 42 thousand of whom are members of Aerospace Machinists Industrial District Lodge 751. Arising from a seven-week strike in late 1989, the new collective bargaining agreement creates a Quality Through Training (QTT) Program that accumulates approximately $12 million per year for skill upgrading and the continuous improvement of the company's human resources. The QTT Program is directed by a Joint Training Policy Board and administered by a full-time, ten-person Joint IAM/Boeing Training Administrative Staff.

The IAM/Boeing program was founded on the recognition that a highly skilled and productive work force is in the interests of both union and company. The contract sets up an organization that is jointly controlled, yet one step removed from the day-to-day conflictual relationship between labor and management on the shop floor. It helps to promote authentic flexibility by creating an ongoing mechanism to oversee training, which is especially important when it comes to the combination of job classifications. There are now up to 1,800 separate job classifications at Boeing, and the company and union have a special jobs committee to whittle down that number. Efforts to streamline the organization of work tend to cause great anxiety among the members, and the QTT Program offers a structure to ensure that workers obtain the necessary training as change occurs. HRDI is working with program administrators to develop a prototype of "work-based learning" for two highly skilled jobs relating to the maintenance of numerically controlled (NC) machine tool equipment.

Another level of commitment is evident at a medium-sized manufacturing firm located in the Northeast. The company produces highly sophisticated, customized machinery for a variety of industrial uses. Union workers there are mainly machine tool operators.

Management at this company is also committed to continuous learning, as illustrated in 1987 by the formation of a training council with members from union and management ranks. In cooperation with the state's adult education system, the council oversees classroom training in a variety of subjects. Unlike Boeing, the training system here has not been institutionalized through collective bargaining language. There is no free-standing organization with its own budget and full-time staff. Although the council is seen as an organization that does good things, union leadership does not perceive it as an equal partnership between both sides.

This secondary level of commitment has hampered the development of authentic flexibility at the firm. The main dynamic is the wholesale transformation of the organization of work into a cellular manufacturing system where equipment is grouped together for the efficient machining of parts (Huber and Brown, 1990). That system has developed alongside the collective bargaining agreement, and the union has had difficulty dealing with it in the course of contract negotiations. Hourly workers tend to feel quite insecure about these changes, mainly because they will eventually be required to operate all the machines in their particular cell. The existing training system focuses on classroom instruction. The absence of a mechanism to integrate both systematic on-the-job training and classroom education has hampered the company's ability to make optimal use of cellular manufacturing.

SITUATED LEARNING

The second characteristic of authentic flexibility is an understanding of the importance of structured and systematic on-the-job training (OJT). This point is closely related to commitment. It also has profound political ramifications, again relating back to flexibility as a reflection of the balance of power between different groups in society, and among management, unions, and workers in individual firms.

In U.S. companies, the employees who obtain job-related training and education are those who already have a high level of education, status, and career mobility (Carnevale and Gainer, 1989). A 1985 survey found that only 22 percent of machine operators, for example, and 14 percent of laborers reported receiving upgrade training on the job (Carey and Eck, 1985). When training does filter down to blue-collar production workers, it tends to be informal training that is not carefully planned, monitored, or evaluated.

At the same time, a number of academic studies in the field of cognitive science have found that the most effective learning occurs in a "practice-based" context when people are interacting with situations and things with which they are familiar in their everyday lives. A classroom is a very artificial setting, and there are great discontinuities between traditional schooling and the learning that occurs at the workplace (Resnick, 1987). As the building and construction trades have understood for a century, effective training means working at the job site with the tools of the trade and with coworkers in a constellation of occupations. In industrial occupations it means working with the machinery on the shop floor and, more and more frequently, under new types of work organization, functioning in teams to organize the conduct of production. And in an office it may mean interacting with your coworkers in a collegial setting in which novices must learn the complexity of the entire organization, negotiate the politics of situations, and master a number of "knowledge domains" throughout the organization (Scribner and Sachs, 1990). Whatever the occupation, some form of OJT is essential.

Yet in each of our demonstration projects, OJT is the least understood part of the learning process. At Boeing, the company has a very extensive selection of classroom courses, and all three major divisions have their own training staffs. New workers and trainees are assigned to work with "lead" workers, yet exactly how OJT operates is unclear and mysterious.

Likewise, the Northeast manufacturing company has a solid selection of job-related classes and diligently promotes its experience in training. Yet little is known about how OJT occurs. In several cases, workers with minimal OJT have been placed on sophisticated NC machinery with no supervision, resulting in costly damage to parts and machinery. Company officials tend to rely upon a traditional classroom model when it comes to ongoing training.

At one of our health care demonstration projects, a personnel manager commented that we should just deliver the trained staff to them without disturbing the existing workers or their supervisor. At another medical care institution: an extensive curriculum, but little sense about how workers obtain work experience and no coaching for their peers who provide the instruction.

Even when some companies devote significant resources to job-related training, they tend to continue thinking in standard concepts of knowledge developed by experts and handed down to a passive group of "students." A revealing example is provided by Motorola, a nonunion company that is praised widely for its high-quality products, open management style, and annual training budget of some $40 million (Rosow and Casner-Lotto, 1985). A recent issue of *Harvard Business Review* contains a thirteen-page

110

article by a company vice-president who recounts the problems (such as worker "complacency") that management encountered when developing basic skills and quality-improvement training. OJT is dismissed at the outset as simply "watching others." Management is especially enthusiastic about the formation of Motorola University, where faculty members teach trainees in a classroom setting; students choose from a catalog of courses; and curriculum is prepared by teams of instructional experts in cooperation with outside educators. Despite the company's highly-touted Participative Management Program, the planning and implementation of continuous learning apparently gives no recognition to the skills, knowledge, and insights of production workers. Nor do the workers have much choice about their involvement. When eighteen long-time employees declined to attend training classes, they were immediately fired (Wiggenhorn, 1990).

The underutilization of on-the-job training is rooted in the dynamics of workplace politics. OJT transpires from one worker to another in a peer-to-peer relationship, all in the context of goods being produced or services delivered. It assumes that workers, through their day-to-day practical experience, have developed a high level of expertise and competence; and that they can compartmentalize their knowledge, dividing it in such a way to effectively transmit it to their "green" coworkers. OJT is out of the direct and immediate control of management; it presumes confidence in the ability of workers to do a good job. The higher value that you place on OJT, the more you accept the legitimacy of workers comprehending the production process. In this sense, OJT is inherently empowering and contrary to the principles of Taylorism, which emphasize management control over all details of the production process and the elimination of worker judgement (Callahan, 1962). Managers who cling to traditional scientific management have difficulty accepting the importance of OJT, and may be threatened by its practice. By restricting job-related training to the boundaries of classroom instruction, managers are able to maintain a greater degree of control over what is taught, who does the teaching, and when education takes place.

Much additional research needs to be done on the intricacies of OJT, especially on its relationship to new methods of work organization. Some cognitive scientists, using theoretical constructs already popular in Europe, are conducting path-breaking research in industrial settings (Scribner and Sachs, 1990; Raizen, 1989). David Stern and Charles Benson are conducting four case studies that investigate the relationship between OJT and incentives, employment security, and worker participation. Through a process they call "informalizing," these researchers found, companies create "opportunities and incentives for employees to learn from each other and from supervisors in the ordinary course of daily work" (Stern and Benson, 1989).

The connection to flexibility is obvious here. As employers bring in new technology and consider changes in work organization, employees are more likely to be flexible and conducive to the change if they are: (1) involved at an early stage of planning; (2) have training and skill upgrading mechanisms available; and (3) perceive that management places a high value on OJT and, therefore, the knowledge and insights that workers develop as they interact with the new machinery and work processes. The level of flexibility here will be partially dependent upon whether management adopts a hierarchical and authoritarian model of education, or whether there is a great degree of openness and meaningful worker participation.

UNDER THE WORKMAN'S CAP

The third leading characteristic of authentic flexibility is the adoption of a program approach that is worker-centered and participatory. The more that workers comprehend the entire production process; the more that they are involved in training and upgrading one another; the more that they perceive that management is receptive to their ideas and insights; and the more that the system of pay and incentives at the company reflect their real contribution to increased productivity; the more that the company, union, and workers will share a kind of mutual flexibility when it comes to adapting to all manner of

111

change.

At the same time that the company gains this authentic flexibility, it loses some of its ability to exercise control over how work is done. Aspects of the production process may become virtually invisible to them, reaffirming Big Bill Haywood's classic statement: "The manager's brains are under the workman's cap" (Montgomery, 1979). Again, this flies in the face of traditional Taylorist principles and requires a major transformation in management philosophy and practice.

A worker-centered perspective is not merely a political thrust advanced by unions, or a tactic to help overcome the "blue-collar blues." Rather, this approach is absolutely essential to make the most productive use of new technology and develop methods of work organization that are truly efficient. The flexibility inherent in computer-controlled technology allows work to be performed in a variety of ways, some that amplify worker capabilities and others that perpetuate management control over production planning and execution (Shaiken, 1984). New technology will never attain its full potential if it serves to further constrain the creative input of the production workers who understand it most intimately.

What do we mean by worker-centered principles? A good example is provided by the State, County, and Municipal Employees (AFSCME) in New York City. District Council 37 has operated a training and basic skills program since 1971, running it unilaterally with funds from the collective bargaining agreement. It has reversed standard program design practices that start with an evaluation of the workplace from a top-down, management outlook. Instead of forcing workers to be flexible and adapt to workplace changes imposed from above, in the words of Education Fund Administrator Katherine Schrier, the union has developed programs that were "designed not only to meet the needs of the work environment but were structured around the experience, skills, and abilities of the present work force. In other words, the central premise of these training programs is not the skills that workers lack but rather the skills that workers have" (Schrier, 1989). Again, this approach takes what you hear about "dumb workers" and the scourge of illiteracy, and turns it on its head.

HRDI has developed a comprehensive description of a "worker-centered learning strategy" in its 1990 volume: *Worker-Centered Learning: A Union Guide to Workplace Literacy*. Briefly stated, there are nine principles:

- building on what workers already know;
- addressing the needs of the whole person;
- worker and union participation in planning;
- a participatory approach to decision making;
- equal access to learning programs;
- reflecting diverse learning styles of adult workers;
- worker involvement in design of tests;
- assessment records kept confidential; and
- integrating basic skills into a larger strategy for adapting to change in the workplace.

The guide then describes a step-by-step process to design and implement a worker-centered program (Sarmiento and Kay, 1990).

These principles, in conjunction with the step-by-step process, provide an outline for translating authentic flexibility into durable systems of "high performance work and learning." This approach is similar to the perspective of the Australian Council of Trade Unions (ACTU) on the "principles of good job design." The council explains in a recent pamphlet that greater skill training will be meaningful only if linked to job redesign, the reorganization of work, and opportunities for workers to move forward on a career path without necessarily joining the ranks of management (Australian Council, 1990). To Australian trade unionists, good jobs possess these characteristics:

- variety of tasks;
- responsibility for decision making;
- adequate payment for skills;
- jobs centering on a group of people;
- good social interaction between employees;
- healthy and safe working environment;
- understanding the total system of production;
- constant learning;
- adequate access to information;
- useful and environmentally-sound product or service;
- equal opportunity for all; and
- career opportunities.

Expanding the number of good jobs, ACTU officers explain, is integral to the evolution of a "new and higher competence social fabric" that encompasses more broad-based education; merging the processes of work and learning; developing new forms of work organization in the educational profession; and offering on-the-job training that produces multiskilling—all with "effective, positive, and independent trade union input . . . " (ACTU Executive, 1990).

REASONS FOR OPTIMISM

The process of U.S. firms developing more enlightened human resource policies—not to mention worker-oriented practices—will be measured not in years, or even in decades, but probably in generations. Despite the problems with commitment and OJT and authoritarian versus participatory approaches, there are some reasons for optimism over the long term.

First, there's the evolution of government policy. The demonstration projects being operated by HRDI are part of an initiative by the U.S. Department of Labor to explore the use of federal resources for training, retraining, and upgrading the skills of currently employed workers. This presents the potential for a major, historic change in federal job training policy, which for thirty years has focused on unemployed, disadvantaged persons, and the welfare-dependent. In effect, federal job training has always been seen as social policy: helping to bring poor people back into the mainstream. The recent consideration of the federal role in skill upgrading is founded on the assumption that a skilled work force is essential to sound economic policy.

When it comes to intervention in the operation of individual firms, state government is way ahead, essentially developing little industrial policies across the nation. As of 1989, forty-six states had programs that combined economic development objectives with plant closing avoidance, retraining, and skill upgrading activities (American Society, 1989). Unions have been integral to many of these efforts (Marschall, 1990).

Second, there are reasons for cautious optimism concerning the future of organized labor. Essentially, the contemporary emphasis on human resource investment is what unions have been arguing for the last century. In the late 1800s, skilled workers in fledgling unions had far more autonomy over how they performed their work (Montgomery, 1979). Frederick Taylor was very explicit in developing his methods to break that control over the work process. Unions resisted for many years, but eventually made peace with standardization and mass production, adopting a role "to eliminate any undesirable consequences of standardization" (Green, 1928).

The pressures of global competition have changed the rules of the game. In many industries, mass-production techniques are anachronistic and counter-productive. American employers are searching for new methods, yet remain reluctant to embrace practices that empower their employees. The philosophy and principles that underlie a union perspective on authentic flexibility also represent a critical component to the revitalization of organized labor in the U.S. By holding up continuous learning as a value to be sought by strong trade unions, and emphasizing skill upgrading and career mobility as a tangible benefit of union membership, unions align themselves with the dreams and aspirations of their members. It is exactly that sort of broad definition of unionism, in the context of many other union services, that many prospective union members are likely to find attractive.

The activities of strong and progressive unions tend to push toward the sort of high-wage, high-skill, and high-performance strategy that has been so successful in countries such as Sweden. As unions forcefully articulate worker-oriented policies, and put forward a compelling vision of the workplace as a learning-place, they are working not only to benefit their members, but to advance the interests of the entire society in an era of acute global interdependence.

REFERENCES

ACTU Executive. "Decision Higher Competence Society." August 21, 1990.

American Society for Training and Development. *New Foundations: State Economic Growth Through Training*. Alexandria, Virginia., ASTD, Fall, 1989.

Australian Council of Trade Unions. *Making Better Jobs: Guidelines for Negotiating Better Jobs in the Workplace*. 1990.

Callahan, Raymond E. *Education and the Cult of Efficiency*. Chicago: The University of Chicago Press, 1962.

Carey, Max L., and Alan Eck. *How Workers Get Their Training*. Washington, D.C.: U.S. Department of Labor, Bureau of Labor Statistics, 1985.

Carnevale, Anthony P. and Leila J Gainer. *The Learning Enterprise*. Washington, D.C., The American Society for Training & Development and U.S. Department of Labor, May, 1989.

Commission on the Skills of the American Work force. *America's Choice: High Skills or Low Wages!* Rochester, New York, The National Center on Education and the Economy, June, 1990.

Dertouzos, Michael L., Richard K. Lester, and Robert M. Solow. *Made in America: Regaining the Productivity Edge*. Cambridge, Massachusetts., The MIT Press, 1989.

European Trade Union Institute. *Flexibility and Jobs: Myths and Realities*. Brussels; ETUI, May, 1985.

Green, William. "The Effect on Labor of the New Standardization Programs in American Industry." *Annals of the American Academy of Political and Social Science* :.43–6, May, 1928.

Hoyman, Michele. "The Joint Labor-Management Training Program: A Useful Innovation." Prepared for the Chicago Assembly Conference *Creating Work, Creating Jobs*, November 12–14, 1990.

Huber, Vandra L., and Karen A. Brown. "Human Resources in Cellular Manufacturing." March, 1990.

Klingel, Sally, and Ann Martin. *A Fighting Chance: New Strategies to Save Jobs and Reduce Costs*. Ithaca, New York: ILR Press, Cornell University, 1988.

Lewin, David. "Expert's Report on the United States." Conference on Labor Market Flexibility and Work Organization, *Organization for Economic Cooperation and Development*, August 8, 1990.

Mangum, Stephen L. "Evidence on Private Sector Training." *Investing in People: Background Papers Vol. I*. Washington, D.C.: Commission on Work force Quality and Labor Market Efficiency, U.S. Department of Labor, September, 1989, 331–85.

Marschall, Daniel. "Union Involvement in State Government Economic Development/Training Programs." Prepared for National Governors' Association Conference, *Training the American Work Force: The Mark of Excellence*. November 14–16, 1990.

Meulders, Daniele, and Luc Wilkin. "Labour Market Flexibility: Critical Introduction to the Analysis of a Concept." *Labour and Society* 12(1):3–17, January, 1987.

Montgomery, David. *Workers' Control in America*. Cambridge: Cambridge University Press, 1979.

Raizen, Senta A. "Reforming Education For Work: A Cognitive Science Perspective." National Center for Research in Vocational Education, December, 1989.

Resnick, Lauren B. "Learning in School and Out." *Educational Researcher*, December, 1987, 13–20.

Roberts, Markley. Remarks presented at the OECD Conference on Labor Market Flexibility and Work Organization, Paris, September 17, 1990.

Rosenberg, Samuel. *The State and the Labor Market.* New York: Plenum Press, 1990.

Rosow, Jerome M., and Jill Casner-Lotto. "The Motorola Training and Education Center." *Training for New Technologies: Part I.* White Plains, New York: Work In America Institute, 1985.

Sarmiento, Anthony R. and Ann Kay. *Worker-Centered Learning: A Union Guide to Workplace Literacy.* Washington, D.C., AFL-CIO Human Resources Development Institute, 1990.

Schrier, Kathy. "Presentation to New York State Governor's Office of Employee Relations Symposium." 1989.

Scribner, Sylvia, and Patricia Sachs. "A Study of On-the-Job Training." Technical Paper No. 13. City University of New York, February, 1990.

Shaiken, Harley. *Work Transformed: Automation and Labor in the Computer Age.* New York, Holt, Reinhart, and Winston, 1984.

Stern, David, and Charles Benson. "Firms' Propensity to Train." Berkeley: University of California, June, 1989.

U.S. Congress, Office of Technology Assessment. *Worker Training: Competing in the New International Economy*, OTA-ITE-457. Washington, D.C.: U.S. Government Printing Office, September, 1990.

Wiggenhorn, William. "Motorola U: When Training Becomes an Education." *Harvard Business Review* :71–83, July–August, 1990.

Australian Union Movement Strategy

MAX OGDEN

Director, Skill Formation and Work Organization Office, Australian Council of Trades Unions

In this article I will briefly outline the macro approach of the Australian union movement to economic restructuring, then discuss more fully changes at the enterprise level. I must emphasize that it is not possible to understand one without the other.

THE ACCORD AND UNION STRATEGY

Australia has pursued the type of strategy that Ray Marshall presents in this volume, a high-wage, interventionist approach. We began to develop it in 1983, just prior to the election, when the Australian Labour Party (ALP) and the Australian Council of Trade Unions (ACTU) signed an agreement that became known as the Accord. This agreement dealt with the maintenance of living standards through wages, job creation, introduction of a national health scheme, and other social policies including industry policy, education, and occupational health and safety.

The Accord arose from the problems confronting the union movement and the economy at the time, as well as from some damaging experiences between 1972 and 1975 when the previous Labour Government and the union movement had been at loggerheads on most issues.

The Australian Labour Party won the election, and the Accord was a very important element in that victory. We have since had a very interesting seven years, with a full ten years of Labour Government by the next election. The Australian Council of Trade Unions and the government are in constant negotiations about almost every issue confronting the economy, including the education system and social services, with unions having a major influence in many government policies. This is not to suggest that there are no problems. There are very strong free market forces both in the bureaucracy, especially Treasury, and amongst some of the ministers, and some of their policies are dominant at times.

The Accord has now gone through six phases and has been modified each year to suit the new circumstances. However, it has consistently supported a centralized wage-fixing system, and the government and unions have been able to agree on overall National Wage outcomes for each twelve months. They jointly pursue their agreed proposals in the Industrial Relations Commission, which is a very powerful organization in Australia, acting something akin to a court that determines wages and working conditions.

We no longer talk about wages as being the sole determinant of living standards, but of living standards packages that can become complex, including such things as tax cuts, superannuation, and improvements to child care. In other words, the social wage.

As a result of the Accord, all Australian workers are now covered by a minimum of 3 percent superannuation that is paid by the employer in union-management controlled funds. The latest agreement requires that this be raised to 6 percent in 1992.

The importance of such living standards packages, especially the centralized wage system, can be shown by the latest research on wages. It demonstrates that low-paid workers, which means mostly women, have received more from the centralized system in terms of real increases in living standards.

However, when compared with wages negotiated at an enterprise level, or when total income is examined, the wages of women and low-paid workers drop behind. The centralized system has been crucial for equity.

While this is a vastly better framework to work within than with a conservative party in power, we still have quite serious arguments and major differences in a number of areas. These include industry policy, where there is a strong push to eliminate all protection without putting any proper structures in place to help Australian manufacturing become world competitive. The deregulation of the finance industry has led to major distortions in the economy through massive amounts of speculative capital, now resulting in all of the big takeover merchants collapsing and contributing in a massive way to Australian foreign debt. The continued high interest rate policy is also problematic, although there is some understanding in the union movement as to the reasons for that. In other words, while there are many good aspects about the Accord, there are some ministers and departments pursuing policies that are in conflict with the direction agreed to in the ACTU/ALP agreement. Nevertheless, one has to say the Accord has been remarkably successful, and has lasted much longer than any of us imagined. It has helped us turn the Australian union movement from a traditional economist movement dealing only with *wealth distribution*, to a union movement that is now concerned with and playing a major role in *wealth creation*. I can't stress enough how important such a fundamental change as this is.

A new union movement is emerging that is concerned with long-term strategies of social change and is not only reacting to issues as they arise. Issues such as training, efficiencies of industry, job design, and the consultative process are now at the very center of negotiations in a way that never occurred previously. This has all been assisted by the macro framework of the Accord.

ENTERPRISE-LEVEL REFORMS

The focus of our work is increasingly at the micro level. Microeconomic reform relating to new skill levels, job redesign, new management methods, consultative mechanisms, and new wage systems have been developed with a view to achieving world competitive enterprises.

We have used the National Wages system, not only for the purpose of maintenance of living standards, but since 1986, to help drive the micro-level changes. There have been several wage decisions from the Industrial Relations Commission, agreed to by government and unions, that have required negotiations for significant change at the enterprise level as a condition of receiving the national wage increases.

Despite employers' attempts at times to see these negotiations as trade-offs for previously hard-won benefits, the unions have been fairly successful in resisting such attempts, and have sought to focus on changes in work organization, improvement in skill, and general efficiency measures to give the enterprises some hope of survival. The linking of the new awards and enterprise change to the national wage decisions has been critical to ensure that progress is made right across industry. Otherwise, it would have taken an impossible amount of time to make significant changes.

We are now in the process of completing the biggest change to our wage-fixing system in history. The largest awards covering the major industries have now been negotiated, and they all have skill levels and career paths as their central and new feature. Most provide for rights to some training leave for each employee and an obligation on the employer to establish, in conjunction with the union, consultative mechanisms such as an enterprise consultative committee and, if the enterprise warrants it, a joint training committee to oversee the training program. Such changes are fundamental as blue-collar workers have previously had no career path, organized training program, or any joint consultative mechanisms.

The biggest award in the country is that covering the metal industry. It had 348 different wage classifications, some of them with differences of only twenty cents. The new award has fourteen skill levels ranging from a semiskilled metal worker, totally new to the industry, through an experienced engineer. There are three streams: mechanical, fabrication, and electrical. All the levels are articulated so that for the first time it is feasible, though difficult, for a person to walk in off the street, completely unskilled in the industry, and eventually emerge at the top of the tree as an experienced engineer. It is expected that there will now be a big increase in the number of engineers rising from the traditional tradesperson level.

Traditional demarcation, which has been such a bug bear for the unions and was largely instituted by management in their pursuit of the Taylorist division of labor, has diminished dramatically, and by the middle to late nineties should be of no significance. We not only seek to eliminate demarcation at the horizontal level, but more importantly, we want to eliminate the traditional divisions of labor, whereby the conceptual is divided from the doing. Therefore, in the metal industry award, for example, a person will be able to move through the various skill levels, which include criteria for responsibility so that some of the traditional skills and tasks of foremen and supervisors are increasingly incorporated in the normal work practices of the shop floor person.

The approximate timetable for these changes is in several rough stages: The conceptual thinking about the new awards from about 1986 to 1988; negotiations with the employers to get the new documents from 1988 to 1991; the implementation phase with special focus on multiskilling and on-the-job training from 1991 to 1993; the job redesign phase arising from the pressures of multiskilling and on-the-job training from 1991 to 1996; and towards the end of the decade, career paths will become embedded in most enterprises. Beyond that, we are looking at fundamental cultural change, and the union movement has established the objective of the high-competence society to emerge in the first decade of the twenty-first century. In nearly all of these changes, it is the union movement that has taken the initiative, although some employer groups, especially those in the metal industry, have responded fairly positively. Others on the new right spectrum, especially in mining and agriculture, have opposed the developments vigorously.

ENTERPRISE-LEVEL PROCESSES

I turn now to the processes that we have used at the enterprise level. We seek a comprehensive approach to enterprise change. The essence of this change is in three basic principles of flexibility. First, many of the employers only want enterprise specific skills and we have said no. People must have skills that give them recognition and the ability to move across the industry because we are interested in assisting the whole industry. The second flexibility must be the enterprise. It is important, given the demands of new markets in terms of quality and uniqueness, to help reinforce those unique and competitive elements that an enterprise might have within the context of the national structure.

The third flexibility will be the one that provides for major economic structural change so that the work force is able to move across to new skills and whole new industries when there are difficulties in their own. In other words, the active labor market policy that Ray Marshall (1991) discusses and is one of the hallmarks of the Scandinavian approach, is now being created within our structure. We now have a National Board of Employment Education and Training that oversees training and education and a National Training Board that sets national standards.

There are five components which seem essential to get effective change at the enterprise level. First of all, there must be a long-term strategy. Eighty percent of Australian management haven't got a clue where they are going. The unions now think in terms of fifteen to twenty years. When you talk to employers about best practice in their industry, they often have no idea. So, we are helping them write strategies for their companies. It is not possible to get change right in the short term without long-term strategies.

Second, the change must be comprehensive. Change has to be from top to bottom. For example, employers have approached unions and asked for help to implement a Just-in-Time or a Total Quality-Control system. Our response has been that we don't have a big problem in principle with these systems. But they have had in mind a little program here and there, disconnected from everything else. This will not work. There has to be change from top management down. A more educated work force is needed, and the members of this work force need to be given a lot more responsibilities. Most of these schemes are seen as a flavor of the month, and have disappeared because management has not understood the essence of what the change is all about. Change, therefore, must be comprehensive. The total culture of the enterprise has to change to ensure devolution of decision making.

Third, there must be a macro framework such as the new awards, the national training network and standards, and some national goals. This ensures that at least to some extent, enterprises in the same industry are heading in the same direction, and there are overall pressures for change.

Fourth, it must be problem centered. Our experience has been that most of the work force is not particularly enthusiastic about the award changes nor about what is happening nationally with the strategy. They are often worried about the new flexibility. However, when we have brought the strategy and new awards right down to solving practical minute-by-minute problems confronting the employee, it starts to make sense, and often generates enthusiasm for the change.

Fifth, the process or methods of work we use are of great importance. The process should equate to the long-term objectives. If we aim for high-quality, high-skilled, democratic enterprises and work organization, *then we must be very democratic in the way change is implemented.*

In numerous cases, a company will request help to put in a new technology, or solve some big problem, and our response is that we will cooperate but only on our terms. The company must first enable us to have a seminar for employee representitives lasting from three days to a week to let them work through the issues and develop an independent position. At this seminar, the employer presents a session to outline their problems and plans. The union provides background such as the history of technology and work organization, the long-term union strategies, the current economic situation, the potential of future change, the new award and training structures, and related topics. From there, the employee representatives develop proposals that relate to their enterprise and become the basis for negotiation with the employer.

The workers come up with detailed, comprehensive, and lengthy documents that often cause concern to management because of their insights and radical proposals. This document is distributed to the work force and is often followed by small meetings conducted by the union to ensure a full understanding and involvement in deciding the final proposals. Then the long period of negotiations and implementation begins.

CONCLUSIONS ABOUT THE FUTURE

Finally, what does the future hold? The strategy we have been pursuing is one of considerable potential. It also has dangers, but then there is danger in everything we do. There is far greater danger in sitting back and doing nothing. What we are really trying to do, and I suppose the sophistication of it, is to balance the interventionist approach into management and industry with the problem of becoming incorporated into management's plans. So far that has not happened because we have been able to set the agenda. The balance between the macro strategy and enterprise flexibility is a real challenge for unions. How we handle this challenge and at the same time maintain a fundamental union position is critical for our future.

The whole process creates a potential for unions to become much stronger on the job through joint training committees and joint consulting committees, and these are part of the new legally binding awards. In that process, the biggest challenge is to develop a rank and file who will turn the union movement more into a facilitative organization than just a servicing one. There is no way we can make this all work if we rely on full-time officials—it finally must be driven by the rank and file.

Flexible Labor Markets and Labor Training—An American and International Analysis

STEVEN DEUTSCH

Director, Center for Work, Economy, and Community; Professor of Sociology, University of Oregon

INTRODUCTION

The United States and all industrial nations experienced the crises of the 1970s and the 1980s: energy, inflation, rising interest rates, changing patterns of international trade, and the resulting decrease in economic growth and rising unemployment. Throughout the 1980s manufacturing contracted and the services expanded with major long-term structural changes, nurtured by microelectronic technologies and the globalization of the economy.

Considerable discussion in the 1980s around what is meant by flexibility generated a high level of concern for how the United States and all nations might be more responsive to the economic crises and address the challenges of unemployment, skills training, productivity, and more flexible work organizations and labor markets (Meulders and Wilkin, 1987). The OECD established a panel of experts to examine the situation and make recommendations concerning flexibility and greater responsiveness in labor markets, along with technological innovation and related social programs to meet human needs (OECD, 1986a). The report stressed flexibility in labor markets linked to labor costs, conditions of employment, work practices and work patterns, labor market rules and regulations, mobility, and education and training.

This paper focuses primarily on formal labor market policies, skills acquisition, and worker training as central features of economic flexibility. Flexible work organizations and work restructuring, while critical to the larger picture, are developed in a number of other writings of mine. The situation in the United States and a survey of international experiences with labor market flexibility and training is presented here, with lessons that might influence American labor policy for the future.

THE ECONOMIC CRISIS OF THE 1980S

Some interrelated trends affected the American economy over the past few decades. The development of the technology of production itself began with the early stages of factory automation in the 1950s and 1960s. In the late 1970s and 1980s, the rapid application of microelectronics at the workplace occurred across all occupational categories, skill levels, and economic sectors. The shift to a global economy brought a severe challenge in the 1970s to the heretofore hegemonic control of the world industrial economy by the U.S.

Foreign competition for U.S. and global markets led over the decade of the 1970s to massive changes in the U.S. economy. American firms moved large amounts of production and assembly off-shore with the resulting loss of facilities and employment in the United States (Bluestone and Harrison, 1982; Reich, 1984). The proportion of steel, autos, textiles and apparel, shoes, television and other electronic products, manufactured abroad and sold in the U. S., grew enormously over the past decade (President's

Commission on Industrial Competitiveness, 1985). This has led to an imbalance in international trade so that the United States is currently the largest debtor nation in the world. These structural shifts in the position of U.S. industry and the international economy had a profound impact on employment.

Greater globalization and economic integration among the industrial nations, higher use of new microelectronic technology in production, and a growing over-capacity in production in many of the basic industries such as auto, steel, and electronics manufacturing characterize today's world economy (ILO, 1983). The impact in the United States unleashed a debate, which started with the recession in the late 1970s, over the need for an industrial policy comparable to that characteristic in most of the competitor industrial nations (Reich, 1984). This discussion focused on the need to plan economic growth and to establish a tripartite approach building on active and joint planning by labor, management, and government so as to limit adverse effects and maximize the benefits of internationalization of the economy and technological change.

While much of the literature, including that coming from the management community, calls for cooperative labor-management efforts to apply new technology and to increase efficiency, productivity, and hence America's "competitive edge" (Manufacturing Studies Board, 1986a, 1986b), few advocate systematic escalation of labor's participation in economic decision making both at the level of the enterprise and in the broader economy (Marshall, 1987; Deutsch and Albrecht, 1983). Rodberg and Tabb make a cogent argument that the market is incapable of leading toward solutions and that the historic role of government in the U.S. is inadequate to assist in economic restructuring. Furthermore, they state that,

> Equity considerations must be given a central role in policy on efficiency grounds, since the cost of ignoring workers' needs is socially wasteful of human capital investment, while natural resistance on the part of antagonized workers slows down the adaptation to change and inhibits the necessary participation by workers in the development of the forces of production (Rodberg and Tabb, 1987, p.29).

The implications of this for shaping a labor market policy and commitment to full employment and for maximizing worker training in response to and in anticipation of technological change is obvious. A policy of reindustrialization and economic revitalization must be built on human resource development, and the application of new technology must occur in partnership with authentic training efforts to produce the highly flexible work force that is part of the lexicon of the current debate on "competitiveness" (Lund and Hansen, 1986; Carnevale, 1985).

The worldwide recession of the early 1980s and the application of new technology in the industrial and newly industrialized nations created challenges that most of the rich nations had not faced previously (President's Commission on Competitiveness, 1985; Reich, 1984; Bluestone and Harrison, 1982). In the past few years concerned parties called for greater productivity, efficiency of production, better use of new technologies, and enhanced flexibility of the work force (*Business Week*, 1986). The last must be understood as the need for a skilled work force with highly developed capacities for learning and adaptation of workplace knowledge in the face of shifting industries, production systems, and technologies (Flynn, 1988). A challenging process of upgrading skills, creatively using existing plant and equipment, applying new production technologies, and making a better match between the work force and the potential and real labor market demand system is required (Deutsch, 1989; Levitan et al., 1981).

The situation in the United States exemplifies a failure to achieve what the Swedes and the Japanese understand as essential for the economic health of the society: the ability to effectively undergo change in the context of global economic competition and massive changes in technology at the workplace. The long record of governmental and private efforts in worker training within the U.S. presents overall results

121

that have been quite dismal (Levitan et al., 1981; OTA, 1986a; National Commission for Employment Policy, 1987). In the United States only about one in twenty displaced workers who are eligible are involved in national governmental programs of assistance and training (Office of Technology Assessment, 1986a). Too few resources have been expended and almost all programs are remedial and posthoc rather than adaptive and anticipatory. The absence of a comprehensive labor market policy and the fact that coordination and planning are seen by many as anathema to a system that relies upon private collective bargaining explains this pattern. Retraining after workers have been made redundant misses the mark and will fail to assist the country in creating a more flexible work force.

LEGISLATIVE ACTION AND NEW PRIORITIES

The situation became sufficiently severe in the early 1980s that reports were issued by the U.S. Congressional Office of Technology Assessment (OTA, 1986a, 1986b) and the U.S. Department of Labor (USDL, 1986) recommending major new legislation mandating large employers to give advance notification before permanent or extended lay-offs and plant closings, and for an initiative in federally supported worker training, targeting workers already victimized but also those employees whose jobs and job skills are in jeopardy. Following years of political resistance, only in 1988 did the U.S. Congress pass an omnibus trade bill with so-called "plant closing" advance notification provisions along with training provisions, thus having the United States join most other industrial nations with such legislation.

The move toward legislative remedies, the search for alternative national models of training, and the increasing resources committed to human resource development were among the most hopeful developments in the late 1980s and suggest some more optimistic possibilities for the future (Marshall, 1987; Deutsch, 1987, 1988). In the course of this policy debate several trends and needs are prominent.

First, many governmental and quasi-governmental reports in recent years have underscored the need for a cooperative labor-management spirit to apply new technologies and effectively manage the work force and human resources to make American organizations efficient, productive, and competitive. This is demonstrated in reports from the National Academy of Sciences (Manufacturing Studies Board, 1986a, 1986b), U.S. Department of Labor (USDL, 1986), and the U.S. Congress Office of Technology Assessment (OTA, 1984, 1985, 1986a, 1986b). This same argument exists in much of the literature in the business community (*Business Week*, 1986) and writings by significant policy analysts (Marshall, 1987).

Second, the impact of new technologies is being felt especially among women workers (U.S. Department of Labor, 1985). Feminization of the work force is an international phenomenon—women constitute 45 percent of the U.S. work force and are highly concentrated in occupational sectors most affected by microelectronic technology (National Association of Working Women, 1985; OTA, 1985). Special attention should be given its impact on women and the need for job training in the face of new technology.

Third, and much overlooked, is the need for societal and enterprise training programs to work toward greater sex equity and opportunity, versus simply reinforcing and extending the victimization of women in the work force. The dominance of men in design of systems of work technology, office computerization, robotics, and artificial intelligence should be clue enough to the challenges in this realm.

"Who will do America's work as the demand for skilled labor outstrips a dwindling supply? The U.S. has lost much ground to competitors, and investing in people looks like the way to retake it. After years of neglect, the problems of human capital has become a crisis" (*Business Week*, September 19, 1988, p.100).

STATE INITIATIVES

In summary, the occupational and labor force shifts, market and corporate structural changes, and the impact of new technologies all had profound consequences in the United States. Policy makers, labor, and management all recognized the need for greater flexibility through skills training and a more active labor market policy, and an altered means of coordinating all of the parties. Some federal programs were introduced, but the magnitude of all federal efforts is far below the need. As a result, significant new initiatives were launched at the state level where there was greater need felt and a more supportive political climate in many cases for government to become more active in working with employers and unions to enhance the flexibility of local and state labor markets and worker training (Deutsch, 1987). An exploration of some of these state efforts toward more flexible labor markets follows.

California

California is the largest state in terms of population with a GNP that exceeds all but a small number of nations in the world. The economy is diverse with significant shares in agriculture, forestry, fishing, and food processing on the one hand, and steel and finished products manufacturing on the other. California spawned the world's first high-technology industrial complex, known as "Silicon Valley," with the largest concentration of firms in the world devoted to microelectronic technology, from manufacturing of chips and semiconductors to advanced computers and industrial machinery.

The state of California experienced a substantial number of plant closings starting in the late 1970s and accelerating in the early 1980s, a pattern similar to that in much of the country. Many of the plants were large manufacturing facilities for Fortune 500 corporations including Ford, General Motors, Kaiser, Firestone, Atari, and others. In large part reacting to the challenge of retraining displaced workers and upgrading the skills of the work force in the context of technological change, the state created the California Employment Training Panel (ETP) in 1982. Funded by a tax on employers linked to unemployment insurance payment, it has had $55 million annually to spend in retraining programs. The ETP "states that a principal goal of active retraining is to encourage the adoption of new technology, thus helping California businesses to stay productive and competitive. The effect, besides avoiding immediate loss of jobs, is to make future employment more secure" (OTA, 1986a, p.207). This makes the ETP different from the federal Job Training Partnership Act (JTPA) Title III programs since eligibility for JTPA requires being displaced or having lay-offs announced. The ETP budget is more than five times that of the California JTPA allotment.

During the first three years ETP trained more than 40,000 thousand workers for jobs in a variety of businesses, from large defense contractors to banks, from architectural firms to bakeries. The statutory provision for ETP established a mandate to assist workers likely to be displaced, which "gave ETP administrators latitude to fund projects that help workers and businesses implement workplace changes made necessary by technological advance or the demands of competition" (Walsh, 1986, p.8). The implicit recognition in ETP is what many explicitly see as the need to regularly upgrade workers' skills in a high-tech society. The state of California also built into the program the capacity to do in-state worker training as incentives to lure and to keep high-tech businesses.

The initial impetus for the ETP legislation was the rash of plant closings, mostly affecting blue-collar production workers in the late 1970s and early 1980s. Yet one-third of the programs of the Employment Training Panel were targeted towards white-collar workers. The electronic firms in Silicon Valley experienced a changed economic climate due to international competition with 17,500 jobs lost from 1984 to 1986 and more predicted (Pollack, 1986). The theory and the practice of the ETP according to one evaluation is that, "... the availability of panel funds provides companies with the incentive to retrain a work force with outdated skills, rather than laying off employees. Companies are encouraged to take a long-range view towards their employees" (Young, 1985, p.31–32). The harsh reality in the electronics industry shows considerable variations between employers, such as Hewlett-Packard, which have attempted to avoid lay-offs to companies that have moved to hiring temporary employees (OTA, 1986a).

The enabling legislation makes it clear that targeted workers include those whose jobs are vulnerable as well as those who have been displaced. It allows for up to eighteen months of training (State of California, 1986a; 1986b). The California evidence suggests that it is 39 percent more expensive to train persons who are unemployment insurance recipients than employed workers who are likely to be displaced (Young, 1985). This gives strong support to the move to provide training prior to layoff and in anticipation of employment changes, one of the strong points of the California program.

Massachusetts

In the 1970s and 1980s the state of Massachusetts suffered substantial job loss in declining industries, more than thirty thousand jobs from 1981 to 1984. While only 12 percent of all state workers are within those industries, in some communities they account for more than one-half of the work force (Commonwealth of Massachusetts, 1986). In that context the state passed Chapter 208 "An Act Alleviating the Impact of Major Dislocations of Employment and to Assist in the Reemployment of Dislocated Workers." This law became operational in 1985 with $15 million state funding designed to assist workers and communities affected by plant closings and major layoffs.

The 1984 act established the Industrial Services Program (ISP) to provide statewide technical assistance and financing to aid business, workers, and communities. First, it provides funding through the Economic Stabilization Trust to assist in corporate restructuring, change of ownership, and employee buyouts and other efforts to save jobs. Second, an early warning system analyzes state economic trends and monitors industries and businesses likely to experience plant closings. Third, the ISP oversees and coordinates dislocated worker programs through the federal JTPA Title III. In addition, state funds are used to provide programs for worker assistance and industrywide job-creation programs. This legislation and programmatic activity is broad and seeks to both ameliorate the problems of dislocation and to be preventive.

Part of the 1984 Act established the Massachusetts "Social Compact" whereby all employers are encouraged to provide ninety days advance notification in the event of an extended layoff or plant closing (Commonwealth of Massachusetts, 1984). This was based on evidence that such advance notice is critical to successful adaptation by the work force to gain reemployment and for the agencies involved in worker assistance, job retraining, and job search and placement. Firms that fail to give such notice must provide some continued pay as severance. A provision of the law mandated that ninety days of continued health benefits would be available after the job loss. In the first year of the operation of the Social Compact most contacts concerning a closing or layoff came to the Industrial Services Program from unions rather than employers, with business associations and affected communities being a second source of inquiry.

The evaluation of the 1983 to 1985 period led the Division of Employment Security of the state to recommend extending the provisions of the 1984 Act to include partial layoffs involving at least 20 percent of the employees in a high unemployment area, where the employer constitutes a large proportion of the work force, or where more than 300 workers are involved in the layoff (Commonwealth of Massachusetts, 1986). This takes the state program an additional step. If the law with this extension had been in effect, 77 percent of the laid-off workers in economically distressed areas or layoffs of more than 300 would have been covered, and 80 percent of workers in declining industries would have been eligible for benefits as well.

The evidence suggests that many of the typical features of worker retraining programs exist in the ISP/

JTPA Title III efforts in this state. The importance of giving advance warning of impending layoffs or plant closings to dislocated workers was a key element in the Massachusetts case and is built into the law and the concept of a "Social Compact." The linkage of worker assistance and training programs to broader programs of management consulting, financial and technical aid, and worker buyout assistance makes this a unique aspect of this operation and one worthy of more national attention.

In addition to programs targeting displaced workers, the state of Massachusetts sought to engage state funding in linked programs of training and economic development. Out of this approach the Bay State Skills Corporation (BSSC) was created as one mechanism for the state to foster technological preeminence. The BSSC states, "As long as government compensates only for its failing industries, it can at best merely slow the rate of economic stagnation. By encouraging its technologically successful companies, Massachusetts controls the transition from declining industries to its future—computers, robotics, numerically controlled machines, biotechnology and others . . ." (Bay State Skills Corporation, 1986).

The BSSC is project-specific and requires private sector corporate participation in each jointly funded effort. State and private funds, channeled through an educational institution, provide training for workers with special emphasis on training in new technologies. For example, these have included a project to train displaced bank tellers as computerized money machine repairers as well as more professionally advanced levels of training. The recent annual report states that the four years of the program have involved more than 600 companies and 200 educational institutions and that 91 percent of trainees received full-time employment in the private sector.

The Expanding Move to State Worker and Employment Training Efforts

As the recession and economic dislocation realities affected states across the nation, efforts evolved at the state level to assist dislocated workers and industries that were experiencing severe shocks, particularly in the industrial heartland of the country. These programs typically were initiated as remedial efforts to provide desperately needed assistance, but gradually were part of a broader economic development package to attract new industries, diversify the state economy, and provide inducement and assistance in the adoption of new technologies.

The Center for Policy Research and Analysis of the National Governors' Association actively promotes new state initiatives. More than twenty states established rapid response teams to assist dislocated workers and industries. While JTPA Title III funds cannot be used until a layoff or closing has been announced, states have been providing funds for worker retraining before firms are threatened with closing (Balderston, 1986).

Michigan, a state devastated by the dislocation in the auto industry, committed over $20 million to assist in worker training geared to high-tech transition. State funds are used for retraining dislocated workers and for assisting firms and workers to obtain consultations and training to adopt new technology. The Michigan Technology Deployment and Modernization Service is specifically geared to help firms modernize and move toward use of programmable automation by use of technical assistance, customized training of workers, and other support services (State of Michigan, 1986; BNA, 1988).

The Customized Job Training in Pennsylvania, established in 1982 to augment the federal programs, during the first three years expended over $12 million to train steelworkers and those in other manufacturing industries that had severe employment cut-backs. The program is also geared to attract new industry to the state by providing funds to be used by educational institutions to train workers to fit new job requirements (Commonwealth of Pennsylvania, 1986).

Washington, also adversely affected in the timber and other industries, enacted legislation in 1983 to create the Washington State Job Skills Program "as an economic development incentive to provide customized, quick-start training to meet the employee needs of new or expanding businesses . . . to train individuals for new jobs, to avoid dislocation, and to prepare employees for upgrade." The funding formula matches state and corporate sources with the training designed to be short term and highly focused on job placement opportunities (Washington State, 1986).

The New York State Regional Education Center for Economic Development provides firm-specific training designed to help dislocated workers as well as to meet the economic development needs of industry. A companion program works in training and education for public assistance recipients, is on-the-job focused, and is operated by local social service districts. It, too, is run in partnership with employers with the training customized in terms of employment needs (SUNY, 1986).

The Oregon Case

The regional economic revitalization strategies in the United States become understandable by making some cross-national comparisons. In the 1970s the Swedish government was made aware that international competition in ship-building put their industry into jeopardy and anticipated that twenty thousand shipyard workers would lose their jobs in the western part of Sweden around Gothenberg. The government, with an active labor market policy, moved to implement a variety of programs including early retirement, job retraining, support of workers to relocate, and government initiatives for new industry to come in to replace the shipyards as a source of economic foundation. The last is illustrated by Volvo's new plant in Uddevalla, built on the ashes of the old shipyard.

Also in the late 1970s, automation and market caused twenty thousand workers in the forest products industry to lose their jobs in Lane County, Oregon. The size of the state of Connecticut, it is the most productive county in the nation in production of timber. In contrast to the Swedish case, nothing was done for the Oregon workers who lost their jobs. Some may have worked for an employer where contractual rights allowed transfer to another location. Some may have been able to take early retirement. Some of the workers were able to enter retraining programs and receive other help. For the great majority, it was simply assumed that they would respond to a free market and move elsewhere if they were unable to find work locally. Indeed, the unemployment rate increased to more than 12 percent, and out-migration was significant in the face of a severe recession at the national and local level. Programs to help companies stay in business, allow workers to buy plants, technical assistance for new industries, and subsidies for new employers in other industries did not exist as in the Swedish milieu.

Legislative and community efforts to mitigate the effects of the economic downturn in the wood-products industry were largely unsuccessful. A strong business campaign against the Employment Stabilization Act in 1981 defeated the attempt to mandate advance notice of plant closings and provide retraining assistance. However, in subsequent years a number of legislative reforms were passed providing for greater state capacity to intervene to promote industrial retention and economic growth.

The Oregon model parallels that in other states and similarly reflects the inadequacies of state solutions without a coordinated national program of action. The Oregon Economic Development Department created an industrial retention service to provide assistance for firms in economic difficulty and threatened with closure or substantial reduction of employees. A company receives technical assistance and consultation in an effort to turn the economic picture around and avoid a closure.

Another program moved ahead to provide technical assistance for employee buyouts as a method to save jobs and production and the economic base of a community. Again, the concept requires advance notice and sufficient state involvement to provide assistance in financing, training, and consultation. A worker manual has been printed and workshops have been run through a private nonprofit contractor in local communities throughout the state to assist in employee ownership ventures.

In the larger picture, there appear to be some contradictory trends and policy implications. On the one hand-much of the new job creation has been in the low-wage sector implying unskilled jobs. Yet there is a concern for the mismatch between labor market needs and labor force skill levels. In Oregon the Economic Development Department, along with the Office of Educational Policy and Planning, understood this challenge and in 1989 initiated an assessment of the projected needs by employers, the skills base of the existing work force (young and midcareer employees), and the future work force (those in school) to ascertain any deficiencies and the implications for altering school programs, vocational preparation, and upgrading employee skills (State of Oregon Economic Development Department, 1988, 1989).

What this adds up to is an effort to gain a holistic economic plan for assisting and revitalizing the Oregon economy. Modest legislative reforms have been enacted, all predicated on some degree of voluntarism with incentives for employers to give advance notice, seek assistance, and work toward retaining production and employment. The ingredients in the Oregon program are comparable to those in most state efforts. These typically include advance notification by employers, voluntary involvement, emphasis on cooperative labor-management planning, technical assistance efforts to help employers, worker training and retraining, some assistance in financing and research and innovation, and programs to facilitate employee ownership. Since few national programs address these needs, and those that do, such as federally supported worker retraining, are able to assist only a very small fraction of those in need, states have and shall likely continue to struggle to seek out their own programs and solutions for economic dislocation and change.

INTERNATIONAL EXPERIENCES

Given the internationalization of the global economy and the common technology across national boundaries, it seems obvious that the issues of technology at the workplace, worker and job training, and labor-management relations are being addressed in industrial nations (OECD, 1986). It is notable that the European Community has stressed job creation (Commission of the European Communities, 1983), job training, and programs to cope with the substantial unemployment and job dislocation within its member states.

While all of the industrial Western states are market economies, they range along a continuum in terms of the degree to which the welfare state has been developed, the size of the work force that is unionized, and the nature of the labor-management relations system. In Scandinavia, a tradition of a more cooperative labor relations approach exists with the work force highly unionized and an advanced welfare state. The more adversarial labor relations model in the U.S., Canada, England, and Australia led to a different pattern of response to technological change in the economy (Deutsch, 1986). A study by an American economist suggested that, "With few exceptions, the European countries have demonstrated a comprehensive and stable institutional structure for addressing employment and training issues" (Haverman, 1982, p.19).

While noting the variations, it also can be observed that changing technology has provoked a common response in collective bargaining arrangements emphasizing advance notification, employee involvement in planning and implementation, forms of job security, employee training and retraining, and other such concerns. So-called technology agreements have been strongly urged by many European unions for a decade or longer and a large volume of publications has flowed across national boundaries (ETUI, 1985).

There are also variations in the tendency to legislate provisions applied to introducing new technology at the workplace and addressing its various consequences, including job protection and worker retraining (ILO, 1985b). These reflect long-standing political traditions, strength of trade unions and labor parties, and the recent trends toward public policy solutions to challenges in the economy (Deutsch, 1986; Markmann, 1985).

The European Communities (EC) Experience

Comments have already indicated several tendencies within the EC nations. First, a stronger trend occurs toward legislation to address structural dislocation and the problems of unemployment than is true for the United States. For example, prenotification of a plant closing or major layoff is legislated in most European states, contrary to the emphasis upon voluntary notice within the U.S. (Harrison, 1984; OTA, 1986b).

Second, an overriding concern exists for the economic advancement of Europe in competition with other industrial leaders, particularly the United States and Japan. This has led to major research and training efforts to innovate and diffuse information technology and advanced manufacturing technology. Emphasis is placed upon application of technology for successful economic expansion and training the labor force to adapt to the changes.

The EC reported 71 demonstration projects in worker training as part of the effort to develop effective training and retraining programs, materials, and effecting program evaluation (Commission of the European Communities and European Centre for Work and Society, 1986).

In this coordinated effort, known as Euro TecneT, 50 percent of the projects are linked to the educational system, 30 percent to the industrial world and 15 percent to particular institutions. Private industry is responsible for no more than 10 percent of these training efforts, while 70 percent fall under the federal ministries. The programs are governmental and federally coordinated with regional and local governments playing a minor role. The preponderance of projects, 70 percent, focus on general job training or retraining, and the remaining 30 percent are focused on upgrading practical skills for the workers enrolled. This is more understandable when we learn that 55 percent of the target groups are youth, and 45 percent are unemployed. The training projects are typically viewed as longer-term courses, most last several months or longer than a year, either part or full time. The projects are typically financed as well as coordinated by the federal governments; only in France and Germany is industry involved as a co-sponsor. The projects cover all of the member states, from Ireland to Greece, Denmark to Spain, and all are focused on "training designed to improve individuals' access to work, to increase the efficiency and stability of existing jobs, and to contribute to the creation of new employment," to quote from the Euro TecneT May, 1986 newsletter.

A brief exploration of developments within some countries is presented below to suggest particulars and possible lessons.

France

Microelectronic technology has had wide application in France. French citizens are more involved with computers in their daily lives as consumers than as workers, but one union argued that four million additional workers needed training in computerized applications by 1990 (ILO, 1985a). In 1979 France initiated a five-year program of introducing computer instruction in the schools with a major program to nurture science and technology training at all levels. A 1983 agreement was signed between the government and the Federation of Metallurgical and Mining Industries, representing employers in iron and steel, for the joint implementation of training projects both for the unemployed and to meet the needs for modernization of the industry (ILO, 1985c). Nevertheless, industry in France has experienced major dislocation and long-term and permanent layoffs, comparable to the United States (Rothstein, 1986).

A National Employment Fund exists that provides up to 70 percent of the expenses in retraining workers in any firm that is being restructured as a result of automation. At the same time the Agency for Development of Information Technology (ADL) assisted training institutions in training engineers and technicians to help meet the labor shortage for high-tech application fields, while the Agency for the Development of Automation (ADEPA) advises and subsidizes enterprises wishing to introduce new technologies (ILO, 1985a, p.101).

The French system of training is the result of a partnership involving the government and the private sector, with both a legislative and contractual foundation for operation. The State finances continuous training activities under regional and local agreements which meet concrete needs of employment assistance with target groups and specified skills training. Employers must contribute 1.1 percent of payroll to such efforts.

The National Employment Agency created courses designed to upgrade skills of job seekers who do not possess the necessary qualifications. Pacts signed with employers are designed to prevent layoffs and provide financing of training programs to upgrade skills needed as the technology and work demands shift in the enterprise. The intention is for such retraining to maintain employment in the firm or fit the needs of another employer (ILO, 1985a, p.99). Also, a legislated worker study leave policy is designed to facilitate adult education.

A Plan for the Future of Youth was launched in France in 1981–1982 with a focus upon both vocational training and targeted programs for the most underprivileged youth in the society. An extension of this provides a mix of training and work available for youth between seventeen and twenty-six through a contractual arrangement whereby the employer gets a federal subsidy for training workers for 120 to 1200 hours or having such training contracted with an outside organization. Early evaluations after 1982 showed that 80 to 85 percent of those who went through such training programs found permanent jobs and 40 to 50 percent in the occupation for which they were trained (ILO, 1985a, p.95). The attention given youth within the French worker training programs is not atypical of the countries in Europe.

England

England, the cradle of the Industrial Revolution, experienced massive structural shifts in its economy as a result of lost markets, contracting industries, outmoded and replaced technology, and other changes. The proportion of manual workers in the labor force declined from 63 percent in 1961 to 54 percent in 1978 to less than 50 percent in 1985. Over the past decade more than one million semi and unskilled jobs were lost and another million jobs were projected to disappear by 1990 (ILO, 1985a, p.101). The result has been a staggering and long-term high unemployment rate with the special problem of youth unemployment. The latter is aggravated by the fact that at the end of the 1970s, 44 percent of youth left the educational system after the age of sixteen without being employed or registered for any training (compared with 19 percent in France and 7 percent in Germany).

The awareness of technology has been high in England, and calls for technology agreements and employment planning were issued by unions and journalists earlier in England than almost any other country. The Trades Union Congress championed technology agreements and urged comprehensive labor market policies and employment training as part of its official body starting in the mid-1970s (TUC, 1979). Training provisions are included in 65 percent of all collectively bargained agreements dealing with technology between 1977 and 1983, and 77 percent of agreements where specific provisions are provided (Williams and Stewart, 1985). Reliance remains heavily on private-sector programs to deal with employee training and at least one study suggests that company policies on technology are likely to be influenced by their employment policy rather than the reverse (Rothwell, 1985).

The existence of high unemployment, particularly among young workers, in no way speaks to the simultaneous shortages of highly trained people, especially engineers with computer expertise, reported in England (Northcott, 1984). Thus, there is a typical mismatch of skill requirements and the labor force. Some argue that insufficient application of microelectronics has hampered England's economic growth.

The Microelectronics Application Program initiated by the government in 1978 was committed to spending $100 million over six years to increase industry's awareness of the new technology and to assist in retraining employees in its use. Firms are allowed up to 25 percent of the cost for applications of microelectronics and grants are given to educational institutions for training. About 30,000 people a year have received training under this program, which seems to have targeted more professional employees than the skilled and semiskilled workers whose jobs are most vulnerable to technical change (Blair, 1985).

Almost one-third of the over three million unemployed are included in some program or other, the largest of which is enterprise allowances. The Department of Employment estimates that all governmental programs were responsible for keeping 485 thousand people in jobs, training, or early retirement rather than claiming unemployment benefits (Spellman, 1986). These programs include allowances to firms for adoption of new technology, hiring and training unemployed workers, temporary public works employment, early retirement incentives to open up jobs, job-share and reduced hours programs, and a range of youth employment and training efforts.

Analysts of England's program conclude that less interest in the technology and employment issues exists than is true in Sweden and Germany, and that only modest activity overall facilitates labor market adjustment (Blair, 1985). "Whether the new training initiatives prove sufficiently flexible to provide for tomorrow's skill needs remains open to doubt" (Spellman, 1986, p.224).

Germany

"In the sixties it was recognized that a preventive manpower policy with appropriate advance training measures would prove both more effective and more economical than subsequent measures to correct structural changes once these had occurred" (Schmidt, 1985, p. 237).

From this premise came the Federal Labor Promotion Act of 1969 which introduced continuing vocational training as an instrument of a preventive manpower policy. A decade later with regional economic difficulties and the onset of a world wide recession, the Manpower Policy Program for Regions with Particular Unemployment Problems was inaugurated. This program was designed to stimulate help to firms and workers in areas of high unemployment or industries and firms undergoing structural change. It served as a long-term stimulus for companies continuing vocational training (Schmidt, 1985). Training takes place in firms and educational institutions and is highly decentralized with more than 50,000 training places created since the early 1970s through a federal government program of investment in group training centers in which 80 percent of the costs are borne by government.

The issue of technology and employment has become a highly visible political concern in the Federal Republic of Germany. This reflects a politicized labor movement representing one-half of the workforce and a high level of concern over unemployment. It also reflects the projection that up to one-half of all jobs in the country will be substantially affected by microelectronic technology by the year 2000 (Blair, 1985). The pattern in Germany has been for an elaborate system of apprenticeship run by industry to train the nonprofessional work force. Structural changes and evidence of a rapidly changing technology pushed the government into stimulating the system with continuing vocational education. This led to governmental funding of experimental high-tech vocational training programs as well as a program supporting corporate application of microelectronics (Chichon, 1986).

The Employment Promotion Act of 1969 and subsequent labor market initiatives took place in a context of a labor market shortage with the importation of immigrant labor. In recent years the international recession and the application of new technology altered the climate in the Federal Republic of Germany as elsewhere in the industrial West. In May 1986 official unemployment in the FRG was 8.5 percent. In the first eight months of 1986, 307 thousand new participants were brought into governmental training programs, including both job training in which two-thirds of the participants were engaged full time and job creation projects that involved 105 thousand persons. Without these programs there would be a 10 percent increase and a 5 percent increase respectively added to the official unemployment figures (Graff, 1986).

Sweden

Before examining program-specific solutions in Sweden, it helps to understand the political and philosophical context within that nation. According to a former Swedish Minister of Labor, " . . . unemployment certainly is the most important political issue today" (Leijon, 1986, p. 175). With almost 90 percent of the labor force organized, unions and employers joined in a commitment to moving rapidly to adopt new technology for the advancement of the economy and new job promotion (SAF/LO/PTK, 1982; Deutsch, 1986). The underlying assumptions are that technological change is essential for the adaptation of the Swedish economy to remain competitive, and that a tripartite approach among government, labor, and industry is necessary to ensure that the transition is effective with workers retrained and supported in this period of transition (Farm, 1985).

The approach stresses control of unemployment through an active labor market policy, which means " . . . job placement services and other more or less selective measures to improve opportunities for people in the labor force to obtain and keep a job" (Swedish Institute, 1985, p. 1). Unions argue that " . . . labor market policies should foresee and facilitate structural changes . . . Such policies make it possible for trade unions . . . and members to accept the necessary structural changes" (Rexed, 1986, p. 1). Similarly, employers support such programs claiming that the " . . . shaping of labor market policy must attempt in various ways to promote geographical and occupational mobility" (Nordlander, 1986, p. 4).

In short, " . . . the Swedish system emphasizes prevention (of unemployment) through labor, educational, and economic policies, with compensation being the policy of last resort" (Einhorn, 1984, p. 80). In this sense the differences in the way the Swedish system operates in comparison with the United States becomes obvious (Ginsburg, 1983; Farm, 1985). Similarly, it is illuminating to point out that only about 30 percent of the federal budget in Sweden goes toward cash assistance to unemployed workers and 70 percent is used for work training programs, while in England the same figures are 90 and 10.

The labor and management concurrence over the strategy of maximum application of new technology is built upon assumptions of job protection, job creation, worker retraining, and active programs to promote full employment (Meidner, 1986; Deutsch, 1986). In addition, a major program supported by the Work Environment Fund is based on a small tax on payroll:

> " . . . to ensure that new technology is introduced in a manner which will improve the environment, develop and expand work content, and promote the creation of more stimulating occupations and work assignments, thereby enabling the technology to be used—in the widest sense—in the most positive manner possible. Only by adapting technical innovations designed to meet human requirements can the competitiveness of Swedish industry and the efficiency of public administrative bodies be given a real boost" (Swedish Work Environment Fund, 1986, p. 4).

Sweden is a nation of just over eight million people, yet it leads the world in per capita use of robots and in many of the new technologies in operation today. The shifts in skill requirements has been dramatic in the 1980s. In 1980, 55 percent of all jobs required vocational education and/or experience; by 1986 the figure was 77 percent. Within manufacturing the corresponding figures rose from about 40 percent to almost 70 percent (Larsson, 1986, p. 9). This reveals a major challenge for Sweden's educational system and a system of training both new entrants into the labor force and upgrading the skills of workers already employed. To accomplish these objectives the Swedes have developed an elaborate

National Labor Market Board, with tripartite oversight, and twenty-four regional employment boards, 300 employment offices, and ninety employability assessment centers. The system employs a computerized network of job registries and placement services (Swedish Labor Market Board, 1984).

A range of other services is provided, including counseling, temporary public work for the jobless, and targeted programs for youth and longer-term unemployed. A system of governmental payments to employers to maintain employment, hire and train workers, and train existing work forces is part of the overall strategy of the Swedish Labor Market Board. In 1985 to 1986, 22 percent of all training was done in-house by the employer and involved 28,000 workers (Swedish Labor Market Board, 1986).

While wage assistance to the unemployed is considered a last resort, 83,700 applicants per month qualified during 1985 to 1986. An unusual component of the Swedish labor market program is the granting of support to unemployed persons who wish to start their own businesses, providing up to six months of support to seek entrepreneurial self-support (Swedish Labor Market Board, 1986).

As in other industrial countries the problem of youth unemployment is especially significant. In May 1985, 5.4 percent of persons between 16 and 24 were unemployed, accounting for nearly 40 percent of total Swedish unemployment (Swedish Labor Market Board, 1985). The majority of applicants (78 percent in 1983) for labor market training are either unemployed or those considered at risk of becoming unemployed and needing retraining (Swedish Labor Market Board, 1985). About 3 percent of the labor force is trained annually, or 140 thousand; and, 40,000 or 1 percent of the labor force is in training at any one time. The training runs from ten weeks to two years resulting in some difficulty in getting workers to enroll in programs without cash incentives for training. Unions and those in favor of such incentives argue that it is in the national interest to facilitate employee skills building to upgrade the labor force. Employers are more resistant to further cash incentives since the results of training presumably are rewarded in the labor market. The Swedish Labor Market Board has succeeded only a modest amount thus far in attempting to stimulate employers on their own to generate more job training for the existing work force, anticipating technological change and the needs for the future (Larsson, 1988).

There are, however, additional programs that have been developed by unions, by educational institutions, and one interesting joint labor-management effort in the SAF-PTK Employment Security Council. Initiated by agreement in 1975, this program is run jointly by the Swedish Employer's Federation (SF) and the Swedish Federation of Salaried Employees in Industry and Services (PTK). Employers pay a 0.65 of one percent of payroll fee, and nonaffiliated employers are able to participate by paying a small surcharge. The prime purpose of the program is to prevent layoffs and engage in job training within firms, paid for by the fund. If jobs are cut, the funds may also be used to assist in relocation and retraining with a new employer. This initiative is over and above governmentally operated programs and it is unclear how extensive the training actually is (SAF-PTK, 1985).

In sum, Sweden has made a commitment to applying new technology at the workplace, and labor and management share in that so as to increase efficiency and Swedish competitiveness. This is achieved through a policy of active efforts to combat unemployment, underwrite worker retraining, improve the work environment, and engage all parties in the planning and execution of programs to achieve these ends (Standing, 1988). This has been accomplished by the resolve and financial commitment of the government, which spends between 6 and 7 percent of its budget on labor market programs, or 2 to 3 percent of Swedish GNP (Leijon, 1986; Larsson, 1986).

Canada

While similarities between the United States and the industrial democracies of western Europe might be drawn, it is the case that the nation to our north bears greatest resemblance to us. Canada's economy is closely tied to that of the United States and the same challenges faced within this country in recent years have been felt there as well. High unemployment, market changes, and the shifts in technology have all been characteristic of the Canadian economy (Newton, 1985). A commission appointed in the early 1980s sought to explore the impact of microelectronic technology on the labor force and in education with the findings debated since their release (Jain, 1983). Some of the recent federal governmental initiatives might be traced to the stimulus of that report. The Canadian Workplace Automation Research Centre, established in late 1985 within the Department of Communication in the national government, is designed to serve as a clearinghouse of information for applied research into computerized office systems. Meanwhile, the Canadian labor ministry, Labour Canada, has established a Technology Impact Research Fund. The language describing the purpose is worth quoting at some length:

> " . . . the government recognizes that the introduction of new technologies has a direct impact on jobs and people. The Technology Impact Research Fund has therefore been developed to support research projects that will broaden understanding of the impacts of technological change and contribute to greater sensitivity on the part of workers, managers, and governments to the human and social factors implicit in the introduction of new technologies in the workplace"(Labour Canada, 1985, p. 1).

While these developments suggest a significant appreciation of the challenges of new technology, even larger questions concern training. One Canadian report focused upon training states that, "A fundamental redesign of training systems is required to facilitate adjustment and promote economic growth . . . There is some evidence that in some industries, the half-life of skills has become so short that the employers must accept the responsibility for providing workers with these skills and with retraining when these skills are obsolete" (Canadian Department of Employment and Immigration, 1985a, p. 87). It is difficult to find evidence that Canadian employers are providing more such training and retraining at their own initiative than American employers, but it is easy to observe that Canadian programs for displaced workers have captured the imagination of many on this side of the border (La Flamme et al., 1989).

The issue of mandated advance notice in the face of a plant shutdown or long-term layoff continues to be debated in the U.S., while three-quarters of the Canadian labor force is covered by advance notice requirements for collective dismissals, through provincial legislation and federal labor codes (OTA, 1986b). That reality has played an important part in the success of the Canadian Industrial Adjustment Service which has been in operation since 1963, targeting its efforts to working with displaced workers. The system of a rapid-response mechanism for dealing with an announced layoff builds upon a voluntary approach, with employer and worker representatives forming a joint committee to attempt to solve the problem of announced layoffs. Since advance notice is typically given, some cushion is allowed in setting up job placement and counseling services and a system of training helps toward relocations. "The Canadian emphasis is on helping workers as expeditiously as possible, not on subsidizing extended unemployment" (Batt, 1983, p.8).

Normally the costs of the program set up by the joint committee with governmental technical assistance is borne evenly by the employer and the Industrial Adjustment Service (IAS), which can also cover half of the costs of relocation for workers who find employment in other locales. Since the notice is typically three to four months before layoff and the IAS moves immediately to establish functioning committees, time exists to set up an effective program of counseling and assessment, advising for training and implementation of training, and job placement. An evaluation of the record from 1971 to 1981 showed that two-thirds of workers affected by plant closing found employment with the assistance of the labor-management committees within a year, with better results than for American workers who have fallen victim to plant closings.

"IAS committees offered adjustment services to about 39,000 displaced workers in fiscal year 1982–

83. This is an impressive number, considering that in the United States, where the labor force is nearly ten times as large, 132,000 displaced workers were served in the 1984 program year by JTPA projects" (OTA, 1986a, p. 221).

The Canadian government provides public funds for education in ways not used in the U.S.; for example, tax dollars go to the Canadian Labour Congress for worker education programs. During 1983–84, 277 thousand people, or 2.3 percent of the labor force, participated in job training funded by the government. This figure contrasts with 1 percent in both Sweden and Germany (OTA, 1986b). Most of these people participated in vocational skills classes with mostly classroom-based instruction. Almost all in full-time job training in Canada receive government income support in contrast with the U.S. experience.

In 1985 a new program of strategies for retraining in Canada was announced with the commitment of substantial federal governmental funds (Canadian Department of Employment and Immigration, 1985b). A mandate of the program is to facilitate the upgrading of job skills, the acquisition of new technology job skills, and career development. This program has several component parts: skill investment ($100 million budget for 1985–96) allows for employee training in concerted planning with the employer, whether on the job, with another firm, or in a school; job entry ($350 million budgeted) targets youth and new job entrants; job development ($700 million budgeted) targets long-term unemployed workers; skills shortages ($50 million budgeted) targets employed workers who need skills updating especially related to new technologies. Additional programs target innovations in labor market policy, communities that have been severely dislocated by plant shutdowns, and other changes. The overall approach is strongly geared to joint government-industry financing and local voluntary involvement and planning. Long-term training is assumed, up to three years, and can be either full time or part time. The worker receives compensation, up to two-thirds of standard wages, paid equally by employer and government while going to school.

Japan

Japan has emerged as the third most powerful economy in the world measured in terms of GNP, while it has successfully adopted advanced technology and demonstrated an efficient, protective, and competitive economy. The adoption of technology and commitment to science and technology has been an important part of the culture and educational system of Japan for some decades. The system of production relies on a group process and structure in which tasks and expectations are clearly spelled out and worker qualifications and job requirements are made to mesh. This requires appropriate education and training before employment and relies on training in the firm that is typically an ongoing process.

"Japan is without doubt one of the countries where continuous training is most developed. The training concept is totally integrated into the life and work organization of enterprises. Continuous training in fact plays a key role in industrial strategy, whether it is intended to improve the versatility and mobility of workers or to support the activities of quality circles or total quality control systems" (ILO, 1985a, p. 100).

This system was stimulated by the 1969 Vocational Training Law which encourages employers to provide training to their work force. The governmentally operated vocational training system provides general training, skills training, and training geared to facilitate updating and upgrading of skills and assisting workers needing to change jobs. Most training in firms takes place off the job and is specifically designed to maximize the flexibility of the work force and develop the ability to change jobs with the changing system of production and the technology (Inoue, 1986).

What is critical to note is the assumptions within Japan that investment in people is of highest priority and essential to ensure productive and flexible work organizations. Education and training are well financed, receive high levels of commitment by the government and private employers, and are part of an over-all strategy of industrial and economic planning (Inoue, 1986).

SOME CONCLUSIONS AND POSSIBLE LESSONS

The United States might learn from the job training and labor market experiences of other nations. Providing governmental funds to help industry and labor innovate with new methods of training the work force is a policy suggested by Sweden and Germany and to some extent by England (Blair, 1985). In the U.S., federal training funds are targeted for the disadvantaged and displaced, and almost no federal funds go to retraining employed workers to upgrade their skills. Such approaches have been adopted by states and may be the future direction as distinct from federal funding.

Federally funded work research centers exist in several countries and, while governmental grants on a project basis are available, the U.S. does not have a federally supported work research institute, either freestanding or in a university or governmental agency. The research program within the Employment and Training Administration in the U.S. Department of Labor was almost terminated in the 1980s and operates on a small budget. The importance of research information in making informed policy is essential.

The Canadian experience has been most heralded in this country due to the modest cost, the joint government-industry financing, the impressive results, and the voluntary and cooperative model (Olsen, 1988). "Although it is far less comprehensive than either the Swedish or the German plan, the Canadian approach should prove more acceptable to Americans" (Batt, 1983, p.7). Considerable interest has been generated in the Canadian experience, ranging from the National Alliance of Business (NAB, 1983, pp. 4–14) to the National Governors' Association. The U.S. Department of Labor sponsored study trips to Canada by JTPA and state agency personnel, and several U.S. government reports favor the adoption of a Canadian Industrial Adjustment Service model in the United States (OTA 1986a, OTA 1986b; U.S. Department of Labor, 1986). Other features of the Canadian labor relations, union, and economic landscape might also serve as useful guidelines for U.S. labor and policy makers.

Certainly the primacy of collective bargaining will remain in labor's tactics for winning American workers benefits on the job and in economic welfare. This will include the critical issues of work organization, technological change, work environment issues, and matters of career development and worker training. Strategies for work restructuring must join collectively negotiated features of job security, skills training, and work tasks with broader policy agendas. Hence, advance notification and efforts to stop plant closings and deal with worker dislocation are key legislative issues. Federal and state initiatives for retraining in advance of and not only in response to changes in technology, market and corporate structures, and global markets are critical. The more active and successful national cases meld public policy concerns with those of labor and management. Hopefully, the United States will continue to be inspired to move in this direction.

REFERENCES

Balderston, Kris M. *Plant Closings, Layoffs, and Worker Readjustment, The States' Response to Economic Change.* Washington, D.C.: National Governor's Association, 1986.

Batt, Jr. William L., "Canada's Good Example with Displaced Workers." *Harvard Business Review* : 4–11, July–August, 1983.

Bay State Skills Corporation. *1986 Report, Bay State Skills Corporation Act of 1981* and miscellaneous flyers and brochures. Boston, 1986.

Blair, Louis Helion. *Technological Change and Employment in Western Europe.* Washington, D.C.: National Commission for Employment Policy, July, 1985.

Bluestone, B., and B. Harrison. *The Deindustrialization of America.* New York, Basic Books, 1982.

BNA. *Training for New Technologies, Success Stories for the 1990s.* Washington, D.C., Bureau of Natonal Affairs, 1988.

Business Week. "The Hollow Corporation." March 3, 1986.

—. "America's Income Gap, the Closer You Look, the Worse It Gets." April 17, 1989.

—. "High Tech to the Rescue." June 16, 1986.

—. "Human Capital, the Decline of America's Work Force." September 19, 1988.

—. "Management Discovers the Human Side of Automation." September 29, 1986.

Canadian Department of Employment and Immigration. "Changing Skill Requirements." In OECD *Employment Growth and Structural Change.* Paris: OECD, 1985a.

—. *Canadian Jobs Strategy.* Ottawa, 1985b.

Carnevale, Anthony P. *Jobs for the Nation, Challenges for a Society Based on Work.* Alexandria, Virginia, American Society for Training and Development, 1985.

—. "The Learning Enterprise." *Training and Development Journal.* January, 1986.

Chichon, Deborah R. "The Labor Market Policies of West Germany." In *Comparative Labor Market Policies of Japan, West Germany, United Kingdom, France, Australia.* Edited by Howard Rosen. Salt Lake City: Olympus Publishing Company, 1986.

Commision of the European Communities. *New Information Technologies and Vocational Training: A Network Demonstration Projects.* Maastricht: European Centre for Work and Society, April, 1986.

—. *The Potential of Information Technology for Job Creation.* Fast Series, No. 16, Luxembourg: 1983.

Commission of the European Communities and European Centre for Work and Society. *EuroTecnet, New Information Technologies and Vocational Training.* Netherlands: April, 1986.

Commonwealth of Massachusetts. *An Act Alleviating the Impact of Major Dislocations of Employment and to Assist in the Reemployment of Dislocated Workers.* 1984.

Commonwealth of Massachusetts, Division of Employment Services. *The Final Report of the Mature Industries Research Project on Partial Plant Closings.* January 1986.

Commonwealth of Pennsylvania. *Customized Job Training in Pennsylvania, A Progress Report.* Harrisburg, 1986.

Deutsch, Steven. "International Experiences with Technological Change." *Monthly Labor Review.* 109(3):35–40, 1986.

—. "Successful Worker Training Programs Help Ease Impact of Technology." *Monthly Labor Review.* 110:14–20, November, 1987.

—. "Unleashing Human Intelligence—More Than a Matter of Computer Technology." In *Culture, Language, and Artificial Intelligence.* Edited by Magnus Florin and Bo Goranzon. London: Springer, Verlag, 1989.

—. Testimony, *Hearings Before the Sub-Committee on Appropriations, U.S. House of Representatives.* Part 8:376–90, April 25, 1984.

Deutsch, Steven, and Sandra Albrecht. "Worker Participation in the United States, Efforts to Democratize Industry and the Economy." *Labor and Society* 8:243–69, July–Sept., 1983.

Einhorn, Eric. "Employment Policies in Scandinavia." *Scandinavian Review* 72(4):75–83, 1984.

European Trade Union Institute. *Technology and Collective Bargaining, A Review of Ten Years of European Experience.* Brussels, ETUI, 1985.

Farm, Goran. "Swedish and U.S. Labor Market Policy—A Comparative Analysis." In *Economic Dislocation and Job Loss.* Edited by Betty G. Lall. New York, Cornell University Press: 1985.

Flynn, Patricia M. *Facilitating Technological Change, The Human Resource Challenge.* Cambridge, Massachusetts, Ballinger Publishing Co., 1988.

Ginsburg, Helen. *Full Employment and Public Policy, The United States and Sweden.* Lexington, Massachusetts, Lexington Books, 1983.

Graff, Albert. "Counteracting Job Loss." *International Association of Personnel in Employment Security News.* October, 1986.

Harrison, Bennett. "The International Movement for Prenotification of Plant Closures." *Industrial Relations.* 23:387–409, Fall, 1984.

Harrison, Bennett, and Barry Bluestone. *The Great U-Turn, Corporate Restructuring and the Polarizing of America.* New York: Basic Books, 1988.

Haverman, Robert H. *European and American Labor Market Policies in the Late 1970s, Lessons for the United States.* Washington, D.C., National Commission for Employment Policy, 1982.

Inoue, Ken. "Manpower Development in Japan, A Study of the Japanese Education and Training System." In *Finding Work, Cross National Perspectives on Employment and Training.* Edited by Ray Rist. London: the Filmer Press, 1986.

Internation Labor Office. "Selected Provisions of Laws and Regulations Relating to the Introduction of New Technology." *Conditions of Work, A Cumulative Digest*. Geneva: ILO 4(1), 1985b.

————. *Technological Change, The Tripartite Response, 1982–85*. Geneva: ILO, 1985c.

————. *Collective Bargaining, A Response to the Recession in Industrialized Market Economy Countries*. Geneva: ILO, 1983.

International Labor Office. *World Labour Report 2*. Geneva: ILO, 1985a.

Jain, Havish. "Task Force Encourages Diffusion of Microelectronics in Canada." *Monthly Labor Review*. October, 1983.

Labour Canada. *Technology Impact Research Fund*. Ottawa: Labour Canada, 1985.

Laflamme, Gilles, et. al. (eds.). *Flexibility and Labour Markets in Canada and the United States*. Geneva: ILO, 1989.

Larsson, Allan. *New Technology and the Labour Market of the Future*. Swedish National Labor Market Board, September, 1986.

Leijon, Anna Greta. "Labor-Management Relations and the Jobs Problem, the Swedish Experience." In *The Jobs Challenge— Pressures and Possibilities*. Edited by Daniel F. Burton, et al. New York: Ballinger Publishing Company, 1986.

Levitan, Sar A., Garth L. Mangum, and Ray Marshall. *Human Resources and Labor Markets, Employment and Training in the American Economy*. New York: Harper and Row, 1981.

Lund, Robert T., and John A. Hansen. *Keeping America At Work, Strategies for Employing New Technologies*. New York: John Wiley and Sons, 1986.

Manufacturing Studies Board. *Human Resource Practices for Implementing Advanced Manufacturing Technology*. Washington, D.C.: National Academy Press, 1986a.

————. *Toward a New Era in U.S. Manufacturing, the Need for a National Vision*. Washington, D.C.: National Academy Press, 1986b.

Markmann, Heinz. "The Role of Trade Unions in Coping with the Labour Implications of Technological Change." In *Employment Growth and Structural Change*. Paris: OECD, 1985.

Marshall, Ray. *Unheard Voices, Labor and Economic Policy in a Competitive World*. New York, Basic Books, 1987.

Meidner, Rudolf. "Swedish Union Strategies towards Structural Change." *Economic and Industrial Democracy*. 7(1):85–97, 1986.

Meulders, Daniele and Luc Wilkin "Labor Market Flexibility, Critical Introduction to the Analysis of a Concept." *Labour and Society*. 12(1):3–17, 1987.

National Alliance of Business. *Worker Adjustment to Plant Shutdowns and Mass Layoffs, An Analysis of Program Experience and Policy Options*. March, 1983.

National Association of Working Women, 9 - 5. *Hidden Victims, Clerical Workers, Automation, and the Changing Economy*. Cleveland, 1985.

National Commission for Employment Policy. *The Job Training Partnership Act*. Washington, D.C., September, 1987.

Newton, Keith. *Employment Effects of Technological Change, Some Implications for Education*. Economic Council of Canada, May 27, 1985.

Nordlander, Ake. *SAF's Views on the Shaping of a Labor Market Policy*. Swedish Employer Confederation, Stockholm, September, 1986.

Northcott, J. "Microelectronics in Industry—What's Happening in Britain." In *Microelectronics and Informatic's Technology and Their Training Implications in Firms*. Edited by Van Kemenade et al. Berlin: European Center for the Development of Vocational Training, 1984.

OECD. *Labor Market Flexibility* (Dahrendorf Report). Geneva, Paris, 1986a.

Office of Technology Assessment (OTA), U.S. Congress. *Automation of America's Offices 1985–2000*, OTA-CIT-287. Washington, D.C.: U.S. Government Printing Office, 1985.

————. *Computerized Manufacturing Automation, Employment, Education, and the Workplace*, OTA-CIT-235. Washington, D.C.: U.S. Government Printing Office, April, 1984.

————. *Plant Closing, Advance Notice and Rapid Response—Special Report*, OTA-ITE-321. Washington, D.C.: U.S. Government Printing Office, 1986b.

————. *Technology and Structural Unemployment, Reemploying Displaced Adults*, OTA-ITE-250. Washington, D.C.: U.S. Government Printing Office, February, 1986a.

Olsen, Gregg. *Industrial Change and Labor Adjustment in Sweden and Canada*. Toronto, Garamond Press, 1988.

Organization for Economic and Community Development. "Technology and Jobs." *Science, Technology, Industry Review*. 1, Autumn, 1986b.

Pollack, Andrew. "A Somber Silicon Valley is Changed Forever." *New York Times.* October 5, 1986.

President's Commission on Industrial Competitiveness. *Global Competition, the New Reality.* Vol. I and II, Washington, D.C.: January, 1985.

Reich, Robert. *The Next American Frontier.* New York: Penguin, 1984.

Rexed, Knut. *The Swedish Trade Unions and Labor Market Policies.* Stockholm: Central Organization of Salaried Employees in Sweden, September, 1986.

Rodberg, Leonard S., and William K. Tabb. "What Can We Learn from the Industrial Policy Debate?" *Social Policy.* 17:27–33, Winter, 1987.

Rothstein, Lawrence E. *Plant Closings, Power, Politics, and Workers.* Dover, MA, Auburn House Publishing Co., 1983.

Rothwell, Sheila. "Company Employment Policies and New Technology." *Industrial Relations Journal* 16:43–51, Autumn, 1985.

SAF-LO-PTK. *Agreement on Efficiency and Participation.* Stockholm, 1982.

SAF-PTK. *The SAF-PTK Employment Security Council.* Stockholm, December 1985.

Schmidt, Hermann. "Vocational Retraining and Structural Change in West Germany." In *Economic Dislocation and Job Loss.* Edited by Betty G. Lall. New York, Cornell University Press, 1985.

Spellman, Ruth. "Education and Training Initiative in the United Kingdom and Macro-Economic Policies." In *The Jobs Challenge—Pressures and Possibilities.* Edited by Daniel F. Burton, et al. Cambridge, Massachusetts: Ballinger Publishing Company, 1986.

Standing, Guy. *Unemployment and Labor Market Flexibility, Sweden.* Geneva: ILO, 1988.

State of California. *A Review of the Employment Training Panel Program.* Sacramento: April, 1986a.

———. *Employment Training Panel Annual Report 1985.* Sacramento, ETP, 1986b.

State of Michigan, Governor's Office for Job Training. *Michigan Business and Industrial Program, the Michigan Industrial Deployment Service, Michigan Job Opportunity Bank.* Miscellaneous flyers and brochures, Lansing, 1986.

State of Oregon Economic Development Department. *A Strategy for Oregon's Development.* April, 1989.

———. *Education and Workforce—Strategic Plan for Economic Development.* October, 1988.

SUNY, State Education Department and Bureau of Economic Development Coordination. *SED Firm-Specific Training Program, Rational Education Centers for Economic Development, New York Training and Assistance Programs.* Miscellaneous flyers and brochures, Albany, 1986.

Swedish Institute. *Swedish Labor Market Policy.* Stockholm, April, 1985.

Swedish Labor Market Board. *Annual Report 1985–86.* Stockholm: AMS, 1986.

———. *Flexibility in Production, Security for Individuals.* Stockholm: National Labor Market Board, 1988.

———. *Labor Market Training.* Stockholm: AMS, 1985.

Swedish National Labour Market Board. *Terminals in Placement Work.* Stockholm, AMS, 1984.

Swedish Work Environment Fund. *The Development Programme.* Stockholm, ASF, 1986.

Trades Union Congress. *Employment and Technology.* London: TUC, 1979.

U.S Department of Labor. *Economic Adjustment and Worker Dislocation in a Competitive Society.* Report of the Secretary of Labor's Task Force on Economic Adjustment and Worker Dislocation, USDL, 1986.

———. *Women and Office Automation, Issues for the Decade Ahead.* Washington, D.C.: DOL, Women's Bureau, 1985.

Walsh, Joan. "ETP, Saving Jobs and Money—But Whose?" In *These Times,* May 21, 1986.

Washington State. *Washington State Job Skills Program, Annual Report.* Miscellaneous brochures and flyers, Olympia, 1986.

Williams, Robin, and Fred Steward. "Technology Agreements in Great Britain, a Survey 1977–83." *Industrial Relations Journal* 16:58–73, Autumn, 1984.

Young, Arthur. *Study of the California Employment Panel.* Los Angeles, California: Arthur Young and Company, 1985.

Flexibility, Job Security and Labor Market Policy

MARYANTONETT FLUMIAN

Executive Director and Chief Executive Officer, Canadian Labor Market and Productivity Centre

INTRODUCTION

The issues in labor market training and adjustment are broadly similar in both Canada and the U.S. In economic terms, we must deal with the need for our economies to be productive and competitive. As capital becomes more global, our jobs depend on it. In demographic terms, we need to deal with the fact that our work force is aging and that new entrants are an increasingly smaller part of the labor force. We will face skills shortages in many industries, and more and more the only place to get skilled workers is among those already working. In technological terms, we need to face the absorption of new electronic technologies, and the replacement in many cases of mass-production models of production with continuous-process production, which requires workers to have different skills and often broader skills.

Each of these changes presents a challenge for our institutions. In the field of technological change, for instance, the spread of new technology depends on a broadly educated and skilled population. New technologies and new procedures can spread most easily when there are fewer skills bottlenecks and people have the tools to allow them to adapt. Providing this kind of generic, transferable education as the foundation for more specific training makes sense for everybody.

What is required are broad and unspecific skills; not just "functional" skills dedicated to a specific purpose, but skills as a generalized, polyvalent resource that can be put to many different and, most importantly, as yet unknown future uses.

The problem is that this kind of broad educational background is not the way we have traditionally gone about educating or training individuals. And we have many people, especially older workers, whose levels of literacy are too low to allow them to continue learning, on the job or elsewhere.

Fortunately, as indicated in studies by the Canadian Auto Workers on technological change in the automotive and aerospace industries and by the work of the Sectoral Skills Council in the electronic and electrical industry, firms in Canada are beginning to come to grips with this orientation. Part of the work of the Canadian Labor Market and Productivity Centre (CLMPC) has been in fostering this discussion, and in dealing with the institutional changes that are required if training and educational practices and institutions are to be reoriented to take full advantage of the wider possibilities involved, for both workers and employers.

The CLMPC, established six years ago, is the only national institution to facilitate consultation between business and labor on national issues of broad social and economic concern, thereby offering a framework for labor market partners to act as agents of change in the Canadian economy. The critical leadership for the center's establishment was provided by business and labor. Shirley Carr, president of the Canadian Labor Congress and Thomas Savage, president of ITT Canada Limited, act as the cochairs of this bipartite structure. It is the mandate of the CLMPC to undertake activities designed to improve Canada's labor market and to enhance joint efforts between business and labor toward improving productivity.

The major theme of the work of the center is that the direct involvement of all those involved in the labor market is essential if we are to improve our ability to manage change. The proposition that the labor market partners should "work together" is often articulated, but rarely translated into a key principle of public policy, although it is commonplace in many other OECD countries.

LABOR FORCE DEVELOPMENT STRATEGY

In 1989, the minister of employment introduced the Labor Force Development Strategy to deal with training as a response to the adjustment problems faced by the Canadian economy. The minister asked the CLMPC to conduct a series of consultations with business and labor, as well as other key groups in the Canadian society, on the nature and the extent of changes needed for the development and administration of suitable labor market policies in Canada.

Seven task forces representing business, labor, and community and social development groups and educators were established. Sixty-four distinguished Canadians gave fully of their time and effort over a period of six months. They were drawn from all regions of the country and reflected the industrial composition of our economy. The task forces dealt with the broad training issues involved in:

- programs for older workers;
- programs for unemployment insurance beneficiaries;
- programs for social assistance recipients;
- apprenticeship;
- co-operative education;
- entry level training, and;
- approaches to human resource planning.

To put these deliberations in their proper context, what is at issue is not only offering details on policies and programs, but also the minister dedicated $800 million for the project. This sum is in addition to the $1.7 billion currently being spent by the federal government on labor market programs. From her standpoint, she hopes this exercise will lead employers, large and small, to double their training efforts over the next half decade.

In Canada, labor markets are a shared jurisdiction, further complicating efforts at reform. The task forces undertook to review the direction of all labor market policies in Canada and in effect addressed the expenditure of all public funds in this area. This represents sizeable expenditure. In addition to the funds mentioned above, the unemployment insurance fund in Canada that is supported by contributions from employers and employees totals $12 billion a year. In addition, we spent $44 billion a year on our education systems. By OECD standards, no one doubts our commitment when measured in terms of dollars; what is in question is whether we are getting enough "bang for our buck."

The Labor Force Development Strategy is a federal initiative, but the task forces did not limit their comments only to federal government policies. Their deliberations led them to consider many factors that affect labor markets in Canada, and for the most part their conclusions address both provincial and federal efforts.

The period of consultation was quite intense. After six to seven meetings, the task forces were ready to submit the results of their work to a wider audience of interested parties at symposia held in different regional centers across the country. Over six hundred people representing a broad array of labor market interests were invited to hear each task force present the results of its work and to evaluate those results in terms of their own experience. Then, task force members went back to the table to revise their work in light of what they heard. The final reports were presented to the federal government in the spring of 1990.

TASK FORCE RECOMMENDATIONS

The task forces based their work on a few fundamental principles. One of these is a belief that training and education is the best means to promote equitable and efficient adjustment in the economy not only for today, but it is also the best way of equipping individuals and the businesses that employ them for the future. This principle is echoed in the De Grandpre Report (Advisory Council on Adjustment, 1989) and also in the final report of the center's own business/labor Task Force on Adjustment, "Working Together to Manage Change."(CLMPC, 1989) Training and education, of course, are not a substitute for economic management and job creation; however, they are a foundation on which economic management is built, since they affect the choices that can be made and the tradeoffs that are possible.

Another principle stems from the conviction that in the past we have relied on passive policy instruments and have turned to education and training only when an individual has been unemployed for a long period of time and has become marginal to the work force. The time has come to take a more active approach that has as its purpose early identification of those most at risk of long-term unemployment and implementation of preventative measures.

Finally, a third principle that was fundamental to all the work done by the task forces was that skills acquired through training that is paid for by public funds should be broad and generic, and that skill certification should be fully transferrable between provinces, and between industries.

Each task force worked independently, and arrived at separate recommendations. However, there were a number of common themes in their work. It is not surprising that all members are of the conviction that there is a need to promote lifelong learning. Although it has been said many times in Canada, it seems to bear repeating. As technology changes, individuals are often required to learn new skills or to upgrade and update existing skills. The increasing pace of technological change means that today's workers may have to be trained for many careers over the course of their working lives. In this context, the importance of lifelong education and training cannot be overstated. Education and training must no longer be perceived as a prerequisite for work, but rather as an integral part of the work process itself. Since Canada and the U.S. have less experience with workplace training than other countries, turning the workplace into a center of learning will require changes in attitudes and changes in some of our institutions.

We are just beginning to realize that a nation's most important competitive asset is the education and skills of its work force. Every factor of production other than work force education and skills can be duplicated anywhere around the world. Capital moves so freely across international borders that the cost of capital in different countries is rapidly converging. The latest technologies flow from one computer to another via satellites. State-of-the-art factories can be erected anywhere. Capital, technology, raw materials, and information are all transferable; the one element that is unique about a nation is its work force.

A second theme identified by all task forces is that more private-sector input is needed for effective labor market programming. Both business and labor have considerable stake in the outcome of any labor market policies and programs. Their role in developing labor market policies has in the past been limited, with governments playing the lead role. Business and labor together now feel they are very well positioned to assist in determining the needs of the labor market and collectively developing the policies and programs that will meet those needs. Their input should be expanded while at the same time the role of educational institutions, as the mechanism that effectively delivers the training, should be made more responsive to the private sector and better integrated with the needs of employers and individuals.

A focus on local needs also emerged as a central theme of the task forces' consultations. Task force members believe that there is a critical need for institutional mechanisms that have a high degree of flexibility in responding to local labor markets and to individual needs. They were acutely aware that there is not only one labor market in Canada, there are many. And the needs of a small community in northern British Columbia are very different from a large urban center like Toronto.

Until we recognize that decisions about the appropriate mix and delivery of training and adjustment programs are best made at the local level with the involvement of all the labor market partners—business, labor, community groups, and educators alike—real reform will not be possible. It is at the local level where individuals and institutions most directly share a sense of community and can best shape a common purpose. It is where young people and adults learn the skills they need for working life, and it is where educational institutions can have a significant impact through expanded continuing education activities.

Therefore, task forces recommended that federal and provincial governments commit themselves to reforming the decision-making process for the delivery of labor market programs by devolving the authority to the local labor market level, and to reform it with the active involvement of all the labor market partners. This applies whether we are talking about publicly funded training programs for social assistance recipients or updating and upgrading education for the existing work force.

This is after all how many of our most successful competitors conduct their affairs. The models may vary whether we are speaking about Germany, Sweden or Japan, but the principle of involvement of all those who have a stake in the outcome of their labor market prevails, both at the national and local level.

Nonetheless, there is no question that a national perspective and national objective criteria must be maintained, especially in the context of responding to competitive pressures that are international. In addition, devolving authority to the labor market partners at the local level is an evolutionary process that builds on existing resources, structures, and personnel.

One final area of task force recommendations concerns issues of access. There are many barriers that prevent individuals from accessing the education and training they need. Sometimes these include program criteria, others are due to a lack of appropriate information, and still others have to do with illiteracy. Income support is also an access issue, and all of the task forces stressed the importance of adequate earnings replacement in education and training.

POLICY IMPLICATIONS

Let me turn now to the outcome of all this. Studies are one thing, but the need is for policies that will be translated into actual programs.

Following the task force consultations, a group of eight individuals, each of whom had served in the original task force exercise, developed a structural framework that would accommodate the various recommendations. Their report includes a recommendation for a National Training Board (CLMPC, 1990).

The CLMPC has been cast in the role of facilitator and secretariat in encouraging the dialogue between business and labor and managing the consultative process over the past few months. But the National Training Board, as it is proposed, will be a separate structure with its own board and mandate. That board will consist of members drawn predominantly from the labor and business communities, with the addition of representatives of the education community as the engine that drives the training and education system in Canada. Since the board will be influencing policy that directs public funds, there will also be representation from each of the designated "target" groups under the Canadian Jobs Strategy, our umbrella federal labor market program, namely women, natives, visible minorities, and the disabled.

One of the first issues that the National Training Board must wrestle with will be finding an acceptable definition of "training." The federal government claims that Canadian businesses spend only half of what American businesses do on training, and one of the clear goals of the Labor Force Development Strategy is to increase the amount of money spent by employers. Some employers, however, claim that the government data are faulty, and that a lot of training goes on that is not documented. At the moment, we have little in the way of our own data to provide a more complete picture. Addressing this issue is a big priority.

Under contract with the federal government, we are in the process of establishing a steering committee for a National Training Survey. Unlike past efforts, the labor market partners will effectively develop the data collection process and will give direction on everything from definitions to methodology.

Information gathering is a necessary first step. The proposed framework outlines a role for the board in monitoring and evaluating the effectiveness of publicly funded training activity, and in gathering and disseminating basic labor market information concerning job vacancies and essential skill supply and demand.

Nationally recognized standards and skill certification that is transferrable across jurisdictions and occupations was an important recommendation in the task force reports. Establishing such standards would also be a critical function for the National Training Board.

Currently, some innovative human resource initiatives are being launched at the sectoral level, particularly in steel, electronics and electrical manufacturing, and in automotive repair and service. The new training board would encourage the establishment of more sectoral initiatives. In addition, the problems of barriers that prevent access to training programs for some groups was a recurrent theme, and task force members see a role for the new board in examining the linkages between income maintenance and training systems in light of these access issues.

Inevitably, a role in allocating funds for training will also evolve. The key word is evolve. We are not talking about recreating bureaucracies currently in place. But we are talking about new relationships and the active input of those labor market partners who have the most to lose or gain in the outcome of any training policies.

And there is a lot at stake. The whole question of workplace literacy is a small example. The Conference Board of Canada estimates this problem costs Canadian businesses $4 billion a year, and it hampers the ability of many workers to get and keep jobs. The results of the recent national literacy survey conducted by Statistics Canada for the Secretary of State are sobering. Approximately 40 percent of adult Canadians do not have sufficient reading abilities to deal with most everyday tasks. Of this group, 22 percent do read; however they do not have sufficient skills to cope with more complex reading situations. As one expert described them, "these people can learn to read, but they cannot read to learn."

Literacy is only one issue; however, it is a good illustration of the competing jurisdictions and fragmented approach to education and training that we have adopted in Canada. We are hopeful that with the proposal to establish a National Training Board will lead to change.

The entire consultative exercise we have undertaken in this last eighteen months suggests that real reform requires institutional change and the active involvement of the workplace partners in labor market policy and program design. Without reform, the question of how to meet these adjustment challenges becomes far more difficult to answer.

The good news is that the consultation exercise and the Phase II recommendations suggest a realistic method of dealing with our adjustment problems. Moreover, as a model for conducting public policy, the lessons we have learned in the past few months will prove useful as we continue to deal with the problems of adjusting to changes in a wide range of areas.

REFERENCES

Advisory Council on Adjustment, Government of Canada. "Adjusting To Win." The report of the Advisory Council on Adjustment, the *De Grandpre Report*, Ottawa, 1989.

Canadian Labor Market and Productivity Center. "A Framework for a National Training Board." The report of the Phase II Committee on the Labor Force Development Strategy, Ottawa, 1990.

Canadian Labor Market and Productivity Centre. "Working Together to Manager Change." The report of the Business/Labor Task Force on Adjustment, Ottawa, 1989.

Canadian Labor Market and Productivity Centre. *Report of the CLMPC Task Forces on the Labor Force Development Strategy.* Ottawa, 1990.

Streeck, Wolfgang. "The Enterprise of the Future." *Work, Employment and Society* 3(1), 1989.

Section 5

LABOR AND GLOBALIZATION DOWN UNDER

The international character of the challenges facing U.S and Canadian labor are well illustrated by the economic and industrial relations patterns in Australia and New Zealand in recent years. Of particular note is the transformation of economic and industrial relations policies that has taken place in both countries under labor governments, a process Ray Harbridge has labeled "a most un-labourlike experience" in the case of New Zealand. The internationalization of investment patterns, by both national firms and foreign corporations, has substantially altered the balance of bargaining power in both countries.

The role of organized labor in the restructuring process in this part of the world is of particular interest to Canadian and U.S. unionists. The Australian Council of Trade Unions (ACTU) shifted course with the 1983 "Accord" with the Australian Labour party. The ACTU asserted a role for labor in management and in wealth creation as well as wealth distribution, including participation in the radical restructuring of industry, training and job classification systems, and the introduction of new technology. Elements of this model have been advocated for Canadian and U.S. unions.

Ted Wheelwright sees in the case of Australia the essence of the globalization of capital and the resultant ascendancy of capital over labor and the state. The post-World War II history of Australia reveals large-scale in-migration of workers and massive investment of foreign capital, primarily from the U.S. at first and, much later, from Japan. While manufacturing peaked in the mid sixties, shifts in trade policy at this time contributed to a rapid rate of deindustrialization. Political events of the 1970s such as a virtual coup d'etat that removed a Labor government from power demonstrated to Wheelwright the power of foreign capital over the Australian state.

The economic problems of the 1970s and 1980s—stagnation of real wages, inflation, unemployment, and increasing inequalities of income and wealth—were accompanied by attacks on trade unions, privatization, and escalating debt. The Labour government that came to power in 1983 reached an agreement with the trade unions, known as the "Accord," a new social contract between labor and the government. (See also Ogden, Chapter 4.) While aspects of the Accord have been successful, continued globalization, deregulation, and income inequality call into question its ultimate benefits for workers. With Australia's continuing integration into the South Asian economic sphere, a combination of building international ties with Asian unions and fashioning coalitions with other citizen organizations within Australia is essential for labor's continued strength.

Ray Harbridge recounts the transformation of the New Zealand economy and industrial relations under the fourth Labour Government, elected in 1984. From 1984 to 1990 New Zealand moved from one of the world's most regulated and protected economies to one of the least. The free market approaches significantly undermined New Zealand's trade unions, and the impact of these economic policies was heightened by major changes to the private and public sector collective-bargaining systems.

Harbridge describes the transition in New Zealand from an arbitration-based, state-controlled model of labor relations established nearly 100 years ago to one described as the "The New Zealand Wagner" model. The implementation of this new model, concurrent with the internationalization of capital investment and the sale of state-owned enterprises, have left unions with little bargaining strength. The transformation of the public sector and its labor relations, under the terms of the State Sector Act of 1988, will be of interest to students of privatization in Canada and the U.S.

The Impact of International Capital on Australian Labor

TED WHEELWRIGHT

Emeritus Associate Professor of Economics; Honorary Associate, Transnational Corporations Research Project, University of Sydney, Australia

Australia has considerable experience of the essence of the globalization of capitalism, which is that it alters the power relationships between labor, capital, and the state. It is much easier for capital to go global than it is for labor, or the nation state. Consequently, globalization strengthens the power of capital and weakens that of labor and the state. The ideology of the free market justifies this change in power relationships; much of what passes for economic theory today is little more than an ideological weapon being used by the forces of capital against labor, and against states, that want to control capital. Hence, the task facing political economists is to demystify economics for the benefit of working people.

Using economic theory, capital argues for a weak state; one that could take us back to the "night-watchman" state of the last century, a "laissez-faire" situation that Charles Dickens described as: "Every man for himself, as the elephant said when he danced among the chickens." In the present climate that has been created, governments that put the interests of labor before those of capital are just about impossible. If they come to power on a labor or semi-socialist platform, they have to change their spots in order to survive, as is true of Australia, New Zealand, France, and Greece.

AUSTRALIA AS A "CLIENT STATE"

Most of the effects of globalization on labor can be seen in the last few decades of Australian history. The major characteristics of globalization in Australia that have affected labor and industrial relations include the following:

- The inflow of people, i.e. the immigration of labor, particularly its quantity and the quality of skills, and the type of culture from which it comes.
- The inflow of capital, especially that which employs much labor and hence is affected by management practices, attitudes to trade unions, and the determination of wages.
- The import of goods that compete with local production and hence affect employment.
- The import of technology that suits global capital, such as communications systems facilitating international financial movements; and flexible manufacturing systems that facilitate smaller plants with fewer workers.
- The import of free market ideology that is antiprotection, antipublic sector, antiwage fixation, antiunion, but procapital, promarginalization, proderegulation, and proinequality of income and wealth.
- Various kinds of export dependence.

In the course of time, the combination of these elements has produced a "client state" of international capital that will do nothing to offend it, and most things to attract it. Hence, globalization affects politics, not only on the level of political alliances and support of dubious military adventures, but also on the level of the political activities of trade unions and their leaders.

Time permits a limited number of examples. Thus, in the early postwar period there was a massive immigration program designed to fill up the country with persons of European origin, as a bulwark against the threat from Asia, particularly Japan, which previously had plans to incorporate Australia into its "Co-Prosperity Sphere in Greater East Asia." Under this plan, Australia was scheduled to take in millions of Indians, Chinese, and Indonesians, to be employed by Japanese capitalists and leaders of industry.

Hence the postwar slogan was "Populate or Perish" and a Labour government persuaded the trade union movement to accept large numbers of semiskilled and unskilled workers from Europe, especially from southeastern Europe—Italy and Greece—on the understanding that they would be employed under traditional Australian wages and conditions. This was largely successful, with a minimum of strife, but what it did in the first instance at least, was to insert a large unskilled component at the base of the work force, which tended to push Australian-born workers into more lucrative white collar types of employment that were less unionized. Also there were few representatives of the new migrants in the trade union leadership position, partly, but not only, because of the language problem. Initially, therefore, immigration reduced union militancy.

This population explosion, created for political reasons, needed many more employment opportunities, and hence capital to create those opportunities. Given the shortage of domestic capital, the doors were thrown open to foreign capital. Britain had very little, so the U.S. filled the breach. Consequently in the 1950s and 1960s U.S. investment came to dominate manufacturing and mining. However, U.S. capital was not happy with Australian industrial relations and wage-fixing practices, and so there was a strong trend toward collective bargaining at the corporate level, as distinct from the previous wage fixation at the industry and national level, on the British model, modified by arbitration.

Most of the manufacturing investment was aimed at the local market, which was protected by quota or tariff. Thus, there was less concern about wage levels, particularly as workers needed adequate purchasing power to buy the product. Indeed it was suggested that there was some kind of "alliance" between manufacturers and unions on this point, at the expense of exporters, mainly farmers and mining companies. In those years full employment was achieved, and governments were threatened whenever unemployment exceeded 2½ percent.

However, by the mid-1960s, the domestic market was saturated and population growth was slowing. Much of manufacturing industry was dominated by multinationals, mainly British and American. For most of them there was no desire to export; this could be done more profitably from subsidiaries in cheap labor countries. The removal of quotas and the reduction of tariffs in the 1960s and 1970s facilitated imports from these countries and others. Consequently, the mid-1960s marks the apogee of Australian industrialization, as measured by the proportion of the work force in manufacturing industry—28 percent. By the mid-1980s this was down to 17 percent, about the same as India, and less than most southeast Asian countries. Hence Australia has suffered one of the highest levels of deindustrialization in the world, in the era of globalization. Most of the employment created since then has been in the service sector, usually at lower levels of pay, much of it taken up by women, especially in tourism.

It was during those decades of the 1960s and 1970s that Australia reached the dubious distinction of being the most highly penetrated country by foreign capital of all OECD countries, except Canada. This now applied across all key sectors—manufacturing, mining, and finance. It is not surprising therefore, that this high level of globalization affected politics. America was outstripping Britain as the dominant foreign investor when the Labour party won the 1972 election. Strongly based on trade unions, it was pledged to remove Australian troops from Vietnam, tighten controls on foreign investment, control the marketing of minerals through a state agency, and suspend the export of uranium.

Three years later that Labour government was removed from office by what amounts to a *coup d'etat*, manipulated by a loose coalition of the opposition, foreign capital and local capital, our security services and the American CIA. This, I think, proved the "client state" thesis: when a critical mass of foreign investment is reached, the state in that country *has* to be a client of foreign capital. The state is no longer the executive committee of the national bourgeoisie but of the international bourgeoisie; or certainly the dominant fractions of global capital (Crough and Wheelwright, 1982).

It should also be emphasized that globalization affects the politics of trade union governance. The dominant fractions of capital seek out potential trade union leaders, who can be molded into minimal hostility to the interest of capital. They are offered overseas trips and suitable training courses, often at prestigious universities, as well as connections with local "safe" trade union leaders. The American labor attache in Australia was believed to be a past master of the part of picking and supporting future labor leaders who might also become influential politicians.

This globalization effect of politics, political parties, and trade unions should *not* be underestimated; where it operates successfully, as in France, Greece, the U.K., New Zealand, and Australia, governments initially hostile to world capitalism can be emasculated. Equally powerful is the "international demonstration effect" of how to deal with unions, roll back the welfare state, and privatize the public sector, in the strongholds of capitalism such as the U.S., the UK, and Japan. There is always plenty of advice available from multinational companies or consultants with plenty of experience in union bashing or privatizing the public sector; always of course, for a substantial fee. Australian is awash with them at the moment.

Irrespective of whatever government has been in power, over the last fifteen years Australia has seen: an acceleration of globalization, the stagnation of real wages, a substantial shift in the share of national income going to capital, a significant increase in unemployment, high rates of inflation, and increasing inequalities of income and wealth. The last few years have brought, in addition, attacks on trade unions by capital *and* the state, contraction of the public sector, the beginnings of privatization, and a rapidly escalating foreign debt.

The unionization of the Australian work force has fallen from 59 percent in 1954 to 40 percent last year. Nine out of ten new jobs are in the private sector, but unionization is down to 32 percent there. The rate of unionization is low among the young, and among female workers. It is also low in the fastest growing industries of clerical work, wholesaling and retailing, finance, property, and business services. Not all of this, of course, is due to globalization, but some of it is, including the decline of manufacturing, the rise of the finance sector, and tourism.

LABOR UNDER THE "ACCORD"

In 1983 the present Labour government came to power largely as a result of the 1982 recession, when unemployment reached a post war high of over 10 percent. To cope with this, the Labour government worked out a deal with the unions, by which they would accept wage restraint and the consequent shift in national income from wages to profits, on the understanding that these increased profits would be *invested in the country*, thus creating more employment.

This was known as the the "Accord"—a kind of agreement of social contract between the unions and the government involving a form of managed collective bargaining. It *was* in the Labour party platform, and it worked reasonably well for a while. But what was *not* in the party platform was the virtual total deregulation of the financial system, beginning after less than twelve months in office (Stilwell, 1986).

This resulted in the negation of a vital part of the "Accord;" there was much less investment in the country than expected—especially in industry—and a lot of it went out of the country, mainly to Britain and North America. Deregulation also meant a large increase in speculation in foreign exchange, the stock market, and the property market (all nonunionized areas). There was tremendous foreign borrowing for this, and for takeovers, mergers, and shonky deals.

There was also a flood of foreign investment into real estate, especially for tourism. The foreign debt quadrupled. In the middle of this bonanza for the upper classes, workers were expected to exercise wage restraint, give up their traditional work practices, and be restructured in the name of economic efficiency and survival.

Trade unions that attempted to break out of the approved level of wage increases, such as the pilots' unions, were destroyed by a combination of forces including the official trade union hierarchy, the government, and public and private corporations.

Some restructuring has occurred, but it is by no means clear that this has benefited labor. So far it has not rebelled, but there is much disaffection in the rank and file, and a falling off in support for the Labour government, which will face great difficulty in being reelected.

The central point is that all can now see there is no equality of sacrifice—the rich are getting richer, the poor are not improving much, and there are more of them. Most workers are like the Red Queen in *Alice in Wonderland*, having to run as fast as they can to stay in the same place (Wheelwright, 1990). Many people can see little difference between so-called Labour policies and those proffered by the Conservatives.

THE IMPACT OF ASIAN CAPITAL

The most recent factor in the globalization of the Australian economy and society has been the rise to prominence of a new foreign investor, Japan. I have just coauthored with a trade unionist a book that attempts to assess what changes this is bringing to Australian labor and trade unions. Our conclusion is that the nature of the dominant investing country *does* make a difference to the impact of globalization (David and Wheelwright, 1989).

By 1989, Japan was the third largest investor, after the U.K. and the U.S.; but in the previous six years, Japan had supplied more investment than the U.S. and almost as much as the U.K. If this trend continues, Japan will soon be the dominant foreign investor in Australia. We decided that it is different in several respects. For example, the Japanese economy is a much more integrated and disciplined system than either the U.S. or the U.K., with stronger linkages to state power. It does not have a long tradition of free trade unions, which were suppressed in the prewar Fascist era, emerged in the late 1940s, only to have the militant ones smashed after 1949, leaving mostly "tame cat" unions almost integrated into the corporate culture. Consequently the hours of work are longer than most western countries, and living conditions are much more cramped. Real wages have increased, but at a lower rate than profits or capital accumulation.

The term "hegemonic integration" has been applied to certain aspects of Japanese foreign investment, to indicate the tendency to control more stages of production. Thus, Japan is importing more beef from Australia but to do so it first buys the cattle stations or ranches in Australia, then the feed lots, then the abattoirs and the meatworks, finally sending the beef to Japan in refrigerated ships owned by Japanese companies. Another example is tourism, which begins by buying up real estate and hotels, goes on to buy up souvenir production, retail shops, locally conducted tours, and finally flies the tourists back to Japan in a Japanese airline. These practices ensure that not much of the value-added in these industries remains in Australia.

In terms of management practices, two things stand out. One is the "management-by-stress" technique, which takes away any remaining control of the work process by unions; the other is the unwillingness to appoint local managers to key positions.

Japan, of course, is not the only Asian investor, but it is by far the biggest. Even so, there is considerable investment from, and trade with, those apt pupils and former colonies of Japan, South Korea, and Taiwan.

149

Similarly, there is considerable investment from southeast Asian Chinese in places like Hong Kong and Malaysia, where they are uncertain of their future. This investment is often accompanied by immigration of Chinese businessmen seeking sanctuary for themselves and their property. This reverses the image of poor and uneducated Asian migrants to Australia.

This is why we have subtitled out book *Australia and Asian Capitalism*, because increasingly globalization means some form of integration with Asian capitalism. So, we face not only the problems of an incipient common market with countries of a not too different culture, as in the case of the European Common Market, or a North-American common market, but problems of some form of integration with a quite different culture of Asia.

Consequently, for Australasia—which literally means South Asia—globalization will mean eventually some form of "Asianization." The sheer force of numbers will dictate this, as Australia and New Zealand have only twenty million people between them, a few hours flying time from the population of half the world. The only relevant comparison for North America is of course, the "Latin Americanization" of the continent, but the discrepancy in numbers and economic power is not nearly so great.

THE COMMON CAUSE OF INTERNATIONAL LABOR

Significant linkages are already being made at the top, at government level, but very little at the level of workers, trade unions, and the common people. In our book we argue strongly for the reversal of this situation, and the need for Australian labor to make common cause with Asian labor. Some unions are beginning to do this, but much, much more needs to be done.

The language barrier has to be overcome to begin with, and this means that unions must train interpreters so that they can converse with Asian counterparts, and read their literature. There has to be much more understanding of each other's cultures and much more knowledge of the way big business operates, especially the multinationals with branches and subsidiaries in Asian countries.

Clearly, what is on the agenda for the rest of this century and well into the next is the development of the existing common market in Europe, and the creation of other regional markets in North America, possibly South America, and certainly in Asia. European trade unions are showing the way forward by their emphasis on the *social dimensions* of the market, i.e., that there are social costs in the extension of the market that should *not* be borne exclusively by labor.

The latest European TUC economic policy paper argues that the European trade union movement must strengthen its capacity for action at all levels. There are now fifteen industry committees concerned to ensure that the favorable terms and conditions in the developed countries are not undermined by lower wage levels in the less-developed nations. There are also links developing between unions in branches of European multinationals for collective bargaining purposes, such as those in the computer company, Bull, and the BSN food conglomerate, to monitor pay and working hours. There is a fear that a half million jobs might be lost as industries restructure, firms merge, and plants close as business adjusts to more competitive conditions. Governments are being pressured into improving social provisions for the economic and industrial casualties that may ensue (The *Guardian*, 1990). This task is difficult enough in Europe in parts of which there is a long tradition of versions of the welfare state, beginning with Bismarck's Germany, but it will be much more difficult in Asia, where there is no such tradition.

The international trade union movement is well aware of the issues, as is indicated by the ICFTU conference in March this year in Denmark, on "The Challenge of Internationalization" (ICFTU, 1990). It is emphasized that international solidarity, while important, should *not* be a substitute for national action; that priority should be placed by all unions on the organization of women, because of the growing proportion of women workers, especially in the service sectors; and that the trade union movement that is declining in many countries must be strengthened by alliances with other citizen's organizations, such as environmentalists, consumers, and antiracist groups.

These tendencies are in their infancy in Australia, and international links with Asia are very weak. Well over a hundred years ago Karl Marx told the workers of the world to unite; unfortunately they have not taken his advice, but the capitalists have, with the consequence we have to live with today, and which our children will suffer tomorrow, if nothing is done. There is a danger that a new form of international fascism could come out of this global "managerial demiurge" to use C. Wright Mill's felicitous and prescient phrase (Mills, 1951). Eventually there may well be more fascists in three-piece suits than in military uniforms.

REFERENCES

Crough, Greg, and Ted Wheelwright. *Australia: A Client State.* Melbourne: Penguin, 1982.

David, Abe, and Ted Wheelwright. *The Third Wave: Australia and Asian Capitalism.* Sydney: Left Book Club, 1989.

ICFTU. *The Challenge of Internationalisation.* Background document for Conference on Trade Unions and the Transnationals. Elsinore, Denmark: March, 1990.

Mills, C. Wright. *White Collar.* New York: Oxford University Press, 1951.

Stilwell, Frank. *The Accord and Beyond.* Sydney: Pluto Press, 1986.

The Guardian. London: August 31, 1990.

Wheelwright, Ted. "Are the Rich Getting Richer and the Poor Poorer? If So, Why?" In *Questions for the Nineties.* Edited by Anne Gollan. Sydney: Left Book Club, 1990.

A Most Un-labourlike Experience— Six Years of a Labour Government in New Zealand and Its Impact on Organized Labor

RAYMOND HARBRIDGE

Senior Lecturer, Industrial Relations Centre, Victoria University of Wellington, New Zealand

INTRODUCTION

In July 1984, the New Zealand Labour Party was elected with a handsome majority to government for just the fourth time ever. Three years later, it had enacted the most "un-labourlike" policies imaginable, yet it was reelected in 1987 to govern for a further term with an increased majority in Parliament. Support for Labour since then however has crashed with opinion polls predicting that in the general election planned for October 27, 1990, the Labour government will be unceremoniously dumped from office and that the Labour party could be represented in Parliament by as few as eight of the ninety-six elected representatives.[1] The irony of the unpopularity of the Labour government is that the Government that would replace it, a National government, promises more of the same policies that have led to voter dissatisfaction with Labour; the National government however, undertakes to implement its economic program more efficiently than Labour has! Little real policy differences are seen between the two parties. As would be expected in these circumstances, voter disillusionment is high with nearly one-third of eligible voters stating that they do not intend to vote or that (just eight weeks before the election) they are uncertain who they will vote for. The situation is summed up by a slogan currently going around New Zealand's trade union movement—"Don't think—just vote Labour." Just seven weeks before the election, on September 4, 1990, the Prime Minister, Geoffrey Palmer, resigned and has been replaced by Mike Moore—a man seen as a traditional Labour politician, and one likely to return to traditional Labourlike policies.

The experience of a Labour government with un-labourlike policies has been an extraordinary experience for many New Zealanders, particularly those in the labor movement, but many of the changes implemented over the last six years are irreversible, and a late change of leadership is seen as unlikely to restore Labour's fortunes. This paper analyses the major economic and labor relations reforms implemented by Labour since 1984; examines the outcomes of those changed policies for the labor movement, and concludes by examining the changing framework of New Zealand's labor relations system.

THE ECONOMIC APPROACH OF THE FOURTH LABOUR GOVERNMENT

The economy that Labour inherited in 1984 was the legacy of many decades of economic intervention and protectionism. New Zealand had one of the world's most regulated economies. A very broad range of industries was protected by subsidies and tariffs, with these being paid for by high taxes and by high consumer prices. But the legacy of these policies, and of poor economic performance over the preceding two decades was a net national debt that amounted to 41 percent of GDP in 1984–85.[2] Moves by the international finance community, particularly related to New Zealand's credit rating and interest charges on further loans, meant that the crisis of this unsustainable debt had to be faced by the incoming Labour government.

Labour resolved to wipe the national debt and set about deregulating the economy and disestablishing subsidy and tariff protection for industry so that now in 1990 New Zealand stands as one of the least-regulated economies in the world. The New Zealand dollar floats freely on international currency markets (one of the few currencies in the world to do so); personal and company taxation peaks at thirty-three cents in the dollar; a raft of specific taxes have been replaced by a consumption tax on all goods and services (GST); tax incentives that had subsidized exporters and regional investment have been abolished; state trading departments have been corporatized and, despite assurances given at the time that corporatization was not a first step to privatization, a number of these enterprises have since been sold to (foreign) interests. The changes implemented are well documented by Easton (1989), Boston and Holland (1987), Roberts (1987), Walker (1989), Bollard and Buckle (1987), and Jesson (1989).

For many New Zealanders the changes implemented came as a surprise. The economic liberalization and general deregulation of all aspects of the New Zealand economy were not at all apparent in Labour's election manifesto(s) (Hubbard, 1990). Labour had developed two distinct strategies for handling the poor performance of the New Zealand economy in the decade prior to its election (Oliver, 1989). The first strategy was the "restructuring option," involving market liberalization and the removal of market protections. The second strategy, the "corporatist strategy," required significant government intervention in selecting and funding industries to be developed; a strategy that the Opposition Finance Spokesperson Roger Douglas had named "picking winners." The two strategies were in conflict but the Labour party's 1984 manifesto "patched up" these differences (Easton, 1989, p. 8). Once elected however, the latter strategy was quickly dropped as Douglas by then believed that the government would be a poor judge of "form" and had no role in "picking winners" (Douglas, 1989). An economist, Geoff Swier, who worked with Roger Douglas while in opposition in 1981, says Douglas came into government in July 1984 with a "very comprehensive plan that as it unfolded over the next four years changed just about every part of the economy and certainly every part of the government sector" (The *Evening Post*, 1990). The free market approaches adopted were planned, and at the outset, accepted willingly by the New Zealand public. Their impact on labor relations was to be very significant and was to irrevocably destroy the base of trade unionism and the position of organized labor in New Zealand. Critical though these economic changes were to the bargaining position of unions, changes to the labor relations systems were enacted that further empowered employers at the expense of unions.

PRIVATE SECTOR COLLECTIVE BARGAINING BEFORE LABOUR

New Zealand's private sector industrial relations wage-bargaining system in the period from the 1960s until the arrival of the fourth Labour government in 1984 had evolved around a number of principles. The first group of principles dealt with the issue of union organization: unions had monopoly coverage; there had been a mix of occupational and industrial unions; and there was a proliferation of small unions. Union membership was, for all intents and purposes, compulsory throughout this period, except for eighteen months from February 1984 when the National government enacted legislation to make unionism voluntary. Second, the wage bargaining process was undertaken through a system of compulsory conciliation that also had a compulsory outcome—and generally the settlement contained a "blanket clause" provision binding other, unspecified parties to the award. Third, where conciliation failed there was a system of compulsory arbitration with no criteria to guide the arbitrator(s). Fourth, awards were minimum rate documents and, in some industries, an extensive second tier of over-award bargaining took place.[3] Fifth, the outcomes of bargaining (awards and registered second-tier settlements, etc.) were enforced by the state. Finally, a minimum wage rate was legislated through the Minimum Wage Act.

When combined, these principles led to two major effects. First, the New Zealand trade union movement, was (and is) a litigious rather than a militant movement with union officials and members relying on the law rather than collective action to provide bargaining outcomes. Legislated compulsory union membership has led to a high penetration of unionism with over 60 percent of the work force being unionized. While that high penetration has provided good income for union organization, it has provided little in the way of membership cohesion. Second, the combination of compulsory unionism and compulsory arbitration led to a highly regulated system of wage bargaining where unions and employers negotiated craft or occupationally based national awards across industries and used a raft of informal relativities to secure wage increases year by year. Where no award was negotiated the minimum wage applied. There was considerable and widespread dissatisfaction with this system, and the former National government moved to review the methods of wage fixing during the last two years of its term. Much of that dissatisfaction was with occupationally based bargaining, and for some time there had been growing pressure for the development of industrial bargaining to replace it. Long before he became Minister of Finance in the fourth Labour government, Roger Douglas (1980) espoused clear views promoting industrial bargaining and, earlier than that, the New Zealand Employers Federation (1978, p. 18) had argued for the "amalgamation of awards and employers into industry groups." Associated with the thrust toward industry bargaining was a belief that such a move would introduce greater wage flexibility—or at least a more diverse range of settlements in any given wage round. The alleged lack of flexibility in settlements and the failure of those settlements to provide adequate minimum standards had been of concern to many key union and employer protagonists (e.g. Douglas, 1983; Bradford, 1983), and of course by the mid-1980s the OECD (1986) had become very interested in greater flexibility in collective bargaining outcomes.

LEGISLATIVE CHANGES TO PRIVATE SECTOR LABOUR RELATIONS: DECEMBER 1984

Shortly after its election in 1984, the Labour government hosted an "economic summit" at which it unveiled a wage-fixing reform package, parts of which had been developed in a tripartite forum over the previous two years. In the single most radical change to labor relations seen this century, the government made arbitration of unsettled interest disputes voluntary rather than compulsory—the process of conciliation remained compulsory but if the parties were not able to agree in conciliation to a settlement, then both parties had to agree to the dispute being referred to an arbitrator before that referral could take place. The removal of compulsory arbitration had not been agreed to in the long-term tripartite forum but, in return for a restoration of compulsory unionism, was accepted by the unions after Labour was elected. Compulsory arbitration had not in fact been widely used in the past two decades but the threat of its use had been. It was argued that this had held together the system of rigid relativities that had forced the New Zealand wage-bargaining system into a straightjacket.

The removal of compulsory arbitration was the first significant move to deregulate the labor market and allow greater flexibility for those employers keen enough to pursue it. This change allowed the possibility of an award lapsing should the parties not be able to agree on a settlement. It ensured that traditional relativities between awards could be broken where employers refused to have the matter referred to a Labour Court. Further, where arbitration was voluntarily selected by the parties, the court was given five market-led criteria to guide it in its arbitrating. These changes shifted the power in award negotiations very strongly in the employers' favor, yet it was a change confirmed by the National Executive of the New Zealand Federation of Labour, all of whom had been invited to attend the economic summit. Around the same time, the Government increased the minimum wage from $2.14 per hour to $2.50 per hour. Later, in 1985, this rate was increased further to $4.25 per hour—a very large increase in percentage terms and one that affected many award rates. The minimum wage has been adjusted from time to time since then and as of September 17, 1990, has been increased to $6.25 per hour. Radical though these changes were, there was limited opportunity for them to have any impact, as within eighteen months the government had issued a green paper reviewing labor relations in New Zealand. In due course, the government released a white paper (Department of Labour, 1986) summarizing its intentions, which were eventually formalized in the Labour Relations Act 1987.

Wage Bargaining and the Labour Relations Act

The Labour Relations Act retains the changes implemented in 1984, particularly voluntary arbitration and market-led criteria for that arbitration. The single most important new feature of the act is that it allows for just a single set of bargaining to take place for any group of workers. The act effectively outlaws second-tier bargaining, forcing unions to decide whether each group of workers should be covered by an award (with its all-important blanket coverage provisions) or an agreement (a single union, single employer settlement). Once a union decides that an employer should be party to an agreement and thus be exempted from the award, then in the future that employer's consent is required before they can come back under the award. For those unions that had been prolific users of second-tier bargaining, this presented a major difficulty.

Unions are encouraged to undertake composite (multiunion, generally single employer) bargaining arrangements under the act. Should a union decide to discontinue a composite agreement then, in contrast to the procedure with agreements, employer consent is not required to return to the relevant award coverage. There are some restrictions on composite bargaining, the main one being that 50 percent of site unions (or a minimum of five) must take part. The old problem of one or two unions standing outside the composite bargaining arrangement and then bargaining separately with the employer is not addressed.

To encourage unions to develop better structures the government legislated that unions must be bigger, stipulating that they must have a minimum of 1,000 members to retain their registration. This meant some critical reorganization for the 117 unions (just about 50 percent of all unions) that at March 31, 1987, had fewer than 1,000 members. The "bigger is better" argument for unionism is not new in New Zealand politics, for the current leader of the opposition, Jim Bolger (1982), discussed the pros and cons of such a move when he was Minister of Labour. Later in the decade, in direct contravention of International Labour Organization Convention 87, (Freedom of Association) and under a Labour administration, the "bigger is better" argument won the day.

These were the major changes implemented but not the only ones. Others include: allowing the parties develop the scope of bargaining by removing the "industrial matters" definition in the old legislation; removing the restriction that the terms of settlements be twelve months; legalizing the right to strike over interest disputes; removing state subsidies for the parties attending conciliation; providing new administrative structures with an Arbitration Commission handling the registration of wage-bargaining arrangements and a Labour Court dealing with interpretation and other matters; allowing a very limited form of competition between unions for members but allowing only one union to have coverage of any one group of workers; and withdrawing a system of Labour Department award inspections and leaving enforcement of registered settlements to the parties.

In terms of structural change to the system, the critical changes were those implemented in 1984, particularly the removal of compulsory arbitration. The changes implemented in 1987 were designed largely to encourage unions toward industry bargaining, with the removal of second-tier bargaining forcing some unions to consider moving to industry agreements rather than occupationally based awards.

LABOR RELATIONS IN THE STATE SECTOR

Personnel procedures and procedures for the negotiating conditions of employment in the state sector were governed by specific pieces of legislation. Particular branches of the state services outside the general public service, such as health and education, had separate legislation, but these closely resembled the public service legislation. Personnel matters were centralized under the authority of the State Services Commission. The public service operated as a unified nonpolitical career service with uniform employment conditions across departments. Appointments were made on the basis of merit with appeal procedures available for a public servant passed over for promotion in favor of the appointment of someone from outside the service. This ensured an internal labor market operated within the public service. Conditions of employment were set nationally on the basis of fair relativity with conditions applying in the private sector (Randle, 1985; Walsh, 1988a). They were renegotiated by applying a percentage-based, annual general adjustment to all wages. Adjustments to compensate for service and seniority were available, often automatically. Separate negotiations could take place for specific occupational groups within the state services but few of these were undertaken within any one wage round. In addition, nonremuneration matters were block-negotiated, covering most if not all occupational groups. As in the private sector, compulsory arbitration was available as a final dispute resolution mechanism, but in practice, it was only ever used for occupational class pay claims.[4]

Reforming State Bargaining Processes: Corporatization and the State Sector Act 1988

By 1986 the Labour government had come to the view that the economic market-led changes that had been implemented elsewhere in the New Zealand economy should be applied to the state as well. The government was a significant employer of labor with over 20 percent of the work force being employed either directly or indirectly by the state. Labour decided to deregulate the state and expose the government's own operation to the influences of the market. A government review of state pay-fixing (Minister of State Services, 1986) found that the nonmarket character of the services provided by the state pay-fixing system and the consequent absence of competition as an accountability mechanism were key features of the system that should be reformed. Specific criticisms were aimed at the automatic annual general adjustment that had created an impression of state pay leadership, and at the payment of national rates throughout the state sector that created regional and occupational labor market distortions. Running through the government's analysis was the ideology that the existing system was cumbersome, inefficient, and incompatible with the government's wider economic policies of deregulation.

The government's deregulatory program in the state commenced in earnest with the implementation of the State-Owned Enterprises (SOE) Act 1986 that established nine new state trading enterprises and brought six existing state trading corporations under its jurisdiction. The legislation required the corporations to abandon the principles that had previously governed their operation. The act stipulated that their principal objective was to be a successful business and to that end to be "as profitable and efficient as comparable businesses that are not owned by the Crown." The act also required each corporation to be a "good employer" and to be "an organization that exhibits a sense of social responsibility by having regard to the interests of the community in which it operates and by endeavoring to accommodate or encourage these when able to do so." These requirements were inserted in the legislation in response to criticisms by state unions and others that corporatization would mean an end to the social service aspect of the organizations concerned and the destruction of hard-won employment conditions.

The business and profit-oriented nature of the SOEs was seen in part as a denial of the legitimacy of trade unions and a determination to restore the primacy of management in the workplace. Issues of power and control, especially at the workplace, have been the central issues in the early period of the new corporations (Walsh 1988b). The SOEs were all required to negotiate a transitional agreement to apply from April 1, 1987, when they began operation. For the most part, the transitional agreements carried over existing conditions of employment. Following the transitional agreements, each SOE had to negotiate a new agreement later in 1987, and then renegotiate these as they expired. In those negotiations wages and salaries have not been very contentious issues, with settlements generally following wage path trends already established in the private sector. It is to be expected that wages and salaries will become a more contentious issue in the future. However, until now, wage negotiations have been largely overshadowed by a number of issues relating to power and control.

Issues of union coverage and managerial prerogative have been key aspects to negotiations. Union coverage has rarely been an industrial issue in New Zealand. In the private sector, it has been resolved by a government-imposed system of union registration, and in the state sector by Ministerial recognition. Neither course was taken in the SOE Act, and the issue of whether any union would have coverage and at what level became a matter of negotiation. The SOEs soon conceded the need to accept union coverage but bitterly resisted the continuation of the high level of coverage the state unions had enjoyed in the past. Many appointees to the SOE Boards came from big business sector backgrounds and believed that weak management and strong unions had hindered the effective performance of state trading enterprises. One reason for this, they believed, was the fact that most senior managers belonged to the same union as their subordinates. The issue was settled by specifying a set of senior managerial positions exempt from union coverage. The coverage loss was not initially great but the trend is that more and more unionists are being excluded from settlements as time goes by.

There has been a consistent and uniform drive by SOE management to restore managerial discretion in all areas. The personnel procedures in the State Services Act 1962 became a key target in all SOEs. Existing provisions with regard to merit appointments, appeals, promotions, transfers, classification, grading, and termination were eliminated and replaced by provisions giving management vastly increased discretion. Sweeping away the state services personnel procedures was seen as essential both to managerial authority and to being a commercially profitable enterprise.

Finally, the decentralization of management control was sought as a mechanism to ensure the SOEs were more businesslike, more profit centered and more like their private sector counterparts. For unions, the challenge posed by the decentralization of managerial authority has been significant. Their structures had developed historically to meet corresponding management structures and the location of management decisions. The possibility of varying conditions and policies being followed in different regions and organizational units means that traditional assumptions about national uniformity have had to be abandoned and new state union structures have had to be developed.

The government's program for deregulating the core state services was implemented through the State Sector Act 1988. This act does more than alter labor relations processes as it reshapes the administrative structure of democratic government in New Zealand. It transforms the upper levels of the public service, changes relations between ministers and public servants and among public servants, alters the character of the public service, and makes possible significant shifts in the manner of its operation and the principles that guide it (Walsh, 1989). The labor relations changes alone are, however, the focus here.

The philosophy behind the State Sector Act was that the private sector system should be applied to the state sector unless there was good reason not to. Thus the disputes procedures of the Labour Relations Act now apply to the state sector. The State Sector Act eliminated the Annual General Adjustment and the criteria that in the past had preserved relativity with the private sector. It also eliminated compulsory arbitration and replaced it with voluntary final offer arbitration, although this is only available as part of a no-strike/no-lockout package. Voluntary conventional arbitration is also available. In the public service, occupational pay claims have been abandoned in favor of departmental agreements. The concept of a unified public service has been jettisoned. Each department is now an autonomous unit, especially for budgetary purposes, and for the first time, different conditions of employment are being negotiated across government departments. The State Services Commission holds its position as the employer party for the negotiation of employment conditions, despite the separation of departments one from the other. The commission is required to consult with departmental chief executive officers and may delegate negotiating authority to them. It appears it is intended to do this once the commission is satisfied departments, which have never carried out industrial relations functions before, have acquired the necessary expertise.

In the personnel area, the most important exception to the application of private sector arrangements lies in the obligation of the state employer to implement an equal employment opportunity program and to be a "good employer." There were other changes to other personnel provisions designed to enhance managerial flexibility. The most important of these was that the chief executive of each department became the employer for all staff with authority to appoint and dismiss without reference to the State Services Commission. The unified public service was indeed finished.

OUTCOMES UNDER THE NEW BARGAINING PROCESSES

Some evidence of changed bargaining structures is available in the three years since the implementation of the Labour Relations Act and the two and a half years of the State Sector Act, but the rate of change is slow. There has been a general reduction in the level of union coverage achieved through the collective bargaining processes. Private sector employers have used the procedural advantages offered by the removal of compulsory arbitration to resist reaching settlement with unions in approximately 10 percent of awards and many of these awards are in the process of lapsing. Further, union coverage has been diminished by the exclusion of many employees from coverage in public sector settlements. These exclusions fall into two groups: exclusions of certain managerial positions and, in some settlements, exclusion on the basis of salary. Most other restructuring of bargaining has been limited to unions that have needed to meet the "1,000 member" requirement, but the development of various new composite awards are useful examples of the potential for restructured bargaining now available to employers and unions. The most important of these new composite awards is in the forestry industry at Elders Resources New Zealand Forest Products subsidiary, NZ Forest Products Pulp and Paper Ltd (ERNZFP).

While bargaining processes are slow to change, bargaining outcomes however are showing considerable change. Considerable flexibility in wage and condition movements (particularly working time arrangements) has been identified and reported (Harbridge 1990a, 1990b). Wage increments have, each year since 1987, been kept well below the rate of inflation as measured by the Consumer Price Index (CPI) and on par with other price movements as measured by the Producers Price Index (PPI).[5] The level of wage settlements provided for in the award system continues to provide the lowest common denominator approach to wage levels, with 50 percent of all registered awards establishing minimum adult pay rates of $295 per week or less (at a time when the minimum wage was $235 per week). The ability of the national award system to produce low wage outcomes is well known to employers. Bob Matthew, the Chief Executive of one of New Zealand's largest companies, Brierley Investments Ltd., while arguing for increased labor market deregulation at a recent Wellington Chambers of Commerce seminar, gave the game away when he stated that "some of you might have been lulled into some degree of satisfaction with the present award system because it seems to be delivering relatively low settlements" (*The Press*, 1990). Matthew identified exactly the point of tension between many rank and file employers and their representatives. The award system which some employers are keen to dispense with provides sufficiently low outcomes that many other employers are keen to preserve it.

There has been increased flexibility in the types of wage settlement reached, with many settlements incorporating straight monetary rather than percentage increases. These have the effect of compressing internal wage relativities and have predominantly occurred in state bargaining settlements. Greater managerial autonomy in the setting of individual wage rates has been negotiated in the majority of public service settlements. Within individual settlements, the number of occupational salary scales has been substantially reduced by the broad-banding of salaries. This has given management much greater discretion over the duties that individual staff members can be asked to perform. In addition, nearly all public service settlements contain mechanisms that shift the emphasis in pay determination away from experience and a career structure, to pay based on performance and the requirements of the position. These mechanisms are available through "ranges of rates" of pay that can be paid staff. Under this new "ranges of rates" regime only the minima and maxima that employees in the new classifications can earn are recorded, and employees are placed on this scale according to performance and job requirements. Taken overall, there can be no doubt that employers have benefited most from the altered bargaining processes, especially during these times of rigorous economic restructuring.

ECONOMIC CHANGE AND ITS EFFECT ON BARGAINING

The overall effect of the changes implemented in the Labour Relations Act and the State Sector Act was the creation of a permissive system of labor relations bargaining that allowed the parties themselves to determine their own bargaining structures and outcomes. In the changed economic environment, however, unions have had little bargaining strength. The internationalization of capital investment and the sale of state-owned enterprises to foreign investors has had a major impact on the outcomes of industrial negotiations. In the forestry industry, for example, the acquisition of forestry investments in both Canada and Chile by one of New Zealand's largest companies, Fletcher Challenge Ltd., enabled that company to place very considerable pressure on their New Zealand work force in a major industrial dispute in 1986. New Zealand unions and their members were quite directly played off against wage and associated labor costs in both North and South America.

The purchase of forestry giant, New Zealand Forest Products, by an Australian-based multinational company, Elders Resources, enabled that company to dispense with parochial work methods and systems and to extract significant gains from the work force. The combined site unions at the Kinleith plant in the central North Island had traditionally provided an important leadership role in national industrial relations bargaining. ERNZFP undertook not to close the Kinleith plant and abandon the New Zealand operation, provided the unions agreed to staff reductions from 4,500 to 1,190, a no-strike provision in the agreement, new disputes resolution procedures, and a term lasting thirty months (McCaw and Harbridge, 1990). Unions that had previously demonstrated great militancy had little option but to comply with these demands.

The structural unemployment[6] that has resulted from the economic restructuring has also led to radical shifts in the balance of power in negotiations. New Zealand's second largest union, the Engineers Union, has been involved in important efforts to implement bargaining reform in the face of a manufacturing environment that has seen that union drop from 55,000 members in 1984 to 40,000 in 1990 (*Metal*, 1990). Those efforts have produced some new bargaining structures and satisfactory outcomes, but limited progress has been made in negotiations despite some quite substantial concessions by the union. Where employers see some benefit from dealing with the union, they do; where they don't, they simply decline to settle talks. Unions are able currently to place little industrial pressure on employers in negotiations. High unemployment, and the reduction in organized work force, has made pressure industrial action extremely difficult for unions to organize as is demonstrated by the decline in official statistics of work stoppages and days lost.

Probably the most significant change that has emerged from the economic and labor relations policies enacted under Labour has been the end of the cost-plus approach to union and employer negotiations. In the private sector before 1985, companies such as NZFP simply passed on increased wage costs to a consumer who had no alternative product market to choose from, and then claimed the appropriate subsidies from the state. In the state sector prior to 1988, wage increases were funded through a system of "supplementary estimates" approved later as appropriations by Parliament. In the economic circumstances of the 1990s companies no longer have the buffer of protectionist economic policies, and state chief executive officers are no longer able to fund wage increases through the supplementary estimates system. The ending of the compulsory arbitration system in both the state and private sectors has enabled employers to pursue lower wage settlements (and nonsettlements) with considerable aggression.

CONCLUSION

It is entirely appropriate for me to address a North-American audience on the difficulties currently being experienced by the New Zealand trade union movement. Boxall (1990) portrays the events of the last six years as furthering a transition away from the model of labor relations that has served New Zealand since 1894. That model was an arbitration-based, state-controlled model of labor relations established at the turn of the last century. That model was based on a series of compulsions: compulsory union membership, compulsory arbitration of disputes, monopoly union bargaining rights, and blanket coverage of awards. That model created a trade union movement reliant on the law and those compulsions for its survival. It is being replaced by what Boxall terms the "New Zealand Wagner" model of labor relations. As the name implies, this new model is similar to the North-American model: a noninterventionist approach to labor relations prevails; union membership is voluntary; bargaining processes are essentially voluntary; bargaining outcomes are changing from being occupationally based settlements to industry- and enterprise-based settlements; the parties are responsible for and enforce their own settlements.

If the North-American experience (e.g. Freeman, 1988) is anything to go by then the future of unionism in the next few years in New Zealand looks bleak. The National party has policies that if elected in October would further advance the North-American model into the New Zealand context. National has targeted the labor market for substantial further deregulation (Birch, 1990). National has undertaken to make union membership voluntary again, remove award blanket coverage provisions, and make union bargaining rights contestable. Such moves will further weaken union penetration and union influence in the New Zealand labor market. The National party promises to finish off what the Labour party commenced. What of course is really extraordinary about the New Zealand situation is that it took a Labour government to behave in an un-labourlike fashion.

ENDNOTES

[1] TVNZ poll reported in the *Dominion Sunday Times*, p.2, May 20, 1990.

[2] In 1989/90, after significant sales of state assets, net national debt had risen to 49.7 percent of GDP.

[3] Whether second tier bargaining was a very widespread phenomenon or not was the subject of considerable conjecture. Despite the rhetoric of both union and employer representatives, the author's research and surveys estimated that less than 50,000 employees (about 6 percent of the workforce) outside the meat processing industry were covered by a second tier arrangement (Harbridge, 1986).

[4] A more extensive analysis of changes in state labor relations, upon which this account draws, is available in Harbridge and Walsh (1989).

[5] In the period 1984–1988/9, CPI increased by 65 percent; PPI by 41 percent and registered wage settlements by an average

of 40 percent. The gap between CPI and PPI is largely explained by the introduction of a consumption tax, GST, in October, 1986.

[6] In June 1990 there were 160,000 workers registered nationally as unemployed. This represents nearly 11 percent of the work force.

REFERENCES

Birch, Hon. W.F. *New Choices in Industrial Relations*. Wellington: New Zealand National Party, 1990.

Bolger, Hon. J.B. "Commentary: the Government's Role in Industrial Relations." *New Zealand Journal of Industrial Relations*. 7(1):35–7, 1982.

Bollard, A., and R. Buckle, editors. *Economic Liberalisation in New Zealand*. Wellington: Allen, and Unwin, 1987.

Boston, Jonathon, and Martin Holland. *The Fourth Labour Government*. Auckland: Oxford University Press, 1987.

Boxall, Peter. *Towards the Wagner Framework: An Interpretation of the Direction of Change in New Zealand Industrial Relations*. Monash University, Melbourne: Management Paper No. 31, 1990.

Bradford, Max. "A Private Sector Employer View." In *The Future of Wage Fixing*. Edited by P. Brosnan. Wellington Industrial Relations Centre, Victoria University of Wellington, 1983.

Department of Labour. *Government Policy Statement on Labour Relations*. Wellington: Government Printer, 1986.

Douglas, Ken. "A Private Sector Union View." In *The Future of Wage Fixing*. Edited by P. Brosnan. Wellington Industrial Relations Centre, Victoria University of Wellington, 1983.

Douglas, Roger. *There's Got To Be a Better Way*. Wellington: Fourth Estate Publications, 1980.

———. "The Ends and the Means." In *Rogernomics: Reshaping New Zealand's Economy*. Edited by Simon Walker. Auckland: New Zealand Centre for Independent Studies, 1989.

Easton, Brian. *The Making of Rogernomics*. Auckland: Auckland University Press, 1989.

The *Evening Post*, August 18, 1990.

Freeman, Richard B. "What Does the Future Hold for U.S. Unionism?" Paper presented to Perspectives 2000, the First Industrial Relations Congress of the Americas, Quebec, August 25–26, 1988.

Jesson, Bruce. *Fragments of Labor*. Auckland: Penguin, 1989.

Harbridge, Raymond. "Collective Second Tier Bargaining in New Zealand." *New Zealand Journal of Business*. 8:40–55, 1986.

——— "Flexibility in Collective Bargaining in New Zealand: Facts and Folklore." *New Zealand Journal of Industrial Relations*. 15(3):241–250, 1990a.

——— *Flexibility in Collective Bargaining*. Labor Market Flexibility seminar, paper presentation, Wellington, August 15, 1990b.

Harbridge, Raymond, and Pat Walsh. "Restructuring Industrial Relations in New Zealand, 1984–1988." *Labour and Industry*. 2(1):60–84, 1989.

Hubbard, Anthony. "Broken Promises." *Listener and TV Times*. Wellington: Broadcasting Corporation of New Zealand, April 16, 1990.

McCaw, Stuart, and Raymond Harbridge. "The Labour Government, Big Business, and the Trade Unions: Labour Relations at Kinelith in the 1980s." *New Zealand Journal of Business*. Forthcoming, 1990.

Metal. 36(2):2, 1990.

Minister of State Services. *Pay Fixing in the State Sector*. Wellington: Government Printer, 1986.

New Zealand Employers Federation. "Balance in Bargaining." Wellington: New Zealand Employers Federation, 1978.

Oliver, W. Hugh. "The Labour Caucus and Economic Policy Formation, 1981 to 1984." In *The Making of Rogernomics*. Edited by Brian Easton. Auckland: Auckland University Press, 1989.

Organization for Economic Cooperation and Development (OECD). *Labor Market Flexibility*. Paris: OECD, 1986.

The *Press*, February 21, 1990.

Randle, David. *Industrial Relations in the Public Sector*. Industrial Relations Centre, Wellington: Victoria University of Wellington, 1985.

Roberts, J. *Politicians, Public Servants and Public Enterprise: Restructuring the New Zealand Government Executive*. Wellington: Victoria University Press, 1987.

Walker, Simon, editor. *Rogernomics: Reshaping New Zealand's Economy*. Auckland: New Zealand Centre for Independent Studies, 1989.

161

Walsh, Pat. "The Buff Paper Revisited: The Development of State Sector Industrial Relations in New Zealand." Industrial Relations Centre, Victoria University of Wellington, working paper, March, 1988a.

————. "The Struggle for Power and Control in the New Corporations: Industrial Relations in the First Year of the State-Owned Enterprises." *New Zealand Journal of Industrial Relations*. 13(2):179–89, 1988b.

————. *An Analysis of the Legislative Process: From the State Sector Bill to the State Sector Act*. Research paper, New Zealand Institute of Public Administration, Wellington, 1989.

Section 6

REPRESENTING THE NEW WORK FORCE

One of the most visible effects of global economic change is the composition of the work force. In the United States, the work force is increasingly female and minority. The famous "Work force 2000" report of the U.S. Department of Labor and other studies estimate that fewer than 15 percent of new jobs will be filled by white males in the next two decades. While the demographic shifts in Canada are not as dramatic, they are steady and important.

Another element of the work force has to do not only with workers but with employer policies in the private and public sectors to shift to part-time and temporary workers or to contract out work altogether. The result is a burgeoning contingent work force that has less attachment to any one job or employer than the regular work force.

The articles in this section deal with the dual aspect of the new work force—its demographic composition and its increasingly contingent nature. Karen Nussbaum is famous as founder of 9to5, National Association of Working Women. Women are a key component of the work force and are disproportionately represented among part-time and low-wage workers. Nussbaum maintains that employers in a global economy respond to competition by squeezing down on workers. The result is a "big squeeze" for workers—more work for less pay, inferior benefits, and inadequate job security. She presents solutions that include higher wages for the new higher skills that are needed, a new social contract that recognizes workers' complicated lives, and pay equality. She urges labor to be more ideological in the struggle to promote worker rights.

Joy MacPhail of the British Columbia Federation of Labour traces the roots of the growing contingent work force. In Canada, contingent workers have increased by 50 percent in fifteen years due to contracting out, growth of the service sector, technological change, and deregulation. These trends have negative effects on unionized workers, so unions must adopt strategies that recognize the growth of the contingent work force. MacPhail suggests that unions puruse legislative and collective bargaining protections for part-time workers, and she endorses the high-skill strategy to enhance jobs and wages.

Jose LaLuz is education director for the Amalgamated Clothing and Textile Workers Union (ACTWU). He describes the multicultural nature of his union and the resulting union commitment to multicultural education and representation. ACTWU is currently concerned with international trade policies and U.S. immigration policies, and it is one of only two unions to formally oppose the U.S. policy of employer sanctions for hiring undocumented workers.

The New Work Force: Management and Labor Strategies

KAREN NUSSBAUM

Executive Director, 9to5, National Association of Working Women; District 925, SEIU

Women have entered the work force in record numbers. Real wages keep going down. The number of marginal workers has skyrocketed.

But some things never change. At least that's the way we felt at 9to5's National Boss Contest, called "The Good, the Bad, and the Downright Unbelievable." Becky's boss at an insurance company didn't like the way she dusted his duck plaques and served coffee. When she complained, he told her "Me chief, you squaw." A boss at a major accounting firm followed his office workers to the bathroom with a stopwatch and timed them. And for originality, we had "The Beeper Peeper" who routinely asked his secretary to visit the local bar looking for attractive women and then beep him if she thought it was worth his while. Enough bosses like these and you wonder, who needs a new strategy for labor?

In this article I briefly describe the new work force, the response by management, and offer solutions for the labor movement.

NEW WORK FORCE

There is a new work force. It's defined by the new workers in it—women, minorities, retirees, and kids—and defined by working conditions: low pay, few benefits, no job security, and heavy discipline. These working conditions, long identified with women, minorities, and Southern workers—are now the norm for most. The old work force is being remade in our image.

The new work force is a result of a business strategy to respond to a changed economy. It dates from 1973: the official end of the war in Vietnam; the first oil shock; the first year of the decline in wages and the beginning of the "U Turn" in income distribution; and—not coincidentally, we now realize—the start of 9to5, the National Association of Working Women in the U.S.

The U.S. faced new competition: from countries like Japan and West Germany on the one hand with their high-skill workers and countries like Korea and Mexico on the other with their low wages.

How did business respond? In 1974, *Business Week* ran a column selling "the idea of doing with less so that big business can have more."

They succeeded. The U.S. is now seventh in wages; we allocate less to training than Singapore; we are nineteenth in infant mortality; we have a uniquely low-paid service sector; we are last among industrialized nations in work and family policy; the U.S. is the only industrial nation without universal health insurance; and one out of three workers are contingent.

Working Conditions

A management strategy such as this—increasing productivity by squeezing workers—has to rely on discipline and control for motivation. Electronic monitoring is one of a growing list of surveillance techniques used in the work place. The Congressional ban on polygraphs last year only heightened the scramble for other methods, including drug testing, handwriting analysis, and "honesty tests." "When lie detector tests were banned," according to the *New York Times*, "a Miami bank substituted a new employee screening program—a written honesty test, a urinalysis and a thorough background check before hiring an employee."

What's the panic? Especially when so many experts point to the questionable value of these methods—drug tests have up to a forty percent error rate; and handwriting is considered to have no correlation to job success. And what is an "honesty test" anyway? One test had questions like "When you were young did you ever hate your mother or father?" Others include questions about your sexual preference, religion, and bowel movements.

How does all this affect workers?

A *Wall Street Journal* headline read "Cynicism Runs High in the American Workplace." The *New York Times* profiled a member of the new work force, a young single mother who can't find work that pays enough to cover child care costs. "It's my own fault," she said. "It's all my own fault."

And in a meeting of 9to5 members in Atlanta, I heard a new sentiment voiced: the workplace is a hard, cold place these days. A long-term legal secretary gave up her permanent job to work temp five days a week, even though she desperately needs the benefits she no longer gets. Sonya explained, "We're suffering from the battered wife syndrome. You go in and get your butt beat every day. I'm working temp now because I didn't want to know anyone at work any more."

Cynicism, despair, alienation. These are the hallmarks of the new work force.

Management Solutions

We are moving through a major transition, faced with real problems. But what are the solutions? Here's what we hear coming out of management.

There's "dumbing down," a management theory that uses technology to bring the skill level down to the appalling level of our educational system. Recently a management consultant boasted about the fast food chain that uses "pictures of hamburgers [on the cash registers], so the cashier doesn't have to know how to read" (*Computerworld*, 1990).

Other management solutions include computer monitoring, surveillance by hidden cameras, and headset monitoring. Are these seen as necessary evils by reluctant managers?

I spoke at a conference of the managers of call-in centers—catalog order houses, airline reservation clerks, customer service representatives. These managers insisted their workers loved monitoring. "We had to close down the monitoring for a few months and my employees came to me begging that we start it up again," one manager declared to wild applause from her colleagues.

Then there's pay for performance, independent contracting, and one of my favorites, "cafeteria benefits." Only in this cafeteria, it turns out you are not choosing between the éclair and the chocolate mousse, but the meat and potatoes.

One popular new approach is "managing cultural diversity." With women and minorities making up 85 percent of the new job entrants in the next ten years, managers can no longer be so literal about hiring in their own image or having people blend into the corporate mold. But this is not a celebration of cultural diversity. This is what it says—a containment policy to diffuse differences.

On the other hand there are the so-called "best practices" companies. These are the companies that follow the work organization found in Europe, Scandinavia, and Japan that puts the emphasis on training, trust, and teamwork, and believe in employee input in decision making and blurring hierarchical lines. (In other countries, these practices are in the context of collective bargaining.)

There are a number of companies in the U.S. that follow this model—Corning Glass and Apple

Computer, for example. But at most only 5 percent of U.S. companies employ "best practices." If it works for them—the Germans, Swedes, and Japanese—why don't more companies pursue this strategy?

That was one of the questions the Commission on the Skills of the American Work Force asked in in-depth interviews of 400 American companies. The answer? Managers aren't interested in a more highly skilled, highly trained work force. What they are most concerned about is finding workers who are more "pleasant." Apparently, these overworked, underpaid, monitored workers who are getting their urine tested are not as nice on the phone as they used to be.

SOLUTIONS FOR THE NEW WORK FORCE: POLICIES FOR A NEW SOCIAL CONTRACT

We need real solutions. The new work force requires a new *Social Contract*—a redefinition of the rights and responsibilities among workers, business, and government.

There are three key points in our strategy:

1. We need to understand that the threads of the last fifteen years—the rise of international competition, the diffusion of new technology, the increase of working women, and the shift from manufacturing to service work—are inextricably woven together. We won't be able to solve the problems if we insist on seeing them piecemeal.

Solving problems out of context will give us incomplete solutions, like maternity leave for women law partners; or our current distribution of in-company training money—75 percent goes to train managers (with not much to show for it, either); or eroding employer paid health care to compete with the Japanese.

2. We have to win a public debate on what it is we want: do we want higher productivity that grows from an educated, highly skilled, high value-added, high-paid work force? Or is it enough to secure return on investment and provide enough workers for the next period? Do we want high skills or low pay?

Creating a high-skill, high-wage work force requires a long-term investment. Since management is not inclined in this direction on its own, we have to create a combination of requirements and incentives: mandated benefits such as child care, elder care, and family leave; higher minimum wage; and parity for part-timers.

We have to redirect the system that provides rewards for maximum short-term profits only: a tax policy that provides incentives for capital investment but none for worker training; or investment policies that can lead to the ouster of a CEO who shows only a handsome return on investment instead of the maximum return on investment.

3. We aim to do something big—rewrite the social contract from a progressive point of view. But policy makers can't hide from the task on the grounds that it is too big. The pieces of it are being worked out at the state and local level and in collective bargaining contracts all over the country. Here I'll discuss some policy options on a few issues that are key to a new social contract, and refer to our book, *Solutions for the New Workforce* (Sweeney and Nussbaum, 1989) for scores of such examples.

Work and Family

Fourteen states have parental leave and have lived to tell the tale. Five states have paid leave provisions, and have not yet been annexed by West Germany. In fact, in a study by 9to5, we found that these "family leave" states outperformed the highest-ranked Grant-Thornton states in employment in the small business sector.

State politicians know family leave legislation is necessary—thirty-three states considered family leave legislation last year. Yet a family leave bill so modest in its provisions as to border on the inconsequential failed to override a Bush veto in 1990.

There is momentum at the state level on family leave; we should push it. And we should make these bills as strong as possible. They should include leave time for the care of elderly parents, spouses, and individual medical leave time. There should be wage replacement during leave—an extension of an existing fund like unemployment insurance or workers' compensation into which employers and employees pay a small payroll tax in order to provide up to two-thirds of a worker's wage while on leave. Five states have temporary disability leave that works on this model. Their funds are solvent and easy to administer.

Unions are making family leave and child care common elements in their contracts. Only 1 percent of employers provide any kind of child care, and a majority of those are the result of bargaining, mostly in the public sector. In a showpiece victory, the contract agreement in 1989 between the Communication Workers of America and AT&T centered on a comprehensive work and family package.

Part-Time Workers and Temps

We need to take the incentive out of part-time work as a way to lower labor costs. One way is through legislation. For example, a New Hampshire bill prohibits insurance companies from excluding part-timers from the group rate. Wisconsin will consider model legislation next year. It will amend the Wage and Hour law to define temporary employment and prohibit the use of long-term temps. Congresswoman Schroeder's Economic Equity Act calls for prorated benefits for part-timers. The goal is parity for part-timers. We are just at the doorstep on this issue, but it's not a bad time to begin the legislative battle.

Unions are also taking up the challenge. The traditional wisdom to stay away from representing part-time workers—who have full-time problems but pay only part-time dues—is changing. My own union, District 925, organized 300 part-time office workers at Cuyahoga Community College when they began to outnumber our full-time workers.

Pay

The most important policy is the one that is least discussed—compensation. In the largest companies during the 1980s, real wages for workers fell 5 percent, while pay for executives in the same companies rose by 149 percent. Last year, average pay for top executives was 132 times greater than that of the average clerical worker.

The income gap between the rich and the rest is bigger than it has ever been and bigger than any competitor. Our CEOs look more like the Emir of Kuwait than their Japanese or German counterparts.

There is new attention now to redefining the poverty level. Economists argue convincingly that the old level is too low. But the issue may not be so esoteric. In 1979, one out of four new jobs were poverty wage jobs—now it is one out of three. The point is to stop the growth of poverty-level jobs at whatever definition.

We need to build from the bottom up, raising the floor through minimum wage legislation and organizing the lowest-paid workers, as in SEIU's Jobs with Justice Campaign that organizes part-time, mostly immigrant janitors. But we also have to break the taboo of talking about the bosses. Their pay is obscene and we need to bring public opinion over.

Monitoring and Surveillance

State and local legislation on monitoring can be successful. Contract language is even more important. We need to turn around the management offensive on the need for surveillance—witness the public relations campaign on the need for drug testing a few years ago. The purpose of surveillance is not to motivate or protect, it is to control and cause fear.

Though legislation is having only limited success at this point—with the significant exception of the national prohibition against lie detectors—it's a useful way to raise the issue and gain support.

Our message is that the problems are vast, profound, and complex, but the solutions are at hand. And it is a message that makes sense to Americans. I've traveled around the country talking about our book, *Solutions for the New Workforce*.

The radio call-in shows are the best. A man named Dwayne in Cleveland said his five grown children have seventeen years between the oldest and youngest. As the older children came of age, they found good jobs. The younger children are making minimum wage and still living at home. "There's no difference between the children," Dwayne said. "The older ones aren't more worthy, or smarter. The opportunities just don't exist now."

Callers all over the country call in with their own solutions: school nurses in Harrisburg think they should be paid at least what the janitors are paid; a retiree in Boston thinks the problem is that management is paid too much; a bank employee thinks we need a national health insurance program.

WHAT LABOR SHOULD DO

How do we advance an agenda for a new social contract when organized labor grows smaller every year and the Democrats appear to have no ability to conceptualize or project any new vision—an unreliable ally at best.

I hope we will look back on the 1980s as a dark period. And there is some reason to think things may be getting better. The popular reinterpretation of the Reagan era as a decade of unprecedented greed and restructuring of the economy in favor of the rich may reveal a desire for more humane social values.

I have three recommendations for labor whichever way we ride the pendulum. *First, speak to a broad audience and go to people—don't insist that they come to us*. For example, 9to5, the National Association of Working Women, runs a job problems hotline. We are flooded with calls. Some months we get as many as 12,000 phone calls—with our small staff we can service only a fraction. These are people who want to do something about their problems. And many become members. At a time when the labor movement longs for hot shops, we are getting loads of people calling us. I think it's because we meet them halfway with a message they can respond to.

Second, be ideological.

9to5's appeal depends on its message—stand up for yourself. We are not just a service organization. The Boss Contest I told you about is a good example. We hold an annual contest to put the spotlight on bad bosses, to make this a social, a collective issue.

Opinion polls can show you what people want to hear, but we also have a responsibility to devise a message that is not just politically popular but politically correct.

Last, dig deep.

Two great labor leaders come from Brazil—Lula, the metalworkers leader who nearly became Brazil's president in last year's elections, and Chico Mendes, the martyred Amazonian rubber tappers leader. Both men were formed during the military dictatorship—Lula, illiterate until he was an adult, was influenced by his brother and other activists in the left opposition during years of right wing military rule; Mendes learned to read at eighteen from Euclides Tavora, an escaped political prisoner.

While we continue to try to move mountains we have to take the time to do thorough leadership or cadre development—to dig deep. Or else we won't move mountains.

168

CONCLUSION

I want to end with the story of an airline reservation clerk with thirty years at the company who called our hotline. The workers were being monitored, they had had their pay cut, she and others were suffering from stress-related diseases. The conditions were terrible. We worked with Harriet, and told her story to reporters. One reporter talked to her, and in disbelief said, "Doesn't anybody ever stand up there?"

She realized that no, they didn't—neither figuratively, standing up for their rights, nor literally, as they were glued to their seats except for painstakingly timed breaks. So she went into the office the next day and organized everyone to stand up—at ten o'clock they all rose, headsets plugged in, still talking with customers, and did the Big Wave. And they have been doing the Big Wave off and on since then.

It's their way of saying "you don't own us." And as Harriet told a national meeting of 9to5 this summer, "They never know when we will stand up next." This act of resistance is so small it hurts, and so big it is breathtaking. It is people like Harriet in a movement who will create the new social contract.

The writer Flannery O'Connor said, "To the deaf you must shout! And to the near blind you must draw large, wild pictures." So beat your breast, and bang it out: This system is broken, and we know how to fix it!

REFERENCES

Computerworld, August 20, 1990.

Sweeney, John, and Karen Nussbaum. *Solutions for the New Workforce: Policies for a New Social Contract.* Seven Locks Press, 1989.

The Contingent Workforce in Canada: Problems and Solutions

JOY MACPHAIL

Assistant to the Officers, British Columbia Federation of Labour

WHY IS THE CONTINGENT WORK FORCE GROWING IN A GLOBAL ECONOMY?

Every country in a global economy produces a number of goods for trading which they can make efficiently and cheaply. This lends itself to the development of a specialized work force; if the goal is solely profit maximization, employees will move to specialized part-time and temporary workers, or a contingent work force.

Riccardo's classic theory of comparative advantage was based on the premise that neither capital nor labor was mobile. The trading nation's comparative advantage was derived from domestic resources particular to that geographic location. Now that capital is totally mobile, it moves to the nation with the absolute advantage. This mobility of capital is enhanced by free trade arrangements that make nation-state borders irrelevant when trade occurs. The Canada/U.S. Free Trade Agreement has, as one of its major thrusts, unfettered mobility of capital between the two countries. Capital can now move to the cheapest labor sources available in any state or province.

Workers have restricted opportunities because of the "narrowing" of the goods produced in a single nation within a global economy. Also, because capital in a global economy is totally mobile, jobs must move where capital moves. Therefore, workers must move too, if they want to continue to be employed.

The impact of this is twofold. First, many communities that exist in Canada now will not be there for our children because the jobs will have gone elsewhere. Second, the social/community structure that we are now used to will disappear, just as nation-state borders disappear in a global economy. These trends are not in the interest of workers.

WHAT IS THE CONTINGENT WORK FORCE IN CANADA?

The origin of the contingent work force traces back to the 1950s when women entered the labor market in large numbers. Today, contingent workers are people who need flexibility in order to cope with other responsibilities such as child care, domestic responsibilities, and education upgrading. Our official government statistics agency—Statistics Canada—says it is a small percentage of the work force, but its statistic measures only those workers employed at temporary employment agencies. Most recent estimates suggest that almost 30 percent of the work force can be identified as contingent.

Contingent workers are mainly women in clerical positions and immigrants who often are non-English speaking and have no idea of their rights. They tend to be over qualified for their work. Some hold down more than one job. Of our youth (aged sixteen–twenty-four), 30 percent hold down more than one job, as do 8 percent of women, 9 percent of men, and 8 percent of unionized workers.

Employers add to the number of contingent workers by hiring employees part-time, and this trend is on the increase. Part-time employment in Canada increased from 9.89 percent of the total work force in 1975 (10.43 percent of the employed) to 14 percent of the total work force in 1989 (15.1 percent of the employed). This is a 50 percent increase over a decade and a half.

The contingent work force is increasing due to:

- contracting out;
- privatization;
- government down-sizing and cutbacks;
- growth in service sector jobs as opposed to goods-producing jobs;
- technological change and the concurrent de-skilling of work; and
- deregulation where companies have less need for a trained, skilled work force because they have no regulations with which to comply.

All of these are major economic policy goals of most of our provincial governments and definitely of our federal government in Canada.

One example of government "downsizing" leading to a growth in the contingent work force is found in the forest industry. In the mid-1980s, the British Columbia Ministry of Forests was ordered by the government to shift toward downsizing and contracting out. This occurred as part of an overall restraint program instituted by that government. In 1981, this ministry's contingent labor force costs were 15 percent of the total salary and benefits paid to regular government employees. By 1990, the contingent labor force costs were 157 percent of total salary and benefits paid to regular government employees.

It is interesting to note that forest industry "deregulation" occurred at the same time as downsizing; the provincial government turned forest management and regulation over to the forest corporations directly. Resource companies became self-monitoring and self-regulating, so the Ministry of Forests no longer needed their expert technical employees. Some of these employees contracted their skills, then, to the resource companies, again expanding the contingent work force.

The forest industry also provides an example of technological change leading to an increase in the contingent work force. When the activity of a forest industry firm changes, the company may well choose not to physically expand its capital investment to deal with the business change. For instance, a mill rough-cutting cedar for the last ten years has a work force trained for that. Rather than build a planer to begin to remanufacture the cedar, the company may take that work and send it off to a mill that already custom cuts as a full-time business with state-of-the-art technology.

This reshuffling of the production process leads to complaints about contracting out and to the erosion of the collective agreement. It also lends itself to the creation of temporary jobs because the actual production is done at a location other than that of the employing business.

WHY IS A CONTINGENT WORK FORCE A PROBLEM?

The contingent work force undermines the benefits of the permanent work force.

The B.C. union representing hotel and restaurant workers recently did a survey of a segment of their membership. Six hundred of a 2,100 person work force in Vancouver's major hotels worked less than eighty hours per month. They were thus ineligible for pension, health, and welfare benefits.

The costs of providing these benefits rise because there is a smaller work force over which to spread "user experience" costs. The irregular contribution to the plans by these contingent workers merely means that full-time workers have to ante up more. These contingent workers, who are union members, then complain, "What does the union get for me?"

Employers in this type of industry no longer suffer the administrative nightmare of having a large number of part-time workers because of computerized payroll systems. The bureaucratic costs of relying on a contingent, temporary work force shrink each year as the administrative technology improves.

Contract and temporary employment in our colleges and universities undermines the tenure system and all of its value. B.C.'s post secondary system now relies heavily on the use of contract instructors. The constant "renewal" of employment contracts keeps these education workers in line and sometimes unwilling to take either independent or collective action. However, in B.C. it is interesting to note that there have been several major strikes recently by college unions who were fighting for job security and benefits for their contract instructors.

The contingent work force works alongside established employees but often earn half their wages and have far fewer benefits and less decent working conditions. This leads to conflict and tension between the two groups. The "necessity for flexibility" argument made by employers really means absolute control over the work force. Contingent workers are excluded from any policy decision-making process and therefore have no available avenues by which to gain any control over their jobs.

The contingent work force can also keep an employer going, or at least immunized against long-term damage, during a strike or lockout.

Many contingent workers are forced to moonlight in order to survive. Family members need two jobs just to make ends meet. However, both jobs cannot be permanent because the individual can't make a permanent commitment to two employers, and this is often exploited by employers. If a worker moonlights, she/he will not need the contractual benefits provided at that job if she/he gets benefits at the regular job. Again, this undermines the provision of benefits to the permanent work force.

The TV sitcom "In Living Color" epitomizes the moonlighting dilemma. It portrays a Jamaican family who are new immigrants to the U.S. Everyone has several jobs and all are killing themselves just to survive. The demands arising within our urban centers now require working people to live their own personal "In Living Color"—this survival pressure lends itself to the expansion of the contingent work force.

SOLUTIONS TO THE PROBLEMS OF THE CONTINGENT WORK FORCE

There are several solutions to the problems of a fast-growing contingent work force that we can advocate for the benefit of working people.

We can lessen the effects of the global economy. We could change the way we run our economy and begin to maximize opportunities internally. We could have community-based production where capital sees no advantage in escaping.

We could enhance domestic (internal) competition by breaking up existing monopolies/oligopolies. We would still trade, but trade would be based on the old theory of comparative advantage—not absolute advantage.

We can develop a skilled work force specializing in value-added production. Employers, by concentrating on the use of a contingent work force, have put Canada at a comparative disadvantage because of our training deficit. Our work force is undertrained in relation to other industrialized countries. We should develop skills that allow us to produce value-added products and processes. No longer should B.C. and Canada's corporations ship out our raw resources and buy back finished products from the Third World.

We can develop a pool of capital for domestic investment. Our pension funds are ideal for this. We can then insist that permanent jobs be created within any investment scheme. This type of "local" investment also counteracts the drain caused by capital fleeing Canada because of the Free Trade Agreement.

We can bargain protection. We can negotiate language that prevents the expansion of the contingent work force. Contracting out can be prohibited. We can negotiate benefits for temporary and part-time workers. We can negotiate flexibility into work rules and hours of work. We can perhaps negotiate a flexible "unionized" employment system and expand the hiring hall concept to function in places of employment that traditionally have not used a hiring hall. We can even negotiate provisions that may allow for employees to work out of their homes.

We can take legal action arising from the collective agreement. We can fight exclusions from the bargaining unit. We can challenge sham contractors who are not bona fide third-party contractors. We can file union grievances wherein a steward brings a grievance on behalf of the union claiming that the union itself is being harmed.

We can lobby for legislated protection. The province of Ontario now has an employer payroll health tax that ensures that every worker receives health care benefits. We can legislate a minimum number of hours of work per employee. We can either lobby for legislation that guarantees portability of pensions or demand a government-run pension plan for contingent workers.

And finally, we can seek legislation that makes it easier to organize the unorganized, including the contingent work force. All workers, regardless of the number of hours they are on the job, should be covered by the bargaining unit's collective agreement.

The contingent work force is a major issue with which unions must contend as our economy grows ever more globalized. There are solutions available to us that maximize the rights of working people in this type of economy, but we must start now toward achieving them. To wait any longer may just mean that the employers' use of a contingent work force will dominate all future labor market policies and industrial relations systems.

A Multicultural Framework for Worker Education

JOSE LA LUZ

Education Director, Amalgamated Clothing and Textile Workers Union

I am a worker educator employed by the Amalgamated Clothing and Textile Workers Union (ACTWU) whose members are very diverse racially, culturally, and linguistically and are employed in rapidly declining industries such as apparel, shoes and leather, headwear and, to a lesser extent, textile.

An increasing number of these men and women are foreign-born immigrants from the Caribbean, South and Central America, Southeast Asia, and, most recently, from eastern European countries. Many more are Black and white textile and apparel workers from small rural areas in the South and the Southwest; others are apparel workers whose ancestors were immigrants from Europe who settled in large cities such as New York, Chicago, Boston, and Baltimore. Women in general and women of color in particular are now the fastest growing and the largest group of members.

In spite of their diversity, they all share one thing in common—they are all members of a union that is fighting back in order to survive in the face of the challenges posed by the rapidly shrinking industries where its members make their living. This union has had to reexamine itself critically, to experiment with new strategies, programs and practices as part of a long and complicated process of cultural and organizational change designed to transform these challenges into opportunities.

Allow me to put this in a context that illustrates both the scope and the magnitude of the changes we envision. ACTWU is in effect four unions in *one*, the result of a merger of four different organizations with their own distinct cultures. One of them, the Amalgamated Clothing Workers of America (ACWA), traces its origins to the struggles of European immigrant workers who built an enduring multiethnic, multicultural, polyglot organization in the men's clothing industry at the turn of this century.

Another, the Textile Workers Union, was founded in the 1930s with assistance from the leadership of ACWA and the Congress of Industrial Organizations of which ACWA was a founding member. The composition of this union did not have the ethno-occupational characteristics of its sister union in the apparel industry and it did not have the same immigrant traditions and multicultural and polygot character of the ACWA.

It did, however, make significant inroads in organizing southern rural industrial workers employed in textile mills that, in many instances, resembled a modified plantation. Organizing the Deep South required the articulation of new union building strategies and tactics that would break down the racial barriers preventing the unity of white and Black textile workers.

The other two unions that became part of this merger process were the United Shoe Workers and the Hat and Millinery Workers. Both trace their origins to the struggles of artisans and skilled workers in the mid- to late-1800s to protect their jobs from the degradation and deskilling resulting from rapid industrialization.

The fact that these four distinct unions with their respective cultures merged into one was indeed part of a strategy to consolidate forces to face the decline of those industries and the massive loss of unionized jobs.

Another important aspect of the union's developing strategy has to do with the nature of the changes taking place in the industries where our members are concentrated. These industries are declining as a result of the interdependent relationship between the restructuring of both the U.S. and the global economies.

One trend is that the apparel industry continues to relocate many of its operations to developing countries that have adopted export-oriented strategies based on their availability of cheaper labor and the expansion of Free Trade Zones. Incidentally, this mobility of manufacturing capital is encouraged by the policies and practices of international agencies such as the World Bank and U.S. government directly. It is no secret that an apparel manufacturer can get far more U.S. government assistance (training program, engineering help, marketing, etc.) for manufacturing in the Caribbean than in Tennessee or North Carolina.

An opposite trend is that, in certain markets such as Southern California and the New York metropolitan area, the apparel industry has become an important pull factor in that it attracts immigrant workers from the very same countries where the industry is relocating, such as the Caribbean and Southeast Asia.

It is estimated that as much as 39 percent of that industry's entire work force now consists of undocumented Asian and Latino immigrants (Hill and Pearse, 1987, p. 5). Partly as a response to the changing demographics of the apparel industry, and perhaps more importantly, because it is a matter of civil and human rights, ACTWU has adopted a policy calling for the repeal of employer sanctions contained in the U.S. immigration laws. The ACTWU thus joins its sister union in the garment industry, the International Ladies Garment Workers Unions (ILGWU), as the only two AFL-CIO unions to oppose employer sanctions for hiring undocumented workers. This is an important step in the process of shaping a strategy to increase and improve the organizing and representation of the growing immigrant work force.

In addition, the union has increased its activities overseas to assist workers in developing countries to organize themselves. Much has been learned from our very successful experience in South Africa where our sister union SACTWU has become the third largest union in the country, partly as a result of our solidarity. Similar programs are now being developed in the Caribbean Basin Region and in South America.

What do all these changes have to do with the union's educational programs? Do these changes affect the mission of the Education Department?

In our report to the union's recent convention this summer, the mission of the Education Department was defined as that of assisting in the "the development of the union's primary resource: its members, officers, and staff by providing them with access to the skills and knowledge and the principles and values that shape its strategy and operations."

What does this really mean? It means that education is central to the life of the union and is not an ad hoc activity subject to whenever the perceived need arises. It is an ongoing, uninterrupted process of building the union itself.

After extensive discussion, convention delegates approved a resolution that conceives education in terms of promoting and aiding the "development of a dynamic, change-oriented organizing culture" that builds on the union's "cultural and linguistic diversity."

In summary, the resolution calls for "empowerment and union building as key objectives for all ACTWU education programs."

The adoption of this policy guideline in the area of education represents a vision that a growing number of top union leaders and rank-and-file members have of an education program that goes beyond providing basic skills and knowledge to one that promotes cultural and organizational changes.

These policies have provided a framework that has allowed us to experiment with what we hope will become a multicultural worker-education program. The following are basic principles that guide us in developing the learning experiences associated with that program.

1. Recognize that "ownership" of the union belongs to all its members and not only those that make policy (elected officers) or to those that are employed by the union (paid staff).

2. Affirm and promote the strength and value of cultural diversity in all aspects of the life of the union and its members.

3. Promote equality of opportunity for all people that belong to the union.

4. Recognize the importance of equity in the distribution of rewards among all members of the union.

5. Insist that eradicating biases and prejudice of all kinds is the task of all union workers.

6. Expose all workers to the contributions that men and women from all racial and ethnic groups have made to build this union and the entire trade union movement.

7. Place special emphasis on the recruitment and training of union members whose participation in education programs has been limited by language and/or cultural differences.

8. Offer basic literacy and multilingual training to all union members as part of an inclusionary and developmental process of education and training.

9. Establish that the union is an agency for social change to improve the quality of life of all its members.

10. Recognize that the responsibility to promote change belongs to all union members.

REFERENCES

Hill, John K. and James E. Pearse. "Enforcing Sanctions Against Employers of Illegal Aliens." *Economic Review*. Federal Reserve Bank of Dallas, May 1987.

Section 7

PRIVATIZATION OF PUBLIC SERVICES—CONCEPTS AND STRATEGIES

Public sector jurisdictions in both the United States and Canada have adopted privatization of public services as one plank in the public policy side of a "competitiveness" strategy and as one method to reduce costs in an era of budget stringency. The issue of privatization burst on public sector unions in both countries during the 1980s. Early strategies to fight privatization included research and demonstration that cost savings were illusory and exposing private sector contractors and certain public officials as corrupt or at least greedy. Recently unions have shifted strategies and have begun to expose the concept of privatization as part of a market-oriented, antiunion and antiworker public policy. The challenge for public sector unions is to organize private sector workers into supporting this formulation.

The papers in this chapter concentrate on the conceptual underpinnings of privatization and union strategies. Laurie Clements of the University of Iowa Labor Center analyzes privatization as part of the political resurgence of the right. He argues that more than jobs are at stake, and that privatization raises the most fundamental questions about the role of government in the economy and society and who controls traditionally public assets. Clements also critiques common arguments offered in support of privatization.

John Shields of the British Columbia Government Employees Union has battled privatization of provincial and municipal workers. He also argues that privatization is mainly a political rather than economic issue transferring public assets to private interests. Shields describes one example dealing with highway maintenance in British Columbia and the union's public campaign to save jobs.

The Politics of Privatization: Public It's Ours, Private It's Theirs

LAURIE CLEMENTS

Program Consultant, University of Iowa Labor Center

Over the last decade workers in many parts of the industrialized world have been subject to a range of strategies and tactics on the part of employers and governments designed to undermine the power of organized labor. Whereas union busting tactics are not new, there have been significant changes in orientation with more sophisticated methods of psychological and legal manipulation.[1] State support of corporate antiunion policies has increased at both the ideological and structural levels. Changes in the economic environment and the legal framework in which workers and unions operate have made the everyday activities of unions more difficult. Domestic economic instability and foreign competition in international trade have both contributed to this antiunion hostility. Within this framework unions have been portrayed as fetters on economic development and a hindrance to the process of rationalization necessary to carry western economies into the twenty-first century.

In this dynamic situation, a new concept has entered into the language, and its overall impact has yet to be determined. Privatization may well be one of the most significant developments affecting public sector workers, public employers, and communities since 1945. Its influence has been felt in many advanced and less-developed economies and in political systems of very different ideological persuasions. Privatization on the global scale is linked to the global restructuring of capital and the world division of labor. As industrial restructuring is occurring on a world scale, the role of the state in the management of economies is also changing. State involvement in the post-1945 era has been characterized by increasing size, increasing intervention, and, with the major exception of the United States, an expansion of the state into the realm of production. Privatization initiatives lead to a modification of this role and offer new opportunities for private organizations to expand their rate of profit. The role of the state has been modified to better facilitate the expansion and proliferation of the "market system" around the globe. The resurgence of the market model has been experienced in the United States, as in other countries, and the American privatization debate has to be located in this context.

The discussion of privatization and the subsequent proposals for privatizing public services, therefore, must be analyzed within this dynamic political and economic landscape. Supporters of privatization advocate reduction in the size, scope and role of the public sector and a consequent expansion of the private sector. The term "privatization" means to make private or to change from public to private ownership and control. The privatization process can take many forms (Pirie, 1988). These include the sale of public sector assets, the contracting out of work previously performed in the public sector, the distribution of vouchers to eligible consumers who would then choose a private organization from which to purchase services, and the deregulation of industries and services.

The elevation of privatization to major-issue status in the political arena has grown with the resurgence of free market economics (Moe, 1987). Privatization has led to questioning economic, social, and political issues that had long been considered settled in the postwar era (Moe, 1988). The privatizers advocate reducing government involvement in many areas of social provision, encourage the purchase of private sector services instead of public, and assert that public service provision has led to the development of a permanent dependent underclass in America. The privatization movement challenges the very premises of public policy in the "New Deal" and especially "Great Society" eras. By fusing the free market with a populist appeal, conservative governments have redefined earlier policy initiatives as misguided.

Privatization, therefore, raises fundamental questions about the role of the state in contemporary society. The massive federal budget deficit provides an environment that has helped popularize privatization as a solution to "excessive" government spending and government "interference" in the economy. Privatization is portrayed as a panacea for future economic well-being by promoting the liberalization of market structures and deficit reduction. At the ideological level it emphasizes "getting the government off the back of the people." The arguments are infused with the view that "the government that governs best is the government that governs least."[2] This Hobbsean approach depicts the role of the state in society as a Leviathan that has to be controlled.[3]

The central argument of this paper is that the real Leviathan is being created as the machinery of government is replaced by a much less accountable form of power concentrated in the private corporation.

Privatization has become a major element in the arsenal of the ascendant conservatives seeking to restructure social, economic, and political relations, in response to the profitability crisis of capital. The overall strategy of the Reagan and Thatcher governments has been to deregulate markets, support corporate policies to reduce the price of labor power, develop fiscal policies favorable to the wealthy, and openly endorse union-busting strategies. Rather than create the free flow of competition, however, this development has led to the "privatization" of economic decision making, a growing concentration of economic power, and bolstering the interests of the economic status quo.

The redefinition of the role of the state has also occurred in many Third World countries. Less developed countries, already hostage to massive foreign debts and dependent upon first world capital, are firmly set in a core-periphery relationship with the dominant economies. The "export" of privatization to these poorer nations has been manifest in the highly restricted constraints on borrowing, as the World Bank, International Monetary Fund, and Asian Development Bank have embraced the privatization model. Privatization has been lauded as a panacea for economic development and debt reduction in Chile, Peru, Malaysia, Niger, and Turkey.

The globalization of privatization, however, is more likely to increase the dependency of less developed nations on western capital. International capital mobility has supported privatization initiatives, and, conversely, privatization facilitates such capital mobility. Eastern European privatization programs will offer further opportunities for western capital to extend its sphere of influence around the globe.

There is a need to go beyond the apparent seductiveness of the argument for privatization and carefully analyze the impact of this development on the structure and process of public sector service delivery in contemporary America. This paper will outline the conceptual debate on privatization and provide an analytical framework for unions and workers to develop programs, strategies, and tactics to defend both their own and community interests against the worst excesses of privatization.

THE CONCEPTUAL DEBATE

Conceptually, privatization can be firmly located in the economics of the "public choice" school and the politics of the "new right." These views were articulated in the Grace Commission Report to President Reagan in 1984. The Grace Commission claimed that implementation of its recommendations would result in savings and revenue enhancements of more than $424 billion over three years. A significant proportion of the "savings" would result from a proposed privatization program that would reduce the size and scope of the federal sector. The Grace Commission targeted such services as the space shuttle program, the U.S. Coast Guard, the Veterans Administration Hospital, and the Federal Power Marketing Authorities as items for sale to the private sector. Following the Grace report, the president established the Presidents' Commission on Privatization in 1987 to investigate the wider range of possible targets for privatization (President's Commission on Privatization Report, 1988).

Much of the discussion of privatization thus centers on the appropriate role of government in contemporary society and whether certain activities are appropriate functions of government. This is clearly stated in Executive Order 12607, which instructed the Presidential Commission to study and evaluate activities of the federal government and identify those functions that:

1. Are not the proper responsibility of the federal government and should be divested or transferred to the private sector, with no residual involvement by the federal government; or

2. Require continuing oversight by an executive branch agency but can be performed more efficiently by a private entity, including the use of vouchers as an alternative to direct service (President's Commission on Privatization Report, 1988).

There is a need to analyze the theoretical underpinning and ideological content of the privatization arguments in order to better understand the rationale, operation, and implications of the privatization process and consider the options open to opponents of privatization.

Supporters of privatization accept the competitive model in nonproblematic terms and contend that the public sector is less efficient and effective than the private sector. They assert that public officials are often more concerned with building up bureaucracy than in reducing costs. Without the discipline of the market there is no economic incentive to prevent the misallocation of publicly funded resources. Public sector institutions therefore lack both the ability and desire to become more efficient.

The economic priorities that flow from this model include a nonintervention strategy by the government in the operation of markets and tax incentives to stimulate economic growth. The irony of government fiscal intervention should not be lost. The market model portrays individuals as profit or utility maximizers best served by the market and the institution of private property. The market, portrayed as a neutral entity, is accepted as the most effective and efficient provider of services. The privatization movement has sought to legitimate the market as a provider of economic and social benefits, and the antistate rhetoric and ideological position embraces a conscious rejection of collective responsibility.

This highly individualistic model has always been important in the United States, but it contains an insidious element that implies that individual self-reliance has been undermined by the growth of public provision and social services. Privatizers assume that the trend towards greater social equality has failed to promote incentives and therefore efficiency. This perspective implicitly and explicitly accepts that a reduction in publicly funded services would be beneficial both for individuals and communities. It suggests that increased individual effort would reduce the dependency of citizens on the state. Supply side economists and the Reagan administration, in supporting tax cuts, shifting resources away from human services, and advocating the substitution of the market for government agencies, embraced an argument for dismantling collective support systems and reducing government responsibility. The fetishism of individualism and the denigration of collectivism displays an important ideological aspect of privatization that has onerous connotations for workers and unions.

An individualizing model diminishes the importance of social class in the debate. The role of state power in any society is framed and structured by the role of class interests and power within that society:

> The threat to the hegemony of the class that controls capital was sufficient to evoke the response represented by the policies of Reagan. In the name of economic efficiency, poverty programs have been cut, regulatory systems dismantled, and entitlements reduced (Hoover and Plant, 1989).

Government policy making is likewise subject to the pressures of various class interests. The policies of privatization in western economies are a reflection of these pressures to sanction and legitimate the interests of private capital. They are a manifestation of the political and ideological conditions for the reproduction of capital in an era of economic decline and the loss of international hegemony of American capital in the post-1973 period. In order to bolster the needs of private capital, the state has become increasingly involved in directing publicly funded resources into the private sector, particularly through massive defense appropriations. Now the infrastructure of government itself is being sold to "for-profit" organizations after being funded by taxpayers dollars. The economic role of the state is thereby redefined not in a neutral or technical way but as a direct conveyor in the reproduction of private capital.

President Reagan focussed on privatization in his 1987 Independence Day Speech. He portrayed privatization as a key element for both the "economic bill of rights" and "a free America." This provides a particularly restrictive view of the meaning of "rights" and "freedom." It is the economic freedom of the marketplace; an atomistic model that accepts the current socioeconomic system in harmonistic terms. In this "privatized" model, wealth and property distribution are governed by impersonal market forces, not by human power relations. Conflicts of interest are marginal and the "invisible hand" of market clearing forces ensures utility maximization. Statements about society are reduced to those about "privatized" self-seeking individuals. There are no irreconcilable conflicts of interest that cannot be accommodated within the existing structure of society. This serves to both justify the status quo and to transpose public issues into personal problems. Individuals are to blame for their own inadequacies; people get what they are worth. The ideological nexus of private ownership and individualism allows the privatizers to castigate those who advocate a strong public sector as being un-, if not anti-, American. Privatization is therefore portrayed as a return to traditional "American" values. The implications are that a strong public sector is "un-American," that basic social safety nets are antithetical to American values, that the modern state is a "Leviathan," and that the concept of "freedom" is limited to the sphere of the individual.

This model of freedom contains a fundamental critique of egalitarianism. Poverty and inequality that result from the operation of market forces are not regarded as infringements on the freedom of the poor. A "neutral" market does not impinge upon freedom, and poverty is not equated with unfreedom (Hoover and Plant, 1989, p. 47). This perspective suggests that the welfare state is the creator of "unfreedom" because it generates a dependency relationship upon the state rather than a mechanism to foster a more equal society. In fact the argument goes further to suggest that:

> Social equality is a destructive value and should be detached from the proper role of government and the place of welfare within that role (Hoover and Plant, 1989, p.51).

This nascent individualism both ignores and undermines the concept of collective freedom that emerges through the coalition of interests in both the political and economic arenas. The concentration upon individualistic solutions undermines the potent arguments for collective solutions and the use and deployment of collective action. The implication for collective organizations such as labor unions are readily apparent in both the economic and political spheres. Privatization and "individualization" provides further ideological justification for the labeling of collective activity as "special interest." The pejorative specter of "big labor" interfering with "free markets" and "free individuals" has become a central argument in the conservative support of the privatization initiatives and union avoidance.

The assertion that privatization will remove the yoke of government, however, has to be tempered by the fact that one structure of control will be replaced by another less accountable form of control. It is the nature of such control that is at the heart of the privatization debate. The transfer of services to the private corporation in an era of oligopolistic capitalism does not guarantee that competition will increase. This may well be one of the heroic assumptions of the entire scheme. The Reagan economic strategy, if it can be called a strategy, fostered and consolidated oligopolistic structures as merger mania became the dominant form of economic expansion. Despite the rhetoric of competition, the reality of the Reagan years was increased economic concentration and the consolidation of differences between rich and poor. The sale of public sector assets is just as likely to confirm this consolidation and further concentrate wealth in the richer echelons of society, as many examples of British privatization testify (Vickers and Yarrow, 1988).

A Critique of the Arguments Supporting Privatization

Advocates of privatization argue that it will lead to:

- An improvement in economic performance of the assets or service functions concerned;
- A reduction in the federal deficit and improved "fiscal responsibility" at all levels of government;
- An accelerated economic recovery;
- A reduction in the power of public sector unions; and
- An expansion of the share owning population and the growth of popular capitalism (Hanke, 1987).

Privatization and Economic Performance

Perhaps one of the most pernicious aspects of the privatization model is the general assumption that services will be more effectively and efficiently provided in the private sector. Does this mean that the productivity and efforts of workers in the public sector consistently fall below that of private sector workers? Does this mean that public sector management, presumably trained in the same business schools and following the same basic principles as their private sector counterparts, are somehow less qualified, able, or productive? It is difficult to sustain an argument that suggests that one sector has a monopoly on skill, technique, or organizational acumen.

"Magic formula management" is a myth that has to be debunked. To suggest that the public sector has been particularly susceptible to bureaucratic inertia whereas similar large-scale organizations in the private sector are somehow immune from any such development is hardly an adequate explanation. The magic formula management often attributed to Federal Express more accurately reflects an authoritarian approach to labor relations under which management, "since the company's founding sixteen years ago has had its way with its work force" (*Wall Street Journal*, 1989, p.10). Yet the United States Postal Service and its unionized work force is frequently extolled to follow a similar pattern of labor-management relations.

Unions in the public sector have been among the most vocal critics of inefficiency and have advocated in-house improvements. This is, however, a very different approach than selling assets or contracting out work. Public sector inefficiency should not be condoned, but privatization should not be embraced as the panacea of efficiency.

Advocates of privatization support the view that private ownership creates greater incentives to improve productivity and performance, and that private property rights will lead to an improvement in performance monitoring (Vickers and Yarrow, 1988). This is problematic. In the case of many publicly owned assets such as federal lands or forestry reserves, it is very difficult to determine if they can be more efficiently operated in the private sector. Paul Starr notes that there is mixed evidence on the comparative performance of public and private sector services such as electrical utilities (Starr, 1988). Starr makes a second point, however, that needs to be addressed:

> ... pervasive differences in services performed by public and private organizations often render simple comparisons misleading. Especially important are differences in clientele. Public and private schools, hospitals, and social services rarely have the same kinds of students, patients and clients .... The burden of public institutions is precisely that they are often the services of the last resort; the freedom of private institutions consists in part from their ability to select the most desirable client populations. To be sure, that selectivity may make them more attractive sources of services, but it does not indicate they perform any better than do the public services when both face the same clients and the same tasks (Starr, 1988, p. 6).

182

Yet when an agency is very successful in providing its service, such as the Federal Housing Administration (FHA) mortgage insurance program, the President's Commission recommended that:

> The Federal Housing Administration should reduce its mortgage insurance activity so that it does not compete as directly with private mortgage insurers. It should direct its efforts toward that market not served by private insurers, that is, toward buyers who have been turned down by private mortgage insurers. (President's Commission Report, 1988, p. 32).

This perspective ensures that a federal agency should not be allowed to play on a level playing field. In the competitive model a logical conclusion would be that private sector insurers unable to compete with the FHA would not deserve to stay in business. In this case the competitive model appears as an emperor with no clothes. Competition is secondary to economic restructuring and profit shifting to the private sector.

Starr also indicates that most studies comparing performance in the public and private sectors concentrate more upon accountants, standards of financial measurement and contain little evidence on the quality of service produced. This makes it difficult to estimate if costs are lower because of efficiency, a reduction in the service provided, or because there is an unorganized work force earning lower wages, receiving fewer benefits, and more likely to be working part time (Starr, 1988, p. 8).

Contracting out does not remove public responsibility for the quality of service provided, and, on a more onerous note, the narrowing of public provision acutely exposes those most in need in our society. Privatization will reduce the protections of disadvantaged members of society by excluding them from privatized services because of the lack of ability to pay. Black and minority workers who have been subject to the discriminatory effects of segmented labor markets in the private sector will also suffer an adverse impact as job opportunities are shifted away from the public sector (Suggs, 1989).

Transferring public services to the private sector places government responsibility on the alter of economic sacrifice, and may lead governments to evade constitutional responsibilities. Harold J. Sullivan suggests that if flexibility is a promised advantage of privatization, it may come at the expense of citizen rights and liberties (Sullivan, 1987, pp. 461–467). Private firms and leaders whose priorities are cost-cutting and deregulation are less likely to follow safeguards and protections that would be constitutionally required of a public entity.

Privatization and Deficit Reduction

It has been suggested that much of the current economic malaise has resulted from profligate public sector spending. A reduction in public financial responsibility via privatization has been heralded as a mechanism of deficit reduction. By any evaluation, the decade of the 1980s has been one of increased deficits and vigorous support by conservatives for increasing defense expenditures. This has been the epitome of "privatized spending" and has ensured that the contradictions of the "Reagan Revolution" are experienced by American workers. Nationalization has never been a major factor in American as compared to European experience. The multibillion dollar sell-offs as experienced in Britain is not an American option. A few agencies such as the Postal Service offer the possibility of a major asset sale, but the sale of assets at heavily discounted prices is not the way to address fundamental budget problems.

On the issue of federal deficit reduction, American privatization has been an inadequate and ineffectual policy instrument. It has failed by all standards and criteria, including the ability to significantly reduce the size of the federal sector work force. Yet it still carries enormous ideological support among the supply siders in the economic debate. A cursory examination of the President's Commission Report also indicates that the transfer of resources to the private sector would amount to stripping assets from the public sector. This erodes the argument that privatization can be used as a significant part of a deficit reduction package because there will be considerable pressure put on the government agencies, by groups with vested interest in the process, to ensure that the asking price is as attractive (low) as possible.

Further, not all transfers will reduce the deficit. The sale of an agency that generates a surplus will have a negative impact on deficit reduction. Yet these are the prime targets of the privatizers. Privatization will thus remove the surplus generating areas from the public sector leaving those that remain to be deficit funded, presumably from tax revenues. The bottom line is that assets can only be sold once. The future revenue earning potential in the public sector is therefore drastically reduced. The massive growth in the American federal deficit has occurred during the incumbency of the most rightwing administration for decades. It is double speak on the part of the government to suggest that a privatization program is a solution to the problem of the deficit.

Privatization and Economic Growth

There is little evidence to suggest that privatization fuels economic growth. The view that private ownership provides incentives for growth is too restrictive. Market structure, regulation, and other relevant economic factors are important. It is inadequate to assume that if private sector firms have lower unit costs than their public counterparts, their contributions to either welfare or growth will be greater. Market power and the lack of real competition can significantly affect output and growth. In the United States the expansion of contractual monopolies, as opposed to a model of competing market forces, has been a regular feature in contracting out situations. Under such circumstances it is not surprising that the impact of privatization on economic growth is limited.

There are other factors that indicate that long-term growth could be hindered by privatization. Privatization has long been recognized by both its most staunch supporters and opponents as a way of cutting labor costs. But this has an adverse impact on purchasing power. Studies in Florida indicate that privatization programs have a "negative income multiplier" effect of 2.4, which means that for every dollar reduction in wages and benefits resulting from privatization, $2.40 is actually lost to the community (Barry, n.d.). The savings to the local taxpayer is therefore more illusion than reality, and the adverse community impact amounts to a tax on the community.

There is little evidence to support the view that privatization will lead to job growth. In fact the advocates of privatization suggest that cost reduction resulting from privatization is because contractors use less labor. Whereas "new" jobs may appear as a result of privatization, the reduction in public sector employment must also be built into the equation, and the relative wage/benefit package paid to workers is also of importance when evaluating the overall impact of the process. The impact of privatization on unemployment has been more a re-structuring of labor markets and growth of lower paying jobs than a solid expansion in the labor market prospects of workers. Fewer jobs at lower wages do not provide a sound base for either economic recovery or growth.

Privatization does not address the trade deficit. There is, however, a relationship between patterns of international trade and privatization. As global privatization continues, more capital flows out of the core countries (United States, Britain, Germany, etc.) into peripheral countries (in Africa, South America and possibly Eastern Europe) in response to these changes. Eventually goods will flow back into the core economies from newly owned foreign subsidiaries located in the peripheral economies. If global privatization increases the export of capital, it will in effect increase the export of employment and the import of goods. The interests of multinational capital are served therefore by privatization programs in less-developed economies. Foreign penetration is intensified and the concentration and centralization of economic power in the hands of foreign capital will increase. The impact on growth in the domestic economy, under these circumstances, is as likely to be negative as positive. As far as domestic privatization in the United States is concerned, there is little evidence to show that the growth in contracting out would have any significant impact upon the trade deficit.

There is little evidence that privatization will help reduce interest rates. The United Kingdom experience reflects the most advanced privatization program coupled with the highest interest rates in the economically developed world. The view that privatizations would lead to a reduction in government financing, and therefore place less pressure on interest rates, has not been sustained in practice.

Privatization programs, at best, appear to provide a short-term prop to an ailing economy. At worst, they allow for governments and employers to increase the control of labor in the production process. What should be of genuine concern to American workers is the way the Thatcher government has used privatization as part of a systematic, state-led union-busting initiative. It is to that we now turn.

Privatization and Union Power

Of the five arguments made for supporting privatization, the attack on the power of organized labor has the greatest credibility. The growth of public sector unions in an era of private sector union decline is anathema to the supporters of privatization. This process has occurred in many countries where the expansion of unionism has coincided with the advances in public employment. In the United States, the precipitous decline in union membership in the private sector has been partially offset by growth in the public sector. The marginalization of unions in the private sector has placed unions outside the decision-making process. Contracting out of bargaining unit work, endemic in the private sector, is an ever expanding element in the public sector. Contracting out is the major form of privatization at city and county levels of government. Supporters of privatization argue that contractors are more flexible and cost effective because they operate without the "restraints" of government or union work rules. Contractors maintain unilateral control of the labor process and are not "encumbered" by the protections afforded workers by seniority, job classification, or just-cause provisions in the contract. Contracting out is a mechanism for circumventing the rules of Civil Service or the labor agreement. This is shorthand for union busting.

The President's Commission described the postal employees' contract with the Postal Service as "union-imposed restrictions," which lends considerable weight to the view that privatization is a union avoidance strategy. Steven Hanke openly suggests that it can be used to reduce the power of public sector unions (Hanke, 1987). And by cutting the public sector, the potential union membership base is also reduced. Clearly this would also put significant downward pressure on the wage and benefit package of workers in both sectors. Research by Valente and Manchester indicates that contractors are more likely to employ fewer workers, employ more part-time and temporary workers, employ younger workers, and pay lower wages (Valente and Manchester, 1984). Their research indicates that contractors apply a "Social Darwinist" approach that emphasizes the survival of the fittest. But the new "leaner, fitter, trimmer" organization is dependent upon a smaller, more tightly controlled and lower paid work force. From a union perspective, privatization tells public workers that they are dispensable; that they are commodities with no premium for skill, experience, or seniority. Privatization also sends a message to public sector unions that they are dispensable. The irony is that the conservative agenda for privatization has provided public sector unions and workers with an issue over which significant organizing can take place, and on which they may also receive the support of public sector management.

Privatization and "Popular Capitalism"

The argument that privatization would encourage the growth of the property-owning democracy and "people's capitalism" also has intuitive appeal among supporters of the process. The expansion of share ownership among employees is possible in cases where considerable asset sales are envisaged. Preferential terms to current employees who are given first option on the share sale can have the effect of reducing resistance to the privatization process. This impact is increased if the offer price is set low enough for workers to "buy in." But the question of expanding the property-owning democracy is more problematic than mere ownership of shares. ESOP developments in Britain have been merely a precursor of corporate control of privatized operations.

Two specific points should be made on this matter. First, the diffusion of share ownership generally leads to a concentration of real control. This is a readily understood paradox in corporate hierarchies and has been used by management to consolidate its control over corporations. Secondly, in Britain the shareholding population increased dramatically with the privatization process, but there has also been a reversal in this trend in the late 1980s. Whereas the government claimed that shareholders would soon outnumber trade union members and that this would reflect a fundamental shift in the balance of class forces in society, Clarke has argued that this is little more than an elaborate facade (Clarke, 1990). Clarke also notes that 70 percent of British shareholders have holdings of less than 3,000 pounds ($6,000) at a time when institutions control over three-quarters of stock traded on the exchange (Clarke, 1990, p. 501). Large corporations and financial institutions usually have a considerable stake in the long-term control of privatized corporations. Even where preferential buying terms are offered to current employees, there is no guarantee that they will remain long-term shareholders. The British privatization process has more effectively smokescreened the transfer of assets from the public sector to large financial and multinational operations under the illusion of the widespread dilution of corporate control (Clarke, 1990, p. 502). While this development is far less likely to occur on a similar scale in the United States, for reasons already outlined, the transfer of assets out of the public sector is likely to follow the British pattern. Shareholder democracy is not a meaningful objective of privatization.

CONCLUSION

Privatization offers the promise of "people's capitalism," but this promise is fraudulent. The expansion of interest in privatization is in line with the dominant economic and political trends of the last decade. Privatization is as spurious a solution to the problems of the public sector as is "trickle down" economics to the economy in general. It is an attempt to appropriate public resources for private profit. Its short-term advantages to conservative governments, however, carry long-term costs to the citizenry. It is a single palliative, not a fundamental cure for the multifaceted problems facing both the public sector and the economy.

Privatization should not simply be regarded as a problem for public sector workers. It raises the more fundamental question of the role of government in modern society and therefore affects all workers. State economic policy has always been affected by the demands of capital, especially in relation to the economic and labor relations climate. "Reaganomics" intensified the demand for state support to bolster profitability and employer control of the labor process. Privatization is part of a power struggle that has unfolded over the last decade. Governments have embraced a model of authoritarian populism that has sanctioned the undermining of collective action on the part of workers and unions in both public and private sectors, and at the same time encouraged the redefinition of the appropriate boundaries for state activity and the parameters of social democracy within our society. Unions need to find their political allies in this struggle and work with them to prevent the worst excesses of privatization. In spite of the free market rhetoric, the politics of this radical policy change is as important as commercial judgement. Unions have to confront the myth that the mere change in ownership will provide a cure-all for the perceived weakness or failure in structure or function of service delivery.

Privatization is a political attack on public services. It is difficult to rebut this attack with traditional trade union methods alone. The basis of the struggle has to be carried to private sector workers and the public in general. Workers will not defeat privatization simply by defending the current status quo. Rather, unions should be involved in a positive strategy to improve public services. The movement to privatize public services is well advanced in many state-provided services. The gurus of privatization have taken the high ground on the issue, and it has been a significant part of the "Reagan Revolution." Its impact at the federal level has been limited, but its ideological rhetoric has been of greater significance than the economic reality. A creeping privatization process has expanded at the state, county, and city levels as local authorities, financially strapped and fiscally bound, have looked for alternative delivery systems. As we enter the nineties, it is important that the labor movement not simply let the debate take place on the terms of the privatizers. There is a need to organize and mobilize around the issue, and to fight to ensure that government does not give up on itself.

The importance of the public sector cannot be evaluated in terms of elementary accounting. This is not to justify inefficient practices. But there is a pressing social and moral need to provide effective public services to those who require them. A profit-centered model will serve only those with the ability to pay. Privatization is an issue to be confronted. A labor movement prepared to defend public services is an important first step. The current range of public sector services emerged and grew because of the support of the labor movement for those less fortunate members of society and because of a belief that some things like national forests were too important to be left in private hands. These perspectives on the quality of public life should not be given up lightly.

ENDNOTES

[1]See, for example, Center to Protect Workers Rights, 1979 and 1980, for a review of the literature and cases in this area.

[2]Ronald Reagan is quoted as saying "I have often that the best government in no government is no government at all." Quoted in *Private Profit Public Risk: The Contraction Out of Professional Services*. AFSCME, 1986.

[3]Thomas Hobbes. *The Leviathan*. Michael Oakshot (ed.) (Oxford, England. n.d.) This text by the seventeenth-century English philosopher likens the emerging modern state machine to the mythical monster Leviathan. The essential message of the text was that government had become too large and powerful and would dominate the lives of the citizens of society. The modern state therefore had to be reduced in size and scope, and is a perspective that is central to the advocates of privatization.

REFERENCES

AFSCME. *Private Profit, Public Risk: The Contracting Out of Professional Services*. 1986.

Barry, D. Marshall. "The Negative Local Economic Impact of Privatization." *Center for Labor Research and Studies*. Miami, Florida: Florida International University, n.d.

Center to Protect Workers Rights, *From Brass Knuckles to Briefcases*. 1979.

Center to Protect Workers Rights. *Union Busting and the Law: From Benign Neglect to Malignant Growth*. September, 1980.

Clarke, Tom. "Socialized Industry: Social Ownership or Shareholding Democracy." In *Organization Theory and Class Analysis: New Approaches and New Issues*. Edited by Stewart R. Clegg. Berlin: Walter de Gruyter, 1990, 485–512.

Hanke, Steve. H. "Privatization versus Nationalization." In Steve H. Hanke (ed.) *Prospects for Privatization*. The Academy of Political Science, 1987.

Hobbes, Thomas. *The Leviathan*. Edited by M. Oakshot. Oxford, England.

Hoover, Kenneth, and Raymond Plant. *Conservative Capitalism in Britain and the United States*. London: Routledge, 1989.

Moe, Ronald C. "Exploring the Limits of Privatization." *Public Administration Review*. 453, November–December, 1987.

———. "Privatization: An Overview from a Public Administration Perspective." *CRS Report for Congress* :88–201.

Pirie, Madsen. *Privatization*. Aldershot, England, Wildwood House, 1988.

President's Commission on Privatization. Report, *Privatization: Toward More Effective Government*. March, 1988.

Smith, Marcia S. "Privatization of the Landsat Remote-Sensing Satellite System: Current Issues." *CRS Report for Congress*

477:4, Spring, 1987.

Starr, Paul. *The Limits of Privatization*. Economic Policy Institute, 1988.

Suggs, Robert E. *Minorities and Privatization: Economic Mobility at Risk*. Washington, D.C.: Joint Center for Political Studies Press, 1989.

Sullivan, Harold J. "Privatization of Public Services: A Growing Threat to Constitutional Rights." *Public Administration Review* 47(6):461–7, November–December, 1987.

The Grace Commission. *The President's Private Sector Survey on Cost Control*. 1984.

Valente, Carl F., and Lydia D. Manchester. "Rethinking Local Services: Examining Alternative Delivery Approaches." *Management Information Service* Special Report (12):12, March, 1984.

Vickers., J., and G. Yarrow. *Privatization: An Economic Analysis*. Cambridge, Massachusetts: MIT Press, 1988.

Wall Street Journal. "Bumpier Flight: Federal Express Faces Test of Pilots' Loyalty Since Purchasing Tiger." A1–4, October 23, 1989.

Wall Street Journal. "Tory Paradox: In Thatcher's Britain, Freer Enterprise Leads to More State Control." October 6, 1988.

Fighting Privitization: The British Columbia Experience

JOHN T. SHIELDS

President, British Colombia Government Employees' Union

At the Douglas border crossing between Canada and the U.S., there is an inscription on the Peace Arch. It reads: "Children of a common mother." Our nations have common roots and traditions. As trade unionists, we share many values. And these days, in the United States and Canada, men and women who care about the common good share a dismay and a despair at the way governments are attacking public services. Our common mother has let us down.

The people who today hold power in the mother country, in England, have unleashed a right-wing, ideological assault on the public interest. Margaret Thatcher's battle cry, echoed by conservative governments in North America, is "sell everything." It doesn't make sense in Great Britain and it makes even less sense here.

A strong public sector is essential to binding together the citizens of geographically large countries like ours. That's even more true in Canada than it is in the United States. We have more acres, more snow, and many fewer people. Without a strong public sector, Canada would not be Canada. Canada exists as a nation because public investment pushed through a railroad from the Atlantic to the Pacific.

Nation building in Canada is enhanced through our publicly owned national radio and television network, the Canadian Broadcasting Corporation (CBC). The CBC gives us a sense of ourselves from coast to coast through public affairs and information broadcasting. It also produces Canadian drama and entertainment programs. The private networks in Canada show mostly American programs, because it's cheaper and more profitable to buy programs than to produce them. Our children know more about the constitution, the laws, and the politics of the United States than their own. Virtually their only opportunity to see themselves is through public broadcasting.

As a Canadian, I am proud of the nation that we have built north of the 49th parallel and conscious of the vital role played by public investment and public enterprise. I share the pride that Americans feel in the public enterprise that lifted humankind off this planet and gave humanity a new frontier in space. I am delighted to be able to travel through the United States on a magnificent interstate highway system, built with public investment to serve the public.

In both the United States and Canada, our societies are built on a foundation of public service: a public health system, public schools, highways, airports, and a whole array of vital municipal and state (or provincial) services. The public sector is the way we work together to improve life for all of us, uphold our common ideals and values, and do the things the private sector can't or won't do. The public sector is the way we say that a four-year-old sexually abused child must be helped, without leaving it to chance or charity. It's the way we say that people are more important than profit.

THE ROOTS OF PRIVATIZATION

So what's behind this push for privatization, contracting out, and deregulation of public services? Who benefits? Who are the people who want polluters to regulate themselves; the people who want the big forest companies to scale their own logs; the people who want to get rid of safety inspections, and meat inspections, and highway maintenance operations? They are right-wing politicians, ideologues, and big business. They don't like government and they don't like unions.

They want to put profit first at the cost of tearing down the institutions we have built together to serve us all. The public institutions that make our countries better, more civilized places to live. They claim that individual greed can somehow add up to collective good. That's absurd. They know the price of everything, and the value of nothing.

Privatization, at root, has nothing to do with economics or efficiency, and everything to do with politics. There are three aspects to that political agenda. First, privatization is a way the right wing can turn over public assets, at fire sale prices, to their supporters in the private sector. Second, through under-funding and under-staffing of public services, governments have promoted the lie that the private sector is more efficient, and that privatization will save tax dollars. Third, privatization attacks unions, which the right wing sees as a way of attacking a major base of support for their political opponents.

In Britain recently, Nigel Lawson, chancellor of the Exchequer, told a group called the Wider Share Ownership Council: "It is interesting to note that as the number of shareholders has risen from three million in 1979 to nearly nine million now, the number of trade unionists has fallen from over thirteen million to around ten million. At this rate, it cannot be long before the two lines cross."

The arguments for privatization, deregulation, and contracting out are political arguments. They are arguments that favor big business, private interests, and government friends and insiders at the expense of the majority of ordinary people. What we have to point out, and what we have to help voters to understand, is this: *Privatization has no economic benefit.* It creates not one new job; in fact, it usually means fewer jobs—nonunion jobs—at lower wages. It means private profit for a few, and poorer quality services for the public.

It is a way of transferring public assets to private interests. It is Robin Hood in reverse, stealing from the people and giving to the rich.

PRIVATIZATION IN BRITISH COLUMBIA

In British Columbia, privatization came out of nowhere. Premier Bill Vander Zalm suddenly decided that it was the trendy, politically rewarding thing to do. There was no public pressure for privatization, nor was there pressure from the people providing the services. There wasn't even any pressure from the business community.

Privatization was sprung on British Columbians unexpectedly on October 23, 1987. On that date, Premier Vander Zalm announced that the first phase of the sale of public services would begin immediately. He announced that ten thousand public service jobs would be eliminated.

The first target was highways maintenance services, affecting 6,000 workers. One of the best highways maintenance systems in North America was dismantled, carved up into twenty-eight separate districts, and put up for bid. Highways maintenance equipment was sold off at firesale prices, with specialized equipment going for 30 percent of its true value.

The lives of six thousand men and women and their families have been disrupted, and for what purpose? Highways maintenance costs the province the same, or more. Service is no better, and may be worse as private contractors cut corners to make a profit. There is no consistency or continuity of service from district to district. In short, the privatization of highways maintenance is detrimental to the public interest, as well as to the thousands of individual workers.

The British Columbia Government Employees Union (BCGEU) continues to represent most of the workers affected under successor agreements with the private contractors. The workers were promised by the government that they would continue to enjoy their existing rights and benefits, but it's not that easy.

Highways maintenance workers in the Fort St. John and Quesnel regions of B.C. were forced into a lengthy strike to fight concession demands. The private contractor is not the most progressive employer we've ever negotiated with. Northland Road Services was refusing to participate in the workers' pension plan and demanding other takeaways, including a five-fold increase in the number of people excluded from the union, among them the entire office staff. They wanted to increase the number of exclusions from five to twenty-five, in a bargaining unit of only seventy-five people.

Shortly after the first privatization announcement, we asked for a meeting with the government to discuss the impact on our members. When we asked for details about the plans, the senior bureaucrat in the premier's office told us that the government was ideologically committed to selling off everything, and that the only thing that would slow them down would be political expediency.

The government of British Columbia jumped blindly onto Margaret Thatcher's bandwagon. They were convinced that privatization was an opportunity to get rid of the union, score political points with voters, and throw some big contracts to their friends. There was no consultation with British Columbians. There was no study of whether privatization was a good thing or a bad thing for B.C.

There was lots of consultation with people from our mother country. Madsen Pirie, one of Thatcher's top privatization hit men, was flown in from England to tell our government how to do it. Representatives from the B.C. government flew to England to see how Thatcher pulled it off there.

But they didn't bother talking to British Columbians, and they went to great lengths to avoid talking to the union. In fact, one of their chief goals was to bypass the BCGEU and try to convince public employees to buy their own jobs. The government set up hit teams that were sent to various work sites around the province to intimidate and coerce employees on government time, and at government expense. The government set up a propaganda branch, and began producing publications that outlined the so-called benefits of bidding on your own job. These were distributed directly to individual employees at work by their supervisors.

For many of our members, it has been a difficult and painful process. Take the Vehicle Modification Depot in Saanich, near Victoria. It's a typical example of how far a government will go when it comes down with privatization fever. Employees at the Vehicle Modification Depot are carpenters and cabinet makers. They convert vans into ambulances. The depot basically assembles the provincial ambulance fleet. One day, a group of senior government officials drove up. They usually arrive in a very large limousine. The officials presented a glowing vision of employees-turned-entrepreneurs. They talked about profits of $10 thousand per vehicle. They held out the promise of a four year guarantee of work from the government. They even talked about developing offshore markets.

They lied. The employees were told they could not choose to remain government employees if the depot were privatized. The workers were told they could join the partnership to buy the operation or take a chance on getting a job with the privatized company. They were told they could not continue to work for the government. That was a lie. The workers were also told they would not get any severance, despite many years of service with the government, which was another lie.

Just imagine how these workers felt. For years, they had been doing a good job, and working at a job that filled a real need. Suddenly, a handful of strangers walk in the door and say, "Sorry, that's not good enough. If you want to keep doing the job you've been doing, you'll have to buy this place. Get a second mortgage on your house. Take out a big loan. If you don't, you may be out on your ear." Eventually, the government convinced the employees their only hope of holding their jobs was to go along.

The government sent in a consultant to help the employees form a partnership and submit a bid that the government then rejected. After all that, the government rejected the bid. For five more months, the government dragged out the negotiations. It had the workers over a barrel, and it kept them there. Throughout these discussions, workers were warned that things would be even tougher if they tried to involve their union.

At this point, the B.C. Supreme Court made a landmark decision. In what has come to be known as the Verrin case, the court upheld the right of a government employee to choose to remain a government employee. Once the Vehicle Modification Depot employees realized they had a choice—to stay in government, or to pursue a privatization bid—they withdrew from the bidding process.

But the turmoil is not yet over. The consultants sent in by the government have presented the employees with a bill for $11,700. They are being threatened with legal action if they don't pay. As a final straw, the government decided not to sell the Vehicle Modification Depot after all.

Now, two years later, the government has announced that it plans to relocate the depot in another part of the province. The government claims this would be a cost-saving measure. The economics don't support that argument. It seems more likely that the move is an attempt to boost government support in an area where it has a chance of winning a seat. The fact that the depot has been in its current location for eighteen years—successfully operated by qualified, experienced employees—is not a factor to a government that puts political survival ahead of everything else.

These privatization zealots are oblivious to the chaos they have caused in the lives of a group of employees who had been effectively providing a service to the public. These workers have faced months of intimidation, threats, lies and stress. They still face possible legal action to try to make them pay for consulting services they accepted under threat and coercion from their employer. And now their jobs are threatened once again by the proposed relocation.

This case is typical. This is the way the B.C. government pushes privatization. There is no public consultation, no evidence or research to demonstrate that privatization is a good idea, and no union involvement. It is a secret, closed process, not open to public scrutiny. There is coercion and intimidation of employees, and there is no limit to the funds the government will spend on propaganda, private consultants, and privatization hit teams.

There are still rumors that the government will privatize the ambulance service—not the vehicle modification depot, but the ambulance service itself. In B.C., this would be a return to the bad old days when some private operators seemed more concerned about your credit rating than your health. Back in the early 1970s, we even had ambulances that were operated by funeral homes. When you were put into one of those, you were never quite sure whether they were going to rush you to the hospital, or drive you slowly to another destination. We don't want to go back to those days.

UNION STRATEGY

Our job, as trade unionists in the public sector, is to demonstrate to the public that privatization doesn't work. The fight must be won, in public debate, at the political level. Before privatization hits, identify with the public interest. Make it clear that unions stand for quality services, that we care, that we want to do a good job.

Remind the voters about the work we do, in very specific terms. Work from areas of strength, such as public safety. Build on the values of community and cooperation, that some things are more important than making a buck.

When privatization is threatened, build on your base. Strengthen your link with the public interest. Identify with the public. Make the voter part of the "we" who is threatened. Don't make it a public sector workers issue. There is no sympathy for vested interest. The members of *public* sector unions are working for the public interest. We are advocates for first-class public services—because families in the United States and Canada deserve nothing less.

If the government still proceeds, make the privatizers pay a heavy political price. Make sure the voters are fully aware of the impact of what the government is doing. Run ads, use polling research to craft effective antiprivatization arguments. Report the horror stories and create news. I think a news report is worth three ads. It gets the story out, and the news media will go to the privatizers, forcing them to defend themselves.

Keep your members well informed and on your side. Some of them may be tempted by the government's tales of instant millions and streets paved with gold. The facts are on our side, but we have to make sure our side is heard.

Privatization of public services in B.C. has been a failure by every measure. When you look at quality of service, public assets, public accountability, overall costs and economic impact, privatization is a failure.

Services in B.C.'s provincial park system—which I think is one of the best park systems in the world—have been turned over to private operators. An in-house document prepared for the B.C. Parks Branch makes no bones about it. In what's called a "Strategy for Establishing Private Sector Operation of Major Park Campgrounds," the B.C. government says one of the benefits is "enabling entrepreneurs to get into business without major capitalization."

Why should our governments help private business interests earn a profit from a park system built with public funds? Why should our world-class parks be a subsidy to private companies? But that's what privatization is: a way for private businesses to make a profit, with no capital investment.

CONCLUSION

Privatization is a mean-spirited, short-sighted policy, which puts profit before people, the few ahead of the many.

Some politicians say we must sell off assets and services in order to pay debts and balance the budget. That is nonsense. It is comparable to selling your house and paying rent to the new owner in order to get rid of your mortgage. In the long run, you will pay more in rent, you won't have the house you started out with, and your family will be worse off.

For the good of the public interest, it is we in public sector unions who must fight and win the battle against privatization. In B.C. more than 100 municipalities and regional districts have passed motions opposing privatization. A recent poll shows that 70 percent of British Columbians are opposed.

We have won some big battles. The government has been forced to reverse its decision to privatize a number of services, such as liquor stores, vehicle modification, the B.C. Systems Corporation and Riverview.

Despite public opposition, the present government of B.C. is determined to continue. It is, however, proceeding more quietly, and taking smaller bites. For instance, it is currently trying to turn over alcohol and drug treatment centers to societies, a process that's come to be known as societization. These are small centers, some with only two or three employees, scattered throughout the province. Another new strategy by the government of B.C. is to privatize jobs one at a time. We've had cases where clerks were advised there were no jobs available—but if they would just set up a little company, they could work on a personal service contract.

They sit at government desks, they use government equipment, they report to government officials. They do exactly the same work as government employees, but the government says they are independent contractors: nonunion independent contractors. In one government ministry alone, there are more than 2,000 such contracts each year.

When these cases go to arbitration, we win. The contractors win pay increases, back pay, and seniority dating back to their first day on the job. They also become members of the union.

There is no issue that you will have to face that is more important than privatization. The public sector is the foundation upon which our societies are built. Without a strong and dedicated public sector, who will protect our environment from plunder and pollution? Without a strong and sharp-minded public sector, who will restrain monopoly and greed from trampling the public interest? Without a strong and compassionate public sector, who will address the needs of the poor and the homeless? Without a strong and intelligent public sector, who will oversee the conversion from a war machine economy to a peace economy?

This is the challenge that has been given to us. I am confident that, together, we will win.

Section 8

LABOR LAW AND ORGANIZING IN THE U.S. AND CANADA

The divergence of success in organizing and staying organized since the 1960s is one of the defining distinctions of the Canadian and U.S. labor movements. Currently about 37 percent of Canadian workers are unionized compared with 17 percent in the U.S. Both countries have experienced significant deindustrialization, greatly reducing the number of workers in traditional strongholds of union organization such as heavy manufacturing. This has been only partially offset by the expansion of public sector unionization.

The authors address several major questions. What accounts for the significant disparity in union density in two countries that share so many outward similarities? What are the implications of sectoral shifts, changes in the gender and ethnic composition of the work force, and challenges of global economic competition? What strategies are unions implementing in the field to promote successful organizing in the face of these challenges?

Stan Lanyon and Robert Edwards practice labor law in British Columbia. They review the existing research and competing explanations of divergence and conclude that public policy, resulting labor legislation, and different levels of employer resistance account for the large disparity in union density between Canada and the U.S. The remainder of their paper is a case study of the evolution of British Columbia labor law regarding organizing and decertification, including major revisions that adopted elements of the U.S. model into B.C. law. Specifically, they address provisions that increase the use of certification elections rather than card check certification and provide greater ability for employers to intervene in the union election procedure. Their analysis of data on certification, decertification, and unfair labor practices shows the negative impacts of these legislative changes on organizing success in the province.

Keith Oleksiuk provides a view of Canadian organizing from the field and as a staff employee for an international union that operates on both sides of the border. Reiterating the importance of the legislative framework, he provides illustrations of elements of the law in English Canada and Quebec that significantly enhance labor's ability to organize. However, the obstacles and challenges posed by deindustrialization, economic downturns, the changing work force, and globalization are substantial. Responses of Canadian industrial unions have included strong initiatives in service sector organizing, and a recognition that successful organizing among new immigrant groups requires a commitment to working with and drawing leadership from those ethnic communities. Finally, a major thrust that labor has come to recognize too late is to promote the public image of unions through the mass media and through greater community involvement.

Katie Quan represents workers in the garment industry. This work force has a high percentage of women, minorities, and new immigrants, including many Asians, and the industry is affected greatly by international competition and imports. Unions are challenged by the pressures of organizing a diverse, multicultural, and economically vulnerable work force with the ever-present threat of runaway shops. Quan emphasizes that organizing immigrant workers involves similar principles to those applied in organizing other groups, such as understanding people's needs and desires and gaining their trust, but unions too often fail to be culturally sensitive and recognize or develop leadership within the immigrant communities themselves. Community issues and workplace issues are frequently one, as in the case of child care and other family issues among urban Asian garment workers. Furthermore, there must be a clear connection between organizing immigrant workers and reaching out to unions and workers in other countries, particularly in the Pacific Rim.

The Right to Organize: Labor Law and Its Impact in British Columbia

STAN LANYON
Labor Lawyer, Vancouver B.C.

ROBERT EDWARDS
Lawyer, Vancouver, B.C.

INTRODUCTION

The right of workers to organize and to form trade unions is recognized today as one of the fundamental freedoms guaranteed under Section 2 of the Canadian Charter of Rights and Freedoms. In both Canada and the United States this right has been recognized for many years in legislation establishing systems of certification, mandatory collective bargaining, and prohibition of unfair labor practices. This right is rendered hollow, however, if it cannot be effectively exercised within the regulatory regime put in place by government.

The primary focus of this paper is the system of certification and associated law, policy, and procedure that has been created and has evolved in British Columbia. The paper is additionally concerned with the law of unfair labor practice in this province, as it is clear that for a labor law regime to protect the right to organize it must deal effectively with the problem of employer interference. In 1983 John Baigent made the following observation:

> "In summary, the board has simply been unwilling or unable to develop meaningful relief in the context of workers' rights to organize. Today there are no real safeguards under the Labour Code which protect an employee's freedom of association" (Baigent, 1983).

Since 1983, the Social Credit government has extensively amended the labor legislation of B.C. Rather than address the concerns raised by Baigent, Bill 28, The *Labour Code Amendment Act* (1984), and Bill 19, The *Industrial Relations Reform Act* (1987), effected changes in certification law that made the organization of workers more difficult. These amendments, being reflective of the values and ideology of the government of the day, represented a change in direction. We would characterize this change as a partial adoption of the American model of certification previously rejected by the authors of the original Labour Code and by the Labour Relations Board that it created. In the United States a representation campaign between employer and union is a fundamental part of the process available to employees seeking the right to bargain collectively with their employer.

Our study of the certification and unfair labor practice statistics published in the annual reports of the Labour Relations Board and the Industrial Relations Council reveal that there have been concrete results achieved by the Social Credit amendments to the Labour Code. Such results have been at the expense of the right to organize, and are reflective of the government's success in importing into this province, and enshrining in legislation, American labor relations assumptions that are effectively hostile to organized labor.

The authors wish to thank David Blair and Iain Benson for their very helpful review of the paper. The views and conclusion of course are solely those of the authors.

THEORIES OF UNION DENSITY TRENDS: A REVIEW OF THE RESEARCH

An examination of the Canadian experience leads to a simple conclusion: a public policy that has been receptive to collective bargaining has resulted in an increase in union density. Conversely, the conclusions drawn from the American experience supports the equally simple conclusion that a hostile public policy, combined with employer resistance and avoidance of trade unions, results in a decline in trade union density.

However, it should be made clear that there is no consensus of opinion as to the reasons for the decline in union density in the United States over the last thirty years. The connection between public policy and union density has been stressed by a number of authors (Weiler, 1983 and 1984; Meltz, 1985; Gunderson et al., 1986; Rose and Chaison, 1985; Chaison and Rose, 1986). Other research includes factors such as public policy, employer resistance and avoidance, and union organizing strategies, but places greater emphasis on such issues as structural shifts in the economy (Troy, 1986). Some researchers emphasize public approval as the dominant factor in the determination of union density (Lipset, 1986).

To summarize, explanations for the decline in union density in the U.S. in absolute terms and relative to Canada, include the following factors:

- Public policy, including the legal environment;
- employer resistance and union avoidance strategies;
- union organizing strategies;
- structural changes in the economy; and
- public opinion and cultural values regarding unions.

This paper takes the view that the dominant factors (but not the only factors) are public policy combined with employer resistance and avoidance and union organizing strategies. Before elaborating on these factors we will briefly review the research related to structural changes to the economy and public opinion.

Structural Changes in the Economy

One common view is that the decline in trade union membership is the direct result of the restructuring of our economy—from an industrial-based economy to a service economy. It is stated that the heavily industrialized industries in the 1970s suffered from low productivity, inflation, high wage costs, freer international trade, and an inability to compete with the Third World, all of which resulted in high unemployment. These employees were predominantly male and blue collar, with a long tradition of collective bargaining.

The service sector, in addition to being highly competitive, also employs a work force that is better educated, younger, with a higher percentage of women. It is a group with little or no collective bargaining history, and therefore is more difficult to organize (Edwards and Podgursky, 1986).

However, Chaison and Rose reviewed several studies looking at the structural transformation of the economy as a determinant of union density and conclude that this factor is not the dominant factor in determining density. They conclude that market shifts would account for approximately 20–40 percent of the decline.

> While these arguments seem quite logical, the importance of market shifts is not supported by recent empirical evidence. Freeman (1985) found little relationship between the decline in union success in NLRB representation elections and the changing proportions of workers in categories of age, education, sex, occupation, and industry. Farber (1985) concluded that structural changes, i.e. the shift toward the

197

South, white-collar workers, and female workers, and away from manufacturing, accounted for only about 40 percent (3.9 of the 9.4 percentage points) of the decline in union density between 1956 and 1978. Farber (1987) found that only about one fifth of the decline in unionization from 1977 to 1984 was the result of changes in labour force structure. Doyle (1985) found that less than one quarter of the decline in the collective bargaining agreement coverage of production workers from 1961 to 1984 could be accounted for by employment shifts between industries (Chaison and Rose, 1988, pp. 9–10).

Lipset (1986) reviews the shift from an industrialized economy to a service economy in Canada, the United States, and nine other OECD nations (the leading industrialized nations) between 1963 and 1981. During this entire period, Canada led all nations in the size of its service sector. It also increased union density approximately 30 percent to its current level of 40 percent. Union density in Canada is now more than twice that of the United States. Of the eleven OECD nations, four countries (including Canada) increased the size of their unionized work force as the service sector expanded, four remained stable and only three experienced a decrease in unionization, with the United States suffering the greatest decline.

Public Opinion and National Values

Lipset (1986) argues that the major determinant of union density is public approval of trade unions and that underlying public approval are the basic social attitudes and values that determine the degree of unionization in the United States. It is very difficult to deny the significance of political and cultural values in determining the well-being of any trade union movement within any country. However, Lipset's argument is narrower than this. He postulates that public approval, as measured by the Gallup Polls, is the most reliable determinant in predicting union density.

His statistical analysis revealed that as public approval of unions declines, so does union density, as does the rate at which unions win certifications. Further, he states that one can predict the degree of union density in any given year by knowing the public approval rate of trade unions in that year. His polling results include only American data.

Canadian polling data does not show the same relationship. Chaison and Rose (1988) compare Canadian and American polling results. Between the years 1950 and 1958, the rate of union density in Canada and the U.S. was comparable (in the low 30s). During this period between 12 and 20 percent of Canadians thought that unions were bad as compared to 14 to 19 percent in the United States. Conversely, in Canada, 60 to 69 percent thought unions were good, while 64 to 76 percent of the people in the United States thought that unions were good. Therefore, during the period 1950–1958, public opinion in Canada and United States concerning the approval or disapproval of unions was comparable, as was the rate of union density.

In the period 1976–1984, 30 to 41 percent of Canadians thought that unions were bad; in the United States during this period 27 to 35 percent thought that unions were bad. During the same period in Canada, 42 to 54 percent of the public thought that unions were good; in the United States public approval ranged from 55 to 59 percent. In both countries, over this twenty-five-year period, public disapproval of unions had approximately doubled. Trade unions in the United States did slightly better at both intervals—less disapproval and more approval. However, notwithstanding the decline in public approval, the degree of union density in Canada increased during this period from approximately 30 to 40 percent and today stands at more than twice the rate of union density in the United States.

Therefore, we return to the original position of this paper: that the decline in union density is the result of the interplay between public or legislative policy combined with employer resistance and avoidance and union organizing strategies.

UNION CERTIFICATION AND DENSITY: RECENT EXPERIENCE IN CANADA, THE U.S., AND BRITISH COLUMBIA

An examination of the Canadian experience, the American experience, and the British Columbia experience is instructive in regard to the issue of union density. It is of particular importance to British Columbia as we move closer to the current U.S. model of certification. Following a broad review of Canadian and U.S. national experiences, we address in detail the changes in certification law and procedure in British Columbia produced by the 1984 and 1987 amendments; we then discuss and analyze statistics compiled in the areas of certification, decertification, and unfair labor practice; and draw conclusions from the data. The data compiled are to be found in a series of tables we have included in an appendix at the end of our paper.

One of our major conclusions is that a relationship exists between the adoption of a policy of mandatory representation votes in 1984, and an increase in the successful use of unfair labor practices by employers. It seems clear that the availability of automatic certification on the basis of membership evidence, under section 45 of the original Labour Code, was a policy critical to the protection of the right to organize.

The Canadian Experience

P. Kumar (1986) has done an extensive statistical analysis of the rate of unionization in the Canadian economy. Most of the figures that appear in the following section are taken from Kumar unless otherwise indicated.

Union Density

In Canada, the first union membership figures were published in 1911. At that time there was a total of 133,000 union members. Union membership grew to 378,000 by 1919, and then steadily declined throughout the 1920s and 1930s. It did not reach the 1911 level again until 1940–41.

In 1935, when the Wagner Act came into existence in the United States, setting out the legislative framework of labor relations that still exists in Canada and the U.S., membership in trade unions was at 281,000—14.5 percent of the nonagricultural work force. Since that time the percentage of the work force unionized has increased steadily to its current level of 40 percent.

Federations

There are five central labor federations in Canada—the Canadian Labour Congress (CLC), the Confederation of National Trade Unions (CNTU), the Centrale des Syndicats Democratiques (CSD), the Confederation of Canadian Unions (CCU), and Canadian Federation of Labour (CFL). These federations account for three-quarters of the total 3.6 million union members. The CLC is the dominant federation of labor in Canada. The CLC has fifty-one international union affiliates (out of seventy-four in Canada in 1983), twenty-seven national unions (out of 146) and seventy-four directly chartered locals, for a total of 2.08 million members—57.6 percent of the total union membership in Canada. The CLC consists of two-thirds of the membership of international unions and one-half of the national unions.

Structure

In the period 1910 to 1920 international unions constituted 90 percent of the total Canadian membership. Between the years 1948 and 1966 international union membership accounted for approximately 70 percent of the total union membership. However, from 1966 to 1983 this percentage declined to 41 percent. In 1963, twelve out of the fifteen largest unions were Internationals. In 1982, it dropped to nine out of fifteen. In 1982, five out of six of the largest unions were public sector, and indeed, the three very largest unions were public sector.

In 1961, fifteen public sector unions had a combined membership of 183,000. In 1981, public sector membership had increased to 1.5 million and seventy-one different unions. In 1967, the federal government passed the Public Service Staff Act, thus extending collective bargaining rights to civil service employees, and thereby giving the first great impetus to unionization in the public sector. During the next ten years provincial governments passed similar legislation, and by the end of the 1970s public sector workers throughout Canada had collective bargaining rights.

Therefore, the growth of union density in Canada during the 1960s and 1970s is largely attributable to the public sector. This is a direct result of a public policy that directed itself to the encouragement of collective bargaining.

Demographics

In 1981, approximately 65 percent of the unionized work force was male, 90 percent worked full time, and 66 percent had grade 12 or less. Among fulltime employees 39 percent of the male work force and 29 percent of the female work force was unionized. Only 15 percent of the part-time workers were unionized, and almost two-thirds of these were female (75 percent of these were in clerical, service, and professional occupations).

During the period of 1965 to 1981, Canada's economy moved to an increasingly larger service sector, with the result that unionized sectors of the service industry also increased—union density among office workers in the service sector increased from 19 to 30 percent during this period and among nonoffice workers in the private sector it increased from 33 to 53 percent. In public administration both nonoffice and office workers increased in union density from 28 to 90 percent.

Certifications

The most common rule in Canadian jurisdictions is that employees must sign a membership card and pay a nominal fee of $1.00 in order to become a union member. If a union signs between 50 and 60 percent of all employees, and such legal issues as eligibility to vote and the appropriateness of the bargaining unit are determined in the union's favor, the union can be automatically certified without a vote. If a union signs up less than 50 percent but more than 35 percent (40 or 45 percent depending on the jurisdiction), there is then a requirement for a vote, and a majority of 50 percent plus 1 is required in order to be certified. Where there is a specific requirement for a vote for all applications for certification, such as in Nova Scotia and British Columbia, such votes are usually held within a period of five to ten days. Chaison and Rose (1988) found that out of more than 30,000 certifications in Canada between 1971 and 1985, nearly 70 percent of these applications were granted. Only 15 to 20 percent of all applications for certificates went to a vote. Between 1974 and 1980 there was a three-fold increase in the number of unfair labor practices.

The Canadian experience, as will be shown, is in marked contrast to the American experience. Its more favorable public policy has encouraged collective bargaining with the result that union density has increased over the last 30 years. This is especially true in the public sector.

However, as British Columbia moves more closely in its public policy to the American model of representation, we can begin to see the more detrimental effects that such a policy can have on a union's ability to organize.

The American Experience

In *What Do Unions Do?* Freeman and Medoff (1984) undertook a multivariate analysis of the effect of trade unions in the American economy. One of their findings is that the percentage of unionization in the private sector work force in the United States has been decreasing since the mid-1950s. In the two decades following the passing of the Wagner Act in 1935, unionization increased from 15 percent to 30 percent; the succeeding years saw a decline to today's level of between 15 and 17 percent. Two of the most important factors to which the decline can be attributed were first, a decline in organizing; and second, an increase in management opposition, both legal and illegal.

In the 1950s, unions in the United States were spending on average a dollar for each worker organized, and would organize 1 percent of the work force annually. By 1974, they were spending only seventy-one cents per worker, and in 1970 were organizing just three-tenths of 1 percent of the work force each year. Freeman and Medoff conclude that one-third of the decline in unionization is due to this decline in organizing activity.

The authors see management opposition to unionization as having taken two basic forms—first, positive labor relations, in the form of offers of wages and benefits comparable to those proposed by the unions, and second, contested certification campaigns. The use of labor relations consultants in the planning and execution of these measures was found to be very common. The usual tactics employed were as follows:

- Communication with the employees would be increased;
- the legal and administrative process would be delayed;
- eligibility to vote in representation ballots was frequently contested; and
- illegal activity was frequently engaged in.

The employment of these techniques was found to result in a decline in work force unionization of between 25 and 50 percent. Employment of labor relations consultants was the major determinant of National Labor Relations Board (NLRB) election results.

Employers used increasingly sophisticated methods to disguise what were in fact illegal discharges. The penalty for this was small, as most employees reinstated with back pay would not return to their jobs; employers would thereby achieve his original goal at a price often budgeted for at the outset. The popularity of the use of illegal tactics amongst employers was reflected in a four-fold increase in unfair labor practice complaints, and a three-fold increase in illegal discharges specifically, in the period from 1960 to 1980. From 1950 to 1980, the increase in unfair labor practices was 600 percent.

An integral component of the overall decline in the unionization of the work force was the rise in decertification. From 5,000 in 1950, the annual figure for decertification in the private sector work force in the United States had risen to 21,000 by 1980.

Weiler (1988) states that if the current trends continue, union density will fall below 10 percent in the next decade. In a review of data on NLRB certification elections from 1950 to 1980, Weiler (1983) observes that unions have not won a majority of NLRB elections since 1974. Indeed, from 1950 to 1980 the percentage of NLRB elections won by trade unions declined from 74 to 48 percent. The number of employees organized dropped from approximately 750,000 a year to approximately 175,000 a year—from 1.92 percent of the workforce organized annually to 0.24 percent annually. Employer resistance to application for certification delayed the vote on application for certification from 1.8 months to 3.5 months.

An application for certification in the United States proceeds as follows: a trade union must convince 30 percent of the work force to sign a membership authorization card (in practice, applications for certifications are not usually filed unless a union has somewhere between 60 and 70 percent support). The

NLRB investigates the union's petition, defines the scope of the appropriate bargaining unit, decides whether the conditions for a valid election exists, and, if so, conducts a secret ballot vote. Employer and union then participate in a political campaign prior to the vote. If the union is successful it is certified and the employer is compelled to bargain in good faith. If the union is unsuccessful it is barred from reapplying for certification for twelve months.

However, even after certification is granted, there is still the hurdle of reaching the first collective agreement. Weiler demonstrates that the rate at which trade unions were able to obtain first collective agreements declined from 86 percent in 1955 to 63 percent in 1980. Combining the rates at which trade unions have won certification votes, with the rate at which they have achieved first collective agreements, unions are only one-third as successful as they were in 1955. As Freeman puts it:

> .... it is apparent that the legally established mode of organizing labor in the private sector of the United States has run dry for trade unions (Freeman, 1988, p. 74).

Illegal tactics by employers account for much of labor's decline:

> A major factor in this decline has been the skyrocketing use of coercive and illegal tactics—discriminatory discharges in particular—by employers determined to prevent unionization of their employees. The core of the legal structure must bear a major share of the blame for providing employers with the opportunity and the incentives to use these tactics, which have had such a chilling effect on worker interest in trade union representation (Weiler, 1983, pp. 1769–1770).

Weiler goes on to state that from 1957 to 1980 there has been a 1000 percent increase in illegal discharges. He concludes the following:

> Astoundingly, then, the current odds are about one in twenty that a union supporter will be fired for exercising rights supposedly guaranteed by federal law a half century ago (Weiler, 1983, p.1781).

After 1980, under Reagan, conditions of course did not improve. According to Chaison and Rose (1988), from 1980 to 1983 the NLRB awarded an annual average of $32.1 million in back pay to employees who were illegally discriminated against or discharged because of their union activities (this reached a high in 1985 of $62.2 million). The annual average for the previous four years (1976 to 1980) had been $14.7 million. Between 1980 and 1983 charges of unfair labor practice averaged 17,036, almost double the 1970 figure.

In addition to "employer resistance," there is "employer avoidance." A new model of industrial relations has evolved that places greater emphasis on employee involvement and participation. Non-union employers have expanded into various states whose labor relations are far more conducive to nonunion operations—"green-field sites" and "right-to-work" states.

> Employee choice through elections became a moot issue; . . . wherever plants were designed and run on the new human resource management model they were essentially immune from unionization . . . Certification elections were never even held in the vast majority of the new employment relationships created in the past two decades (Chaison and Rose, 1988, p.20).

Furthermore, employers are showing a greater tendency to continue operations during a strike (approximately 40 percent continue to operate during strikes) and to replace strikers (Chaison and Rose, 1988).

One exception to this rule in the United States has proved to be the public sector. According to Freeman (1988), from 1975 to 1982, union density increased in state and local governments from 26 to 35 percent. Public sector unionization has increased during the 1960s and 1970s because many states passed laws that were favorable to employees gaining collective bargaining rights. The variation that appears in different states is due to the differences in labor law—more favorable legislation results in higher union density; unfavorable public policy results in lower union density. Further, Freeman states that local governments rarely participate in illegal activities or hire antiunion consultants in order to defeat employees' applications for certification. For public officials there is always a threat of removal from public office should any of them contravene the National Labor Relations Act or state collective bargaining statues. "Put crudely, management opposition to unions can gain profits in the private sector; in the public sector it can cost votes" (Freeman, 1988, p. 85).

There has been a dramatic increase in employer animosity towards unions in the United States. Employers have increasingly abandoned their commitment to unions and to collective bargaining. Employers increasingly view them as a threat to managerial control and to profits:

> ... rather than being embraced as a social partner, organized labour finds itself to be the object of the most forceful assault on its integrity in more than half a century (Adams, 1988, p.115).

THE BRITISH COLUMBIA EXPERIENCE

The Labour Code and the Industrial Relations Act, 1973–1987: The Law of Organizing

Certification

Under the original Labour Code, where (pursuant to Section 39(1) and 43(2)) a union applied for certification with between 35 and 50 percent membership support in the unit, the Labor Relations Board was directed to conduct a representation vote. If, however, the board was satisfied that an applicant union enjoyed majority membership support in a unit appropriate for collective bargaining, the union was entitled to be certified under Section 45(1) without a vote being held. (In 1977 these sections were amended to require proof of 45 percent support before a vote would be conducted, and to require proof of 55 percent support for certification without the use of a vote).

Although under Section 43(1) the board appeared to possess the discretion to conduct a representation vote for any application for certification, it was decided in *Plateau Mills Ltd. and International Woodworkers of America, Local 1-424 and Group of Employees of Plateau Mills Ltd.* (1977), that a vote would be held under this section only where the validity of the union's membership evidence had been placed in doubt (evidence of fraud, undue influence, or intimidation, or other flaws in the membership cards submitted). Chair Paul Weiler, writing for the panel, reasoned that while there may have been "considerable appeal" to the adoption by the board of a policy of more extensive use of representation votes—where, for example, employee opposition to certification exists and there is a request for a vote from such a group— such votes often produced "a messy campaign" during which the antiunion employer " ... may fire some employees, threaten or intimidate others, or promise wage improvements to the entire group, all in order to avoid unionization." Often the momentum of the organizing campaign is halted, or the relationship between the union and employer made too acrimonious to allow for successful collective bargaining. Inevitably the employees, caught in the middle, are the losers.

No matter how extensive the legal control of such unfair labour practices, this kind of conduct simply cannot be stamped out. Thus, the law has had to adopt some strategies to reduce these incidences and protect the right of employees to choose collective bargaining without employer interference, a right enshrined in Section 2 of the code and its predecessor legislation. One such strategy is contained in section 45. That Section simply finesses the problem by rendering these employer tactics useless. By the time the union has surfaced with its majority membership and made the application for certification, the die is cast—the statutory condition of majority membership is satisfied and the union is entitled to certification (*Plateau Mills*, 1977).

The use of certification without a vote as a means of preventing illegal employer interference in the certification process was predominant in Canada. In contrast, in the United States the representation vote, with a lengthy and often lively campaign between union and employer for the loyalties of the workers in the unit, was the rule. The American model assumed that the union representation vote was analogous to a political election campaign. Weiler rejected this analogy:

> Political campaigns produce a verdict about who is going to govern the citizens who participate in that election. The employer is not governed by the trade union chosen by the employees. The employer still has the right to pursue its own interests in dealing with the employee, whether this be on an individual basis or through the trade union. That is why the employer has no rightful role to play in the process by which the employees make up their minds about how they will deal with their employer (*Plateau Mills*, 1977).

Moreover, "the employees are not making a momentous choice," said Weiler, because the union that is successfully certified must continue to work to maintain support within the unit if it is to win a first contract. If the employer should prove to be less than accommodating to the demands of the negotiating committee, the union must be able to secure a solid strike mandate. If it does not, more often than not the experiment with collective bargaining fails (Weiler, 1980).

The proclamation of Bill 28 in 1984 (Labour Code Amendment Act, 1984) introduced mandatory representation votes to the certification procedure in B.C., by way of amendment to Section 43. (Section 45 was repealed.) Following the board's determination that an applicant union possessed not less than 45 percent membership support, and that the unit applied for was appropriate for collective bargaining, it was directed to hold a vote. Certification was to be issued where a majority of "the votes included in the count" (a reference to an amended Section 55) were cast in favor of trade union representation.

In response to these amendments the Chair of the Labour Relations Board, Stephen Kelleher, on June 15, 1984, issued a Memorandum of Procedure for the taking of representation votes. The time lag between the receipt of the application by the board and its hearing was to be seven days. Representation votes, if ordered, were to be held three days later. Adjournments, other than by consent, were not easily obtained. The purpose of Kelleher's ten-day rule was clearly to lessen the impact of the removal of automatic certification upon the organizing union by limiting the period of time within which the employer could conduct a campaign of influence.

The proclamation of the Industrial Relations Reform Act (1987) brought further refinements to the new course charted three years before. Kelleher's ten-day rule, previously a matter of board practice only, became a mandatory time limit under an amended Section 43(1)—a legislative confirmation that there would not be a lengthy representation campaign of the American type. However, the addition of subsection (3), as a qualifier to the right to organize contained in Section 2, confirmed that a shift toward the American model was intended nevertheless:

(3) Nothing in this act deprives a person of his freedom to express his views provided that he does not use undue influence, intimidation, coercion or threats.

Such a provision is commonly seen to relate to a right of "employer free speech." To the extent that its adoption was to mark the end of the requirement of strict employer neutrality in organizational campaigns and representation votes, it represented the adoption of the American political model; employers are assumed to have a legitimate interest in the outcome of the representation vote, and should therefore be allowed to express their views.

In *Focus Building and S.E.I.U.* (1987), the panel concluded that there was no longer a requirement of strict employer neutrality. As long as employers do not exert "undue influence," or use intimidation, coercion, or threats, they were free to communicate their opinions to the employees on the subject of unionization. Undue influence is akin to intimidation, according to the panel, and its boundaries will depend on the circumstances of the individual case. Where the influence used pertains to sensitive areas such as job security, and the sophistication of the employees is not great, the standard of allowable employer communication was to be stricter.

At the very least Section 2(3) represented an encouragement to employers to become actively involved in representation votes, in the hope that they could exert some influence upon the decision to be made by their employees.

In the construction industry, important changes in the law of certification were the result of policy decisions of the Industrial Relations Council. In *Cicuto and Sons Contractors Ltd.* (1988) the council set out four different ways by which a construction union can bring an application for certification, each of which can in turn be accomplished on a project basis, or a permanent (or provincewide) basis. These are the craft, the poly-party, the all-employee, and the joint council. In addition the council stated that where the different forms of certification resulted in conflict between affiliates and nonaffiliates of the Building Trades Council, they would not enforce nonaffiliation clauses, even though lawfully exercised. Moreover, the Industrial Relations Council stated that if such nonaffiliation clauses were to be exercised with some regularity, it would recommend to the legislature that it reassess their lawfulness. The effect of this policy has been to encourage the establishment of "mixed-bag sites"—sites that have both Building Trades Council affiliated and nonaffiliated unions present.

Unfair Labor Practices and Remedies

The unfair labor practice sections of the Labour Code were amended only once since 1974. In 1977, Section 3 (3) (a) was strengthened, and subsections (f), (g), and (h) were added. The leading decision remains *Forano Ltd.* (1974); employers bear the onus of proof in the hearing of complaints, and must show that their conduct was untainted by antiunion animus.

The original Labour Code made provision for the certification of a union outside of Section 45, "notwithstanding that . . . the true wishes of the employees cannot be ascertained." By virtue of Section 8(4)(e) and Section 43(1) and (3), the board, when confronted by illegal employer tactics that had caused an organizing campaign to collapse, could conduct a representation vote notwithstanding an absence of sufficient membership evidence. If it concluded that, as a result of the unfair labor practice, a vote would not reveal "the true wishes of the employees," it could certify directly, without a vote.

The standard of proof to be met by the applicant union underwent some change following the early cases under these sections. Whereas in *Forano Ltd.* (1974) the test of causation to be met was said to be "the momentum of the drive made a majority very likely," the board—because of its concern that this test encouraged the employer to launch an early "preemptive strike"—said in *Beechwood Construction Ltd.* (1977) that the applicant would thereafter be required to show that it "would be reasonable to assume that, in the absence of the unfair labour practice, the union would have achieved majority support within the unit."

Section 8(4)(e) remained unchanged through both the 1984 and 1987 amendments (Sections 43(1) and 43(3) were repealed), although the cases appear to diverge on the correct test to be met by an applicant after the introduction of mandatory representation votes in 1984. Whereas some cases suggest that an applicant under this section was required to prove that the true wishes of the employees would not be revealed in a representation vote (such a vote being seen as a right granted to employees under the amendments of 1984), others made no mention of this (*St. Jude's Anglican Home Care Society*, 1985; *J&L Meats*, 1985).

The primary test from *Forano* and *Beechwood Construction* is one of causation. The applicant is required to show that an organizing campaign failed, or was "chilled," as a result of an unfair labor practice committed by the employer. According to the Council in *Sandbar Construction* (1989), the inefficaciousness of a representation vote can usually be proven by inference:

> If the employer's behavior has had a chilling effect on the organization campaign or otherwise frustrated its progress it is probable that a representation vote (based on this membership drive) would not reflect the true wishes of the employees.

The test is difficult and somewhat artificial because it must deal with circumstances existing before the employer acted as it did—or with what might be described as the collective mental state of the employees prior to the unfair labor practice. In *Beechwood Construction* the panel described the 8(4)(e) remedy as "not a working reality" in the labor relations environment of the late 1970s, largely in light of the unrealistic evidentiary demands made upon an applicant. Recently, in *United Used Auto and Truck Parts Ltd.* (1989), the council has effectively made these demands yet heavier by suggesting that it will not readily infer the required proof under this section from the commission of serious unfair labor practice, in the face of opposition to automatic certification from employees at the time of hearing. In that case the employer, in response to the organizing campaign of the union, fired all 115 employees, and invited all but nineteen back as contractors. All of the nineteen worked as dismantlers, the group within which the bulk of the organization had taken place. The council found that an unfair labor practice had taken place. However, sixty of the fired employees hired a lawyer and were granted intervener status at the hearing. They introduced evidence of the results of a secret ballot vote conducted amongst themselves, indicating their unanimous opposition to certification without a vote. The council denied the application, relying heavily on the evidence of the "certain employees" who had intervened. (We are not suggesting that the council's decision to grant standing to these employees was in error; we do take issue, however, with the weight given to their evidence in the final decision.) The council's reasoning implies that "the true wishes of the employees" are to be gauged not strictly by what their decision would have been in the absence of the unfair labor practice, but largely by the submissions of employees who have already been subjected to the illegal interference of the employer. We are being no more than slightly facetious in suggesting that "true wishes" can perhaps now be defined as "thoughts expressed by employees under the influence of employer unfair labor practice."

Decertification Under Section 52

Under Section 52 of the original Labour Code, the board possessed a discretion when addressing the issue of the decertification of a bargaining unit; there was no right to decertification, and no obligation to conduct a representation vote as a means of determining the extent of the union's support. In *Hiram Walker and Sons Ltd.* (1974), the board declared that the intention of the legislation was to allow them to form a decertification policy on "an individual, case-by-case basis, taking into account fundamental principles and policies running through the code." When presented with evidence of the lack of majority support for the union in the form of an employee petition, the board would investigate the case and attempt to determine to what extent the petition reflected the true wishes of the employees involved. If the employees indeed desired decertification it would not be denied; however, if there was evidence of employer antiunion tactics the board—pursuant to Section 53(2) and by analogy to Sections 8(4)(e) and 43(3)—would consider whether a representation vote would be efficacious, and could exercise its discretion to disregard the petition and decline to order a vote (See also *Century Plaza Hotel Ltd.*, 1975).

Under the original code the employer was not able to obtain the decertification of a unit in which there were no longer any employees. In *Lifway Foods* (1979) the board, when faced with an application from an employer who had laid off all of the employees in the unit and who asserted that they would not be rehired, denied the application; the panel reasoned that the continuing obligations of the parties flowing from the certification were more important than the fact of the layoffs—to hold otherwise "would destroy the permanency of the position of certified bargaining agent particularly in those instances where employment is seasonal" (p. 495).

The amendments to Section 52 were extensive. The most important change saw voting made mandatory in all applications for decertification where the applicant had the support of 45 percent of the employees in the bargaining unit.

A second major change was Section 52(8), allowing the employer to apply for decertification of the union where it could show that it had not "employed any person as an employee in the unit" in the preceding two years. The board retained a discretion to refuse to cancel the certification under this section where in its opinion the conduct of the employer had been "unfair or unreasonable." The board's policy of not decertifying empty units on application by the employer, first stated in *Lifway Foods*, was thereby limited to a two-year period.

In *Tri-Power Construction* (1984) it was suggested that if an employer had diverted work to another company, or had unreasonably refused an offer of concessions by the union and had chosen to rely on the decertification remedy, the application would be refused.

In *Wall and Redekop Corporation and Trizec Construction* (1988) the board denied applications under 52(8) by two companies that had been contracting out all of their construction work more than two years. Although neither company had in fact directly employed anyone falling within the unit description, the board—quoting from *Tri-Power*—reasoned that what is unfair or unreasonable under this section should be determined "in the context of the Labour Code as a whole and its overall purposes." It was apparently on this basis that it concluded that Section 52(8) was enacted for the benefit of inactive employers, and that the companies in question—who continued to operate and to cause people in the construction industry to be employed—were to be denied relief.

In *Trizec Construction Ltd.* (1989) the council, following the 1987 amendments to this section, confirmed that an employer who has emptied a unit by subcontracting its work will be denied decertification under 52(8).

Eligibility to Vote—Section 55

Prior to the 1984 amendments to the code, the eligibility of an individual to vote was determined by his or her status as an "employee," as defined by section 1, on the date of the application and the date of the vote. In addition to the traditional exclusionary arguments—such as managerial or confidential status—the issue of the status of employees on layoff came before the board in its early years. As outlined in *Western Canada Steel* (1976), the test became known as one of "sufficient continuing interest" in the bargaining unit. It remained through the 1984 amendments (*J&L Meats*, 1985; *Trophy Foods*, 1984), and the amendments of 1987 and the coming of the Industrial Relations Council (*Superior Contracting*, 1988).

In 1984, however, Section 55 was amended by the addition of subsections 3, 4, and 5. A major change in eligibility rules was produced by Section 55(4), whereby persons hired after the certification application is received may be eligible to vote. In *Ladysmith Chemainus Chronicle* (1984) the board stated that individuals who can be shown to have been hired for *bona fide* reasons and do not represent an attempt to "pack the unit" will be eligible to vote.

Section 66(1).1

This section was included in 1987, allowing employers to obtain the cancellation of collective agreements in circumstances where decertification would be denied (*B.C.E. Developments*, 1988). Where rights under a collective agreement were acquired prior to the enactment of this section, (the date of its execution having preceded the proclamation of Bill 19), 66(1).1 was not applicable (*Horizon Developments Ltd.*, 1989).

Statistical Analysis

"We essentially had two aims in mind in drafting the changes that are before us today: to broaden the decision-making process for the working people and make it more democratic; and to try to encourage economic recovery by allowing workers to share in the recovery's awards." —The Honorable R.H. McClelland, Minister of Labour (Legislative Assembly, 1984).

"(It) imports absolutely the worst feature of U.S. labour law and represents a backward step in Canadian labour law."—Paul Weiler, former Chair of the Labour Relations Board of British Columbia (Quoted in the *Current Industrial Relations Scene in Canada*, 1984).

These two comments represent the divergence of views on the Labour Code Amendment Act of 1984.

An examination of the statistics published by the Labour Relations Board and by the Industrial Relations Council suggest that the amendments to the labor legislation of British Columbia analyzed in the previous section of this paper have had a significant—and, on balance, a negative—impact on the right to organize. (Data displayed in Figures 1-8 are also provided in Tables 1-5 in the Appendix).

Certification

At the outset, it should be said that the following figures for certification applications disposed of should be viewed with the business cycle in mind. In 1982 there was the onset of a severe recession, which drastically affected the level of construction activity taking place in this province. An economic downturn may have an effect upon the attitudes of workers toward union organization, and such a phenomenon, if it exists, would also have been a factor bearing upon the numbers we have compiled here.

That aside, the pattern of variation in these figures is well aligned with the major changes in labor law and procedure that took place in 1984 and 1987.

With respect to the certification figures, a number of observations can be readily made. In the 1974–1983 period the numbers of applications fluctuates fairly widely, probably in tune with the business cycle (Figure 1). The figures for success rate (Figure 2) are fairly steady, however, with a range of 88.1 percent to 94 percent, and a ten-year mean of 90.8 percent for unorganized employees. In the 1984–1987 period the numbers of applications reaches a fifteen-year low of 223 for unorganized employees in 1987. More interesting here are the figures for success rate in this period; in 1984 there is a 10 percent drop from the previous year. The mean for this four-year period is 75.6 percent—a decline of more than 15 percent. In 1988 the picture appears to improve significantly, with an increase to 83.4 percent; however, if the applications disposed of that year for teachers (they enjoyed interest arbitration prior to receiving the right to apply for certification) are removed, a figure of 79.5 percent is arrived at. (See Table 1.) In 1989 there was a slight decrease to 75.5 percent, placing it right within the previous four-year mean.

The figures for certification in construction (see Figures 3 and 4) provide a good illustration of the hard times upon which the union sector fell in the mid-1980s. The construction unions would have felt the loss of certification without a vote more acutely than those in the industrial sector, due to the constant renewal and reaffirmation of bargaining relationships that is required in the former by its nature. As new contracting companies come into being (in fact or in mere form, as means of avoiding unionization), the construction unions have to be prepared to respond by means of organization and certification. Whereas prior to the 1984 amendments they were assured of certification at a site where a majority of their members were working, with the coming of mandatory representation votes the antiunion message from the employer was a threat to this support; the union member could be intimidated and could vote against the union as readily as the nonmember. In addition, the short period within which many projects are completed make delaying tactics very effective.

Looking at the figures for applications filed in construction, in the 1974–1983 period we find the expected cyclical variations, within a range of 422 in 1982 to 260 in 1977, producing a mean for the ten-year period of 325.7. In the 1984–1986 period (these data for the years 1987 and 1988 were unavailable) there was a drastic decline in the number of applications filed, with the range in the period being 114 in 1984 to 83 in 1985, and a mean over three years of 96.3.

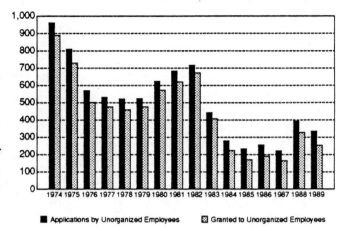

FIGURE 1. CERTIFICATION, APPLIED FOR AND GRANTED

■ Applications by Unorganized Employees   ▨ Granted to Unorganized Employees

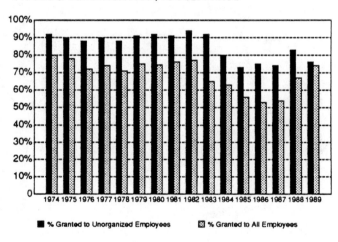

FIGURE 2. CERTIFICATION, SUCCESS RATE

■ % Granted to Unorganized Employees   ▨ % Granted to All Employees

The figures for success rate in the construction industry (Figure 4) show a decline after 1983 that is significantly greater than the comparable figures for the economy as a whole. The range in the 1974–1983 period is 91.1 percent in 1974 to 73.0 percent in 1978 and 1981, with the ten-year mean being 79.9 percent. In the three succeeding years for which we have data, the success rate drops to new lows of 71.9 percent in 1984, 50.6 percent in 1985, and 47.8 percent in 1986. The mean of 56.8 percent for this period is 23.1 percent lower than that for the previous period. This can be compared to the 16.3 percent decline that is displayed by the data for certification generally in the same period.

We note that it would be useful to have access to data for project certifications and unfair labor practice complaints compiled separately for the construction industry.

Unfair Labor Practice

The figures for Section 3 unfair labor practice complaints against employers in the 1974–1987 period show a relatively steady increase in absolute numbers, this faltering only in 1984 and 1985—two years with very low certification application figures. The pattern formed by a comparison of the figures for certification applications and Section 3 complaints— the latter being expressed as a percentage of the former—is quite startling. In the 1974–1983 period, the mean for all employees is 15.9 percent, and for unorganized employees only is 20.6 percent. In the 1984–1987 period, these figures are 42.7 and 62.4 percent. It should be noted that the success rate for Section 3 discharge complaints filed by unions in the 1984–1987 period was 53.7 percent, only slightly below the fifteen-year average of 54.5 percent. This suggests a dramatic increase in the use of illegal tactics by employers in the course of organizing campaigns.

In 1988 there was a sharp decline in these figures, to a level close to that of 1983. At 38.4 percent for unorganized employees (31.1 percent if teachers are included) it remained far above the average level of 20.6 percent for the previous period.

In 1989 the percentage of unfair labor practices for unorganized employees once again increased to 49 percent, thus approaching the previous four-year mean.

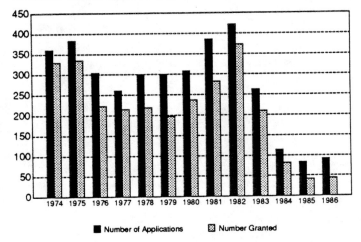

FIGURE 3. CERTIFICATION IN CONSTRUCTION

■ Number of Applications ⊠ Number Granted

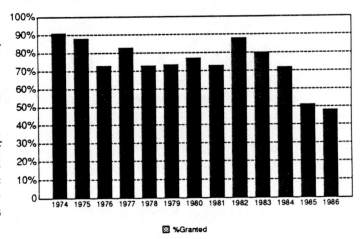

FIGURE 4. CONSTRUCTION CERTIFICATION SUCCESS RATE

⊠ %Granted

Union density in British Columbia in 1983 was 45.6 percent. In 1989 this has fallen to 37.5 percent. The ten-year average from 1974 to 1983 was approximately 45 percent. This decrease is the greatest since the year 1945–46 when it dropped from 38.9 in 1945 to 33.6 in 1946. It is the lowest union density since 1947 when the percentage was 35.7 percent.

Although the contribution of the introduction of mandatory representation votes in 1984 to these disturbing trends cannot be ascertained definitively within the scope of this paper, the data strongly suggest a relationship between mandatory votes, employer unfair labor practices, and declining union density. The vote requirement meant that the employer has had at the very least several days in which to take whatever measures he and his advisers deemed appropriate in the circumstances. Whereas under the original code the union could secure its certificate by conducting a successful sign-up campaign without the employer's knowledge, after 1984 it was necessary to hold on to the support of the unit for a week to ten days after the application, often (as the data show) in the face of illegal employer interference. The ten-day rule, an administrative measure enacted by the board to mitigate the harmful effects of the mandatory vote, is not an adequate substitute for automatic certification on the basis of membership evidence. Where votes are used, as they were under the original Labour Code where majority membership support was not shown, this time limit would be a valuable safeguard.

The Effectiveness of Unfair Labor Practice Remedies

As Paul Weiler observed in *Plateau Mills* (1977), experience has shown that the traditional remedies awarded against offending employers are ineffective; the rewards to be gained from defeating the union far outweigh the cost of legal fees and negative publicity. This was the rationale underlying the primary use of membership evidence to assess employee true wishes, and the rejection of the American political campaign model of certification. The removal in 1984 of this means of protecting the right to organize, given the employer's propensity for the use of illegal interference, made the availability of an alternative remedy of proven effectiveness a matter of some importance.

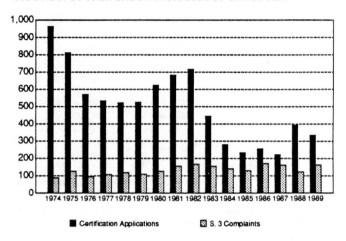

FIGURE 5. UNFAIR LABOR PRACTICE BY EMPLOYER

■ Certification Applications   ▨ S. 3 Complaints

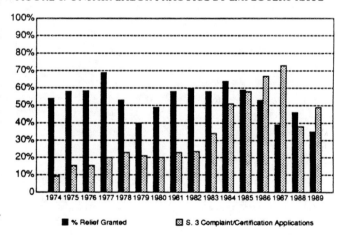

FIGURE 6. UNFAIR LABOR PRACTICE BY EMPLOYERS RATE

■ % Relief Granted   ▨ S. 3 Complaint/Certification Applications

The data in Figure 7 indicate that the remedy of automatic certification under Section 8(4)(e) was not up to the task. Its use has consistently been rare.[1] In *Beechwood Construction Ltd.* (1977), the board observed that the remedy was not, in 1977, "being utilized nor complemented by a decline in the incidences of precertification unfair labor practices." The modification of the board's policy under that section that was undertaken in that case had no appreciable effect on the number of applications granted in the succeeding years. There was certainly no improvement in the precertification unfair labor practice figures; in that regard the worst was yet to come.

The test to be met by an 8(4)(e) applicant has always been too onerous for the remedy to have been relevant and effective; in light of the most recent decisions of the council this will continue to be the case. Yet the need for an effective remedy of this type has never been greater.

Finally, the procedure and remedies under Section 3 for illegal discharges must be reexamined. We make two suggestions: first, any employee fired should retain their status as an employee until the hearing; second, all hearings should be held within five days. We note that there is currently a provision under the Industrial Relations Act (Section 2(5)) for an expedited hearing, to be held within five days of the filing of a complaint.

Decertification

Figure 8 indicates that rates of decertification increased gradually in the 1974–1983 period, before rising dramatically in the succeeding years—from an average of 80.4 to 224.2 annually, a figure approaching 200 percent. (Between 1955 and 1980, decertification in the United States increased 300 percent.) The rapid increase in decertification in British Columbia can be seen to have arisen directly from the 1984 amendments. The legislation reflects an ideological conclusion—that employers should be relieved from their obligations under a certification or a collective agreement after the passage of a two-year period of inactivity.

CONCLUSION: THE ADOPTION OF THE AMERICAN MODEL

The statistical trends in the area of certification and unfair labor practice in British Columbia have developed a disturbing resemblance to those in the

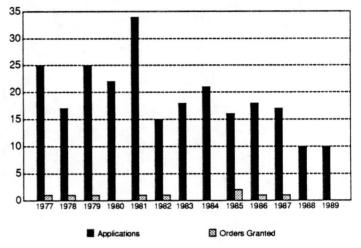

FIGURE 7. APPLICATIONS PURSUANT TO SECTION 8(4)(E)

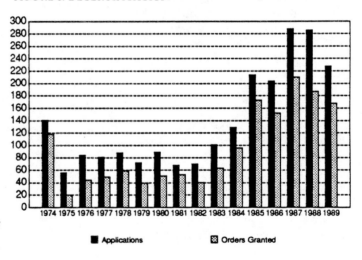

FIGURE 8. DECERTIFICATION

United States. In addition to the import of antiunion attitudes and methodology from that country by the business and employer community of this province, the role played by the 1984 amendments to the Labour Code in this development cannot be discounted. The adoption of a policy of mandatory representation votes—what former Labour Board Chair Paul Weiler had described as "the worst feature of U.S. labour law"—has increased the level of employer involvement in the certification process, with the result that the opportunity for illegal employer activity has been enhanced.

We maintain that the available data show a link between the abandonment of the use of union membership evidence as a basis for certification, and a rapid rise in the successful use of illegal tactics by employers against the organizing employee. The use of representation votes as a condition of certification does not further democratic rights, but instead serves the interests of the employer who would wish to influence his employee's decision on the question of union representation.

Our concern is that today there is no effective means of preventing illegal employer interference in trade union organization. Automatic certification on the basis of membership evidence, as provided for by Section 45 of the original Labour Code, was an effective means of protecting the right to organize, and remains today a relevant policy option.

Finally, we note that in this paper we have undertaken a simple and straightforward compilation and analysis of data contained in the Labour Relations Board and Industrial Relations Council Annual Reports. The utilization of the computerized facilities of the IRC would allow a much more detailed and sophisticated analysis of the effect of the current legislation, and of the IRC's policy, upon industrial relations in British Columbia. Such research would give policy makers and the labor relations community an objective—rather than an ideological—basis for policy development.

ENDNOTES

[1]The unofficial policy of the Labour Relations Board with respect to the use of this remedy can perhaps be best described as the selection of one or two "sacrificial lambs" from a given year's flock of employers guilty of egregious unfair labor practice. The board did not view the remedy as one that they should use on anything more than a token basis; the possibility of being the one chosen in a particular year was held out as a threat to recalcitrant employers during informal discussions the the board's officers. The pattern formed by these figures shows little indicating of being tied to the actual level of unfair labor practice in B.C. in a given year, and is a manifestation of the arbitrariness with which this section was administered.

REFERENCES

Adams, Roy J. *North American Industrial Relations: Divergent Trends in Canada and the United States*. McMaster, 1988.

B.C.E. Developments, BCIRC C269/88.

Baigent, John. "Protecting the Right to Organize." In *The Labour Code of British Columbia in the 1980s*. Edited by J. Weiler and P. Gall. Toronto: Butterworth's, 45–59, 1983.

Beechwood Construction Ltd. BCLRB 32/77, 2 Can LRBR 13.

Century Plaza Hotel Ltd. BCLRB 68/75.

Chaison, G., and J. Rose. "Continental Divide: The Direction and Fate of North American Unions." In Faculty of Business, McMaster University, *Working Paper No. 309*:9–10, September, 1988.

Cicuto and Sons Contractors Ltd. IRC C271/88.

The Current Industrial Relations Scene in Canada, 1984. Queens University at Kingston, Industrial Relations Centre, 94, 1984.

Doyle, Philip M. "Area Wage Surveys Spread Light on Declines in Unionization." *Monthly Labor Review*. 108:17–20, September, 1985.

Edwards, Richard, and Michael Podgursky. "The Unraveling Accord: American Unions in Crisis." In *Unions in Crisis and Beyond: Perspectives from Six Countries*. Edited by Richard Glover, Paolo Garonna, and Franz Todtling. Dover, Massachusetts: Auburn House, 1986.

Farber, Henry S. "The Extent of Unionization in the United States." In *Challenges and Choices Facing American Labor*. Edited by Thomas A. Kochan. Cambridge, Massachusetts: MIT Press, 1985.

Farber, Henry S. "The Recent Decline in Unionization in the United States." *Science*. 238:915–20, November, 1987.

Focus Building and S.E.I.U. IRC C90/87.

Forano Ltd. BCLRB 2/74; 1 Can LRBR 13.

Freeman, Richard B. "Why are Unions Faring Poorly in NLRB Representation Elections?" In *Challenges and Choices Facing American Labor*. Edited by Thomas A. Kochan. Cambridge, Massachusetts: MIT Press, 1985.

———. "Contraction and Expansion: The Divergence of Private Sector and Public Sector Unionism in the United States." *Journal of Economic Perspectives*. 63:74, 1988.

Freeman, Richard B. and James Medoff. *What Do Unions Do?* New York: Basic Books, 1984.

Gunderson, Morley, and Noah M. Meltz. "Canadian Unions Achieve Strong Gains in Membership." *Monthly Labor Review*. 109:48–9, April, 1986.

Hiram Walker and Sons Ltd. 1 Can LRBR 517.

Horizon Developments Ltd. BCIRC C87/89.

Industrial Relations Reform Act, SBC 1987 c241.

J&L Meats, BCLRB 121/85.

Kumar, P. "Union Growth in Canada: Retrospect and Prospect." In *Canada Labour Relations*. Edited by W.C. Riddell. 95, 1986.

The Labour Code Amendment Act, SBC, 1984 C24.

Ladysmith Chemainus Chronicle BCLRB 428/84.

Legislative Assembly. Debates, Hansard, 4661, 10 May, 1984.

Lifway Foods 3 Can LRBR 4&2.

Lipset, Seymour Martin. "North American Labor Movements: A Comparative Perspective." In *Unions in Transition*. Edited by S.M. Lipset. San Francisco: Institute for Contemporary Studies, 1986.

Meltz, Noah. "Labor Movements in Canada and United States." In *Challenges and Choices Facing American Labor*. Edited by

Thomas A. Kochan. Cambridge, Massachusetts: MIT Press, 1985.

Plateau Mills Ltd. and International Woodworkers of America, Local 1-424 and Group of Employees of Plateau Mills Ltd., 1 Can LRBR 82.

Rose, Joseph B., and Gary N. Chaison. "The State of the Unions: United States and Canada." *Journal of Labor Research*. 6:97–111, Winter, 1985.

Sandbar Construction IRC C9/89.

St Jude's Anglican Home Care Society 8 CLRBR NS 257.

Superior Contracting BCIRC C313/88.

Tri-Power Construction BCLRB 442/84.

Trizec Construction Ltd. BCIRC C13/89.

Trophy Foods BCLRB 347/84.

Troy, Leo. "The Rise and Fall of American Trade Unions: Labor Movement from FDR to RR." In *Unions in Transition*. Edited by S.M. Lipset. San Francisco: Institute for Contemporary Studies, 1986.

United Used Auto and Truck Parts Ltd. IRC C109/89.

Wall and Redekop Corporation and Trizec Construction BCLRB 174/86; affd. 30 BCLR (2d) 74 (BCCA).

Weiler, Paul. "Striking a New Balance: Freedom of Contract and the Prospects of Union Representation." *Harvard Law Review*. 98:351–420, 1984.

———. "Promises to Keep: Securing Workers' Rights to Self Organization under the NLRA." *Harvard Law Review* 96:1769–1827, June, 1983.

———. *Reconcilable Differences: New Directions in Canadian Labour Law*. Toronto: Carswell, 1980.

———. "The Transformation of the Law at Work." In *Law in the Workplaces of North America*. (casebook) University of Toronto Faculty of Law, 1988.

Western Canada Steel 1 Can LRBR 25.

APPENDIX

ANNUAL REPORTS: History of Applications for Certification, Unfair Labor Practice Complaints, and Decertification Applications, Labour Relations Board and Industrial Relations Council 1974–1988

TABLE 1—APPLICATIONS FOR CERTIFICATION PURSUANT TO SECTION 39(1) AND 39(2) (ORIGINAL APPLICATIONS AND "RAIDS"), 1974–1988:

a) applications for certification disposed of (all employees);

b) applications for certification granted;

c) percentage of applications for certification granted;

d) applications for certification disposed of (unorganized employees);

e) applications for certification granted;

f) percentage of applications for certification granted.

Year	a)	b)	c)	d)	e)	f)
1989	355	263	74.1	335	253	75.5
1988	512	345	67.4	392*	327	83.4*
1987	343	184	53.6	223	165	74.0
1986	385	206	53.5	255	191	74.9
1985	333	187	56.1	234	171	73.1
1984	376	238	63.3	279	224	80.3
1983	678	441	65.0	445	407	91.5
1982	916	706	77.1	717	674	94.0
1981	848	643	75.8	684	622	90.9
1980	790	593	75.1	625	574	91.8
1979	662	502	75.8	526	478	90.9
1978	672	479	71.3	523	461	88.1
1977	670	498	74.3	533	478	89.7
1976	735	529	72.0	571	504	88.3
1975	965	753	78.0	812	731	90.0
1974	1147	920	80.2	963	892	92.6

*In response to the passing of Bill 20, B.C. teachers filed seventy-five applications for certification. Deducting these from the total number of applications for unorganized employees decreases the success rate for 1988 to 79.5 percent and increases the unfair labor practice percentage to 38.4 percent.

TABLE 2—APPLICATIONS FOR CERTIFICATION IN THE CONSTRUCTION INDUSTRY, 1974–1986 (THERE ARE NO DATA FOR 1987 AND 1988):

a) applications filed in the construction industry;

b) employees involved in the applications filed;

c) applications granted;

d) employees involved in the granted applications;

e) percentage of successful applications in construction.

Year	a)	b)	c)	d)	e)
1986	92	928	44	456	47.8
1985	83	557	42	236	50.6
1984	114	708	82	417	71.9
1983	263	1371	210	1027	79.8
1982	422	2334	373	2109	88.4
1981	386	2414	282	1669	73.0
1980	308	1601	237	1086	76.9
1979	270	1231	198	847	73.3
1978	300	1310	219	989	73.0
1977	260	1204	215	1039	82.7
1976	304	1370	223	1009	73.3
1975	383	1860	335	1640	87.5
1974	361	1755	329	1601	91.1

TABLE 3—UNFAIR LABOR PRACTICE, 1974–1988:

a) Section 3 unfair labor practice complaints disposed of;

b) complaints involving discharge of employees:

c) discharge cases granting relief to at least one employee, including settlement;

d) 8(4)(e) applications filed;

e) 8(4)(e) applications granted;

f) certifications issued under other sections of the legislation where an 8(4)(e) application was dismissed.

Year	a)	b)	c)	d)	e)	f)
1989	164	37	13	10	0	n/a
1988	122	53	25	10	0	n/a
1987	162	77	30	17	0	4
1986	171	74	39	18	2	8
1985	139	62	36	16	2	4
1984	141	80	52	21	3	10
1983	155	81	47	18	0	4
1982	167	107	65	15	2	7
1981	156	99	58	34	2	16
1980	126	77	38	22	0	14
1979	110	69	27	25	1	14
1978	119	71	37	17	1	7
1977	108	64	44	25	1	12
1976	94	72	42	n/a	0	n/a
1975	126	86	50	n/a	0	n/a
1974	90	61	33	n/a	n/a	n/a

TABLE 4—APPLICATIONS FOR DECERTIFICATION, 1974–1988:

a) applications for decertification disposed of;
b) applications for decertification granted;
c) percentage of applications for decertification granted.

Year	a)	b)	c)
1989	228	168	73.7
1988	286	187	65.4
1987	288	210	72.9
1986	204	152	74.5
1985	214	173	80.8
1984	129	96	74.4
1983	101	63	62.4
1982	70	40	57.1
1981	68	53	77.9
1980	89	51	57.3
1979	72	39	54.1
1978	88	59	67.0
1977	81	49	60.5
1976	84	44	52.4
1975	56	20	35.7
1974	141	118	83.7

TABLE 5—UNFAIR LABOR PRACTICE COMPLAINTS AS A PERCENTAGE OF APPLICATIONS FOR CERTIFICATION (UNORGANIZED EMPLOYEES).

a) applications for certification disposed of (unorganized employees);
b) Section 3 unfair labor practice complaints disposed of;
c) b) divided by a).

Year	a)	b)	c)
1989	335	164	49.0
1988	392	122	38.5
1987	223	162	72.6
1986	255	171	67.1
1985	234	139	59.4
1984	279	141	50.5
1983	445	155	34.8
1982	717	167	23.3
1981	684	156	22.8
1980	625	126	20.2
1979	526	110	20.9
1978	523	119	22.8
1977	533	108	20.3
1976	571	94	16.5
1975	812	126	15.5
1974	963	90	9.3

Organizing in Canada: Adapting to Changing Conditions

KEITH OLEKSIUK

Technical Assistant, United Steelworkers of America, District 3, Vancouver, B.C.

INTRODUCTION

Let me begin by commenting on the general nature of the industrial relations system that exists in Canada. In particular I note that it is not a national scheme. Instead, each of the provinces has its own industrial relations legislation. As a result, interesting differences emerge even though the various schemes have common roots.

Following that, I will touch on the issue of union behavior in the world of organizing, particularly in the private sector, and how the development of the material conditions in Canada has begun to force unions to adjust their behavior. Finally I will briefly address the issue of global economics and changes in the work force.

THE CANADIAN INDUSTRIAL RELATIONS SYSTEM: LEGISLATIVE FRAMEWORK

The underlying common theme in the Canadian industrial relations system has been an acceptance of state activism in the design and behavior of the various regulatory systems. The prominence of the provincial role in labor relations in Canada also distinguishes Canada, relative to the U.S. While there are many common threads nationally, if you look at the various provinces such as Ontario and Quebec, it becomes apparent that quite different initiatives have come from that common theme.

There are numerous ways in which the Canadian system, although inspired by the Wagner Act principle, has varied from the U.S. model. I will briefly point to one discrete example of how this has worked to the advantage of Canadian labor.

In Canada the unions assume responsibility for the prosecution of unfair labor practice complaints against employers. They have carriage of the case, they can take the initiative, and that means significant differences in the timing factor. Unions are not dependent in the same way as they are with the state initiative structure of the National Labor Relations Board (NLRB). I know from discussion with counsel in the United States the immense amount of frustration that emerges because of the dependence on the NLRB and its procrastinations. This "administrative" distinction has proved to be advantageous for unions in Canada and is one area where one can look to make changes in the U.S. without entering into major legislative overhaul. That said, I want to address some of the Canadian statutory initiatives, in particular the Quebec experience.

Quebec provides a very interesting case of how state activism can be developed in a way that is positive not only for labor, but is also perceived as positive by the public. A major example of this is the decree system. The decree system involves a geographic and a sectoral way of distinguishing elements of the work force—for instance, the needle trades or the garment trade in the Sherbrook area of Quebec. A union must organize a "significant percentage" of the work force for the particular sector in the chosen geographic area. Once certified, the union applies for a decree. The decree, once granted, establishes that all employees in that region, for that sector of industry, will receive the same basic wages, terms and conditions of work as the people who were certified and obtained a contract. They don't get all the benefits enjoyed by the unionized segment under the collective agreement, but the basic wages, rights, terms and conditions of employment are mandated. This "bottom line" equality of wages and conditions has several interesting consequences. In many sectors of the economy, like security guards and office cleaning, the competition changes from "low-wage bidding" to "quality-of-service bidding." A second consequence is the message by unions to the non-organized components that their wages and terms and conditions of employment depend on what can be negotiated, and that success in negotiations depends on how strong we are. That can have significant benefit in organizing drives.

Quebec has also implemented antiscab legislation. Effectively, it provides that if a strike occurs, the employer is not allowed to bring to that location anyone who wasn't a regular employee prior to the onset of the industrial dispute. They can't bring in new employees, they can't bring in strikebreakers. They can't even bring in employees from another location of the same employer. That particular piece of legislation is given credit for Quebec having one of the lowest incidences of private sector strikes and picket line violence in the country. Those two factors affect how labor is perceived, both in organizing drives and within the communities.

This makes for a very interesting proposal to market to governments. You can put forward the idea that collective bargaining and the decree system reduces industrial relations conflict and provide data that supports that proposition. This goes to support Lanyon and Edwards' basic thesis that while we're talking about organizing we must keep our focus clear as to the kind of political initiatives that enhance the success of organizing (Lanyon and Edwards, 1991). While we're setting the framework within which organizing is going to take place we should not limit the scope of that framework.

HISTORICAL ROOTS AND CURRENT REALITIES

Before talking further about the design of the legislative framework, it will be useful to recall, at least in rough outline, the historical development of the principles that underlie our labor relations systems. The labor relations story in North America started with a background of the British common law system and a reality of vicious opposition by employers and the state to the existence of unions. This highly antagonistic relationship with its overtones of class struggle was replaced by the Wagner Act which put into play new ground rules. This new industrial relations system was based on a mostly unarticulated but historically logical deal. Labor's unrelenting struggle forced the employers and the state to compromise. That deal arose out of the early organizing efforts of trade unions, where, despite everything that employers did, people took to the streets, workers went on strike, organized in the community, and brought the employers' operations to a halt. Despite the efforts of police or anyone else, workers struggled to organize even where there was violence and bloodshed. The strength of labor prompted saner minds to prevail and look for a better way. Employers made a deal because they had to, and the Wagner Act was enacted.

Now the system that developed from the Wagner Act is showing slippage. That whole system has been almost completely betrayed in the United States and serious efforts to undercut it are under way in Canada (Lanyon and Edwards, 1991). Employers think they are back in the driver's seat and maybe they are to some extent. Labor certainly can't count on the deal holding firm. We must remember the lessons of the past, particularly that the deal was there only because of our struggles. We forced employers to make a deal, and they won't continue to honor it just because we raise moral issues. They will keep or improve the deal only if they're concerned about our strength.

However, we cannot look only to past lessons in our strategies for keeping sufficient pressure on employers and the state. Aside from the obvious concerns about the desirability of having to return to physical struggles to protect our interests, we have to ask whether the gradual and continual erosion of massive manual labor workplaces has also reduced our ability to successfully engage in this form of struggle, the Pittston strike notwithstanding.

In the reality of today's world, we must also focus on a different strategy, one that has shown, at least in Canada, some significant promise, and that is the ballot box. Unions should, I think, see the ballot box as a very real weapon on the political battleground. If we allow ourselves to be isolated from electoral politics and pretend that workplace issues and union work are not political, we may guarantee our own demise. If, however, we succeed in placing workplace issues on the political agenda, we will be able to take to the streets in a far more promising and positive fashion.

ORGANIZING IN THE CURRENT CLIMATE

As the structure of our economy has changed so has organizing. As I am primarily familiar with the private sector and our major industrial unions—the United Steelworkers and the Canadian Auto Workers (CAW), I will focus on them. Generally, labor stayed within what I will call traditional jurisdictions up to the recession of the early 1980s. Along with traditional jurisdictions went traditional organizing methods. We sent in the guys who worked in the same kinds of shops when new shops opened, we chatted up things, talked better wages, dealt with whatever challenges the employer put forward, and more often than not we were successful. We felt, with some justification, that we had a fair amount of clout.

That confidence, that unquestioned form of behavior, started to falter when the recession hit. Both auto and steel started to look at the impact of new technology as well as the impact of higher productivity and recognized that down the road there were not going to be as many jobs in the traditional sectors. If these unions were going to grow and succeed they were going to have to look into new areas. In Canada, the CAW has very successfully moved into the fishing industry on the East Coast and into the service element of the airline industry. Steel has 15,000 security guard members, most of them in the province of Quebec (a testimony to the decree system). Wages have increased over 50 percent in the first two contracts. A hotel and restaurant component of the Steelworkers now exists, and the union has also organized nursing homes and ski hill workers.

These successes, however, must not blind us to even greater challenges ahead. Recent developments fostered by the transition to a more global economy pose perhaps even greater threats than the recession of the last decade. Free trade has contributed to the loss of more than 50,000 industrial jobs in Ontario alone in the last year. We must all pay attention to that blunt message.

One lesson learned from these new organizing experiences is that, along with new areas of organizing, unions must learn something new about their organizing techniques, and the way they approach those new, often unorganized, constituencies.

For example, I think that it is obvious when you move into major urban areas, immigration is giving a whole different pattern to who is working in the sweatshops and the low-wage industries. If we want to organize successfully there, we have to be part of the community and we have to have people from those communities as part of our organizing teams.

Another important element goes beyond the techniques of organizing. We have to deal seriously with the image of the unions. We have not been our own best friends. In marketing ourselves and in putting our image out to the communities we live in and are a part of, we're just beginning to learn about the world of advertising ourselves. We are going to have to improve our performance in this area in a hurry. Unless we reverse the negative tendencies shown in recent studies about how unions are perceived, we are going to be in trouble.

Our opposition is more and more sophisticated. A growth industry in both Canada and the U.S. is that of antiunion consultants. They are good at what they do and they want to become much richer. In order to meet their challenge we have to develop a coordinated effort at selling unions to the public through our federations and through our labor congresses. We have to put forward a positive image of unions.

We are all painfully aware of what is and isn't said about unions in the school systems and what newspapers and the general media do with their images of unions. Anyone living in our society and getting these messages, unless they live in a union household where they get a completely different image firsthand, is not going to be in favor of unions when they come out and get into the work force. The reason that they become more interested in unions later is because they suffer and learn through the realities of work. But I think we can and must do some things to change that dynamic, and it has to do with conveying our message at the mass media and the local levels. To succeed we must become more active than ever—in our communities, in our school systems, and in our dealings with the press.

CONCLUSION

If labor wants to grow and remain a viable force in society, its tasks are clear. Politically, in addition to lobbying for improved labor laws that deal with the rights to organize, we must start talking in our communities about laws that are going to impose some social responsibility on the corporations. We are discovering allies out there that we've never had before. Environmentalists, educators, women's rights activists, poverty groups, and immigrant groups are all potential allies. But they are going to have to trust labor and we are going to have to build links that we didn't have before. We have to take on a much more responsible, much more complete role in society as unions and become involved members of an overall community if we are going to succeed.

REFERENCES

Lanyon, Stan, and Robert Edwards. "The Right to Organize: Labor Law and Its Impact in British Colombia." In *Labor in a Global Economy: Perspectives from the U.S. and Canada.* Edited by Steven Hecker and Margaret Hallock. Eugene, Oregon: U of O Books, 1991.

Organizing Immigrant Workers in the Global Economy

KATIE QUAN
Manager, Pacific Northwest District Council, International Ladies' Garment Workers' Union

By the end of this year, my first year as manager of the International Ladies' Garment Workers' Union (ILGWU) Pacific Northwest District Council, I will have lost more than a quarter of my membership due to plant closures. Four hundred jobs were lost during the first half of this year at Koret of California, a fifty-two year-old company that has found it cheaper to manufacture its sportswear in Guatemala, El Salvador, the Philippines, and other parts of Asia. One hundred thirty jobs will probably be lost by December at Sawyer of Napa, a 120-year-old tannery and coat factory, where our union has spent two years fighting union busters while trying to organize and negotiate a first contract, and where the company has found it cheaper and less environmentally restrictive to tan sheepskins in Hungary and elsewhere around the world.

The members and staff of the ILGWU put up a hell of a fight to keep the plants open—so that forty-year employees at Koret who were too young to retire and too old to learn another trade might be able to work with dignity without going on welfare; and so that immigrant workers with limited ability in English and few job skills might be able to hold on to what precious little they have earned with union-scale pay and not be forced back to the sweatshops.

But in the end, despite unprecedented public pressure against Koret, rallies, demonstrations, and boycotts, letters from the community, resolutions from City Hall, and editorials in the major daily newspapers, Koret's profits prevailed over people, and the plant closed. Although the final chapter at Sawyer of Napa has not yet been written, and we are currently fighting for plant retention studies and mobilizing community support, the promanagement laws of the U.S. make fighting plant closures defensive battles, and union-busting companies such as Sawyer will use every means available to prevail.

Garment workers are among the most tragic victims of the globalization of capital. The Koret workers in San Francisco were mostly immigrant Asian, Latina, and Black women who made $15,000 a year in a good year. In a way, it is absurd to think that in the U.S. we have to fight to keep poverty-level $15,000-a-year jobs from running away. But the reality is that the workers making Koret garments in Guatemala make a dollar a day, without any benefits and without a democratically elected trade union. For every jacket produced in the U.S., Koret can produce the same garment for eight dollars less in Guatemala. Koret workers here are exploited, and the Koret workers overseas are super-exploited.

For the union, the loss of membership is yet another blow in the face of a fast-expanding, overwhelmingly nonunion garment industry. In the San Francisco Bay Area, there are 20,000 garment workers making $7,000 to $8,000 a year in nonunion sweatshops. Most are immigrant women from Asian and Latin-American countries. As long as 95 percent of the industry is nonunion with workers earning half of what union members earn, there will always be pressure from the Korets and Sawyers of the world to go to nonunion sweatshops, whether in the U.S. or overseas.

Conditions are not very different in the Pacific Northwest and western Canada. I know from having organized garment workers in Vancouver, B.C., that the garment industry is expanding rapidly there, and that most of the workers are Asian women who are working in substandard conditions. And in Portland there are perhaps several thousands of unorganized garment workers, most of whom are from Vietnam and

China.

The challenge, then, is to develop organizing strategies that will successfully bring union wages and working conditions, together with a sense of dignity, to workers who need and want it—whether those workers come from places like Vietnam, China, El Salvador, or Mexico. And in organizing locally, the challenge is to think and act globally.

ORGANIZING THE UNORGANIZED

I spent many years organizing garment workers in New York City, and when people listen to me tell horror stories—about basement sweatshops that don't have walls or windows, about industrial home workers working for top-name designers making $2,000 per hour, about rats so voracious that they bite big chunks out of polyester fabric stacks—people often ask, "How could they live like that? Why don't they fight back? Aren't they willing slaves?" Well, let me relate a story. In 1982 in New York's Chinatown, 400 Chinese garment shop owners decided not to sign a new three-year contract with the ILGWU. They claimed that they had been discriminated against by the non-Chinese garment shop owners, and called upon the 15,000 union workers in Chinatown to support them in their protest against discrimination.

This immediately threw the industry into chaos. It was the talk of the community in the shops, in the grocery stores, in the streets, in the subways, and in late-night phone calls. The workers were angry that the bosses were jeopardizing their families' health benefits, their retirement benefits, and their ability to argue with the boss over piece rates without being fired. Chinese or not, the workers wanted to strike. In the shop where I was working at the time, all fifty seamstresses attended planning meetings, passed out leaflets in the street, spoke at radio stations, and took other actions.

When the union called for the first rally, 15,000 Chinatown garment workers jammed the site with picket signs chanting for a union contract. Two weeks later on the morning of the strike deadline, again 15,000 Chinatown garment workers rallied, marched, sang "Solidarity Forever" in Chinese, and then struck the garment shops that had not yet signed the contract. By 1:00 p.m. that day, all 400 shop owners had signed the new contract.

It was a proud day for us as Chinese garment workers. And it taught everyone—the bosses, the union officers, and most importantly ourselves—a humble lesson: Chinese garment workers, low-paid immigrant women, *do* fight. And though this was a case of union workers fighting for a contract renewal, the lesson should not be forgotten as we strategize to organize the unorganized.

Is organizing immigrant workers different from organizing native-born workers? Do unions have to take different approaches when organizing immigrant workers? Some people would answer "no" to both questions, saying that a worker is a worker, no matter what color of skin or national origin, and that they shouldn't be treated any differently. Any organizer who takes that approach will need a lot of luck because they are missing the boat entirely. The point is not whether or not to treat people differently. The point is that union organizers must approach immigrant workers as they approach all workers, by trying to understand what's going on in the workers' minds, what issues concern them, what kinds of things will motivate them, which individuals they will follow, and similar factors. Furthermore, we must respect those different interests and incorporate them into our labor agenda. By definition, immigration issues are important to immigrant workers, and a union that is seen in the forefront of immigrant workers' rights will find it easier to win workers' trust. Right now, repeal of the employer sanctions provisions in the Immigration Reform and Control Act is a major policy debate, and because the ILGWU has seen how this provision discriminates against all immigrants, we are fully supporting its repeal.

In an industry such as ours, where most of the workers are women, family issues are a major concern. Many trade unionists still think that child care and parental leave are "soft" issues that you negotiate about when you have the luxury of money left over at the bargaining table. But to women (and men) with small children who are faced with financially needing to work on the one hand, and the abysmal lack of high-quality child care on the other, bargaining about child care may be more critical than wages, pension contributions, or any number of other issues routinely raised at the negotiating table. In fact, when I first began organizing for a child care center in New York Chinatown in the early 1980s, it was an issue which immediately won the support of not just the workers, but the Chinatown community as a whole.

This brings me to the most important group of issues of concern to immigrant workers: community issues. If you ask a Chinese worker which identity she feels more strongly—being Chinese or being a worker, she will 99 percent of the time say that she feels a stronger identity with being Chinese. Whether it is because of strong ethnic heritage, historical discrimination, social isolation, or inability to speak English well, most immigrants would feel the same way. Understanding this leads us to appreciate how vital immigrant community issues are to the workers we are trying to organize. The more trade unions are seen in the community fighting against gentrification, against police brutality, or for badly needed social services, the more the unions will gain the trust and respect of immigrant workers.

Having said this, you have to put your money where your mouth is. This requires hiring Latino and Asian organizers and training them from the rank-and-file, in Portland, Seattle, Vancouver, or wherever you have immigrant workers to organize. In San Francisco, the ILGWU will soon be opening an organizing office in the heart of Chinatown, so that we can be part of the community and the community can be part of us.

If you have got the commitment and you're creative, you can do it. I am impressed with the efforts of organizers in Portland from the Amalgamated Clothing and Textile Workers Union, the Service Employees, and other unions who have formed a team of immigrant volunteer organizers by training rank-and-file activists and by reaching out to local immigrant community activists.

Something that will help all unions organize Asian workers will be the formation in 1991 of an AFL-CIO affiliated Asian labor committee. Though it is only in the formative stages right now, we hope that among other things it will become a resource for translating literature into various Asian languages, conducting leadership training in their native languages for rank-and-file activists and for union staff, and that it will be a general resource to unions on multilingual and multicultural issues among Asian workers.

CONCLUSION

How does organizing immigrant workers tie into a global perspective? I have already discussed how the Koret workers lost their jobs when the company moved production to Guatemala and elsewhere. It would have been easy to fall into the trap of blaming the Guatemalan workers for stealing our jobs. But in the midst of fighting the plant closure we invited a Guatemalan trade union leader to address the Koret workers, and it became clear that at a dollar a day, the Guatemalan workers certainly weren't the enemy. Wouldn't we in fighting our plant closure, and wouldn't the Guatemalan workers, in struggling to organize a union, be a thousand times stronger if we had a network of support among all the Koret workers around the world, a network that would enable us to take coordinated action to support each other when necessary? Wouldn't the tannery workers at Sawyer of Napa fighting their plant closure be put in an offensive position if the Hungarian tannery workers refused to tan Sawyer's sheepskins? The concept of international solidarity is certainly not new. The longshoremen have been refusing to unload coffee from El Salvador and goods from other countries that violate human rights for years. Several years ago the 3M workers in South Africa walked out in support of the 3M workers in New Jersey who were threatened by a plant closure. However, these activities, while important and admirable, were seen as an adjunct to the daily business routine.

I believe that we have to do more than that. The globalization of capital is here to stay. Labor has to catch up with that fact, and to make its international strategy an integral part of its whole strategy. What good will it do if I go out and organize 20,000 garment workers in the San Francisco Bay Area if the manufacturers just turn around and move the production offshore? This Labor in a Global Economy conference is a good beginning in putting this issue on labor's front burner, but we must pursue international strategies as an integral part of the present and future labor movement.

We hear often, especially on the west coasts of the U.S. and Canada, that we are part of a rapidly developing Pacific Rim economy. Whether North-American companies are investing in Asia, or whether Asian companies are investing in North America, the economies of the various nations on the Pacific Rim are becoming linked in many different ways.

A couple of months ago, a Japanese company opened a sake plant in Napa, California, employing contract workers from Japan, which led to resentment from the local work force. Last month a Chinese-American garment shop owner brought in sixteen young women from mainland China to work under sweatshop conditions and live in barrack-style housing. The potential for ugly racial hatred to become mixed up with the ongoing fight for labor justice is there.

I believe, therefore, that it is incumbent, especially on those trade unions on the west coast of North America, to take a leading role in building ties with workers and trade unions in Asian countries. In this way we can lay the foundation for action based on common worker interests in the global context, and especially in the Pacific Rim, in a way that fosters unity rather than divisiveness.

Section 9

OCCUPATIONAL SAFETY AND HEALTH IN A CHANGING ENVIRONMENT

Occupational safety and health fits our themes of globalization and U.S.-Canadian comparative industrial relations on several levels. While it has emerged as a major workplace and public policy issue in the last twenty years, and considerable resources have been invested, the movement for workplace safety and health remains controversial, subject to ideological pressures, and unfulfilled in its promise. In the international context, the issue of uniform standards for workplace conditions is, like environmental standards, central to labor in the free trade discussion, especially between industrialized and developing nations. Revelations about terrible working conditions and environmental contamination in Mexico's Maquiladora zone, where hundreds of U.S., Canadian, and other foreign corporations operate, have heightened concerns about what globalization and competition really mean to the conditions of work.

There has been considerable sharing of ideas between safety and health specialists in the U.S. and Canada, and both countries have also been influenced by Western European concepts and policies. As with labor relations, much of the Canadian legal framework of safety and health is provincial. In the U.S., while states have a role, the overall legal framework is established by the federal Occupational Safety and Health Act (OSHA) of 1970. OSHA has emphasized a regulatory/enforcement approach with some worker involvement measures built into the law. Various Canadian provinces, borrowing especially from the Scandinavian countries, have generally put greater emphasis on worker involvement. Government policies in both the U.S. and Canada have embraced voluntary compliance and tripartite models as political winds have shifted over the last twenty years. In both countries, labor's agenda now includes a more explicit and direct role for workers in safety and health, embodied in a movement dubbed the "right to act" in the U.S.

Our contributors in this section address safety and health at the public policy level and specifically the rights of workers. Robert Sass, formerly director of occupational health and safety for the province of Saskatchewan, argues that Canadian public policy in most or all jurisdictions is de facto based on a voluntary compliance model, which views health and safety as a problem suitable for nonadversarial solutions worked out by labor and management. The failure to make major improvements in reducing injuries and illness is attributed to the insufficiency of standards and enforcement and to the lack of other powerful incentives for employers to institute safety measures. He poses short-term reforms including criminalizing safety and health violations and transforming joint safety and health committees into "work environment boards" with stronger rights and resources enabling workers to participate beyond the current consultation level of most joint committees.

As a long-term strategy Sass advocates a thorough reexamination of the sources of illness and injury at work and of the conflict between property rights and workers' "inalienable" right to health and safety. The former includes a holistic view of health and safety linked to work organization, the design of the workplace, and the "intrinsic" nature of work. The latter demands that the "large ethical problems of social life," including the right of workers to their health and safety, be reintroduced to the public policy arena and the responsibility of governments, and not left to "voluntarism or the untrammeled market."

Robin Baker recounts the policy battles over safety and health in the U.S. and specifically in the state of California since the passage of the OSH Act, drawing lessons about the political vulnerability of the occupational safety and health system. She links the effectiveness of the government safety and health apparatus to the labor movement's strength and ability to exert real pressure on employers and the government for improved workplace conditions. While policy initiatives such as the right-to-know movement have been largely successful in achieving new legislation and standards, the reality of the workplace is that knowledge alone has not meant power for workers. The labor movement is now demanding OSHA reform centered on worker empowerment in the workplace—the "right to act." She warns, however, that the ultimate success of safety and health reform rests on the ability of unions to organize and mobilize. At the same time, unions are recognizing the organizing potential in workers' legitimate safety and health concerns.

The Deficiency of the Voluntary Compliance Model as a Public Policy Instrument in Workplace Health and Safety in Canada

ROBERT SASS

Director, Labour Studies Program, University of Saskatchewan, Saskatoon

INTRODUCTION

Each Canadian provincial jurisdiction and federal government made major statutory, regulatory, and policy reforms pertaining to occupational health and safety during the decade of the 1970s. For instance, by the early part of 1980 every Canadian jurisdiction including the two territories had statutory provisions regarding a worker's right to know about hazardous substances in the workplace, the right to participate on joint health and safety committees pertaining to work environment matters, and the individual right to refuse to work under unsafe conditions, contrary to the previous "work now, grieve later" rule. While the substantive requirements of these provisions range widely in each jurisdiction, they all, nonetheless, incorporate a role for workers in the inspection and monitoring of their working conditions.

Further, we have more occupational health and safety construction, mines, and general inspectors; as well as industrial engineers, occupational health physicians, toxicologists, and varied scientific experts such as ergonomists accompanied by a plethora of policy technocrats in this expanding area. As a result, during the last twenty years we have had an enormous number of health and safety regulations passed, and more recently a "right-to-know" regulation promulgated by the federal government and adopted with modifications by each of the provinces. Occupational health and safety departments or branches within government have evolved from relatively small units in ministries of public health during the early 1970s to become a central part of the Ministers of Labour portfolio throughout Canada with the possible exception of Prince Edward Island.

These changes have been justified and accompanied by an acknowledgement of the socially unacceptable dimensions of industrial disease and injury, and the growing awareness of these issues by the public. Thus, there has been a continuous promulgation of regulations, especially pertaining to toxic substances. For instance, in 1987 a regulation was enacted in Ontario that set legislative standards in respect of more than 600 substances at one stroke. The standard reflected the guidelines suggested by the American Conference of Governmental Industrial Hygienists (ACGIH). Labor activists in that province have taken issue with the adoption of ACGIH standards because of recent academic allegations that they represent employers' interests. Nonetheless, almost all Canadian jurisdictions are responding to growing public concern pertaining to workplace and environmental pollution.

How effective has this paroxysm of protective legislation and policies been in reducing the frequency and severity rates of industrial accidents and diseases?

Despite increased government intervention during the 1970s, there were 1,280,000 occupational injuries in 1980, which was 52 percent above the 1971 level. When the increase in the labor force is accounted for, accidents per employed worker still rose by 16 percent. In 1980, some 5,000 workers were injured each day, compared with just over 3,000 ten years earlier. Total costs in 1980 stood at over $6.7 billion, a rise of 320 percent in the ten years. This represents 2.3 percent of the gross national product and $5,560 per claim or $745 per employed worker; even after adjustment for inflation costs doubled from 1971 to 1980 (Brody et al., 1986).

The situation has not improved during the decade of the 1980s. This is significant to know in evaluating the policy changes that occurred throughout the decade of the 1970s. For example, in 1982 the Ontario Workers' Compensation Board allowed 203 claims in respect of deaths found to be work-related; it allowed 219 in 1983, 103 in 1984, 195 in 1985, and 220 in 1986 (cited in Glasbeek, 1989, p. 11).

Canadian statistics for 1985 indicate that there was a 9 percent increase in allowed claims from the previous year, and Dr. Anna Lee Yassi found that in Ontario alone, as many as 6,000 people per year die earlier than they otherwise might because of their occupations (cited in Glasbeek, 1989).

Professor Glasbeek stated in his prestigious Meredith Lecture that:

> Worse still, there may be a good argument to the effect that we cannot even be sure that there has been a marked improvement in the situation if it is compared to that which prevailed around the turn of the century (Glasbeek, 1989).

Glasbeek has persuasively argued that the situation in Canada has been worsening throughout the last two decades, and governments and employers have apparently been unable to stop this trend. Trade union activists have also focused upon the questionable efficacy of existing governmental policies before debating what new regulations are needed to curb the use of particular substances or which toxic substances need to be looked at next. More and more critics of the system are asking whether our elaborate and sophisticated occupational health and safety regimes are truly different in structure and focus than the preexisting approaches. It is becoming more and more apparent that provincial governments still decide what risks shall continue to be borne by workers, and employers fundamentally determine the level of risks experienced by workers in their respective workplaces.[1]

A FLAWED PUBLIC POLICY

Canadian public policy regulating risks and hazards in the workplace have relied upon the following instruments: (1) worker involvement in joint health and safety committees; (2) the setting of acceptable levels or limits for toxic substances; (3) enforcement and compliance by an inspectorate; (4) workers' compensation levies as an economic incentive for employers to reduce hazards; and (5) the ultimate sanction of prosecutions. While these policy initiatives are necessary in controlling hazards and risks in the workplace, they have been shown to be insufficient in bringing about the necessary reforms that workers, unions, and students of occupational health and safety desire.

The shortcomings of the above policy instruments are becoming more obvious to observers of the Canadian scene. Presently, the inadequacy of existing threshold limit values is being debated by labor's representatives to the Canadian Labour Congress' Health and Safety Committee. There is a general consensus that standards are not scientifically determined, but primarily reflect political decisionmaking and the power relations in production. There is also a growing consensus that Workers' Compensation Board penalties have been a disincentive rather than an incentive for employers to improve working conditions. This, in part, rests upon the fact that workers' compensation is a collective insurance scheme for employers and a bar to individual suits. And while all jurisdictions allow some form of employee "participation" through joint health and safety committees, worker involvement has been primarily consultative rather than of a participative nature.

Professor Swinton wrote:

> ... the legislation's commitment is to consultation, but no more. There is a strongly held belief that health and safety come within management's prerogative, unless bargained away, and the OHSA was not meant to shift the balance of power in the workplace to the worker's side, either by granting actual decision-making power to joint health and safety committees or by turning government inspectors into interest arbitrators (Swinton, 1983, p. 143).

Glasbeek (1989, p. 32) has correctly observed that "we do not have enough inspectors, do not prosecute enough, do not convict enough, do not impose harsh enough penalties because we have decided not to do any of these things."

As former executive director of the Occupational Health and Safety Branch in Saskatchewan, I fully concur with this assessment. No government will tolerate "flooding" the courts with occupational health and safety prosecutions. The inspectors know this, and if they tend to get "out of line" their superiors will interpret their behavior as vindictive, militant, or over-zealous, lacking the ability to cajole, negotiate, and persuade employers to correct hazardous conditions. This is the real politic regarding the enforcement and compliance procedures in Canada. It is political naivete to think otherwise!

In effect, all Canadian jurisdictions have tacitly adopted a voluntary compliance public policy model based upon a nonpunitive approach. Their rationale has, on the whole, been that voluntarism would best ensure employer obligation to adhere to legal standards as opposed to a system of compulsion. This rationale is further defended by the view that occupational health and safety represents a nonadversarial relationship between the two major "actors" in our industrial relations system. Both employers and employees have a "shared goal" in making working conditions safe. Thus, it is not a fit subject for collective bargaining.

This rationale transforms the inspectorate into facilitators and, at times, arbitrators between supposedly autonomous, juridically equal partners to the contract represented by statute and accompanying regulations. This approach ignores the structure of command in almost all Canadian workplaces, and it is devoid of any sociological analysis pertaining to the social relations in production. Little is said of management's authority to discipline and fire workers, and their surveillance system to ensure their expected standards. In light of the unequal power relations in industry, government regulators and administrators talk about a "balance" policy administered with equanimity. This internal responsibility system reflects this voluntary compliance model that has come to be acclaimed as the main achievement in the Canadian approach to occupational health and safety. This approach has at least given workers "weak" rights pertaining to any effective participation in work environment matters (Sass, 1988).

There are, of course, contrary examples. For instance, the director of the Workers' Compensation Board (WEB) and Occupational Health and Safety Department in the Province of British Columbia during the early 1970s demonstrated a more aggressive administration of occupational health and safety enforcement. The director, Terrence Ison, effectively used the penalty section against the recalcitrant employers under the B.C. Workers' Compensation Act. The Province of British Columbia is the only jurisdiction in which the inspectorate are directly under the authority of the Workers' Compensation Board. I am of the opinion that the British Columbia WCB has the best enforcement record of any health and safety jurisdiction in Canada today. In part, this is because they do not have to rely on the ineffective, time consuming, and costly prosecution enforcement mechanism that exists in the other jurisdictions. Instead, regulators in British Columbia are able to use the penalty assessment system, and in 1988 the board penalized 517 employers for violating health and safety regulations for a total penalty assessment of $2,086,750. This is just short of the entire occupational health and safety budget in the Province of Saskatchewan. The population in Saskatchewan is under one million people, with a nonagricultural work force of about 250,000. The B.C. population is about three million, with registered employers of approximately 98,523, compared to about 35,000 in Saskatchewan.

The minimal penalty in British Columbia in 1988 was $1,500 and the maximum levy so far has been $122,000 for a tunneling violation, primarily for excessive levels of silica dust (Walker, 1990). While these figures are impressive in comparison to other jurisdictions, they are by no means embraced as a "beacon" by representatives of the British Columbia labor movement. While there seems to be some advantage in joining the regulatory agency with the compensation board, this pre-1970 approach is generally opposed by provincial federations of labor outside British Columbia.

While the British Columbia record does stand out, there is, nonetheless a general dissatisfaction by labor pertaining to the enforcement record of governments in all Canadian jurisdictions. In this regard, Glasbeek has been an outspoken critic of the voluntary compliance model and the fact that there has been no successful criminal prosecution of any employer even after multiple fatalities (Glasbeek and Rowland, 1979).

Students of occupational health and safety agree that present public policy instruments need to be strengthened. For instance, empirical studies do suggest that an inspectorate enforcing standards and regulations have an appreciable effect on the incidence of workplace accidents. Braithwaite (1985) noted that fatalities in the workplace vary directly with the amount of resources expended on safety education and monitoring, and the number of inspectors used. Similar studies show positive correlations between a decrease in fatalities in mining and provisions for an inspectorate with enforcement rights (Lewis-Beck and Alford, 1980). Braithwaite has reviewed studies indicating correlations between budget allocation, inspectors, enforcement, and accident rates (as opposed to fatality rates). There seems to be little doubt that the more serious injuries and fatalities can be reduced by increased government inspections. At the same time, Braithwaite cautions against drawing the conclusion that there is also a correlation between reduced fatality and accident rates and the imposition of punishment. Glasbeek, on the other hand, attributes the absence of this correlation to the failure of regulators to prosecute employers under the Canadian Criminal Code.

PRACTICAL SHORT-TERM POLICY REFORMS

Criminalization of Violations

The criminalization of occupational health and safety violations has truly been rejected in all Canadian jurisdictions as a policy instrument because it is contrary to the voluntary compliance model. Needless to say, employers would resist this regulatory power more vigorously than the strengthening of other policy instruments. On the other hand, flagrant violations represent corporate crimes against workers' health and safety. And these socially injurious acts arise from the management or ownership of capital or from those occupying positions of trust in institutions that are to facilitate capital accumulation. The present extent of harm and violence created by corporate decisions about investment and construction are not criminalized because they reflect the very interests of owners in our political economy. Yet, a worker is much more likely to die from conditions at work than from an assailant in a common homicide crime (Reasons et al., 1981).

It has become evident that existing policy is not yielding very positive results from the worker's point of view and there is a need for more aggressive government intervention because of the inequality of workers and owners/managers. This is why we regulate health and safety in the first place. Intervention has been necessitated because the terms and conditions reached by untrammelled private ordering cannot be seen as voluntary in any way. There are at least four basic reasons for advocating the utility of using criminal prosecutions in work environment matters.

First, it would give needed recognition to the fact that intentional and reckless deviations from workplace health and safety standards are criminal acts and will serve to remind policy makers and implementers of their policies that society's acceptance of harm-causing conduct is an antisocial act. It would give a clear signal to employers that society values the life and limbs of workers as much as they do the life and limbs of ordinary citizens.

Second, repeated departures from existing standards would be seen as criminal conduct. Consequently, an inspector's order would be seen in a new, compelling light; immediate compliance might become the norm rather than the exception. This is all the more important when we consider the fact that we do not have enough inspectors to ensure compliance with existing standards and regulations. For instance, in the Province of Saskatchewan we have over 30,000 employers with roughly seventeen inspectors. While proportions are higher in other jurisdictions, they are not appreciably greater.

Third, mere assertions by employers of "too costly" will not do, any more than assertions of poverty do not aid the mugger. Better proof that a higher standard cannot be afforded than is at present offered might be required (Glasbeek, 1989).

Finally, criminal prosecution would lead to sufficient pressure on investors for a change in the existing order. And the door will be opened to give workers a better "right to know, participate, and refuse" requirement than presently exists. I believe it will encourage their greater participation and decision-making rights (Glasbeek, 1989).

Glasbeek and Rowland (1979) elaborate the legal issues involved in readjusting our enforcement and prosecution policy in this direction in their article entitled "Are Injuring and Killing at Work Crimes?"

Work Environment Boards

The second practical short-run policy proposal is the statutory transformation of joint occupational health and safety committees that presently exist in all Canadian jurisdictions into work environment boards (WEBs) with public funds to allow worker members on these committees to research their own concerns and visit other plants in their industry to learn firsthand how improvements can be made in their own firms.[2] An experiment along these lines was established in one of the major provincial crown corporations in Saskatchewan—Potash Corporation of Saskatchewan (PCS). The WEB was composed of a parity of representatives of the three certified trade unions, the director of mining, and managers from each of the four mines at PCS. The WEB also negotiated a Work Environment Fund to assist financially with all work environment matters, including psycho-social considerations (Potash Corporation of Saskatchewan, 1981).

As a result of this experiment, there was an agreement between the Saskatchewan minister of labour and the chairperson of the Workers' Compensation Board to transform the existing Joint Health and Safety Committees into WEBs with the power to negotiate monies from the employers for a "Work Environment Fund" as well as to receive monies from the Workers' Compensation Board. This would allow the worker members of the committee to bring in their own experts and make visits to other plants to see varied and alternative technical solutions to the problems they identified.

This experiment was short-lived since the change of government in the Province of Saskatchewan in 1982 resulted in its demise. The new Conservative government rejected this experiment as one of its first political acts regarding revisions to existing labor legislation in that province. It was evident that this approach would "activate" health and safety committees at each of the mine sites. Also, it was seen as an initial experiment which, if successful, would be the basis of the next step in occupational health and safety policy in the province (Sass, 1989).

I am of the opinion that a policy along these lines would strengthen worker activation on joint health and safety committees, and promote a long-term public policy of strengthening worker rights in work environment matters, especially the addition of an appropriate amendment to the workers' compensation legislation in each jurisdiction allowing for a rebate or monies to work environment boards. (I do not wish to go further than this recommendation because I believe it would be in the best interest of workers and society to transform existing workers' compensation legislation into a universal sickness and accident plan along the lines that presently exist in New Zealand.[3])

It is desirable to give WEBs a group or communal right within the enterprise in the same sense that workers under their respective provincial *Trade Union Acts* have presently the right to engage in concerted activity for mutual aid or protection. In the manner that a worker's right to engage in concerted activity represents a communal value, then the same argument would apply to workers' participation on shop floor committees and work environment boards. After all, the most "effective" committees are those where a high degree of solidarity among the workers exists or where there is a sense of community among the workers in a particular plant or operation. In such workplaces, workers more effectively utilize the occupational health and safety legislation, especially their right to participate in joint committees, to know about hazardous substances associated with their work, and to refuse work they believe to be harmful to their well-being. These rights are conditional upon the degree of solidarity or community within the workplace.

This should, of course, come as no surprise since it is the central historical experience of workers and the labor movement for individuals to band together when they are too weak to protect themselves. This is still evident by the language that trade union members use when they address one another as "brother" and "sister," and the analogy is consistent with the solidaristic phrase used by labor that "an injury to one is an injury to all."

A necessary and sufficient basis for a transformative policy would strengthen worker community and solidarity on the shop floor through informal work organizations. And representation from these committees on work environment boards would enable input into board of directors' decision making, which shapes the work environment. This is one way in which workers can have some sense of being industrial citizens and have an opportunity or be free to choose the work environment so that it embodies their conception of "unacceptable risk" and/or appropriate level of "common decency." After all, if workers do not have "common decency" they do not have their health and safety. A group right would better ensure effective advocacy of the individual workers both at the shop floor level and at the board level, although work environment boards or any other structures should in no way deny the individual worker the right to refuse hazardous work. At the same time, Lynd has made a most persuasive argument that the individual right of free speech by way of refusal must also be seen as a communal right. He argues that:

> . . . rights do not come neatly divided into inherently individual and inherently communal rights. Most rights are sufficiently ambiguous that they can be pushed in different directions by political and intellectual struggles. Thus, the point may be less to identify and champion peculiarly communal rights than to fight for communal content in as many rights as possible. Even more important, "communal rights" are not the opposite of "individual rights." Communal rights, whether exercised by groups or individuals, are rights characteristic of a society in which the free development of each has become the condition of the free development of all. The opposite of a communal right is any right which presupposes that what is accessible to one person is therefore

unavailable to another. (Lynd, 1984, p. 1417)

A public policy that takes into consideration rank-and-file workers' experience will find ways to strengthen worker rights with regard to work environment matters; and to force us to focus on the kind of control workers can reasonably have over their work environments and the level of risk; and to introduce an analysis of the social relations in production as well as the modes of production as a factor in shaping the level of risks in our work environments.

PROMISES UNMET: THE NEED FOR A LONG-TERM POLICY STRATEGY

Workplace Design and the Social Relations of Production

To examine the shape and character of the workplace, we need only to start from the beginning—the initial design of the work space. Here it is most evident that the owners have undisturbed authority to shape the work environment and the levels of risk. For example, they make the decision as to how much of their capital to invest, for how long, and where they want to invest it. They determine what kinds of products they wish to manufacture, and for what markets. They also make decisions that bear directly upon the work environment; that is the kinds of sites, substances, processes, techniques, and machinery they are going to use in their productive activity. This will also affect the number of employees they would use and the kinds of skills these employees would be required to have. In making these decisions, the investors in the first instance determine the nature and level of risk to workers and, therefore, any thoughtful public policy must begin at "square-one." It is too simplistic and superficial to merely state that existing public policy instruments and standard setting is taken into consideration by industrial engineers and planners. Where one confronts industrial engineers and designers with this proposition, they can reasonably respond by stating that standards and regulations are always changing, as do governments who enforce them.

Further, it would be naive to think that efficiency and control are not the primary design considerations. Bowles and Gintis go further and state that there is a difference between hiring the work and hiring workers. In effect, employers rent "labor power," which is the worker's capacity or ability to do a job, and when the job is completed, the employer no longer has need of the worker. After all, the worker is treated the same as any resource or as part of any other commodity exchange. Thus, there is little incentive to invest in the skills and the development of the worker, since that will increase their bargaining power so that any potential efficiency advantage is lost. This, of course, also provides a rationale why it is prudent for employers to invest in machines and to keep jobs as menial as possible (Bowles and Gintis, 1986). This argument provides a rationale for the incentive for "de-skilling" of workers and why increased worker participation or democratization of the workplace has not been advanced as economists might predict, given the increase of efficiency and worker satisfaction that accompany it (Klare, 1981).

That managers do, in fact, hire work and not workers is by no means tangential to the study or consideration of an effective public policy pertaining to worker health and safety. At this point, I am merely suggesting that such a public policy requires an analysis of the actual social relations that exist in modern-day capitalist production. Of course, the same analysis would also be required of bureaucratic socialism.

Because the initial production design can be crucial in shaping the workplace and work space, public policy must regulate all stages of the productive process, and develop knowledge that is primary in informing producers how they shall conduct their businesses. In so doing, they must give greater attention to a preventative scheme, rather than a compensation system for those injured or made ill "in the course of employment."

Presently, we argue that if all policy instruments are properly adjusted, the interplay is supposed to bring about appropriate incentives to bear upon the investors and owners to ensure socially acceptable levels of risks; and these risks, more importantly, would be acceptable to the risk-takers. This hypothesis, I believe, is exaggerated. In fact, very little thought has been given to the practical problems associated with "properly" functioning policy instruments. I am now of the opinion that our present public policy instruments pertaining to workplace health and safety when "properly" functioning will not produce socially acceptable levels of injury or illness. More specifically, they will not be acceptable to the risk-takers. And by "properly" functioning instruments, I mean also an enforcement policy that ensures that employers meet existing present-day standards. While this, of course, is necessary, I do not believe it is sufficient. To meet the test of sufficiency, I would add the necessity of extending worker participation into the corporate board rooms for effective input on all work environment matters. The findings from both industrial psychology and sociology relevant to worker health and safety support this hypothesis.

While there are significant correlations between the labor process and industrial injury (Dwyer, 1983), existing regulations rarely deal with job design questions, nor the organization of work itself. Also, there are no regulations whatsoever pertaining to wage-payments systems—i.e., bonus pay, piece rate, or other incentive systems intended to speed up the worker. Yet we know there is a direct relation between such systems and industrial injury.

More importantly, the very structure of command pertaining to the social relations in production remains outside the purview of regulation and standards. At the same time, there is very little pertaining to psycho-social problems experienced by workers although the evidence is unassailable as to the increase of coronary heart disease. Regulators may counter this criticism by cynically pointing to their right to refuse dangerous work, but my own experience suggests that such refusals are infrequent because of the structure of command. Workers have consistently brought to my attention "that management can always get them if they want to." And if these refusals are seen as insubordination, workers are thereafter monitored by their foremen and supervisors, putting their very employment at risk. It is, of course, the reason why this legal right for workers in Canada has been underutilized.

When one examines the psychological findings pertaining to worker health, we again see a very important link to the "intrinsic" nature of work or work process. Studies suggest that:

- Individuals with psychologically demanding jobs that also limit autonomy and social interaction at work are less likely to take part in organized and goal-oriented activities outside work requiring planning and cooperation with others (Gardell, 1982);
- enriching job content and increasing autonomy at work has been associated with increased participation in voluntary associations, studies, and labor union activities (Karasek, 1976 and 1981); and
- job complexity has been found to increase intellectual flexibility, perceptions of self-control, and participation in intellectual leisure time activities, and to decrease resistance to change (Kohn and Schooler, 1983).

The conventional wisdom now suggests that both physical and psycho-social health is related to a high degree of worker involvement and control. And where workers have little autonomy and control, Karasek and others found that high-strain occupations (jobs that are highly demanding but afford workers little control) are associated with elevated prevalence of myocardial infarction even when blood pressure, smoking habits, and serum cholesterol are taken into account (Karasek, 1981). And workers who are without autonomy and control also resist change pertaining to lifestyle matters and their "wellness" (Green, 1982). Gardell and his Swedish associates have clearly demonstrated the adverse effects of worker underemployment (Gardell, 1982).

Worker Rights and Property Rights

There is sufficient evidence to justify a public policy responsibility in regulating more broadly those corporate decisions when it comes to work environment matters. Worker health and safety must be viewed as a serious public issue and not a private matter. The exclusion of worker participation at the governing level of companies results not only in alienation and worker distrust of management, but puts these managers outside the range of worker health and safety concerns.

The continuing maintenance of the public-private split and the respect of public policy makers for the privacy of the boardroom constitute a major illusion and barrier in effectively regulating worker health and safety. Unfortunately, the courts have legitimatized this public-private split and our elaborate structure of law maintains this distinction legitimatizing the priority of acquisitiveness and competitiveness in the private sphere over work environment issues. Thus, the activities of the boards of directors and the private ordering of the economy are, in effect, protected from public reach. Corporate boards where fundamental decisions are made pertaining to the character of the work environment and the levels of risk experienced by workers, are, to a large extent, an exclusionary zone where minimal social control exists regardless of the social consequences of its decisions.

Further, governments and the courts have rejected the argument that the work force of a firm had gained a recognizable property "right" in the enterprise because of the fundamental overriding right to their health and safety. Clearly, at the present time, all three major political parties in Canada would consider the proposal of a "form" of industrial democracy in work environment matters as beyond public reach. They would not want to publicly be seen as having to make a choice between two mutually exclusive rights—the rights associated with private property and those associated with worker health and safety.

Even in contract law it is not clear where self-interest ends and concern for another's security begins. The failure to legally ensure "strong" worker rights in regard to work environment matters at all levels of the enterprise reflects governments regulating in behalf of the owner's free exercise of self-interest based upon property rights. If confronted with this matter directly, they will side with employers, arguing the firm's good faith protection of their workers. And when this is not the case, our present public policy instruments will bring about the desired aims. To date, this assertion has been contradictory, and policy makers have been immobilized in making the primary, rather than secondary, moral choice. This contradiction underlies our present policy choice, which is antagonistic to worker interests. Thus, the core right of worker health and safety is collapsed into a contradiction by the state rendering incoherent the vocabulary of rights in the whole area of workplace health and safety.

The internal governments of economic enterprises are flatly undemocratic both *de jure* and *de facto*; and genuine political equality within economic enterprises has been rejected by representatives of Canadian industry as well as the public as a proper principle of authority within firms. Hence, the ownership and control of enterprises creates enormous inequalities among managers and workers in their capacities and opportunities for participation in governing these enterprises, including matters specific to the work environment and worker health and safety.

Employers will vociferously justify their prerogatives and rights by their claim that economic liberty is just as valid—and more so since it contributes to greater efficiency than some sort of industrial democracy or political equality. And that economic liberty includes a right to private property and their right to control or to delegate control over their firms as they see fit. Many corporate leaders and their spokespersons have argued that the corporate structure of modern capitalism rests ultimately upon an "inalienable" right.

This stance, I believe, conflicts with the workers' "inalienable" right to their health and safety in the workplace. The real politic today, although modified, favors the owner's ideology and defense. This is even more so under the existing neoconservative political agenda. Consequently, existing worker rights in all eleven Canadian jurisdictions are at best "weak rights" with little possibility of any change toward the direction of "strong" rights in the short, medium, or even long run.

The union's argument that health and safety rights are to override or "trump" economic considerations or property rights has, for the most part, been an effete attempt to introduce a mild form of industrial democracy. Their participation is confined to the shop–floor level after management introduces the level of risk in the first instance. Clearly, no one would rationally argue that workers in joint occupational health and safety committees have by law the right to effective participation as opposed to consultation. This "formal" requirement should not be confused with "real" bargaining power or equality.

It could be argued, however, that even from a purely utilitarian perspective, the consequences of private property specifically in terms of workplace health and safety is harmful, and public policy should regulate property so as to void these consequences. Any exercise of power that has significant social consequences should be seen as public. Thus, the democratic process could properly claim the authority to regulate property to the extent of instituting "strong" worker rights pertaining to matters affecting the level of worker risk in the enterprise.

It is my contention that a right to private ownership of corporate enterprises can properly be curtailed by the democratic process when justified by a superior fundamental moral right. And worker health and safety is justifiable grounds to regulate corporate activities to the extent of affording workers "strong" rights of effective participation in those activities affecting the level of risk in work spaces.

Robert Dahl raises the question as to whether those who provide capital must necessarily own and control the enterprise to which they supply capital. He concludes that in principle the task of supplying capital to enterprises can be separated from the rights of ownership and control (Dahl, 1985). In practice, capital supply through loans and bonds does not entail ownership and control of the enterprises that take on the debt. The argument for unilateral or unshared control on the grounds that investors sacrifice the use of their money is not justified (Dahl, 1985). This is especially so with regard to worker health and safety, since workers sacrifice more of their lives by working than investors sacrifice by investing.

Further, Dahl persuasively argues and cites numerous empirical studies demonstrating that a wider form of worker participation and democratization in the enterprise will have a positive effect on the creation, production, and distribution of end products. He states that:

> The best analysis of a broad range of experiences in a number of different countries appears to support these conclusions: participation by workers in decision making rarely leads to a decline of productivity; far more often it either has no effect or results in an increase in productivity (Dahl, 1985, p. 79).

It is not my intention to support a limited form of worker democratization on boards of directors regarding work environment matters on economic grounds. Rather, I do so as a matter of right! A fundamental moral right that "trumps" the economic values of efficiency and productivity. To reiterate and be perfectly clear, the argument that "strong" worker rights and effective participation on the enterprise level regarding work environment matters need not in the last analysis be justified entirely by its consequences. Acceptance of the proposition that workers have an "inalienable" right to their health and safety in the economic enterprises affirms their corresponding right to democratically participate in effecting the level of risk in their work spaces. I am not so foolish to use the term "inalienable" right as an absolute standard. This can never be the case in public policy matters. Rather, I do so in order to impress upon policy regulators the need to establish the right in such a fashion that if it is to be undermined, a very strong argument must be made. As I have already stated, public policy necessarily is utilitarian subject to trade-offs. Nonetheless, a policy can be directed by egalitarian principles based upon the inherent worth of the individual. In taking this line it is my purpose to weaken the present basis of public policy regarding workplace health and safety based upon the rational and moral argument that our economic order must be efficient in all instances.

DEMOCRATIZATION AND WORKPLACE HEALTH AND SAFETY

What arguments can justify limited worker democratization on governing boards as producing positive outcomes pertaining to the incidence of worker injury and disease? Clearly, there are few empirical studies in North America to defend this assertion. At best, the justification for democratization of the sort I am talking about is the *potential contribution* it might make to the value of worker health and safety. I am advocating this approach, nonetheless, because I believe it is reasonable to suppose that worker members on governing boards would optimize occupational health and safety matters in decision making. Although it is flatly impossible to predict what they would choose, the *probability* of their minimizing potential harms and risks strengthens the defense of democratization or effective participation as a strategy of reform. I assume that workers would vote to allocate more funds to healthful conditions and be less short-sighted than privately owned hierarchically run firms that seek to maximize total profit for shareholders. If nothing more, worker participation in enterprise decision making would counter or moderate managerial authority and introduce greater understanding of their own work force (Dahl, 1985).

CONCLUSION

I have some sympathy with the conservative instinct that shrinks from giving up any of its established management prerogatives or rights even with regard to worker health and safety. But the present neoconservative defense of individual liberty and property rights represents not only a mutilation of twentieth-century mainstream liberal thought and social conscience, but senility. Its individualistic theology reflects nineteenth century "gospel of wealth," and its reverence for economic libertarianism is a kind of ancestral worship of Carnegie, Astor, and Rockefeller as well as a starving of the intellect.

Every forward step in public policy during the twentieth century regarding working conditions has been marked by a closer union of economics and ethics. Reagan, Thatcher, and Mulroney together with the majority of provincial premiers in Canada have instead reverted to an unrestrained corporate economic agenda and its economic "trickle down" theory as the greatest social good. For over a decade we have witnessed their ceremonial actions and orthodox beliefs that have widened the gap between rich and poor, and further degraded the worst off in society. They have been indifferent to the large ethical problems of social life.

It is, therefore, more urgent that we revitalize a reformatory force inside our public policy domains with a renewed focus on the ethical problems of social life. They cannot be left to voluntarism or the untrammeled market. Nor can they obviously be left to our present-day corporate leaders. After all, how many have promoted the advance of democracy in their own industrial kingdom when autocracy seemed safer and more efficient?

ACKNOWLEDGEMENT

I wish to acknowledge my enormous debt to Professor Harry Glasbeek of Osgoode Hall Law School, York University, Toronto, Ontario, for his assistance and insightful observations regarding occupational health and safety in Canada. He has been the singularly most outspoken person for criminalizing violations of occupational health and safety in Canada.

ENDNOTES

[1] Outspoken worker health and safety activists are Colin Lambert, director of Occupational Health and Safety for the Canadian Union of Public Employees; Linda Jolly, director of Workplace Health and Safety for the Ontario Federation of Labour; Dave Bennett, director of of Health and Safety for the Canadian Labour Congress; and Cathy Walker, head of Health and Safety for the Canadian Association of Industrial, Mechanical and Allied Workers' Union.

[2] I have elaborated on this scheme in a forthcoming publication on *The Blakeney Years* edited by Dr. James Harding, University of Saskatchewan, Saskatoon, Saskatchewan, Canada.

[3] Terrence Ison, Osgoode Hall Law School, Toronto, has been a major proponent of such a scheme. His writings in this area are most persuasive and illuminating.

REFERENCES

Bowles, S., and H. Gintis. *Democracy and Capitalism*. New York: Basic Books, 1986.

Braithwaite, J. *To Punish or Persuade*. Albany: SUNY, 1985.

Brody, B., P. Rohan, and L. Rompre. "Les Accidents Industrielles au Canada: Les Portrait d'une Décienne." *Relations Industrielles*. 40(3):545–66, 1986.

Dahl, Robert A. *A Preface to Economic Democracy*. Berkeley: University of California Press, 1985.

Dwyer, Tom. "A New Concept of the Production of Industrial Accident: A Sociological Approach." *New Zealand Journal of Industrial Relations*. 8(2):247–60, 1983.

Gardell, B. "Scandinavian Research on Stress in Working Life." *International Journal of Health Services*. 12:31–41, 1982.

Glasbeek, H. *The Meredith Lecture*. Unpublished, delivered at Osgoode Hall Law School, York University, 1989.

Glasbeek, H., and S. Rowland. "Are Injuring and Killing at Work Crimes?" *Osgoode Hall Law Journal*. 17:507–94, 1979.

Green, K.L. "Issues on Control and Responsibility in Workers' Health." *Health Education Quarterly*. 15(4):473–86, Winter, 1988.

Karasek, R.A. "Job Socialization and Job Strain: The Implications of Two Related Psychosocial Mechanisms for Job Design." In *Working Life. A Social Science Contribution to Work Reform*. Edited by B. Gardell and G. Johansson. London: Wiley, 1981.

Karasek, R.A. "The Impact of the Work Environment on Life Outside the Job." Doctoral dissertation, Massachusetts Institute of Technology, distributed by Institute for Social Research, University of Stockholm, 1976.

Klare, K. "Labor Law as Ideology: Toward a New Historiography of Collective Bargaining Law." *Industrial Relations Law Journal*. 450-481, 1981.

Kohn, M.L., and C. Schooler. *Work and Personality: An Inquiry into the Impact of Social Stratification*. Norwood, New Jersey: Ablex Publishing, 1983.

Lewis-Beck and Alford. "Can Government Regulate Safety? The Coal Mine Example." *American Political Science Review*. 74:745–756, 1980.

Lynd, S. "Communal Rights." *Texas Law Review*. 62:1417, 1984.

Potash Corporation of Saskatchewan. "Work Environment Board Agreement." Saskatoon, Saskatchewan, Canada, March 25, 1981.

Reasons, C., L. Ross, and C. Patterson. *Assault on the Worker: Occupational Health and Safety in Canada*. Toronto: Butterworths, 1981.

Sass, R. "Implications of Work Organization for Occupational Health and Safety: The Case of Canada." *International Journal of Health Services*. 19(1):163, 1988.

Swinton, K. "Enforcement of Occupational Health and Safety Legislation: The Role of the Internal Responsibility System." In *Studies in Labor Law*. Edited by K. Swan and K. Swinton. Toronto: Butterworths, 1983.

Walker, Cathy. (Canadian Association of Industrial, Mechanical and Allied Workers Union). Letter, March 1, 1990.

Occupational Health and Safety Twenty Years after OSHA

ROBIN BAKER

Program Director, Labor Occupational Health Program, University of California—Berkeley

This year, the U.S. Occupational Safety and Health Act (OSHA) is twenty years old. It is a time for many of us in the labor movement and the occupational health field to reflect on what we have achieved over the past two decades, and to consider where we need to go from here. In this paper I will share some of my own thoughts on our experiences in California, including our successes and our frustrations. I believe that California offers an interesting case study, since we once soared to the top, providing one of the best worker protection programs in the U.S. We have also plummeted to the depths, having lost our state OSHA program for a while, as one of the many casualties of the Reagan era. I hope that the California experience can offer some lessons on the political vulnerability of the occupational safety and health system in our country, and suggest what we need to do to create a more reliable system for protecting the lives and health of U.S. workers.

A BIT OF HISTORY: OSHA AS A POLITICAL ANIMAL

When the federal Occupational Safety and Health Act (OSHAct) was passed in 1970, it established a health and safety apparatus composed of three agencies: the Occupational Safety and Health Administration (OSHA), the National Institute for Occupational Safety and Health (NIOSH), and the Occupational Safety and Health Review Commission (OSHRC). OSHA was given responsibility for establishing and enforcing workplace health and safety standards, and for providing information and assistance to employers and employees. NIOSH was mandated to conduct research on workplace hazards, to make recommendations for new and improved standards, and to train more occupational health and safety professionals. The review commission was established to hear appeals when employers contest citations issued by OSHA.

The OSHAct gives each of the states the option of establishing its own OSHA program, as long as it is deemed to be as effective as the federal program. Once such a state plan is approved, federal OSHA funds 50 percent of the state program's operating costs. The labor movement was originally opposed to this provision allowing for state plans, based on the dismal record of many states in such areas as civil rights. There was a serious concern that in "right-to-work" states with a prevailing antiunion atmosphere, enforcement of OSHA standards by the state would be lukewarm at best.

The actual experience with state plans has been mixed. About half of the fifty states have opted to run their own OSHA programs. Some states have performed so poorly that federal OSHA has had to apply substantial pressure to bring them up to minimum federal standards, although no state plan has ever actually had its approval withdrawn. Yet there are advantages to state plans as well. First, they offer protection to significantly more workers. Public employees (other than federal) are required by law to be covered by any state OSHA program, while they are excluded from federal OSHA coverage. A second advantage is that some state OSHA programs go well beyond the federal program, providing substantially greater protection in terms of standards and enforcement.

California, which has more than 10 percent of the U.S. population, is an example of a state that developed an OSHA program that was in the forefront of worker protection. Cal/OSHA was established in 1973, and quickly outstripped federal OSHA in just about every area. A special report by the National Safe Workplace Institute (1988, p. 4) stated that, "under its state plan system, California clearly had the strongest safety program in the U.S."

Examples of California's superior performance include the following:

- Cal/OSHA developed more and better standards, especially in the area of toxic substances. Cal/OSHA issued exposure limits for 170 toxics not regulated by federal OSHA, and limits stricter than OSHA's for an additional 100 toxic substances, many of them cancer-causing substances and/or reproductive hazards.
- Cal/OSHA's "Right-to-Know" law covered millions of workers who would have been excluded under federal OSHA's original, more limited Hazard Communication standard. The original federal standard (which has since been expanded due to court challenges) afforded the right to know about toxic substances used on the job to workers in only a limited number of industrial settings.
- Cal/OSHA's Bureau of Investigations successfully pursued more than 200 criminal investigations in the state, while federal OSHA completed only fourteen cases nationwide in the same period.

Why did Cal/OSHA do so much better than its federal counterpart? The answer lies in the political power of the labor movement. If we look at the history of both federal OSHA and Cal/OSHA, it is clear that the success of such programs is closely linked to who is in office. Interestingly enough, both the federal and California OSHA acts were passed by Democratic legislatures, but signed by Republicans—former President Nixon and former Governor Reagan. Not surprisingly, both programs got off to a slow start under Republican administrations, with the business community vociferously denouncing them as an infringement on private property rights and as unnecessary government interference. It was not until a liberal Democratic governor with strong ties to labor, Jerry Brown, took office in California in 1975, that Cal/OSHA began to take the lead in standard setting and innovative programs.

In 1977, when Jimmy Carter became president of the U.S., federal OSHA also was invigorated. Numerous efforts to improve standards and enforcement were undertaken under the leadership of the new OSHA head, Eula Bingham. During this period, the New Directions program was started—a grants program that funded important worker education efforts by labor unions, universities, nonprofit groups, and employer associations around the country. This golden age for OSHA was short lived. The Democrats held the White House for only four years, before the 1980s ushered in the Reagan era.

Under the antiregulatory Reagan administration, federal OSHA changed course and began to backtrack. The standard-setting process, already quite slow, was hamstrung by interference from the Office of Management and Budget and its emphasis on cost-benefit analysis. Cooperative, voluntary compliance was emphasized over mandatory enforcement efforts. The number of willful violations cited by OSHA decreased by more than 50 percent from 1980 to 1987 (Woodman, 1990). The New Directions program was slashed, and there was even an effort to censor educational materials that had been produced under the previous administration. This period also saw an increasing emphasis on individual, rather than organizational, responsibility for safety and health, reflected for example in the new emphasis on drug testing and "wellness" programs in the workplace.

Meanwhile, California's program continued to progress under the Brown administration in the early 1980s. Cal/OSHA was run for a total of eight years under a Democratic leadership that was responsive to the labor movement, while federal OSHA had only four years under a supportive administration. This fact, more than anything else, probably accounts for the stronger program developed in California.

But the California program, too, underwent a steady decline after a Reagan-style governor, George Deukmejian, took office in California in 1983. For the first several years of this Republican administration, there was a slow erosion of labor input into Cal/OSHA standards and administration. Resisting several years of pressure to maintain California's standing as the premier health and safety program in the nation, Governor Deukmejian finally announced the unilateral elimination of the Cal/OSHA program. In February of 1987, the governor informed federal OSHA that California was withdrawing its state plan, alleging that federal OSHA was adequate to protect California workers and that Cal/OSHA was an unnecessarily duplicative program.

Ultimately the labor movement in California had the political clout to override the governor. An initiative was placed on the 1988 state ballot asking voters to restore the Cal/OSHA program. With the support of a far-reaching labor-environmentalist-community coalition, and with surprisingly little opposition from industry, the measure passed handily. Cal/OSHA was restored, but by this time it was badly crippled—it had lost most of its staff; it had fallen behind in the standard-setting process; and it was still being run by the very administration that had tried to eliminate it.

IS A DEMOCRATIC ADMINISTRATION ENOUGH? THE CASE OF THE "RIGHT TO KNOW"

Based on both the federal and the California experiences, it is clear that OSHA programs can only make progress during periods when labor has a significant political voice. Under conservative, antilabor administrations, their performance has been dismal. What is less clear is whether OSHA, as we know it, can live up to its promise, even under Democratic leadership. While experience has shown that OSHA does better under the Democrats, its record of effectiveness has been less than overwhelming even in the best of times. Is this because the Democrats have never held office long enough to get their programs fully up to speed? Or is our basic approach lacking in some way?

Many labor advocates have come to question the very premise of the OSHA system, which relies on government inspectors rather than workers to enforce workplace safety. Not only is OSHA overly dependent on political swings, but even in the best of times there are too few inspectors and average fines are far too low to provide a reasonable deterrent. Many OSHA standards are inadequate and there are also significant hazards that are not covered by standards at all. Cumulative trauma disorders resulting from ergonomic hazards is a large, growing category of occupational disease,[1] yet there are no OSHA standards regulating repetitive motion, posture, and lifting. These problems have led to a great deal of interest in exploring alternative approaches that would rely on more active worker participation.

The "right-to-know" movement of the late 1970s and early 1980s was an early effort to promote the involvement of an informed work force in the health and safety system. This labor-backed movement simply called for the right of workers to be informed about toxic substances they encounter on the job. This seemingly indisputable "right to know" was surprisingly difficult to obtain. Employers strongly objected to the notion of sharing "proprietary" information and raised concerns about "scaring" workers and promoting "toxic hysteria." What industry feared about the right to know was exactly what labor advocates hoped for: that knowledge would be power. That is, if workers knew about the hazards in their workplace, they would be able to demand proper protection; if workers were well-informed, they would be in a better position to demand an active role in determining health and safety practices.

The right-to-know movement was successful in many respects. The first right–to–know law to be passed was a local ordinance in Philadelphia in 1980 promoted by the local COSH[2] group. Since then, California and twenty-nine other states have passed right-to-know laws. More than eighty communities have passed local right-to-know ordinances, often as the result of lobbying by coalitions of labor and environmentalists seeking to secure the right of both the work force and the community to information about industrial chemicals.[3] Even federal OSHA finally was forced to issue a Hazard Communication standard under the Reagan administration. The administration tried to lessen the standard's impact by limiting coverage to workers in the manufacturing sector only. Reagan's OSHA also took the position that the federal standard preempted state right-to-know laws, many of which were significantly stronger.

Ultimately, the courts forced OSHA to abandon the coverage restrictions and to extend the Hazard Communication standard to all workplaces covered by OSHA. The courts also upheld the right of states with their own OSHA plans to retain more stringent right-to-know laws.

Despite the numerous successes, many of the original advocates of the right-to-know movement have been sorely disappointed by the overall impact of these laws and regulations. There are certainly some notable instances where unions have been successful in obtaining information about workplace toxic chemicals and have used the information to achieve substantial improvements, such as substitution of less toxic materials or improved ventilation. Yet there have been enormous problems. Perhaps even more than with most OSHA standards, there has been a significant gap between the standard and its enforcement—few U.S. employers are in full compliance with the standard, which requires that material safety data sheets (MSDSs) for chemicals be available in the workplace, that the information on the MSDS be complete and accurate, and that workers be trained on the contents of the MSDS. What many workers have found is that, even if MSDSs are available, they may or may not be accurate—there is very little quality control, and information, especially about chronic effects, is frequently missing. Even if MSDSs are adequate, they are virtually incomprehensible to most working people who lack any technical background. Training to make this information accessible to the workers is conspicuously lacking in most workplaces, and the training requirements of the Hazard Communication standard are general and vague.

Beyond these practical problems, however, there is an essential flaw with the right-to-know. In practice it has turned out that knowledge is not power. While knowledge is admittedly essential, it is certainly not sufficient. Knowing about toxics in the workplace is one thing, but doing something about them is quite another. Even armed with information about toxics what should a worker do? Speak out and risk being fired? File an OSHA complaint, hope that an inspector will come, hope that there is an adequate OSHA standard that addresses the problem, and then, at best, see the employer face a minor fine? While these problems are significant for unionized workers, they are overwhelming for the vast unorganized workforce.

FROM THE "RIGHT TO KNOW" TO THE "RIGHT TO ACT"

Experience with the right to know, and with OSHA in general, has led the U.S. labor movement and health and safety activists to the conclusion that it is time for a change. Even under Democratic leadership OSHA has not been as effective as it needs to be. The AFL-CIO is now calling for wide-ranging reform of the federal Occupational Safety and Health Act including:

- Coverage of more workers;
- improved standard setting;
- increased compliance incentives (such as larger fines and expansion of criminal liability); and
- the "right to act," placing greater control over health and safety conditions into the hands of workers.

In California, Worksafe (a coalition of labor, health professional, environmental, legal, and other community organizations that was instrumental in the effort to restore Cal/OSHA) has called for similar changes in the state's OSHA act. Its reform proposals emphasize worker empowerment through means such as:

- Mandated health and safety committees in each workplace, with full labor participation and well-defined duties and powers;
- health and safety training for all workers and special additional training for health and safety committee members;
- strengthening the right to refuse hazardous work; and

- full protection from discrimination for exercising health and safety rights.

In seeking ways to achieve greater worker participation in our health and safety system, there are many international models to draw on, including examples from Australia, Sweden, and Canada. Here in the United States, in the state of New Jersey, there is an active campaign for the right to act. As with the right-to-know movement and the California campaign to restore Cal/OSHA, coalition-building between labor and community environmentalists has been the key to an effective campaign in New Jersey. These efforts have led to the introduction of the Hazard Elimination through Local Participation (HELP) Act in the New Jersey legislature. The HELP Act calls for labor-management committees in each workplace that are mandated to inspect for hazards, plan worker training programs, and temporarily stop life-threatening operations. The proposal also allows community-based organizations to participate in plant inspections and in follow-up efforts to reduce pollution.

In California, a new standard will soon require employers to implement comprehensive Injury and Illness Prevention Plans. These plans must include, among other things: health and safety training for all employees; a system for communicating with workers about health and safety (in a language that they understand), and for encouraging workers to report hazards *without fear of reprisal*; periodic inspections of the workplace; and investigations of all injuries and illnesses. Health and safety committees are encouraged, but not mandated under this new standard.

THE NEED FOR A STRONG LABOR BASE: ORGANIZING FOR HEALTH AND SAFETY

While these proposed reforms are laudable, the difficult question we have to ask ourselves is, how likely are they to succeed? Without a strong labor base, passage of progressive reforms is unlikely. Successful implementation of such reforms in the workplace is even less likely. The right-to-know experience provides one example of the disappointing gap between health and safety policy and its implementation in the workplace during an antilabor era.

Another example can be found in the concept of workplace health and safety committees. Many "right-to-act" reform proposals rest on the notion of using committees to promote worker control over health and safety conditions on the job. Yet many union contracts and some state laws already require labor-management health and safety committees and, on the whole, labor's experience with these committees has been frustrating. Committees are frequently used as window dressing and are not permitted to be involved at a decision-making level. Frequently the weak advisory-only role of such committees, along with the absence of needed training for committee members, lead to the committees disbanding or falling into dormancy. While a good OSHA standard in this area might help address some of the past deficiencies of health and safety committees, it is unlikely that the committee approach will be any stronger than the labor movement that puts it into practice.

Ultimately, the success of health and safety reform rests on the ability of the labor movement to organize and to mobilize its members. The bad news is that with a decreasing rate of unionization, we are experiencing an erosion in the power of the labor movement. The good news is that health and safety reforms don't have to wait for greater unionization. Rather, they can play an active part in union organizing.

Some unionists have held that regulatory agencies like OSHA are counterproductive to organizing. If OSHA is there, why should the workers pay dues to the union for protection? But, in fact, using the OSHAct can be an excellent organizing tool. A health and safety campaign can be a successful way to identify potential union supporters, to show what the union can do to make OSHA work better, and even to increase the involvement of current members in the union's activities.

Health and safety campaigns, like all organizing campaigns, must take into account the changing nature of the work force:

- Most new jobs in the U.S. in recent years have been, and will continue to be, in the service sector. Thus we need to pay attention to the "new hazards" such as office technology, indoor air pollution, asbestos-contaminated buildings, infectious disease transmission, and stress on the job.
- The proportion of women in the U.S. work force continues to rise, so many of our efforts must be targeted toward predominantly female occupations and workplaces.
- The number of ethnic minorities and immigrants in the work force is also dramatically rising— predictions suggest that between half a million and a million new immigrants will enter the U.S. work force each year. We have to develop the ability to address the health and safety concerns of non-English-speaking workers, and involve a multicultural team in this effort.
- Finally, this is a time of tremendous technological change. Rapid changes in the design and organization of work provide excellent opportunities for labor to get in on the ground floor. Labor needs to participate in designing and implementing these massive technological changes that so dramatically affect health and safety and working life.

I would like to share two stories that illustrate how health and safety campaigns can be used to address the needs of a changing work force and to support union organizing. The first involves the Service Employees International Union (SEIU), which has been actively conducting a Computer Health and Safety Campaign in support of their organizing efforts in California. SEIU has been attempting to organize the "new work force"—predominantly female office workers, most of whom have been affected by the widespread introduction of computers into the workplace in recent years. Many video display terminal (VDT) operators throughout the country have been suffering from musculoskeletal problems, repetitive strain injuries, vision problems, and concerns about reproductive hazards.

SEIU has been conducting an innovative campaign aimed at identifying potential members and locating office sites to target for organizing. The union also hopes to make itself highly visible in the community as a force for worker protection. In one northern California county, the union's activities have included information campaigns using postcards, fliers, and a newsletter to get the word out about office hazards and particularly the hazards of working on VDTs. They organized a communitywide coalition of labor, women's groups, and politicians to work for a county VDT ordinance. The ordinance would require protection for VDT operators, including adjustable workstations and user training.[4] Organizers went to office parks throughout the county to collect signatures on a petition supporting the local ordinance, and used the opportunity to talk with hundreds of office workers. A union-sponsored vision screening clinic was offered for office workers. The union is now training "member organizers" on VDT health and safety issues. They will be prepared to talk with groups of workers at house meetings and conduct lunch-time workshops aimed at identifying the hazards of VDTs and at exploring how the union can help to create better working conditions for office workers.

The second story is about a tannery in northern California where the International Ladies' Garment Workers' Union (ILGWU) recently won a representation election after twenty-five years of union organizing efforts. The stakes were high for this predominantly non-English-speaking, immigrant work force. The winning campaign emphasized health and safety conditions in the tannery, where noise levels are high and toxic chemicals are used in the tanning, finishing, and dyeing of leather. Once the union won the election, they were stalled by management. The company contested the results and refused to negotiate. In order to maintain support for the union during this critical period, the ILGWU pursued a campaign to tackle the health and safety problems that had been identified during the organizing campaign.

The workers at the tannery formed a health and safety committee and began documenting hazards.

They used a variety of methods such as "risk-mapping," whereby workers drew a large-scale floor plan of the tannery and marked the hazards that could be found in each work area. Exercising their right to know, they collected material safety data sheets on the toxics used in the tannery, as well as the results of all noise and air monitoring that had been done in the plant. The union sponsored medical screening, bringing occupational medicine experts into the union hall. The committee used all of this information to draw up a list of health and safety demands, which they circulated to their coworkers, collecting signatures. The workers also gained support from the community when they uncovered environmental threats from the tannery's hazardous waste and disposal practices. After a year, the union was finally certified and negotiations began.

These organizing stories do not offer any panaceas. For example, SEIU's Computer Health and Safety Campaign is a long-term strategy that may not result in any specific successful unionization campaign in the near future. At the tannery, where the health and safety organizing effort did result in a victory for the union, the company is threatening to close down, citing increased environmental regulation as a major reason. In the meantime, they have already started shifting operations to Hungary, a new hot spot for off-shore production. The union is now involved in a vigorous fight against the plant closure.

Yet, despite the slow and difficult pace, it is only through efforts such as these that we will successfully promote the health and safety of working people. Recent history has made it clear that legislative and regulatory protection can only be as strong as the labor movement that backs them.

ENDNOTES

[1] The Bureau of Labor Statistics recently reported that work-related injuries of the arm and hand, due to repetitive motions, accounted for over half of all work-related injuries and that these disorders have been increasing at an annual rate of 20 percent.

[2] COSH groups are Committees on Occupational Safety and Health, local coalitions of labor, and occupational health professionals who advocate for improved worker protection.

[3] The national Superfund Amendments and Reauthorization Act (SARA) of 1988 also contains a community right-to-know provision (Title III).

[4] An ordinance similar to this was recently adopted in San Francisco as a result of an extensive, coordinated multiunion campaign. The San Francisco ordinance is the only currently standing regulation in the U.S. for the protection of VDT operators.

REFERENCES

National Safe Workplace Institute. *Safer Work: Job Safety and Health Challenges for the Next President and Congress.* Chicago,
Wooding, J. "Dire States: Health and Safety in the Reagan-Thatcher Era." *New Solutions.* 1(2):42, Summer, 1990.

Section 10

LABOR AND FOREST PRODUCTS: AN INDUSTRY IN TRANSITION

The wood-products industry provides the backbone for the manufacturing sectors of the Pacific Northwest United States and British Columbia. Based on the extraction and processing of natural resources, it has created high-wage jobs in the lumber/sawmill and pulp/paper industries. Many communities have been supported by these industries, but they have also suffered the uncertainties of cyclical and structural changes. "Boom and bust" is a very real experience in this region, often leaving behind communities and an environment stripped of their resources.

On both sides of the border this uncertainty for workers and their families nurtured a militant union tradition, common to "extraction"-based economies like mining and logging. While creating some of the strongest labor agreements in either country, the wood-products unions in northern California, Oregon, Washington, and British Columbia found themselves under siege in the 1980s as short- and long-term economic changes converged with environmental and international trade issues to create a serious challenge to their bargaining power.

The articles in this chapter examine the changes in the industry and how unions in both countries have reacted to them. They illustrate both the similarities and differences between the American and Canadian labor movements, and point to the long-term strategic choices that must be made by workers on both sides of the border if their living standards are to be maintained.

Marcus Widenor's paper deals with the breakup of pattern bargaining in the Pacific Northwest lumber and sawmill industry during the 1980s. Tracing the relationship between the unions and the industry from the late 1940s, he concludes that timber companies took advantage of the weakened power of unions to strike in the mid-1980s, and imposed historic concessions despite an improving economic situation. This weakened bargaining power was due to a multiplicity of factors, including cyclical and structural changes in the industry, inter- and intra-union conflict, and changes in timber supply and import/export policy.

Norm MacClellan is an official of the Canadian Paperworkers Union. His paper contrasts the success of his and other Canadian wood-products unions in maintaining industrywide contracts during the 1980s. He observes that in British Columbia there is a closer relationship between the different unions and their negotiated settlements in the two sectors of the industry—pulp/paper and lumber/sawmill. Centralized pattern agreements have remained the standard despite the recession of the 1980s. While MacClellan does not view American wood products workers as being less militant than their Canadian brothers and sisters, he emphasizes that pattern agreements create a stronger "culture" of solidarity to resist concessions. Canadian workers will need to maintain this solidarity if they are to resist the downward pressure on wages and benefits resulting from the recent Free Trade Agreement with the United States.

Denny Scott, a researcher for the United Brotherhood of Carpenters, whose Western Council of Industrial Workers represents many Pacific Northwest lumber and sawmill workers, looks to the future to suggest strategic alternatives for wood-products workers and their unions. Given the long-term structural changes in the industry, Scott sees the need for new approaches at the bargaining table. Like unions in other "smokestack" industries that contracted in the 1980s, the wood-products unions will need to place job security and worker retraining issues higher on their negotiating agenda. He offers practical strategies for recreating a nationwide bargaining pattern in the United States industry by increasing coordination between unions and between the different regions of the country where large, vertically integrated firms have moved their harvesting and production facilities. This regional diversification enabled employers to whipsaw the unions with different contract expiration dates during the late 1980s.

Finally, Scott's paper acknowledges the need for a national timber supply policy that will ensure future employment for American woodworkers. This issue involves the conflict over environmental protection of endangered species and old-growth forest, and will be a crucial issue for both environmentalists and workers in the next decade.

Pattern Bargaining in the Pacific Northwest Lumber and Sawmill Industry: 1980–1989

MARCUS WIDENOR

Senior Instructor, University of Oregon, Labor Education and Research Center

During the 1980s the structure of collective bargaining in many manufacturing industries collapsed and unions found themselves with dramatically reduced bargaining power. Concessions were made on a wide range of wage, benefit, and work control issues, and traditional forms of pattern bargaining fell apart in situations where employers were no longer willing to meet industry or area "standards."

This paper examines what happened to the bargaining pattern in the Pacific Northwest lumber and sawmill industry during the decade. It will concentrate on the "hardwood" side of the industry. However, some references will be made to pulp and paper labor relations, where large, vertically integrated firms have come to dominate the industry.

While pattern bargaining did not completely disappear in the lumber and sawmill industry, it was severely damaged. This was a result not only of cyclical labor market conditions due to the recession, but also of permanent structural changes in the industry that changed the playing field for collective bargaining. Finally, the unions' ability to maintain a bargaining pattern was seriously hampered by their own internal structural contradictions. Differences in structure and internal divisions made it difficult for the two dominant unions to coordinate bargaining strategies. These contradictions became so great that the International Woodworkers of America (IWA) ended up breaking into two national unions in early 1987.

CURRENT THEORIES OF PATTERN BARGAINING

The literature on the nature of union concessions and pattern bargaining during the 1980s has generally expressed two theories. One group has argued that the setbacks for unions represent a temporary readjustment in the bargaining process, from which new patterns will reemerge (Dunlop, 1982; Kassalow, 1982; Mitchell, 1982). One set of data for the early 1980s even indicates that patterns may not have broken up at all (Ready, 1990).

A second point of view on pattern bargaining contends that the 1980s marks a true sea change in collective bargaining. This group holds that structural changes in the domestic and international economy were so far reaching that they may have permanently destroyed labor unions' ability to take wages out of competition through the use of bargaining patterns (Freeman, 1981, 1982, 1985; Cappelli, 1982; Kochan, 1980).

Part of the problem in determining how the lumber and sawmill industry fits into these trends results from the large number of variables at work in determining bargaining power in the industry. In many industries it is possible to identify one or two particular variables that appear responsible for the shift in collective bargaining power that occurred in the 1980s. The list is familiar to us by now: for trucking/ airlines, the key issue was deregulation; for auto/steel, low-wage import competition; in construction, nonunion competition. Unfortunately, there are too many variables at work in the wood-products industry to identify one particular "smoking pistol" that accounts for the loss of union negotiating power. A review of the industry's changing circumstances during the decade reveals numerous factors.

BARGAINING POWER DETERMINANTS IN THE LUMBER AND SAWMILL INDUSTRY

During the 1980s, while the employers maintained their "ability to pay" union wage and benefit demands, the unions had lost their ability "to make the employer pay." While the industry suffered losses during a brief period in the early 1980s, its profitability increased significantly by 1986, the year that the bargaining pattern began to crumble and large concessions were made by the unions. In this way the employers pursued a "me too" approach to bargaining, demanding concessions in part because this was the national trend, whether or not they were needed for the health of the industry. This was a common tactic by employers during the decade in numerous industries (Mitchell, 1985, 1986; Kochan, McKersie, and Cappelli, 1984).

Six major variables affected the bargaining power of the unions:

1. *Housing Starts.* This is the primary index for demand of dimensional lumber. During the early 1980s housing starts collapsed, from a record high of 2.2 million in 1976 to a low of 1.06 million in 1982 (*Crow's Weekly*, 1986b, p. 2). High interest rates and the recession created a significant decline in demand for wood products, leaving the unions with less bargaining leverage.

2. *Rising Raw Material Costs.* While demand for lumber and plywood was stagnant during the early 1980s, raw material costs continued to rise. Much of this was due to the fact that during the late 1970s, many manufacturers had bid up the price of futures on timber harvest. Stumpage prices were grossly inflated, and when timber contracts came due in the 1980s, costs were well above prices in the wholesale and retail lumber markets. This led the unions to reluctantly support legislation that would relieve manufacturers from their overpriced contracts (Scott, 1982). This issue predated the timber supply and cost issues raised by the proposed protection of the northern spotted owl in the latter part of the 1980s.

3. *The Import/Export Double Bind.* While many unions in the postwar era lost bargaining power due to import competition (garment, auto, steel), the wood-products unions were unique in experiencing pressure on their bargaining power on both the import and the export side. With weakened domestic demand during the early 1980s, employers increased their export of raw, unfinished logs to Asia where they were manufactured to Japanese lumber specifications or chipped for pulp and paper. Bypassing the milling process in the Pacific Northwest cost many workers their jobs (Wyant, 1985).

While raw logs were being shipped to Asia, the high value of the American dollar in the international trade market made imports of Canadian finished lumber increasingly attractive to retailers and consumers. Between 1975 and 1985, Canadian lumber increased from 19 percent to 33 percent of the U.S. domestic market (Wyant, 1985). Most tragically, this situation helped divide the International Woodworkers of America (IWA), which represented workers in the Pacific Northwest of the United States and in British Columbia, Canada. The loss of jobs in the U.S. was seen by some as caused by their own union brothers' and sisters' gains in Canada. While market forces made it difficult to maintain wage and benefits standards at the bargaining table, the contradictions within the international union served to weaken solidarity.

4. *Technological Change.* Technological change had been reducing employment in the wood-products industry since the 1950s (Levinson, 1966). The pace accelerated during the 1970s and 80s, which further reduced union bargaining power. First, new computerization and automation of labor intensive jobs such as sorting and grading reduced the number of jobs in dimensional wood products production (studs and lumber). Secondly, changes in production technology, such as the introduction of new resins in the

plywood industry and the development of waferboard and oriented strandboard, reduced employment and expanded the industry into new areas of the country. The existence of "product substitutes" like these creates a potential challenge to union bargaining power (Gagala, 1985). In addition, southern timber, once regarded as unsuitable for manufacturing many products, was now adequate for production. Between the mid-1970s and 1980s plywood production doubled in the south while dropping one billion square feet on the West Coast (Wyant, 1985). The movement resulted in a loss of unionized jobs to the largely unorganized southern states and created a wage differential that would be a constant threat to bargaining power in the Pacific Northwest.

The higher productivity resulting from technological change would also contribute to the overcapacity experienced by the industry in the 1980s (Smythe, 1986). The Weyerhaeuser Corporation (WEYCO) used this as a rationale for its contract concession demands during the 1986 round of negotiations (Weyerhaeuser Memo, 1986; IWA Archives, 1985a).

5. *Nonunion Wage Competition.* While the lumber and sawmill industry was one of the most heavily unionized in the country after World War II, union density had eroded considerably by the early 1980s. As new ways were found to utilize the Southern Pine, there was less need to rely on Pacific Northwest Douglas Fir. Many manufacturers shifted production to the south where unions were weaker. Despite a long-time presence in the southern states by the International Woodworkers of America and the Southern Council of Industrial Workers, wages lagged far behind the Pacific Northwest pattern. In 1986 a wage differential of $2.89 per hour existed between woodworkers in the two regions (BNA, 1986).

Furthermore, even in the Pacific Northwest some employers were encouraged to operate nonunion during the 1980s. While it may not have been the determining factor, the Louisiana Pacific Corporation's (LP) breaking of its unions in a lengthy strike in the mid-1980s encouraged other employers to resist making pattern settlements with the unions.

6. *Institutional Union Strengths and Constraints.* A final variable that affected union bargaining power during the 1980s was the different structures of the two dominant unions, the International Woodworkers of America and the Western Council of Industrial Workers (WCIW). As Hoxie has noted, unions seek to change their structure in order to meet changes occurring in the industry and the employers' structure (Hoxie, 1917). As political institutions, though, unions may be influenced by internal conditions that pull in various directions. Bargaining strategies may be based purely on the maximization of economic benefits for the membership (Dunlop, 1944) or other internal or external political concerns (Ross, 1956). The two unions had different histories (based on their old CIO/AFL rivalries) and internal structures that sometimes made it difficult for them to maintain a united front during bargaining. This would be a crucial factor when they attempted to coordinate one pattern agreement with a group of employers.

For all of the above reasons, an analysis of "ability to pay" and "ability to make the employer pay" shows that, while plagued by a multiplicity of structural and cyclical problems in the market, the vast majority of companies had recovered enough to meet union wage and benefit demands in 1986. At the same time, however, cyclical changes in the Pacific-Northwest economy radically decreased the unions' ability to make the employer pay by using economic sanctions in the form of the strike. This was further frustrated by the internal differences of the two unions.

THE SOURCES OF UNION BARGAINING POWER: THE WOOD-PRODUCTS PATTERN, 1948–1979

While the system of pattern bargaining in the auto and steel industries has probably been most studied (Levinson, 1960; Seltzer, 1951), it was the Pacific Northwest wood-products industry that negotiated the first strong settlements after World War II. Patterns in the industry have always been regional rather than national or companywide in scope. Despite the national markets of the larger manufacturers, the variable prices and types of raw materials in each part of the country have helped determine ability to pay in each region (MacDonald, 1956).

A second overall characteristic of wood products bargaining has been the historic division between the hardwood (lumber/plywood) and the softwood (pulp/paper) sides of the industry. Despite the growing vertical integration of the larger firms during the 1960s–80s, there was not a close relationship between bargaining patterns or unions in the two sectors of the industry. This is quite different from the situation in British Columbia, where lumber/sawmill and pulp/paper bargaining patterns are closely related (Frost, 1990).

The strong rivalry between the IWA-CIO and the Lumber and Sawmill Workers-AFL, the predecessor to the Western Council of Industrial Workers, led not to pattern bargaining, but to years of "leapfrogging" of employers using whipsaw tactics. With 80 percent of the Pacific Northwest industry organized, this tactic worked quite well in the immediate postwar era (Levinson, 1966). However, it became increasingly ineffective by the late 1950s when technological change had cut jobs and the dimensional lumber markets were less profitable. In the early 1960s the IWA and the Lumber and Sawmill Workers (LSW) buried their old rivalries and began to coordinate bargaining in the hopes of establishing a uniform pattern in the Pacific Northwest (Dana, 1965).

Throughout the 1960s the two unions introduced joint bargaining proposals to an increasingly larger major employer association, the Northwest Forest Products Employers Association. After settling with the larger employers, they took the agreement as a "pattern" to be used in settling contracts with a second and third tier of smaller manufacturers. The pattern reached its height in 1980 when the two unions negotiated jointly with an employer "Big 10" group, nominally headed by Weyerhaeuser, the most powerful company in the industry.

THE DECLINING PATTERN: 1980–1989

Following the strongest period in the industry's history, the 1980 Pacific Northwest negotiations set wages and benefits for 65,000 workers at ten companies. The three-year contract called for wage increases of $.80, $.75, and $.70 per hour, increases in contributions to the health and welfare and pension funds, and improvements in holiday pay (the *Woodworker*, 1980). The contract represented the highest and most uniform set of wage, benefit, and working condition standards in any part of the U.S. or Canada, including the more highly organized workers in British Columbia (IWA Survey, 1981).

Despite the huge success of the 1980 negotiations in extending a uniform pattern settlement throughout the industry, there were already cracks beginning to show in the bargaining structure. Two members of the employer association, Louisiana-Pacific and Simpson Lumber, had urged the association to resist union wage demands (Bledsoe, 1990). Their position did not prevail within the association, but it did prompt them and some other companies to leave the bargaining group prior to the 1983 round of negotiations.

At the same time as these rumblings of disunity among the employers, the nation and region were entering the worst economic recession since the 1930s. Housing starts plummeted, mills laid off workers, and the Western Council of Industrial Workers lost fully 50 percent of its membership (Draper, 1990). The loss of dues-paying members was so serious for the IWA that its international union office laid off staff in the spring of 1981. It was further troubled by the growing crisis within the union over Canadian lumber exports to the United States. The high value of the U.S. dollar brought an influx of Canadian lumber, and with it demands by American woodworkers for a tariff on Canadian imports. This was an issue guaranteed to split a binational international union, and IWA president Keith Johnson (a Canadian) sought to walk a middle path by calling for lower interest rates, a new stumpage policy in the U.S., and a national housing policy (Scott, 1982).

1983 Negotiations

By the opening of the 1983 round of negotiations the employers' association had shrunk to six large employers. Some left because they were getting out of the hardwood side of the industry for more profitable pulp and paper production, while others, like Louisiana Pacific, had decided to take on the unions individually.

The unions managed to settle a three-year agreement with the Big Six that called for a back-loaded wage package of 0 percent, 4 percent, and 4.5 percent over the term of the contract. Management dropped its demands for a two-tier wage structure, and it looked as though the unions may have bought enough time to look for an overall economic recovery (the *Woodworker*, 1983a). However, Louisiana Pacific (LP) insisted on 8 to 10 percent wage rollbacks and refused to drop its two-tier wage proposal. In June 1983, nearly 1,500 members of the WCIW and the IWA struck LP's fifteen mills on the West Coast. WCIW bargaining spokesperson Jim Bledsoe described LP's position as " . . . a classic operation to bust the union" (the *Oregonian*, 1983, p. D-9).

Whatever LP president Harry Merlo's motives were in taking on the unions, it was clear that he was in a strong position to do so. LP's debt structure was lower than most of the other large employers because they had not been involved in the inflationary bidding on timber futures during the late 1970s. Furthermore, Merlo was considered an aggressive maverick within the industry, willing to take on the unions (*Business Week*, 1986, p. 63). At least two smaller employers in the second tier of the bargaining structure also refused to agree to the Big Six pattern and took positions similar to LP's. The IWA struck two Oregon companies, Willamina Lumber and the Timber Forest Products Co., in the summer of 1983. A year later there were still no agreements at the three companies, and the WCIW and IWA locals were decertified at all fifteen LP facilities (the *Oregonian*, 1984).

1985–1986: Defending the Pattern

The recession within the wood-products industry deepened during 1984 and 1985, with both Weyerhaeuser and Champion closing many mills and laying off thousands of IWA and WCIW members (the *Woodworker*, 1985a and b). With demands by the employers to reopen the contracts and provide wage and benefit cuts of up to $3.00 per hour, the unions found their pattern settlement under siege (IWA Archives, 1985b).

Region III of the IWA held firm against wage rollbacks and argued that they were not the source of the industry's problems, as labor represented only 15 to 20 percent of production costs (the *Woodworker*, 1985a). Just the same, there were rumblings from local unions in small communities that had been suffering devastating layoffs. In some cases the locals refused to consider Weyerhaeuser's concession demands and whole facilities were shut down (e.g., Klamath Falls). In others, like Enumclaw, Washington, workers agreed to new flexible scheduling and "crew concepts" in lieu of wage cuts. However, in a third group, Local 3-130 in Raymond, Washington, and 3-261 in North Bend, Oregon, the workers were forced to agree to mid-contract wage rollbacks of $3.88 per hour during the summer of 1985 in order to keep their mills open (IWA Archives, n.d.). The first breach of the pattern was felt within the Weyerhaeuser Corporation agreement.

In order to head off an avalanche of takeaway demands, the leadership of the WCIW and the IWA sought to defend the pattern by proposing an extension of the 1983 agreement, foregoing the last year's 4.5 percent wage increase. Three floating holidays would also be eliminated and a temporary two-tier wage structure would be implemented. The key to the whole "accommodation package," as it was sometimes referred to, was a provision that all concessions would be fully restored in 1987, at the end of the extension (the *Woodworker*, 1985a). As politically difficult as it was for the union leadership to endorse wage rollbacks, it seemed preferable to the domino effect that might occur if the pattern continued to erode mill by mill, company by company. It was an attempt at an orderly retreat. Unfortunately, the extension proposal ran aground due to the different internal structures of the IWA and WCIW. More importantly, though, it failed because the companies saw they could extract more by waiting until 1986.

The WCIW sought to get an agreement from the employers before taking the package to its membership. All of the large companies except Simpson and Roseburg Lumber turned down the extension. Many of the second-tier employers agreed to the terms, and the WCIW voted local by local to accept the extension, with 40 percent of its membership ultimately coming under the agreement.

The IWA, on the other hand, voted all locals at once on the extension proposal, and it went down by a 70 percent vote (the *Woodworker*, 1985b). This left the union in a situation where the companies, especially Weyerhaeuser, could approach individual locals and attempt to gain concessions from them on a plant level, as they had at North Bend and Enumclaw. This climate laid the groundwork for Weyerhaeuser's attempt to expand enterprise, or plant level bargaining at the 1986 round of negotiations. The constitution of IWA Region III provided for periodic delegation of bargaining authority from the locals to the Regional Council. This was different from the structure of the WCIW, where bargaining authority was permanently vested in the council's office. In IWA locals that had suffered deep layoffs, there was much membership and community pressure to break away from the region's pattern settlement and make their own local concessions to keep facilities open. This decentralization of bargaining was not possible under the WCIW's structure. The difference became a structural impediment to the two unions making a strategic retreat in a uniform fashion.

The pattern was in serious peril, and the two unions' inability to approach the extension package in a unified manner was one cause. However, it is important to point out that the initial rejection of the proposal was by the companies, not the rank-and-file membership. In the summer of 1985, the WCIW accurately predicted that the fall would bring a huge new round of plant closings, aimed at softening the membership for even larger takeaway demands in 1986 (the *Union Register*, 1985). Weyerhaeuser ended up closing mills in Cottage Grove, Springfield, and North Bend, Oregon, where wage and benefit cuts of $3.87 to $4.62 per hour were demanded (the *Woodworker*, 1985c).

1986 Negotiation—The End of the Pattern

In early 1986 the large employer association dissolved and the unions were forced to take their proposals to each employer in turn. The most powerful company in the industry, Weyerhaeuser, took its proposal for wage and benefit rollbacks on the road in a public relations campaign that visited every town with a WEYCO mill in the Pacific Northwest United States. Central to the campaign was their argument that permanent wage relief was necessary due to the structural, rather than cyclical, changes that had buffeted the industry (Weyerhaeuser Memo, 1986). In presenting their demands to local union leadership the company insisted that it needed to realize a return on invested capital of 15 percent, something the union argued was an anomaly that had not occurred since the boom years of the late 1970s (IWA Archives, 1985a).

Despite Weyerhaeuser's claims, some industry analysts pointed out that the wood-products markets were actually improving in the spring of 1986. Housing starts were up and interest rates were down (*Crow's Weekly*, 1986a). While Weyerhaeuser's profits in 1985 had declined from $266 million to $200 million, the first half of 1986 showed a dramatic improvement (AWPPW, 1989). Production in the industry was up 12 percent from the first half of 1985, and WEYCO's profits rose 21 percent over the same period (the

Oregonian, 1986b).

Despite this seemingly clear improvement in the industry's ability to pay, prices for dimensional lumber remained stagnant (*Crow's Weekly*,1986b). This encouraged Weyerhaeuser to demand wage and benefit rollbacks of $4.30, or approximately 25 percent. Its offer also included an elaborate profit-sharing plan that would adjust wages based on plant productivity. This was a clear threat to pattern bargaining and the union's attempt to create a level playing field by taking wages out of competition. Despite some eleventh-hour concessions by the WCIW and IWA, including elimination of Sunday overtime, a reduction in holidays and health and welfare contributions, and substitution of grievance arbitration for the right to strike, Weyerhaeuser walked away from the bargaining table and the unions struck the company. Strikes followed at Willamette Industries and Champion, where takeaway demands included smaller hourly wage cuts ($1.25), but no profit-sharing mechanism to recoup losses. The Willamette and Champion offers also included a two-tier wage structure (the *Woodworker*, 1986).

With the strikes underway the dynamics of collective bargaining power shifted from the employers' ability to pay, to the unions' ability to make them sign agreements without concessions. Despite both unions' history of militancy they were in a very weak position here. Unemployment in Oregon stood at 9.4 percent when the union set up pickets (the *Oregonian*, 1986a). Weyerhaeuser indicated that if their final proposal was not accepted they would implement it on July 23. The possibility of WEYCO reopening with replacement workers for its union members was strong, and a repeat of the LP scenario was likely. While the WCIW was able to seek strike support assistance from its parent international union, the Carpenters, the international IWA was in disarray, and the Region III strike fund was severely depleted. The unions did not have the strength to sustain a long strike, and this forced them to settle with Weyerhaeuser and the rest of the struck employers in late June.

The final settlement with Weyerhaeuser included the company's commitment to reopen some closed mills in return for the package of wage and benefit cuts of $4.00 per hour and implementation of the profit-sharing plan. Industry analysts termed the settlement a "sea change" in labor relations for the industry (*Random Lengths*, 1986). While the settlements at the other companies included smaller across-the-board wage cuts, the uniform pattern of wage payments was now broken. WEYCO's plant-based profit-sharing system clearly broke the standard for the industry in the region. The pattern was further disrupted by the fact that many of the smaller employers had signed the 1985 extension agreement. Contracts in the industry now had different expiration dates, with the one group to be renegotiated in 1988 and another in 1989. It was now possible for either the union or the industry to use whipsaw tactics in the next round of negotiations, something that hadn't been effective since the late 1950s.

1988–89 Negotiations

Reestablishing a pattern would be a difficult job, and the WCIW and IWA started early on the task by initiating an extensive internal organizing campaign among the rank and file in late 1986 around the theme "Wait Till '88." No multiemployer bargaining took place in 1988 and the IWA and WCIW bargaining committees took their jointly developed bargaining proposal from company to company in the opening rounds of negotiations. The proposal called for full restoration of the 1986 cuts plus a 6 percent wage increase in a one year contract (the *Union Register*, 1988a). Without an employer association representing the companies as a group, it was necessary for the union to target an employer with whom they believed they could make a settlement that would serve as a pattern for the others. Weyerhaeuser was clearly too strong, and their profit-sharing system made comparison with the other contracts difficult. Ultimately, the unions settled first with the Bohemia Company. Bohemia was more vulnerable to a strike threat because they did not produce paper and were unable to shift production there to maintain sales. Furthermore, they had suffered a few bad years and could not afford to take a strike (Scott interview,

1990). Unfortunately, the other companies balked at signing contracts based on the "Bohemia pattern"— a four-year agreement with increases of five percent, four percent, four percent, and four percent plus restoration of holidays, health and welfare, and pension contributions (*The Union Register*, 1988b).

Rejection of the pattern by the other large companies pushed the unions to strike Willamette, DAW, Champion, and Boise Cascade, while negotiations at Weyerhaeuser continued. Two months into the strike, settlements were reached at all the struck companies, but with two different formulas, both of them less than the Bohemia pattern. Most agreements were for four years, like Bohemia, but contracts at Boise Cascade and Champion called for three-year agreements, further fragmenting the expiration dates for contracts in the industry (the *Union Register*, 1988b).

The confusion within the pattern continued into 1989, and strikes at the Roseburg Lumber company occurred when the company demanded wage relief to bring them back down to the patterns set in 1988. Having signed the extension package in 1985, with its full-wage restoration, Roseburg's wages remained ahead of the rest of the industry, where the 1986 cuts were not fully restored. A long WCIW strike resulted in a narrowly ratified agreement calling for wage cuts of sixty cents in the first year, with a restoration of eleven cents in 1992 (the *Union Register*, 1989).

Roseburg had effectively used the pattern against the union. Entering the 1990s, the industry was now composed of four different patterns:

1. Weyerhaeuser's agreement, with its plant-based, profit-sharing system;
2. Bohemia's wage leading agreement;
3. The Willamette pattern, followed by a large part of the industry; and
4. Champion and Boise Cascade's shorter agreement, expiring in 1991 instead of 1992.

CAN WAGES STILL BE TAKEN OUT OF COMPETITION IN THE PACIFIC NORTHWEST LUMBER AND SAWMILL INDUSTRY?

The shattered bargaining structure presents a formidable challenge to the unions. During the 1980s, the rate of industrial change outstripped the ability of the unions to keep pace. Much of the industry's contraction was due to structural changes over which the unions had little control. Nonetheless, there are some things the labor movement might consider as key problems that can be addressed in order to reassert union bargaining power:

1. *Restructure bargaining relationships with sister unions to deal with structural changes in the industry.* While the vertical integration of the "hardwood" and "softwood" sides of the industry has continued, cooperation between the IWA and WCIW and the two paper worker unions, the Association of Western Pulp and Paperworkers (AWPPW), and the United Paperworkers International Union (UPIU), has been inconsistent. The larger companies have used this to whipsaw the unions in the past, shifting production between the two markets. While the merger of all four organizations into "One Union in Wood" seems unlikely at present, more could be done to coordinate bargaining and share information. The relationship between the IWA-Canada and the two paper worker unions in British Columbia might give some useful examples here.

2. *Increased emphasis on inter-regional bargaining between the Pacific Northwest and the South.* The regional advantages that insulated the Douglas Fir market in the Pacific Northwest have been partially eclipsed by product technology changes and the shift of large companies into the southern states. Protection of the Pacific Northwest's bargaining power will entail eliminating, over time, the wage differentials between the two regions. It will also require coordinated contract expirations between the two regions in order to prevent the employers from whipsawing the two regions. The two unions clearly saw this problem when they attempted, in the 1986 round of bargaining, to negotiate common expiration dates

for Weyerhaeuser's mills in both regions. It may be that the unions will need to line up contract expiration dates company by company before attempting to reassemble a multiemployer pattern. Obviously, closing the wage gap will also entail efforts in organizing in the South as well as closer coordination of negotiations themselves. Joint organizing campaigns by the Southern Council of Industrial Workers and the IWA-US might be one way to more effectively utilize the resources of the unions.

3. *Public policy changes that increase industry stability and contribute to employer ability to pay.* The recent history of wood products collective bargaining is complicated by the various public policy issues affecting the industry: housing policy, interest rates, timber supply questions, and import and export policies. The recent crisis over timber supply due to the proposed environmental protection of spotted owl habitat is one graphic example. In some instances these policy concerns might be approached in joint union-management initiatives, while in others it will require independent action in alliance with other stakeholder groups in the community. The unions' ability to create their own agenda, rather than having it dictated to by the industry, will be crucial.

4. *Recapturing the power of the strike.* Wood products workers were not the only union members to watch their power to strike the employer dissipate during the 1980s. PATCO, Phelps Dodge, Eastern Airlines, and the Greyhound strikes are all good examples of how the power of economic sanctions has been compromised by structural economic as well as political circumstances. Recapturing this power is at once a political and internal organizational task. Some curb on the ability of employers to permanently replace economic strikers would help prevent the wholesale destruction of collective bargaining that characterized the Louisiana Pacific dispute. Legal changes are no panacea, however, and their likelihood is not strong given the present political and judicial environment. All unions in the wood products industry will need to continue organizing their own members and their communities. Only this type of social consensus—a "culture of solidarity" like that created by the United Mine Workers at Pittston, for instance—can protect the future of woodworker wages and benefits in the Pacific Northwest over the long run.

REFERENCES

Association of Western Pulp and Paper Workers, *1989 Economic Report.* Portland, Oregon, 1989.

Bureau of National Affairs (BNA). "What's New in Collective Bargaining." Washington, D.C.: Bureau of National Affairs. March 13, 1986.

Business Week. December 22, 1986.

Cappelli, Peter. "Concession Bargaining and the National Economy." *Thirty-fifth Annual Meeting,* Industrial Relations Research Association, Madison, Wisconsin, 1982.

———. "Plant-Level Concession Bargaining." *Industrial and Labor Relations Review.* 39(1):90–104, 1985.

Craypo, Charles. *The Economics of Collective Bargaining.* Washington, D.C.: Bureau of National Affairs, 1986.

Crow's Weekly Letter. 1, May 23, 1986a.

Crow's Weekly Letter. 2, June 13, 1986b.

Dana, John L. "Bargaining in the Western Lumber Industry." *Monthly Labor Review.* August, 1965.

Dunlop, John. *Wage Determination Under Trade Unions.* New York, Macmillan, 1944.

Dunlop, John. "Working Towards a Consensus." *Challenge* 25, July–August, 1982.

Freedman, Audrey. "A Fundamental Change in Wage Bargaining." *Challenge* 25, July–August, 1982.

———. *Labor Outlook 1982.* New York: the Conference Board, 1981.

———. *The New Look in Wage Policy and Employee Relations.* New York: the Conference Board, 1985.

Frost, Ann C. "Influences on Bargaining Structure in the B.C. Forest Products Industry." Paper presented to Canadian Industrial Relations Association, Victoria, B.C., June, 1990.

Gagala, Ken. *Labor Guide to Negotiating Wages and Benefits.* Reston, Virginia: Reston Publishing Company, 1985.

Hoxie, Robert F. *Trade Unionism in the United States.* Chicago: University of Chicago Press, 1917.

International Woodworkers of America. "A Sampling of Concessions Made by IWA Locals to Weyerhaeuser," Knight Library Archival Collection. University of Oregon, Eugene, Oregon, n.d.

International Woodworkers of America. Knight Library Archival Collection. University of Oregon, Eugene, Oregon. Box 126, Folder 77:n.d.(a).

International Woodworkers of America. *Survey of IWA Collective Agreements*. Knight Library Archival Collection. University of Oregon, Eugene, Oregon. January, 1981.

International Woodworkers of America. Knight Library Archival Collection. University of Oregon, Eugene, Oregon. Letter from G.H. Yockert to Red Russell. Box 123, Folder 77, February, 1985a.

International Woodworkers of America. Knight Library Archival Collection. University of Oregon, Eugene, Oregon. Letter from Denny Scott to Chris Short. North Bend Local 3-261, October, 1985b.

Kassalow, Everett M. "Concession Bargaining Something Old, but Also Something Quite New." *Proceedings of the Thirty-fifth Annual Meeting*. Madison, Wisconsin, Industrial Relations Research Association, 1982.

Kochan, Thomas. *Collective Bargaining and Industrial Relations*. Homewood, Illinois: Irwin, 1980.

Kochan, Thomas A., Harry C. Katz, and Robert B. McKersie. *The Transformation of American Industrial Relations*. New York: Basic Books, 1986.

Kochan, Thomas A., Robert B. McKersie, and Peter Cappelli. "Strategic Choices and Industrial Relations Theory." *Industrial Relations*. 23(1), 1984.

Levinson, Harold M. *Determining Forces in Collective Wage Bargaining*. New York: John Wiley & Sons, 1966.

Levinson, Harold M. "Pattern Bargaining: A Case Study of the Automobile Workers." *Quarterly Journal of Economics*. May, 1960.

McDonald, Robert M. "Unionism and the Wage Structure in the United States Pulp and Paper Industry." In *The Evolution of Wage Structure*. Edited by Lloyd G. Reynolds and Cynthia H. Taft. New Haven: Yale University Press, 1956.

McKersie, Robert B. "Structural Factors and Negotiations in the International Harvester Company." In *The Structure of Collective Bargaining*. Edited by Arnold Webber. Glencoe, Illinois: The Free Press of Glencoe, 1961.

Mitchell, Daniel J. B. "Concession Bargaining and Wage Determination." *Business Economics*. 20(3):45–50, 1985.

Mitchell, Daniel J. B. "Why Are Wage Concessions So Prevalent?" *Personnel Journal*. 65(8), August, 1986.

Random Lengths. August 1, 1986.

Ready, Kathryn J. "Is Pattern Bargaining Dead?" *Industrial & Labor Relations Review*. 43(2):272–279, 1990.

Ross, Arthur. *Trade Union Wage Policy*. 1956.

Scott, Denny, International Woodworkers of America. "The Impact of Housing Depression on the Lumber and Wood Products Industry." Testimony before the Forest Subcommittee of the House Committee on Agriculture, Washington, D.C. September 16, 1982.

Seltzer, George. "Pattern Bargaining and the United Steelworkers." *Journal of Political Economy*. August, 1951.

Smyth, Douglas. *The Impact of Technological Change on Production and Employment in the Softwood Lumber Industry of British Columbia*. Vancouver, B.C., IWA-Canada, 1986.

The *Oregonian*. June 25, 1983.

The *Oregonian*. p. E-1, June 23, 1984.

The *Oregonian*. p. C-2, June 12, 1986a.

The *Oregonian*. p. D-7, June 22, 1986b.

The *Union Register*. 48(11):1, June 7, 1985.

The *Union Register*. 51(4):1, April 22, 1988.

The *Union Register*. 51(6):1, June 24, 1988a.

The *Union Register*. 51(8):1, August 26, 1988b.

The *Union Register*. 52(5):1, May 26, 1989.

The *Woodworker*. 45(6):1, June 30, 1980.

The *Woodworker*. 48(7):1, July 22, 1983a.

The *Woodworker*. 48(10):1, October 25, 1983b.

The *Woodworker*. 49(4):1, April 11, 1985a.

The *Woodworker*. 49(5):1, May 16, 1985b.

The *Woodworker*. 49(9):1, September 12, 1985c.

The *Woodworker*. 50(8):1, April 14, 1986.

Troy, Lee and Sheflin, Neil. *U.S. Union Sourcebook*. Industrial Relations Data and Information Services, West Orange, New Jersey, 1982.

Weyerhaeuser Memo. *Western Labor Communications*. Confidential, January 29, 1986.

Wyant, Dan. "Northwest Timber: After the Fall." *Eugene Register- Guard* Special Report, November, 1985.

Interviews:

Bledsoe, Jim; Mike Draper, Western Council of Industrial Workers, AFL-CIO, 1990.

Hubbell, Bill; Roy Ockert, International Woodworkers of America, AFL-CIO, 1990.

Scott, Denny, United Brotherhood of Carpenters and Joiners, AFL-CIO, 1990.

Thompson, James A., Association of Western Pulp and Paper Workers, 1990.

Swanson, Gordon, United Paperworkers International Union, AFL-CIO, 1990.

Pattern Bargaining in the Wood Products Industry in Western Canada

NORMAN MACLELLAN

Vice-President, Region 4, Canadian Paperworkers Union

In this paper I discuss the collective bargaining experiences and policies of Canadian forest products industry unions over the past decade or so, with particular focus on the maintenance and scope of pattern bargaining; the relationships between unions in the industry in Western Canada; the differences we see in our industry relative to the U.S. Pacific Northwest—our concerns and the threats that we see for the future—and what can be done to increase control over wages and working conditions in the interests of workers in the forest products industry in the Pacific Northwest and Western Canada.

BARGAINING AND INDUSTRY STRUCTURE

Before addressing these questions, it might be helpful to review some of the factors that influence collective bargaining in the forest-products industry in Western Canada. The forest products industry in Western Canada exhibits varying degrees of concentration of ownership depending on sector.

The highest concentration of ownership is in the pulp and paper sector. There is less concentration in saw and planer milling, particularly in the British Columbia Interior; and less concentration again in logging, although lumber and fiber supply is largely controlled by the major integrated companies through ownership of timber cutting rights.

The major companies in the industry are large integrated U.S., Canadian, and Japanese transnational corporations. Several of the majors are common to both Canada and the U.S. Pacific Northwest, such as Daishowa, Louisiana Pacific, Weyerhaeuser, and Champion-Weldwood. In the past decade, ownership of the largest corporations in Western Canada has changed significantly. MacMillan Bloedel came under the control of the Canadian resources giant Noranda, and B.C. Forest Products and Crown Forest Industries both came under the control of Fletcher Challenge of New Zealand.

The forest products industry in Western Canada is highly unionized in all sectors except logging in the interior regions. There are three major unions in the industry in Western Canada. The largest union regionally is the International Woodworkers of America (IWA)—Canada, which has 34,000 of its 45,000 national membership in British Columbia. The largest union nationally is the Canadian Paperworkers Union (CPU), with 8,500 of its 70,000 national membership in British Columbia. The third union is the Pulp, Paper, and Woodworkers of Canada (PPWC), with its entire membership of 7,200 in British Columbia.

The IWA—Canada and the CPU are affiliated to the Canadian Labour Congress and the British Columbia Federation of Labour. The PPWC, the first forest-products union to break away from international unions based in the U.S., is affiliated to the smaller Confederation of Canadian Unions.

Reno Biasutti, Staff Representative, Canadian Paperworkers Union, assisted in the preparation of this paper.

The CPU severed its relationship with the United Paperworkers International Union (UPIU) and became an autonomous Canadian union in 1974. The IWA—Canada became an autonomous Canadian union in 1987. The IWA—Canada represents workers in logging on the British Columbia Coast, and workers throughout Western Canada in saw and planer milling, shingle milling, plywood milling, and lumber remanufacturing. The CPU and PPWC both represent workers in pulp and paper milling, secondary paper products manufacturing, and to a lesser extent sawmill operations associated mainly with pulp and paper mills.

While the volume of timber harvested in British Columbia is about two thirds of the volume harvested in the U.S. Pacific Coast region, pulp and newsprint mill capacity in the two regions is about the same.

Sixty-two percent of Canada's softwood lumber production is shipped from British Columbia mills, along with 85 percent of Canada's softwood plywood production, 80 percent of Canada's shingle mill production, 28 percent of Canada's pulp production, and 16 percent of Canada's newsprint production.

Logging/Sawmill Structure

In the logging/sawmill sector in British Columbia, the majority of workers for many years have been covered by two industrywide master agreements negotiated by IWA—Canada with two employer associations. The broadly based master agreement is with coastal industry employers represented by Forest Industrial Relations Ltd. The other master agreement is with interior industry employers represented by Interior Forest Industrial Relations Association.

These two master agreements provide a common standard of wages and working conditions for all workers with each region, with the exception of small companies covered by separate agreements. In the early years of master agreement bargaining, there was a significant difference in wage rates and benefits between the coastal and interior regions, the coastal agreement being superior. Over the past decade, the IWA has been able to all but eliminate these differences and establish a provincewide standard of pay and benefits.

In addition, in 1972, the IWA was able to bring the trades mechanic/millwright rate of pay under the coast master agreement up to the level of the pulp and paper industry's trades mechanics rates.

Pulp and Paper

For well over two decades, the CPU and PPWC in the pulp and paper sector have been able to negotiate multiemployer, provincewide agreements with common base and trades mechanic rates of pay and standard benefits. Consequently, since 1974, we have developed and maintained common base and trades rates in all sectors of industry. CPU and PPWC contracts in pulp and paper expire at the same time and within one month of the expiry of the IWA coast and interior master agreements. Settlements for both wages and benefits in all sectors have followed a fairly constant pattern over the last decade. All three unions have successfully resisted employer attempts to fragment bargaining and break this pattern.

Bargaining in pulp and paper differs very little from bargaining in logging/sawmilling, except that we negotiate with the Pulp and Paper Industrial Relations Bureau instead of Forest Industrial Relations (although the two employer associations occupy the same office and represent similar groups of employers). The two unions in pulp and paper (CPU and PPWC) negotiate jointly at the same table with the same employers group. In addition, although both the pulp and paper and logging/sawmill sectors have sectorwide job evaluation systems to determine the wage structure for the jobs above negotiated base rates, the pulp and paper job evaluation system is different from the logging/sawmill system.

The Pulp and Paper Industrial Relations Bureau and Forest Industrial Relations are also the employer agents through which most industrywide plans are jointly administered. This includes job evaluation plans, safety and health research, health and welfare plans, and pension plans. In both sectors, therefore, union-employer relations have continued to become highly centralized and structured.

The CPU's philosophy and strategy concerning pattern bargaining over the past decade and a half has been to coordinate bargaining in pulp and paper in British Columbia with the PPWC to strengthen and extend the B.C. industrywide standard of pay and benefits.

In this period, the two pulp and paper unions negotiated standard agreements with fifteen major employers operating twenty mills with twenty-five local unions. We established a jointly trusteed industrywide portable pension plan for all of our B.C. members, which negotiates the same increase in pension benefits for retirees as received by working members. The pulp unions have been successful in extending the standard pulp and paper base and trades rates and benefits to every sector of the industry not covered by master agreements (including, for example, box plants, bag plants, plastic plants, warehouses, fine paper plants, and tissue plants). The CPU has carried the pulp and paper pattern of wage rates and benefits in British Columbia east to the Manitoba-Ontario border, so that base and trades rates are the same in all pulp and paper mills.

East of the Ontario-Manitoba border, the CPU is now engaged in tough bargaining struggles and strikes to continue to extend the Western industry wage pattern into Central and Eastern Canada, where the majority of our members are.

Relationships between the three forest products unions in British Columbia have improved over the last sixteen years. As the new CPU vice-president for this region, I see the development of even better relations as a priority task for our union over the period ahead.

The CPU's relations with PPWC have been very good since we started bargaining relationships in varying degrees industrywide in B.C. in 1974. The CPU's new independence in 1974 was a contributing factor to closer relations and cooperation. However, in the main, it was the realization by both the members and leaders of both unions that the divisions of the past were only benefitting the employers at the expense of the workers. Another contributing factor has been the threats by some employers to pull out of joint negotiations; therefore, it was clear that cooperation, coordination, and bargaining solidarity was the only way to go to protect the hard-fought, industrywide standards, and to make further improvements to those standards.

Relations Across Industries

Relations between the pulp and paper unions and the IWA have been strained for some time for a number of reasons. Communications have not been good and mistakes have been made. Bargaining strategies and coordination between the pulp unions and the IWA have been attempted, but have not been successful to any significant degree in the face of centralized coordination by the employers.

While there have not been good relations and coordination between unions in the two sectors, it is nonetheless significant that the IWA was able during the devastating depression in lumber products in the early 1980s to maintain wage structure parity with the pulp and paper unions and to retain the master agreement structure of collective bargaining. This can be attributed in part to the relative buoyancy of the pulp and paper sector during that period, the solidarity and determination of the IWA members, the growing unity and cooperation between the pulp and paper unions, and the general attitude of the industrywide solidarity among all forestry workers.

As I mentioned earlier, one of my priorities is to maintain and improve relations between the CPU, the PPWC, and the IWA. If this does not happen, we will be faced with the same destructive conditions as I observe to exist in the U.S. Pacific Northwest. I can report that relations between the pulp and paper and logging/sawmill unions are already improving. For the first time ever, the three unions have presented a joint brief on forestry policy to the provincial government.

I am not well informed of the relationships and relative cooperation between unions in the wood products industry in the U.S. Pacific Northwest. Unfortunately, when the CPU became an autonomous Canadian Union in 1974, almost all relations with UPIU were severed. However, I observe that over the last two decades, multiemployer bargaining has all but disappeared in the U.S., and as a result, many concessions have been won by employers. Bitter, isolated strikes have been conducted and broken by widespread scabbing, there is no industry standard of pay and benefits, long-term agreements are being signed, and bonuses and lump-sum payments have replaced negotiated wage increases.

All of this information tells our members that the unions have become weakened by the fragmentation of bargaining relationships. We know that there have been attempts to coordinate strikes among employer groups in the U.S. with varying degrees of success, but success is difficult when there are different wages and benefits even among the same employer in the same sector in the same geographical area.

U.S.-CANADIAN RELATIONS AND WAGES

These developments are of growing concern to all the forest industry unions in Canada. The rapid decline of unionization, the nature of collective bargaining and the type of settlements being reached in the U.S. industry are, with greater frequency, being used against us at the bargaining table throughout Canada.

Of great concern to us is the growing disparity in wages and benefits between the U.S. and Canadian industries. I have developed a couple of statistical tables to demonstrate the divergent trends in base and trades rates in unionized pulp and paper mills in Western Canada and the U.S. Pacific Northwest.

Table 1 tracks the trends in industry base rates since 1968. Twenty years ago, there was virtual parity in base rates on both sides of the border. Since 1970, Canadian base rates grew steadily ahead of U.S. base rates until 1982, when the trend began to reverse; and for a period of five years, discounting for the exchange rate differential on the Canadian dollar, in U.S. dollar terms, the Canadian rates were lower than U.S. rates.

However, in the past three years, two things have happened to restore the long-term trend of divergence and to accentuate the positive difference in Canadian base rates: U.S. unions have settled for little or no change in base rates over the past four years, while Canadian unions obtained increases accumulating to 21 percent; and the Canadian dollar has appreciated in U.S. money terms by another 21 percent. As a result, we have an all-time record high differential in Canadian base rates this year of plus $2.32 per hour in U.S. money. Table 2 shows a similar pattern relative to trades mechanic rates of pay.

This development, in conjunction with the Canada-U.S. Free Trade Agreement, poses a very serious threat to our members in Canada. Already, we see major companies in secondary wood-products manufacturing closing down operations in Western Canada and moving south of the border because of significantly lower labor costs in the U.S. We have a mutual interest in seeing a reversal of bargaining trends in the U.S. Pacific Northwest.

I offer a few observations on factors behind the divergent trend in bargaining strengths, pattern bargaining, and wage rates between our two regions.

First, I do not believe that there is very much difference in the militancy of Canadian and American forest products industry workers. American workers have demonstrated their willingness to strike in the face of overwhelming odds against them, odds that do not yet exist in Canada. Surely, there must be a dampening effect in the extreme when an employer, when struck, can immediately hire scabs and legally keep them.

The difference in union behavior and bargaining strength stem more, I believe, from the following factors:

- Differences in the membership culture of industry solidarity and unity, reinforced in Canada by the institutions of industrywide pension and welfare plans;
- differences in membership attitude toward employers, where in Canada our members in general do not see their interests being bound up with the interests of particular employers (e.g., employee stock ownership programs, team concept programs, quality of work-life programs);
- differences in the degree of organization of our work force, both within the industry and nationally; in Canada, union membership continues to grow in absolute terms and to remain fairly constant in relative terms versus steady decline in the U.S.; and
- differences in the organizational strength and activity of central labor bodies, such as the Canadian Labour Congress and the British Columbia Federation of Labour.

In the political life of Canada, the labor movement actively associates itself with democratic socialism and the New Democratic Party, a party that does not receive or seek financial support from the corporate sector. The New Democratic Party has, in the past, elected governments in the Provinces of British Columbia, Saskatchewan, and Manitoba. They are presently elected as governments in the North West Territories and the Province of Ontario, which has approximately 40 percent of the population of Canada and is the engine that drives the national economy. The New Democratic Party federally is in the number three position, and it is within the expectations of many Canadians that they could in the future form the federal government.

The strong, widespread support in Canada for a party that supports labor's objectives, and to an extremely large extent is directed and influenced by labor, causes right-wing governments to hesitate in passing extreme antilabor legislation. This is not to say that dangerous labor legislation does not exist in provincial and federal law.

We, in Canada, do not see the same political relationship on the U.S. side of the border. The political heritage of party platform politics in Canada makes it easier to distinguish which political party labor should or should not support.

CONCLUSIONS

Relative to the future and how American and Canadian unions in forest products in the Pacific Northwest can assist each other, I recommend the following:

1. We need to establish and maintain strong bargaining patterns to obtain greater control of the industry in the interests of workers on both sides of the border.
2. Without being overly ambitious and unrealistic, we need to establish formal forums or associations so that on a regular basis, we can hold conferences, talk to each other, learn about each other's problems and achievements, and build the basis for mutual cooperation and information exchange in an atmosphere of trust and mutual respect.

Simply said, we should get to know each other better. Before we can begin to think about coordinated collective bargaining strategies, we have to establish good lines of communication and cooperation across sectors and borders and between unions. We are working toward these strategies in Canada, and we need to start to do the same across the border.

TABLE 1—WOOD PRODUCTS INDUSTRY COMPARATIVE BASE WAGE RATE DATA: WESTERN CANADA AND PACIFIC NORTHWEST U.S.—1968 TO 1990

1 Year	2 Exchange Rate C$ in U.S.$	3 B.C. Base in C$	4 B.C. Base in U.S.$	5 Pacific Norhtwest Pulp and Paper Base Rates in U.S.$	6 Difference Between W. Canada and U.S., in U.S.$
1968	1.077	2.940	2.730	2.855	-0.125
1969	1.077	3.120	2.897	2.995	-0.098
1970	1.044	3.420	3.276	3.245	0.031
1971	1.010	3.720	3.683	3.440	0.243
1972	0.991	4.085	4.122	3.740	0.382
1973	1.000	4.450	4.450	4.000	0.450
1974	0.978	5.100	5.215	4.325	0.890
1975	1.017	6.140	6.037	4.755	1.282
1976	0.986	6.890	6.988	5.255	1.733
1977	1.063	7.610	7.159	5.960	1.199
1978	1.141	8.160	7.152	6.580	0.572
1979	1.171	9.060	7.737	7.245	0.492
1980	1.169	9.960	8.520	7.895	0.625
1981	1.199	11.460	9.558	8.525	1.033
1982	1.234	12.960	10.502	9.295	1.207
1983	1.232	12.960	10.519	10.195	0.324
1984	1.295	13.480	10.409	11.045	-0.636
1985	1.366	14.085	10.311	11.710	-1.399
1986	1.389	14.085	10.140	12.410	-2.270
1987	1.326	14.485	10.924	12.500	-1.576
1988	1.231	15.335	12.457	12.500	-0.043
1989	1.184	16.180	13.666	12.500	1.166
1990	1.152	17.070	14.818	12.500	2.318

(July)

From 1988 to 1990, the U.S. rates do not reflect the net annual take-home wage due to the widespread settlements of bonuses and lump-sum payments.

Source: B.C. Pulp and Paper Industrial Relations and Forest Industrial Relations Bureau and Stats Canada.

TABLE 2—WOOD PRODUCTS INDUSTRY COMPARATIVE TRADES MECHANIC WAGE RATES: WESTERN CANADA AND PACIFIC NORTHWEST U.S.—1968 TO 1990

1 Year	2 Exchange Rate C$ in U.S.$	3 B.C. Mechanic Rates in C$	4 B.C. Mechanic Rates in U.S.$	5 Pacific Norhtwest Pulp and Paper Average Mechanic Rates in U.S.$	6 Difference Between W. Canada and U.S., in U.S.$
1968	1.077	4.120	3.825 *	3.970	-0.145
1969	1.077	4.350	4.039*	4.270	-0.231
1970	1.044	4.785	4.583	4.520	0.063
1971	1.010	5.250	5.198 *	4.795	0.403
1972	0.991	5.700	5.752 *	5.145	0.607
1973	1.000	6.295	6.295 *	5.555	0.740
1974	0.978	7.505	7.674	6.055	1.619
1975	1.017	8.545	8.402	6.770	1.632
1976	0.986	9.295	9.427	7.740	1.687
1977	1.063	10.015	9.421	8.475	0.946
1978	1.141	10.515	9.216	9.480	-0.264
1979	1.171	11.765	10.047	10.420	-0.373
1980	1.169	12.885	11.022	11.360	-0.338
1981	1.199	15.280	12.744	12.270	0.474
1982	1.234	17.265	13.991	13.375	0.616
1983	1.232	17.265	14.014	14.425	-0.411
1984	1.295	17.955	13.865	15.325	-1.460
1985	1.366	18.765	13.737	16.540	-2.803
1986	1.389	18.765	13.510	17.530	-4.020
1987	1.326	19.195	14.476	17.650	-3.174
1988	1.231	20.015	16.259	17.650	-1.391
1989	1.184	21.115	17.834	17.650	0.184
1990	1.152	22.275	19.336	17.650	1.686

(July)

From 1988 to 1990, the U.S. rates do not reflect the net annual take-home wage due to the widespread settlements of bonuses and lump-sum payments.

NOTE: *Pulp and Paper trades rates only (until 1974 higher than Lumber Industry).

Source: B.C. Pulp and Paper Industrial Relations and Forest Industrial Relations Bureau and Stats Canada.

Current Issues and Future Strategies for Forest–Product Unions

DENNY SCOTT

Collective Bargaining Specialist, United Brotherhood of Carpenters and Joiners of America

This paper discusses the direction that labor-management relations is likely to take in the U.S. forest-products industry and how unions will attempt to influence that path.

CURRENT TRENDS

First, I will present key trends that I believe will most heavily influence the issues that organized labor and wood products corporations will confront during the next decade.

1. Reduced Timber Supply

There is little doubt that the Pacific Northwest timber industry will be operating with a smaller volume of raw material during the 1990s. Numerous studies (U.S. Forest Service, 1973; Beuter, Johnson, and Scheurman, 1976; Rahm, 1981) project timber supply declines in the range of 21 to 30 percent during the 1980–2010 period. The decline will occur primarily on lands owned by forest products corporations because old growth timber on those lands was previously liquidated on fast-harvest rotations. As a result, a significant time lag will occur before the second growth trees, planted since the 1950s, will be sufficiently mature to harvest.

More recently, the U.S. Forest Service announced cutbacks in harvest levels from federal lands in the Pacific Northwest region. For national forests in northern California, Oregon, and Washington, the annual cut is projected to decline by 14 percent in the 1995–2000 period (U.S. Forest Service, 1990). These reductions are related to the resource planning process mandated by law which requires the public agency to balance timber values more evenly with wildlife, watershed, recreation, and other nontimber values. This action alone is estimated to reduce direct employment by 20,000 jobs.

In April 1990 a federal interagency scientific committee published a report (commonly referred to as the Thomas Report) that recommended a strategy for conserving the northern spotted owl (Thomas et al., 1990). This report carries the force of law since it was performed under the provisions of the Endangered Species Act. It recommends reserving 8.4 million acres of old-growth timberlands for spotted owl habitat. These lands are primarily public lands under the jurisdiction of the U.S. Forest Service and the Bureau of Land Management in the states of California, Oregon, and northern California. About 40 percent of the owl habitat areas occur in lands already preserved in wilderness areas, national parks and other set-aside land. Thus, the Thomas report would set aside an additional five million acres currently being used for multiple purposes, including timber production.

At least two major studies have been conducted to assess the economic and employment loss impacts of withdrawing this large acreage from the timber production base in the Pacific Northwest (U.S. Forest Service, 1990 and Beuter, 1990). A Forest Service study estimates the Thomas report would cause timber harvests on federal lands to decline by 2.4 billion board feet by 1995. This represents a drop of 40 percent from harvest plans now scheduled for the 1995 period (4.4 million board feet). As a result of this precipitous decline in volumes, the Forest Service study estimates that 25,500 direct jobs would be eliminated in the Northwest timber industry.

The Beuter study, on the other hand, projects direct timber industry employment losses of 63,700 for the three-state area. Some of the job loss reflected in this figure, however, is due to the already planned harvest reductions (without the impact of the Thomas report). Beuter attributes 44,250 of those jobs to the effects of the Thomas report alone. When both direct and indirect employment declines are considered, job losses escalate to 102,750 for just the effects of the Thomas report. If other declines caused by U.S. Forest Service "program" reductions are factored into the calculation, losses are projected to reach 147,200 by 1995.

In addition to the timber harvest restrictions involved in these measures, there were several bills introduced in the Congress that would reduce Pacific Northwest timber availability even further. Congressman Jim Jontz (D-IN) introduced the "Ancient Forest Protection Act" in 1990 that would prohibit logging of any kind in Pacific Northwest old growth forests. A similar bill introduced by Congressman Bruce Vento (D-MN) would have similar far reaching effects. While these measures did not pass during the 101st Congress, it is reasonable to assume they will be reintroduced in the next Congress and in future years.

2. Technological Change

The second major factor that will significantly affect labor negotiations in the wood-products industry is technological change. The industry went through a period in the early 1980s of drastic structural change, coupled with the rapid introduction of new automated equipment. The primary purpose of the capital investment was to increase recovery from the increasingly expensive raw material. One effect was to reduce unit labor costs and to reduce the output to hours ratio. Systems introduced in the sawmilling industry link computer decision making to automated equipment.

One school of thought advanced is that the technology binge has reached a plateau and, thus, capital investment will curtail in the next several years. My personal view is that this "quiet revolution" will continue at or near the same pace as occurred in the 1980s. Increasing stumpage prices will pressure mills to continue investment in automated systems in order to be cost competitive. One federal study (U.S. Forest Service, 1990) predicts that employment declines in the wood-products industry due to automation and the substitution of capital for labor will be in the 12 percent range over the next ten years. This translates into 60,000 jobs.

Automation and technology have a heavy impact not only on aggregate employment, but also the organization of the work and skill mix of the remaining jobs.

3. The Business Cycle

The third challenge is one that has always been central to negotiating labor contracts in the forest-products industry: the business cycle and the resulting demand for building products.

The economy in 1990 is showing signs of weakness with a strong possibility of recession. As the oil price shock works its way through the economy and affects virtually all manufacturing and agriculture sectors, economic growth will slow even further. Interest rates remain rather high considering the soft economy, but the Federal Reserve Board does not appear anxious to take steps to reduce interest rates. This is bad news for the building products industry since demand is driven largely by construction activity.

4. Corporate Restructuring

Consolidations, mergers, and subsequent spin-offs will continue to plague the forest products industry

271

for many years to come. The merger of Georgia-Pacific (G-P) and Great Northern Nekoosa (GNN) in late 1989, which began as a hostile raid, marked a new era for the industry. The merger created the largest integrated forest products corporation in the world. It was financed with conventional bank borrowing, not high-interest junk bonds, and broke the "gentlemen's agreement" that forest corporations would not prey on one another. Prior mergers were between willing partners (St. Regis and Champion to defeat a hostile takeover bid by Rupert Murdoch of Canada) or they were hostile acquisitions by companies outside the forest industry (such as the Sir James Goldsmith takeover of Crown Zellerbach and Diamond International).

After a settling out period, the G-P/GNN merger will likely cause other combinations to be initiated. This is due to the mill capacity, economies of scale, and price-setting capabilities in certain paper lines gained by G-P with this merger. Other companies are likely to undertake similar raids or friendly mergers to narrow the advantage obtained by G-P. Some observers of the industry predict that the next round of mergers and takeovers will be international in scope. We could well see European forest companies combining with U.S. companies or an influx of Japanese or New Zealand investment in the U.S. industry. Fletcher Challenge, a New Zealand-based company, already has major holdings in Canada.

UNION BARGAINING AGENDA

These issues clearly lead to the conclusion there will be major worker dislocation and unemployment in the Pacific Northwest industry. How do the unions respond?

The unions are, in fact, already responding to the specter of disruptions in the forest industry with a broad array of bargaining proposals and structural bargaining changes designed to (1) mitigate the employment decline with a proactive political strategy on timber supply; (2) enhance strength at the bargaining table; and (3) develop job security and worker adjustment programs through collective bargaining and other public and private means.

It is noteworthy that the United Automobile Workers and General Motors recently concluded a new collective bargaining agreement that set job security as the number one priority. I look at this as a bellwether settlement. It's a sign of the times for many manufacturing industries, including forest products. The UAW agreement establishes employment guarantees for each auto plant with required "replacement ratios" for attrition.

While the forest industry may be some distance from the notion of employment guarantees, the bargaining agenda presented the last ten years has contained several important job security measures. Severance pay packages were added to the labor agreements in 1986. This was the year the industry extracted major wage and benefit concessions from West Coast wood-products workers. The union negotiators made the best of a bad situation by obtaining severance pay language as a partial offset to concessions.

The bargaining agenda in future years will include successor language to ensure that when a company or plant is sold the owner either guarantees the transfer of the contract and work force to the new owner or pays liquidated damages for wages and benefits that would have been earned under the full term of the agreement.

A supplemental unemployment benefit plan has received great attention at the bargaining table in the past and will continue to be pressed. SUB plans establish a fund from employer contributions that are used to fill in the gaps that unemployment compensation misses, such as the waiting week and an add-on to bring total compensation to approximately two-thirds of regular take home pay.

Every effort will be made to improve and expand the availability of early retirement benefits so workers will be encouraged to retire early with a comfortable income and, thus, open job opportunities for younger workers.

Corporate by-laws provide lucrative severance payments for top corporate officials (known as golden parachutes) in the event of a job loss due to a hostile takeover. Production workers deserve similar consideration.

Unions in the industry have proposed "neutrality in organizing" to forest industry giants in several rounds of bargaining the last five years. This will remain on the table so that, hopefully, at some point workers in nonunion plants can make a decision on union representation without undue fear and intimidation. It's clear to us that workers will need union representation even more in this climate of contracting jobs.

Workers should be given the "right of first refusal" when a plant goes on the sale block. This means that before the operation can be offered for general sale it must first be offered to the employees. There are laws now on the books, under the heading of Employee Stock Ownership Plans (ESOP), that make employee buy-outs more feasible than ever. But for workers to take best advantage of this option they need time to form the ESOP, conduct feasibility studies, and secure financing or partners. The contractual right of first refusal would provide a necessary bridge.

There is great need in the lumber, plywood, and wood-products industry for formal skill upgrading, ongoing training, literacy training, and computer training. These areas have, sadly, been largely neglected. The tendency in the past has been for companies to introduce sophisticated technology and then go outside the existing work force to find qualified personnel rather than looking at the present employees as a valuable, trainable resource. If training were integrated into the daily work operation, the transition to new technology would be smoothed.

It is my view that management can be persuaded to see the wisdom of integrating a training function into daily operations. This notion fits perfectly with an emerging management philosophy that equates quality, reliability, and speed of delivery with success (Corporation for Enterprise Development, 1990). It takes a high-quality work force to meet these new realities of world competition. The Japanese recognize this fact, and it helps to explain their preeminent economic position in the world today.

Pacific Northwest timber companies are a bit behind the learning curve concerning this management philosophy, but they can be educated. The Italian conductor Toscanini said, "There are no bad orchestras, only bad conductors." Likewise, I feel there are no bad employees, only bad managers. Our job is to make them better managers of human resources. Just as the goal of a sawmill manager is to obtain the highest and best use from timber with recovery and value added, so too should this idea be extended to human resources.

It is also time for labor to make proposals to industry regarding the management of timber resources and how those resources are best used to increase labor input and value added. I am suggesting a labor-management task force to do several things, including making input on how corporate timberlands are managed and promoting research with universities and public and private groups to upgrade value-added manufacturing in the West Coast timber industry. On this score, management is too important to be left only to managers.

More worker input and voice is needed with the design, organization, and implementation of technology. Forest industry unions have never opposed the introduction of automated systems, but often, workers become victims of technology instead of beneficiaries. Many of these problems could be corrected by early notification, consultation, systematic worker input, and a willingness to put appropriate adjustment and training programs in place.

Those are the objectives that will fill labor's agenda for the next decade. The next question is how to achieve those goals.

UNION STRATEGY

Since 1986, major planning efforts have been carried out by the two major wood-products unions, industrial affiliates of the United Brotherhood of Carpenters (called the Western Council of Industrial Workers in the Pacific Northwest) and the International Woodworkers of America-U.S. The planning has revolved around bargaining programs and bargaining structures.

These unions have concluded that current bargaining structures must undergo some alteration in order to provide a closer fit with the economic realities of the 1990s. For example, there has been a concerted effort to link bargaining in southern units with West Coast negotiations for the national multiplant corporations. This strategy has been moved forward and will continue to receive a great deal of attention in the future.

Closely associated with the national companywide strategy is the principle of establishing settlement patterns and extending those patterns as broadly as possible. This means that, in the future, we will be looking at national patterns with special adjustments that begin to eliminate regional wage and benefit differentials.

Currently, in the South, the same two unions plus several plants represented by the United Paperworkers International Union, are attempting to expand joint bargaining programs within the region. Local unions that have never before participated in joint strategies are being brought together to learn about and to adopt a three-union coordinated bargaining program. These efforts will grow in importance.

Will efforts by wood products unions to consolidate the bargaining structure lead to more acrimony at the bargaining table? It's fair to say that the relationship between the major forest corporations and the two wood products unions has been less than harmonious in the recent past. The unions were forced to strike Weyerhaeuser in 1986 to reduce the concession package demanded by the company. A profit-sharing plan was introduced by Weyerhaeuser at that time and was represented as a "wage recovery" plan. Regrettably, the plan didn't live up to its "recovery" promises in most logging and mill operations and, as a result, it remains as a contentious issue to this day, even though modifications were made during the 1988 negotiations.

There were strikes at Willamette Industries, Boise Cascade, and Champion plants in 1988 as the unions showed determination to recapture a major share of the concessions extracted two years earlier.

Despite this rather stormy relationship in the recent past I believe that the labor-management relationship can reach a higher plane during the next ten years. It depends primarily on the power relationship that evolves between the parties. As the unions continue to develop joint bargaining strategies across the nation, some balance in the power relationship will be restored. As this occurs the industry will likely adopt a less contentious approach at the bargaining table. It is my view that, as the balance of power begins to reach equilibrium, a higher degree of labor-management cooperation will develop. That's not to say, however, that the adversarial relationship will, or should, ever be completely eliminated.

It's interesting to note that cooperation is already taking place on at least one front. A labor-management committee was recently formed for the express purpose of addressing the timber supply problem. The committee is working primarily on federal legislation that will promote a stable timber supply and do it within the constraints of sound environmental and timber management considerations.

Labor in the forest-products industry must become proactive with respect to capital strategies. The unions are novices when it comes to ESOPs and how to use them to enhance job security. The unions are, however, learning as they go. The Western Council has been involved with an ESOP sawmill in eastern Washington and the experience provided valuable lessons. The mechanism also represents a viable option and, thus, is being proposed in a situation where a privately owned wood-products company has been put on the sale block. These approaches will be expanded in the future.

The United Brotherhood of Carpenters also has the capability, through its Special Programs Department, to marshal voting power of stocks held in jointly administered worker pension plans. This is another capital strategy that has been, and will be in the future, used to influence the outcomes of corporate raids and to supply the leverage needed to place labor at the table as an active participant when one corporation goes after another. The union's role, of course, will be to protect the interests of working people in any such transaction.

REFERENCES

Beuter, John H. *Social and Economic Impacts in Washington, Oregon, and California Associated with Implementing the Conservation Strategy for the Northern Spotted Owl: An Overview* (draft). July 9, 1990.

Beuter, John H., K. Norman Johnson, and H. Lynn Scheurman. *Timber for Oregon's Tomorrow*. Forest Research Laboratory, Oregon State University, Research Bulletin No. 19, January, 1976.

Corporation for Enterprise Development. *Playing by New Rules, Nine Economic Realities for the 90s*. 1990.

Rahm, C.M. *Timber Supply Analysis and Baseline Simulations*. Boking Computer Services Co., Module III-A, Forest Policy Project, Washington State University, March, 1981.

Thomas, Jack Ward, E.D. Forsman, J.B. Lint, E.C. Meslow, B.R. Noon, and J. Verner. *A Conservation Strategy for the Spotted Owl* (draft). 1990.

USDA Forest Service. *The Outlook for Timber in the United States*. Forest Resource Report No. 20, 1973.

USDA Forest Service. *Forest Service Estimates Effects of Spotted Owl Strategy*. News Release, May 7, 1990.

USDA Forest Service. *An Analysis of the Timber Situation in the U.S.: 1989–2040, A Technical Document Supporting the 1989 RPA Assessment* (draft). 1990.

Section 11

HEALTH CARE: THE U.S. CRISIS AND LESSONS FROM CANADA

Within the last decade, health care benefits have become the number one issue at the bargaining table and in labor-management relations in the United States. Formerly consigned to benefit specialists and consultants, health care now is a matter of concern to union leaders and employers at all levels of the organization. The crisis in the U.S. health care system has had a direct and powerful impact on labor-management relations and bargaining. The nature and cost of health plans is a matter of intense discussions, and there are increasingly strong voices that call for major reform. Many leaders are looking to Canada for lessons on how to provide universal access to health care at a reasonable cost.

FROM COST CONTAINMENT TO STRUCTURAL REFORM

The U.S. health care crisis is not new; it is merely unyielding. For over a decade, unions and employers have been grappling with escalating costs. There has been a parade of "cost containment" measures that have been adopted in practically every health care plan. These measure include:

- Plan redesign, shifting use from high cost services, and utilization review;
- claims control, administrative reforms, and new financing arrangements;
- alternative delivery systems;
- cost sharing, including higher copayments and deductibles;
- flexible spending accounts and flexible plans;
- case management;
- new purchasing arrangements and tougher bargaining with providers, including purchasing groups and contracts with providers for particular services; and
- wellness and substance-abuse programs.

Despite years of such reforms, health care costs continue to increase faster than the cost-of-living index. Premium increases in negotiated plans now range from 10 to 30 percent per year, and increases of 50 percent were not uncommon in the 1980s.

Labor and management negotiators cannot control the system and its costs, and this fundamental fact has led them to move beyond an analysis of their own plans to examine the health care system itself and possibilities for reform. There is increasing recognition that the problem of health care costs is not caused by the party across the table. Cooperation on health care cost containment has convinced many that "beating up" the other side will not solve the problem. There is a certain illogic to a system in which employees go out on strike against the employer in order to preserve a decent health care plan and a system in which employers force more of the escalating costs onto the users of the plan. While labor and management have been fighting each other, the health care system itself has remained largely unaffected.

The United States has the only health care system in the industrialized world that is based on individual employer plans. Thus, employers and labor are the major consumers of the health care system, and they pay the freight, along with taxpayers through Medicaid and Medicare. As Cathy Schoen points out, our fragmented system has led to individual bargaining on plans. This leaves each plan in a weak bargaining position, and the only escape valve is dumping people from the plan and passing on higher costs. A united effort by labor and management to change the system rather than each other could be very successful.

THE NATURE OF THE CRISIS

The papers by Cathy Schoen and Richard Brown demonstrate that there are two main dimensions to the crisis in the U.S. health care system: *cost* and *access*. It is not sufficient to attack only one, for this leads to negative effects on the other. For example, fixing hospital fees will hurt hospitals that serve low-income patients and exacerbate the access problems. Likewise, insuring more people without controlling costs will perpetuate the cost spiral in health care. Schoen and Brown outline the reasons for spiraling costs and the nature of our access problem.

There are several common themes to the papers as the authors diagnose the crisis in the health care system and the root causes of the cost and access problems. The U.S. system differs greatly from those of other industrialized countries, and these differences are now being identified as part of the problem:

- It is a voluntary system, not a universal system.
- It is fragmented, based on employer plans with multiple financing and delivery arrangements.
- Providers have relative autonomy to set fees, with few procedures for uniform pricing.
- There is no public debate on how much to spend on health care, no procedure to set health care budgets, access, and services provided.

These structural factors contribute to problems related to costs (including cost shifting), access, quality, and accountability.

POSSIBILITIES FOR REFORM

Richard Brown outlines a continuum of possible reforms, each with advantages and disadvantages. Generally, suggested reforms range from proposals to insure the uninsured to complete structural reform and adoption of a universal system with public financing.

The authors of the articles in this section all agree that national reform is necessary, but none are willing to wait for Congressional leadership. David Schreck and Paul Petrie note that Canadian health care reform began in the provinces, and John Kitzhaber persuasively shows why states better understand the problem and are more motivated to act that national leaders. Indeed, the action on health care reform in the U.S. is at the state level.

Several states are discussing structural reform, from reforming the private insurance market to adoption of a universal system that is publicly funded, such as Canada's single-payer system. Proponents of a single-payer system contend that major reform is necessary to reduce administrative inefficiencies, provide universal access, contain health care costs, and provide choice to consumers. The article by David Schreck and Paul Petrie outline the principles of the Canadian system: universality, comprehensiveness, accountability, public administration, and choice.

Such proposals have a number of vocal critics, including current insurance carriers and providers. Critics of the Canadian system are publishing reports on its weaknesses. However, as Schreck and Petrie point out, these weaknesses prompt a public debate in Canada on how to improve the system—the Canadian system has strong support in Canada, and there are no serious proposals to alter its fundamental nature. They summarize their position by stating that the "most important lesson to learn from the Canadian experience is that health insurance is better run as a public monopoly." Schreck and Petrie also present the origin of the Canadian system and its current controversies.

Dr. John Kitzhaber, a physician and President of the Oregon State Senate, explains why states better understand the health care crisis and are more motivated to act than the federal government. He discusses three realities involving fiscal limits, providing health care versus achieving health, and the debate about *what*, rather than *who*, should be covered in the health care system.

Paying Too Much, Buying Too Little: U.S. Medical Care on the Critical List

CATHY SCHOEN

Economist; National Policy and Finance Advisor, Service Employees Internatinal Union

THE DIMENSIONS OF THE CRISIS

The United States, for a variety of historical reasons, is the only major industrialized country that continues to rely on voluntary, private insurance and market price mechanisms to provide affordable health care. Although every public opinion poll since the 1930s has shown broad public support for universal coverage, enactment of Medicare in 1965 for citizens over sixty-five remains the first and last step the U.S. has taken on the road to entitlement (Blendon, 1990).

Until the late 1970s, there was still some hope that we could reach most citizens through voluntary efforts. From World War II on, bargaining demands by unions pushed the voluntary, employment-based approach to cover more and more families. With costs relatively low compared to wages, nonunion as well as union employers began signing on to an implicit social contract that health insurance should be a basic component of all jobs.

By 1976 the proportion of uninsured had plummeted from 70 percent in 1950 to 11 percent—leaving "only" twenty-three million people with no coverage (USDHEW, 1975, 1978). The 1980s have rewritten the end of the story. Today the U.S. experiment is on the verge of collapse. Exploding costs and declining access now threaten basic coverage for middle-as well as lower-income families.

Costs: The U. S. Is Number One

For insured workers the relentless escalation in costs is the most visible sign of the crisis. Average premium costs for basic plans have been rising 20 percent or more per year for the majority of health plans. Plan costs are doubling every three to four years, and all forecasts indicate the trends will continue. Today a typical single-person plan costs $2,000 a year and a family plan over $5,000—double the rates in 1987 (SEIU, 1990).

Nationally, per person spending on health care has soared from $205 in 1965 to $1,059 in 1970 and to over $2,500 in 1990. With increasing health plan costs dwarfing wage increases, each year an ever larger share of our income is transferred out of our pockets into the pockets of physicians, insurance and drug companies, and hospitals. We now spend 11.5 percent of our national income on health compared to 6 percent in 1965 (Levit et al., 1990).

Costs have soared despite major changes in insurance coverage designed to control costs. Free choice of physicians and hospitals is now the exception, not the norm. HMO enrollment has increased dramatically, and even traditional fee for service plans now include preferred lists of doctors and hospitals with major financial penalties for selections off the list.[1]

We have added layers of administrative controls to try to slow costs. It's a rare plan that doesn't require anoutsidereviewer'sapprovalbeforeadmission to a hospital or second opinions on expensivecare.

Meanwhile,insurancebenefitsaredown: we'repayingmoreofthebillsoutofourown pockets. Deductibles,copayments,and eligibility restrictions force patients to pay moreoutoftheirownpockets (Short,1988; Department of Labor, 1989). Nationally, directpaymentsbypatientsaccountfor21 percent of all spending; private insurance accounts for only 32 percent (Levit, 1990).

We'vecreatedthemostexpensivehealth systeminthe worlddespitealloureffortsat costcontrol.Ourannualperpersonspending is double that of Europe and Japan and 38 percent more than Canada, the next mostexpensivecountry.

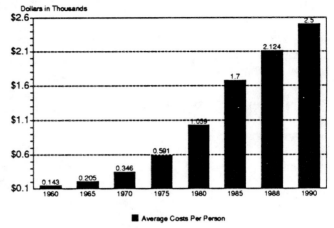

FIGURE 1. HEALTH COSTS SOAR

Dollars in Thousands

Source: Health Care Financing Administration

Furthermore, the gap is growing. U.S. and Canada, for example, both spent roughly the same proportionofnationalincomeonhealthcareatthebeginningof1970whenallCanadianprovincescame intoCanada'snationalplan. (Webothspentslightlyunder7.5percent.) By1990theU.S. wasspending 11.5percent,andrising,whileCanadaspent8.6percentandheldtheproportionrelativelysteadyinthe 1980s. (Schieber, 1990)

Forunions,escalatingcostsmeanthatwenowmustfightwithemployerstosimplykeepwhatwe've hadforyears.Whileunionsinallourmajorindustrialtradingpartnerstookhealthcareoffthebargaining table years ago, health benefits have become a major strike issue and a major source of labor and management friction across the U.S. In 1989, health care strikes accounted for at least $1.1 billion in lost production (SEIU, 1990). The long-term corrosion of U.S. labor and management's ability to work togetherinthefaceofstiffinternationalcompetitionislikelytobedevastating.

Rise in Uninsured and Underinsured

Soaringcostshaveputanendtoanyhopethatvoluntarycoverage wouldbringaboutuniversality. Despitethehighestaverageperpersoncostsintheworld,todayelevenmillionmorepeoplearetotally uninsuredthanadecadeago.Therearethirty-fivetothirty-sevenmillionpeoplewithnocoveragefrom anysource.Thisamountstonearlyoneoutoffivepeopleunderagesixty-five (Chollet,1989,Monheit 1989).

Another20to50millionpeopleareinadequatelyinsuredagainstthecostofseriousillness.[2]Yesterday's standardplanisquicklybecomingtoday'sremnantofthepastasplansimposehigheremployeepremium shares,higherdeductibles,copayments,and totaldollarlimitsperservice.

Takentogethertheuninsuredandunderinsuredrepresent30to40percentofthepopulation.Thevast majority(75to80percent)ofuninsuredandunderinsuredareworkingfamilies—includingfamilieswith full-time, year-round jobs. Escalatingcostsarerippingapartthe implicitsocialcontract with U.S. employersthattheywouldvoluntarilyprovidedecentcoverageforalltheiremployees.

Someemployershavedroppedcoveragealtogether—orasnewbusinessesneverofferedaplan.Others havelookedtoescapebyconvertingjobstopart-timeortemporarystatus,byhiringcontractlabororby contracting work to nonunion, nonbenefit employers.[3] The latest strategy is to encourage employees to move to their spouse's plan. Cash bribes for dropping coverage and high premiums have lured and shoved families from one plan to another.

Public programs have also cut back eligibility. Medicaid—the federal-state program for low-income elderly and families—now covers 46 percent of the poor, compared to nearly two-thirds in the late 1970s (Blendon, 1986).

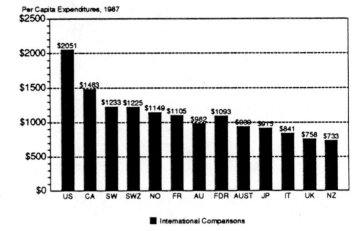

FIGURE 2. U.S. MOST EXPENSIVE

Per Capita Expenditures, 1987

■ International Comparisons

Source: Shieber, FCFR 1989

FORCES DRIVING COSTS UP: DISPELLING THE MYTHS

Some would argue that our high costs are simply the price we must pay for quality or that insurance itself is a problem because it protects families from the immediate costs of their illness. Such arguments are used worldwide by those who would erode coverage or argue for reduced controls on medical care providers.

We can use the U.S. experience to dispel such myths. The two lessons we can teach are that: (1) paying for whatever the medical community bills does not buy quality; and (2) making patients pay when they are sick does little to control costs.

Quality: High Price, Poor Results

Apologists for the dual crisis of costs and access will often respond, "Yes, but we have the best care in the world—and you have to pay a lot for the best."

The facts tell a different story. Virtually every study of the health outcome of care finds the U.S. buys less measurable health status. U.S. babies are twice as likely to die before they reach their first birthday than in countries with the best records—and we're behind twenty-one other countries. Our life expectancy is two to three years shorter than the world leaders, and survival rates from heart disease are worse than twenty-three other countries (USHHS, 1990; WHO, 1989; OECD, 1987).

Moreover, new research studies repeatedly find that much of what we do buy in the name of health care is either pure waste, ineffective, or even harmful to our

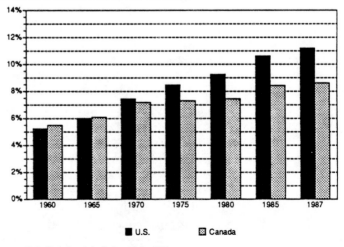

FIGURE 3. WHAT PRICE PLURALISM

■ U.S.   ▨ Canada

Note: Canada puts in single payer by 1970
Source: OECD, Health Affairs, Fall 1989

280

health. The National Leadership Commission on Health Care summarized its review of the evidence:

> As much as 20 to 30 percent of all things done by well-meaning physicians in good hospitals is either inappropriate, ineffective, unnecessary, or sometimes harmful (National Leadership Commission, 1989).

Patients: Overuse Not the Problem

Consultants urging further erosion of benefits often cloak the effort to shift costs to patients by claiming patients will become better "consumers" and that too much insurance is the cause of escalating costs.

Comparison with the rest of the world should by itself put the lie to rest. We are the only major OECD country that restricts choice and makes patients pay significant fees when they use hospital, surgical, and medical care—yet every other country covers everyone for less.

Detailed health insurance data in the U.S. help shatter the myth altogether. Most U.S health plans do not cover bills in full and have erected complex controls to discourage patient decisions to seek doctor or hospital care unless necessary.

In SEIU we've examined plans with controls and without, and we've found a similar story—patient visits to the doctor and admissions to hospitals simply are not rising. If anything, use is down per person compared to earlier years.

In fact, the vast majority of the women, men, and children covered even by generous plans use few or no services during the year. For example, New Hampshire state employees found that 50 percent of the people covered by their plan had no claims paid during the year; 83 percent had claims of $1,000 or less—and these claims accounted for only 10 percent of total plan expenses (New Hampshire, 1989). Costs were high because prices, tests, and procedures were high for very sick patients and surgery—heart attacks, cancer, premature infants, C-sections. Put simply, it takes a lot of doctor visits for possible ear infections to come close to the cost of one $250,000 premature infant.

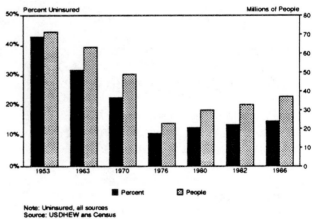

FIGURE 4. REVERSAL IN COVERAGE TRENDS

Note: Uninsured, all sources
Source: USDHEW ans Census

Forces Behind Escalating Costs

There are three major forces driving up costs—all having little to do with quality or patient decisions to seek medical care.

1. Excess Inflation: Prices Charged by Medical Care Providers Rise at Twice the Rate of General Prices

The separate efforts of employer plans, trust funds, and public plans have left each plan in a vulnerable position in negotiating prices with insurance carriers, physicians, hospitals, or drug companies. Each plan runs the risk that providers will simply walk away from patients or charge patients the "excess" the plan will not pay.

The result is that medical care prices and administrative charges continue to soar well above general inflation rates. Excess inflation accounts for roughly one-third of our premium increases each year (Hewitt, 1989).

Expenditures for administrative waste are also increasing. Private insurance company charges add an average 13 percent to the costs of coverage. For small groups the add-on costs can be as high as 40 to 50 percent. In comparison, administration of the U.S. Medicare program adds only 2.7 percent to claims costs (Levit, 1990). The difference is the costs of marketing, profits, constant turnover in the insured group, and inefficient administration.

The contrast with Canada is startling. Eliminating marketing, eligibility tests, and complex benefits has held administrative costs to .1 percent of national income compared to .6 percent in the U.S. (Evans, 1986). If we were as efficient as Canada in running our insurance programs, we would have saved over $20 billion in 1988, more than we spent as a nation on public health and home health care.

This excludes the effect on hospital and doctor costs of more than 1,500 different private insurance carriers and millions of different group plans using different claims forms, different fee schedules, and different control methods. Every hospital and every physician's office must separately track each patient's bills.

The paperwork costs are enormous. Physicians in Massachusetts, for example, found that while their hospital required 300 billing clerks and a multimillion dollar computer to link patients to each cost item, a similar hospital in Toronto needed only two clerks—and these two clerks are mainly busy billing U.S. citizens who happened to become sick in Canada (Bernard, 1990).

2. Cost Shift

For employee plans, prices rise even faster than national trends due to providers' ability to shift costs not paid by large public plans and the uninsured onto privately insured patients' bills. A discount demanded by a big plan with large market share becomes a cost to smaller, less powerful groups. The spread in prices can be dramatic. In California we found that private plans paid over $11,000 for coronary bypass surgery while Medicare paid $5,500 and Medicaid paid only $2,300 (SEIU, 1990).

Estimates put cost shifting at some 30 percent of the increase in premium costs for employee plans.

3. Volume

At the same time, providers are submitting more bills per patient each year despite relatively constant or declining hospital admission rates. Lab tests, prescriptions per patient, MRI scans, out-of-hospital surgery, and the like are all increasing. Some of this increase in claims per patient results from billing for each separate item instead of a comprehensive rate. Some is the result of duplicate tests, and some results from increased procedure rates across the board.

The growing practice of physicians entering into joint ventures as co-owners of diagnostic testing facilities encourages such increases—profits increase with use of the center.

Volume increases account for 12 percent or more of premium increases.

DIVIDED WE FALL

As individual unions or employer plans, we are rapidly coming to the end of in-plan controls that offer any potential of cost control without loss of benefits or quality. As individual plans, our bargaining position is too weak to challenge the ongoing transfer of income from us to the medical industry.

Divided into multiple groups and among multiple insurance carriers, any plan trying to drive a hard bargain risks providers turning away from patients or billing patients over and above what the plan will pay. With the exception of the federal government, no single plan has enough clout to make a take-it-or-leave-it offer.

Employers and public plans could, of course, embark on collective action to increase their power relative to insurance carriers, physicians, drug companies, and the like. However, building alliances, agreeing to collective action and policing voluntary compliance requires discipline and work.

The voluntary nature and fragmented structure of U.S. health care has given each payer an easier solution—escape rather than solve the problem. Each of our plans is mainly concerned with its own budget. Once a plan has exhausted the in-plan laundry list of administrative or structural savings, no rules prevent payers from trying to dump people or cut benefits as the next "easiest" cost control strategies. Yet, communitywide total costs continue to escalate. Costs have been moved, not controlled.

The rapidly growing U.S. consultant industry feeds into this narrow focus. Deductibles, copayments, premium sharing, eligibility restrictions, limits on coverage, waiting periods, and cafeteria plans limiting employer payments head the list of strategies. Meanwhile, only a rare consultant can tell you how much more the insurance carrier has made this year than last or how much prices charged to the plan have increased or where medical providers are double or excess billing. And even rarer still is the consultant advising employers to stop the erosion of coverage and instead build communitywide all-payer coalitions.

Divided, we focus on narrow budget concerns rather than the difficult task of building a power base to negotiate with those who make their living from our health care dollars. We know from our U.S. administrative cost experience alone that diversity and fragmentation come with a high price tag. Far more devastating is the fact that as long as the escape door remains open, access and cost are pitted against each other as competing rather than complementary goals.

The Potential of Collective Action: Lessons from Canada and Europe

It doesn't have to be this way. Canada and Europe have taught us that for the money we now spend we could bring everyone in and improve quality of care. While countries differ in how they structure their systems, all share key concepts:

Universality—everyone's in: The escape door of cutting benefits or people has been closed, forcing community and national efforts to focus on control while guaranteeing access.

Uniform pricing: In any given area, prices are negotiated for all citizens together. Physicians or hospitals cannot charge different prices for the same service. Patients enter on an equal footing and, even where there are multiple plans, plans are united when it comes to bargaining with medical care providers.

Budgets: Budget controls and targets limit the potential that increased volume will undermine efforts to control costs.

Capital: Communities decide collectively on the need to expand expensive equipment

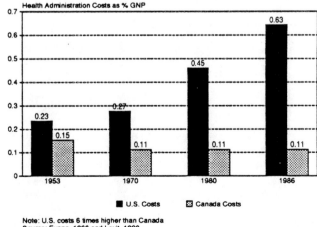

FIGURE 5. U.S. ADMINISTRATIVE COSTS SOAR

Health Administration Costs as % GNP

Year	U.S. Costs	Canada Costs
1953	0.23	0.15
1970	0.27	0.11
1980	0.45	0.11
1986	0.63	0.11

■ U.S. Costs ▨ Canada Costs

Note: U.S. costs 6 times higher than Canada
Source: Evans, 1966 and Levit, 1990

283

and buildings rather than pay first and evaluate later.

From Understanding to Action

We need to move now from understanding to action. Labor and management in the U.S. are locked in bitter battles over who will pay for escalating costs while all of our major competitors have taken the issue off the bargaining table. It is in none of our interests to pay ever-escalating costs, regardless of whose budget shows the price tag. Ultimately all of our incomes and the nation's health are at stake.

We need to join together to mobilize for change. We have three key strategies to turn crisis into opportunity.

First, we must stop the cuts in coverage and benefits. We need to keep employer and public plans in the game and remove the option of simply not playing.

Second, we need to educate each other and the general public. We can draw from the experience of Canada and Europe to give us a vision of what is possible. This vision will be critical to counter the media campaign by those who make their living from the high cost of U.S. health care.

Finally, we need to mobilize a broad coalition. Children's groups, civil rights groups, senior citizens, churches, the women's movement, and even business all share organized labor's dream of securing affordable health care. The polls tell us the support is there. Nine out of ten U.S. citizens believe fundamental change is necessary; two-thirds would prefer the Canadian system to the one we have (Blendon, 1990).

Mobilization can turn opinion polls into action. Visits to legislators, visible public actions, workshops, and coalition building to fight specific cuts all offer opportunities to build political pressure. Our common demand is that politicians put comprehensive reform on the top of their list and stop defining the problem only in terms of the uninsured.

ENDNOTES

[1] For example, the California State Employees Blue Shield plan will pay 90 percent of the costs of hospital, surgery, and medical care after a $200-per-person deductible with a cap of $1,000-per-person total out-of-pocket costs if the patient uses the preferred list. If the patient goes out of the network she must pay 40 percent of the bills after the deductible, with a cap of $3,000 out of pocket. The plan's 60 percent is only for allowable charges. Out-of-network providers can and do charge more than the plan's fee allowances.

[2] Studies of insurance adequacy compared the extent of protection against costs relative to family income. For middle- and lower-income families, Pamela Farley, for example, rated a family inadequately covered if illness costs not covered by insurance would amount to 10 percent or more of income (Farley, 1985).

[3] Including self-employed single workers, contract, part-time, and temporary jobs now account for 35 percent of all jobs compared to 26 percent at the beginning of the 1980s (Sweeney and Nussbaum, p. 56, 1989).

REFERENCES

Bernard, Elaine. National Education Association meeting remarks, September, 1990.

Blendon, Robert J., et al. "Satisfaction with Health Systems in Ten Nations." *Health Affairs.* 185–92, Summer, 1990.

———. "Uncompensated Care by Hospitals or Public Insurance for the Poor: Does It Make a Difference?" *New England Journal of Medicine.* 314(18):1160–63, May, 1986.

Blendon, Robert J., and Karen Donelan. "Special Report: The Public and the Emerging Debate over National Health Insurance." *New England Journal of Medicine.* 323(3):208–12, July, 1990.

Chollet, Deborah. *Uninsured in the United States, 1987–88.* Employee Benefit Research Institute, 1989.

EBRI. "Government Mandating of Employee Benefits." Employee Benefit Research Institute, 1987, 161.

Evans, Robert G. "Finding the Levers, Finding the Courage: Lessons from Cost Containment in North America." *Journal of*

Health Politics, Policy, and Law. 11(4):585–620, 1986.

Farley, Pamela J. "Who Are the Underinsured?" *Milbank Memorial Fund Quarterly.* 63(3):476–503, 1985.

Hewitt Associates. "Sources of Premium Cost Increases." Data, 1989.

Levit, Katherine R., Mark S. Freeland, and Daniel R. Waldo. "National Health Care Spending Trends." *Health Affairs.* 171–84, Summer, 1990.

Monheit, Alan C., and Pamela Farley Short. "Mandating Health Coverage for Working Americans." *Health Affair.* 22–38, Winter, 1989.

New Hampshire State Employees Health Plan. Blue Cross Blue Shield, data, 1989.

Organization for Economic Cooperation and Development, (OECD) Health Data File, 1987. Health Care Financing Review, International Comparisons of Health Care Financing and Delivery. Annual Supplement, 1989.

Schieber, George J., and Jean-Pierre Poullier. "Overview of International Comparisons of Health Care Expenditures." *Health Care Financing Review Supplement.* 1–8, 1989.

Service Employees, International Union (SEIU). *California Health Care: On the Critical List.* March, 1990.

SEIU. "1989–1990 Survey Data." Internal Public Policy Department.

SEIU. *Labor and Management on a Collision Course Over Health Care.* February, 1990.

Short, Pamela Farley. "Trends in Employee Health Benefits." *Health Affairs.* 186–208, Summer, 1988.

Sweeney, John J., and Karen Nussbaum. *Solutions for the New Work Force: Policies for a New Social Contract.* Seven Locks Press, 1989.

U.S. Department of Health Education and Welfare. Health: United States, 1978 Table 164, 1978.

U.S. Department of Health Education and Welfare. Health: United States, 1975 Table A.23, 1975.

U.S. Department of Health and Human Services, Health U.S. 1989.

U.S. Bureau of Labor Statistics. "Employee Benefits in Medium and Large Firms." 1989.

Winslow, Constance, et al. "The Appropriateness of Carotid Endarterectomy." *New England Journal of Medicine.* 318:721–27, March 24, 1988.

World Health Organization. *Annual Health Statistics.* 1987.

The Uninsured and Rising Health Care Costs: The Problems and What We Can Do about Them

E. RICHARD BROWN

Professor, UCLA, School of Public Health; Associate Director, UCLA Center for Health Promotion and Disease Prevention

During the 1980s, the United States has been battered by two fundamental problems related to the financing of health services. One problem is the growing number of people who are uninsured for health care expenses. A second problem is the soaring cost for health care and for health insurance. The combined pressure of these two forces has generated growing political support for broad reforms.

THE UNINSURED

The uninsured increased dramatically between 1979 and 1986.

Between 1979 and 1986, the number of Americans without any health insurance coverage—without private insurance, Medicare, Medicaid or other coverage—increased from twenty-nine million to thirty-seven million, 17.6 percent of the population under age sixty-five.[1]

Three-fourths of these eight million additional uninsured were added by the growing rate at which people had no health care coverage. If the proportion of the population without health insurance had remained at the 1979 level of 14.8 percent of the nonelderly population, six million fewer people would have been uninsured.

The problem in some regions and states is even more severe than for the country as a whole. Larger proportions of the populations of Southern and Southwestern states are uninsured.

The Uninsured are Disproportionately Young, Low-income and, Ethnic Minorities

One-third of all the uninsured are children under the age of eighteen, another third are between eighteen and twenty-nine years of age, and the rest are between thirty and sixty-four years of age. One out of every five American children has no private insurance, Medicaid, or any other coverage. Young adults are most at risk for being uninsured; one in four persons between eighteen and twenty-nine years of age were without any protection in 1986.

Half of all the uninsured are poor or near-poor children and adults (in 1986, less than $16,800 for a family of four). Nevertheless, a large proportion of the uninsured are not poor at all: 23 percent of the uninsured have family incomes at least three times the poverty level ($33,600 or more for a family of four).

Low-income persons are much more likely to be uninsured than the more affluent population. In 1986, 38 percent of those with family incomes below the poverty line ($11,200 for a family of four) and 35 percent of those just above the poverty line had no coverage from private plans or public programs, compared to 18 percent of those with family incomes between 150 percent and 299 percent of the poverty line and just 8 percent of the more affluent population.

One in every three Latino children and adults was uninsured in 1986, the highest rate among all ethnic groups. Although lower than the rate for Latinos, the proportions of uninsured Blacks and Asians and other ethnic groups are also higher than the rate for non-Latino whites.

A Majority of the Uninsured Are Workers

The uninsured are predominantly workers and their families. Working people themselves constitute more than half the uninsured (51 percent)—nearly nineteen million persons in 1986. Working people and their children together represent at least three-fourths of all the uninsured. The proportion of all workers who had no health care coverage increased from 12 percent in 1979 to 15 percent in 1986.

Three-fourths of all persons with any private or public health benefits get their coverage through their own or a family member's employment. It is not surprising, therefore, that 77 percent of full-time full-year employees were covered by their employer's health plan in 1986. Although 15 percent received coverage through the insurance of another family member or some other source, 8 percent of full-time full-year employees were completely uninsured—and they account for 35 percent of all uninsured employees. The uninsured rates for full-time part-year and part-time employees are three times the rates for full-time full-year employees. The lack of insurance coverage is especially great among self-employed workers.

Employees of small firms are much more likely to be uninsured than those in medium- and large-size firms. One-third of all persons who work for an employer with less than ten employees are completely uninsured (Short, et al., 1989; Small Business Administration, 1987).

The decrease in employment-based insurance coverage among workers and their families is due in large part to a decline in employment in manufacturing and other high-wage, union firms and to an increase in the retail and service sectors of the economy. Among all workers whose employers do not offer health benefits, 38 percent worked in retail firms with fewer than twenty-five employees (Small Business Administration, 1987).

FIGURE 1. UNINSURED BY WORKING STATUS, UNDER AGE 65, U.S., 1986

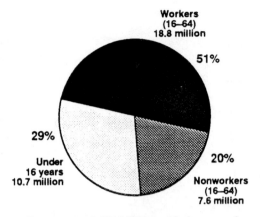

Percent of 37 Million Uninsured

Current Population Survey, 1987

FIGURE 2. PERCENT WITH HEALTH BENEFITS AND UNINSURED BY FULL–TIME, PART–TIME STATUS, EMPLOYEES, AGES 16-64, U.S., 1986

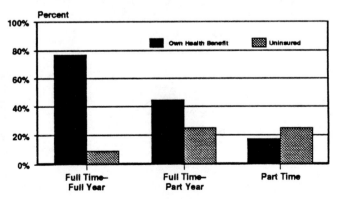

Full–Time, Part–Time Status

Current Population Survey, 1987

287

WHY IS THE GROWING LACK OF HEALTH INSURANCE A PROBLEM?

First, compared to people with health insurance coverage, the uninsured have much less access to necessary medical care. They are less likely to see a physician in a year, less likely to get their young children adequately immunized, less likely to receive prenatal care in the first trimester of pregnancy, less likely to have their blood pressure checked, and only half as likely to see a physician within thirty days if they have serious symptoms, such as persistent high fever, nausea, or bleeding (Davis and Rowland, 1983; Freeman, 1987; Freeman, et al., 1987).

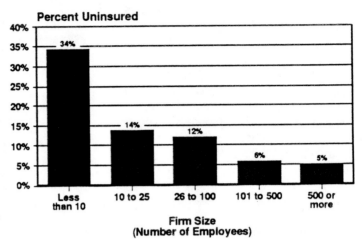

FIGURE 3. UNINSURED ELPOYEES BY FIRM SIZE, UNDER AGE 65, U.S., 1987

Nat'l Medical Expenditure Survey, 1987

Second, reduced access to medical care due to lack of insurance coverage may contribute to a severe decline in individuals' health status. Research studies have found that pregnant women and their children and persons with chronic illness are especially at risk (Lurie, et al., 1984 and 1986; Braveman, et al., 1986).

Finally, although the uninsured get less care than the insured population, everyone pays for care that the uninsured do receive. When the uninsured need urgent care, they usually go to hospitals and clinics. Uncompensated care (bad debts and charity care) cost hospitals in California, for example, $975 million in fiscal year 1985–86, 84 percent more than in 1981–82, 49 percent more after adjusting for inflation. Individual and business taxpayers shoulder the financial burden of uncompensated care provided by public hospitals—$468 million in care given by California's county hospitals in 1985–86 (Sofaer, et al., 1988). Despite these large sums and dedication of their staffs, state and county programs and services for the medically indigent are depressingly underfunded, understaffed, and ill-equipped to meet this population's needs for medical care (Brown and Dallek, 1990).

Employers and employees pay for much of the uncompensated care provided by private hospitals. But as such "cost shifting" has become more difficult over the last few years, more and more private hospitals have found ways to keep out uninsured patients. Hospitals in many cities throughout the country have sporadically closed their emergency rooms, others have downgraded them permanently, shutting their emergency room doors to "911" rescue ambulances, and many have closed their trauma centers. These actions affect the entire community—people with insurance as well as the uninsured.

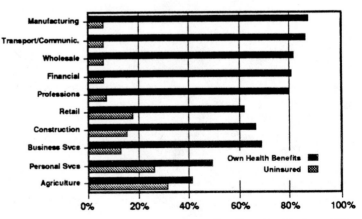

FIGURE 4. HEALTH BENEFITS & UNINSURED BY INDUSTRY, FULL–TIME, FULL–YEAR EMPLOYEES, AGES 16-65, U.S., 1986

Current Population Survey, 1987

288

RISING HEALTH CARE COSTS

The other major health insurance problem that plagues the United States is the rapid increase in expenditures for medical care. Health care in the United States has been consuming an ever greater share of our economic resources, from 6 percent of our gross national product in 1965 to more than 11 percent today. Part of the increase in total expenditures is due to the rapid increase in the costs and prices of medical care, which have been growing at a faster rate than inflation in the rest of the economy. Much of the increase in total medical care spending is due to an increasing "intensity" of services provided to each patient, many of which are neither necessary nor effective.

The United States spends more than any other country in the world on health care—38 percent more per capita than the second most expensive health system, Canada's, which covers its entire population through a universal government-run, tax-funded health insurance program in each province.

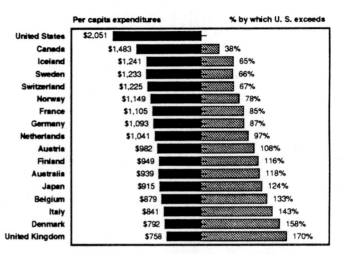

FIGURE 5. PER CAPITA HEALTH SPENDING, SELECTED OECD COUNTRIES, 1987

	Per capita expenditures	% by which U. S. exceeds
United States	$2,051	
Canada	$1,483	38%
Iceland	$1,241	65%
Sweden	$1,233	66%
Switzerland	$1,225	67%
Norway	$1,149	78%
France	$1,105	85%
Germany	$1,093	87%
Netherlands	$1,041	97%
Austria	$982	108%
Finland	$949	116%
Australia	$939	118%
Japan	$915	124%
Belgium	$879	133%
Italy	$841	143%
Denmark	$792	158%
United Kingdom	$758	170%

OECD Data, Health Affairs, *Fall 1989*

Do We Get Adequate Value for Our Higher Spending?

Despite greater per capita health care spending, health indicators in the United States demonstrate that we should be getting more for our money. Many less-developed countries have lower infant mortality and as good or better life expectancy than the United States. Nineteen other industrialized countries, for example, had lower infant mortality rates in 1987 than the United States.

One reason we get less value than we should for the amount we spend is that more of our health dollars are spent on administration than in other countries. The United States has the most expensive "system" of administration and financing in the world. Much of this excess is due to our fragmented insurance and payment system. Canadian health economist Robert Evans estimates that the costs of running our myriad insurance and payment systems, not including any expenditures for patient care, "may account for more than half the difference in cost between the Canadian and the U.S. systems" (Evans, et al., 1989).

During the 1970s and 1980s, administrative costs have increased further as a share of total health care spending, pushed up by intensive marketing by insurers and by the rising economic burden of cost-containment efforts in a system in which financial incentives on providers encourage excess utilization and discourage cost control.

Health Insurance Has Become Unaffordable for Many

Higher medical care costs mean higher premiums. As costs of care escalated, health benefits costs rose accordingly. Between 1977 and 1987, average premium contributions for employment-based health benefits per person covered increased 49 percent in inflation-adjusted dollars, from $1,111 to $1,656 (both figures in 1987 dollars) (DiCarlo and Gabel, 1989). Every year, employers get hit with substantial double-digit increases in the costs for health benefits (Gabel, et al., 1989).

Small firms have been hit very hard by rising health care costs and insurance premiums. Certainly one factor that contributes to the high cost of insurance for individual firms and employer trusts is experience rating,[2] which has isolated smaller risk groups and exposed them to ever-escalating rates.

Rising costs have made it difficult for small businesses to purchase insurance. The health insurance market for small groups is drying up throughout the country: since 1988, at least thirty-four insurers have stopped selling group policies to small businesses in California (Reich, 1989; White, 1990). Finding health insurance for small groups in which one or more members have a preexisting medical condition is difficult for even the most dedicated insurance broker. Moreover, as more insurers move from community to experience rating, employers have seen their health insurance premiums skyrocket.

Employers who do provide insurance have responded to rising health benefits

FIGURE 6. BUSINESS HEALTH SPENDING AS SHARE OF WAGES/SALARIES, U.S., 1965-1987

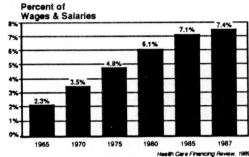

FIGURE 7. BUSINESS HEALTH SPENDING AS SHARE OF CORPORATE PROFIT, U.S., 1965-1987

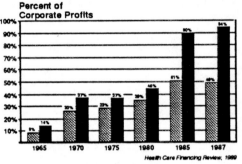

costs by encouraging or forcing their employees to join managed-care plans and by shifting more of the costs of coverage to employees. Employers have been increasing required cost sharing by employees for premiums and for medical care (Short, 1988; Jensen, et al., 1987). Despite these efforts to control their own costs, many employers are at their wits' end. As Clark Kerr, the president of the California Council of Employer Health Care Coalitions, has said, "We have tried a lot of things—utilization review, case management, cost sharing with employees, health maintenance organizations, preferred provider organizations, hospices—and costs are still going up 20 to 30 to 40 percent" (Holzman, 1989, pp. 54–55).

These cost increases have extracted a greater share of workers' earnings and of corporate profits. Between 1965 and 1987, the cost of health benefits has grown from about 2 percent of wages and salaries to more than 7 percent. And it has jumped from 14 percent of after-tax profits of corporations to 94 percent. The financial losses inflicted on business and labor, together with increasing labor-management conflicts and strikes over health benefits, have pushed political support for solutions to the problem to an all-time high.

SOLVING THE PROBLEMS: PUBLIC POLICY OPTIONS

These two health care financing problems are inextricably linked. A large and growing uninsured population has little access to necessary medical care. When they do get care, the uninsured add to the hospital bills, insurance premiums, and taxes of others. Universal coverage of the population would provide more equitable access to health care and end uncompensated-care cost shifting to employers, employees, and government.

Rising health care costs, the second major health care financing problem we face, are straining the economic resources of employers, workers, and their families, as well as all levels of government. The high costs of health care and health insurance make it increasingly difficult for small employers and low-income people to pay for health benefits. This problem, like the problem of insurance coverage, can be solved most effectively by major reforms in our health care financing system.

The approaches to the problem now being considered range from incremental, targeted strategies—proposals that would extend coverage to some groups of the uninsured—to strategies that would completely reform the financing of health care—proposals that would provide insurance to the entire population by completely reforming the health insurance market or by establishing a universal health services financing program.

The Failure of Voluntary Approaches

Some states and private groups, hoping to avoid enacting mandatory programs, have been experimenting with tax credits to encourage employers to cover their uninsured employees. Small employers' participation is influenced by the very factors that now discourage them from providing this fringe benefit—low-profit margins and the high cost of insurance—adding up to a competitive disadvantage for those who would add increased labor costs to their products or services (Small Business Administration, 1987). Few small employers are buying into such programs because the cost remains high, for both employer and employee, and because participation remains voluntary. In the end, relatively few of the uninsured can be expected to participate in and benefit from these programs (Brown and Dallek, 1990).

Employer Mandates

The most dramatic incremental policy option that is being considered is to require employers to provide health benefits to their workers. The high cost of government-subsidized health coverage programs has encouraged legislators in many states and members of the Congress to propose laws that would mandate employers to provide coverage to their employees and dependents. This strategy would place the full cost of such health insurance on employers and their workers. An employer mandate in Hawaii, enacted in the mid-1970s, has helped to maintain a relatively high rate of coverage in that state (Brown, et al., 1987). This has obvious advantages for the state, but it has significant limitations.

One limitation of a state-enacted mandate is that it would require a Congressional exemption from the federal Employee Retirement and Income Security Act (ERISA). Hawaii is the only state that has been exempted by the Congress from ERISA's provisions, which preempt state regulation of employers' self-insured health plans. Most observers are not optimistic about Congress opening up the ERISA Pandora's box, despite the interest of several states that are exploring this option.

Another limitation of the employer-mandate strategy is that it would not cover the entire uninsured population, although it would obviously cover far more than strategies that rely on voluntary participation of employers. The effectiveness of this strategy depends upon what cut-points are adopted: how many hours per week an employee would have to work to be covered; whether small employers would be exempted, and if so, how small; and whether coverage would have to be extended to employees' dependents. The Kennedy-Waxman and Stark bills in the Congress would apply to firms of all sizes and would cover employees who work at least seventeen and a half hours a week and their dependents. The Kennedy-Waxman bill has been estimated to cover about two-thirds of the 37 million uninsured in the U.S., although recent versions have included a public program to cover those left out of the employer mandate.

A variation on the employer-mandate approach is the "play or pay" strategy that was recently adopted,

291

but not yet implemented, by Massachusetts. "Play or pay" would require all employers to pay a special health care payroll tax to the state, but employers would receive a credit against this tax for the amount they spend on comparable health benefits. With the revenues from this payroll tax and other taxes, the state would purchase health insurance from contract health plans and sell it, at subsidized rates, to otherwise uninsured people.

By aggregating coverage from several different public and private financing sources, the federal or state governments theoretically could extend coverage to their entire populations, many of them heavily subsidized by tax dollars. But the substantial share of cost required even from fairly low-income employees and individuals would make such coverage less than universal. And the high cost of government subsidies makes the whole approach less attractive politically, undermining the main impetus for this strategy.

Still another limitation of employer mandates is that they would not control health care costs for employers, employees, or others. Rather, they would impose a significant cost on small employers and their employees, and they offer no reason for optimism that the double-digit inflation in health care premiums experienced by large as well as small employers would be restrained. Employers, together with their employees, are very frustrated by their inability to control the costs of their health benefits, and they want some relief. Because of its impact on small businesses and general business opposition to government regulation, business groups have heavily attacked employer mandate proposals.

Comparison of Reform Strategies' Advantages and Disadvantages
Advantages and Disadvantages

	Employer Mandate	Market Reform	National Health Insurance
Employment-Based?	Yes	Yes	No
Population Coverage	Some left out	All have access to insurance	All are covered
Coverage of Poor	Separate programs/plans	Separate programs/plans	One universal program for all
Revenue Sources	Highly regressive	May be more progressive	Much more progressive
Cost Containment	None or very little	Moderate, but complex	Effective and less complex
Allocation of Resources	Market only	Market only	Planning and market
Accountability	Market insularity	Market plus some regulation	Direct political control plus market

Universal Coverage through Total Reform of the Financing System

A more comprehensive reform strategy would establish a universal national health insurance program, an approach that long has had a core of political support in the U.S., but that has been defeated when periodically proposed. National health insurance (NHI) proposals typically would replace the payment of premiums by employers and individuals to myriad private insurance plans with a government-run health care financing program supported by tax revenues (Brown, 1988). These NHI proposals would provide a comprehensive package of benefits covering essentially the entire population in one financing program that would pay for care obtained from independent practitioners and facilities or organized health plans. Canada has served as a model for several NHI proposals[3] (Himmelstein and Woolhandler, 1989).

A much more limited proposal would reform both the supply and the demand for private health insurance. A market reform, it would impose, instead of a government-run national health insurance program, a combination of play-or-pay employer mandates with heavy government subsidies and stricter regulation of the insurance industry (Enthoven and Kronick, 1989). There are state variations, introduced into many state legislatures, of these basic national NHI and market-reform approaches.

The complete NHI approach has several advantages. First, NHI proposals would permit effective control of health care costs and spending. They would channel most health care dollars through a government financing program with negotiated fee schedules for doctors and some form of budgeted payment of hospitals. These are methods that have been used effectively by other industrial democracies to control their health care expenditures.

Second, tax financing would shift the burden of paying for health care from a very regressive system of premiums, which are essentially a flat amount irrespective of income or earnings, to a system that is more progressive, related to ability to pay. Third, employers' and employees' liabilities for health care expenditures would be limited and their total health benefits costs greatly reduced to a specified tax. Employers' administrative costs related to their present role of health insurance brokers would be completely eliminated.

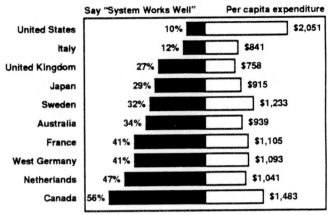

FIGURE 8. PUBLIC VIEWS & HEALTH SPENDING IN TEN COUNTRIES

Harris Poll & OECD Data
Health Affairs, *1990*

Fourth, health insurance coverage would no longer depend on or be tied to employment. People would be covered because they are residents of the country, and their coverage would not terminate or change due to changes in their employment status or marital status. Fifth, cost shifting between payers would end because providers would receive adequate payments for each person they serve.

Finally, a tax-funded government financing program would be more accountable than the present financing system that relies on many privately run insurance corporations. Employer mandates and insurance market reforms leave people vulnerable to the "accountability" of the marketplace, a particularly weak position given the regressiveness of the financing system and the limited choice of plans made available to most employees by their employers. A public financing program could actually expand market accountability by providing a virtually unlimited choice of providers, like the Canadian system, or by giving each person a very wide choice of health plans.[4] Of course, any large organization or program, whether a government agency or a private corporation, has a tendency toward bureaucratization and unresponsiveness. But government financing and operating control are subject to the accountability of the democratic political process, while oligopolistic insurance companies are not. A public financing program with expanded market choice and political accountability is thus far more likely than the private marketplace to serve society's needs, as well as the interests of private providers and health plans.

The market-oriented approach would be a halfway reform, greatly ameliorating access and cost conditions caused by the present chaotic collection of very regressively financed health plans and programs. Even the authors of this proposal, however, acknowledge that an employment-based financing program is far from ideal. (Enthoven and Kronick, 1989) The administrative costs of this system would be substantial, and the control over health care costs would be much weaker than in a full NHI program.

PUBLIC SUPPORT FOR NATIONAL HEALTH INSURANCE IS GROWING

There is clear and consistent evidence of strong public support for national health insurance.

Satisfaction with the existing health care system is lower, and support for dramatic restructuring is greater, in the United States than in most other industrialized countries. Of ten industrialized democracies surveyed in a recent study, fewer Americans were satisfied with their system, despite the fact that the U.S. spends more money per capita on health care than the citizens of any other country (Blendon, et al., 1990).

Public opinion polls have found support for national health insurance among about two-thirds of Americans (Parachini, 1987 and 1988; Pokorny, 1988; Blendon and Taylor, 1989). In the multicountry survey noted above, 89 percent of the U.S. respondents believed that fundamental changes are needed in the nation's health care system (compared to 69 percent of Britons and 43 percent of Canadians), including 29 percent of Americans who believed that the system was so bad that it needs to be completely rebuilt (compared to 17 percent of Britons and only 5 percent of Canadians). A majority of Americans (61 percent) said they would prefer a Canadian-style national health insurance system supported by taxes with the government setting doctors' and hospitals' fees and paying most of the bills.

The public is growing impatient with elected officials for not taking firm action to extend coverage to the uninsured and to control health care costs (Roan, 1990). At the same time, there is great concern that new coverage would increase fiscal demands on already strained government tax revenues or would add costs to private businesses and fuel inflation in health care prices and total expenditures. This apparent political dilemma can be solved by legislation that addresses both problems together in a comprehensive way. Providing coverage to the entire population and controlling health care spending can best be accomplished together, rather than separately. National health insurance is rapidly gaining political support as the most rational, perhaps the only rational, solution to our health care financing problems.

ENDNOTES

[1] The figures on the uninsured are based on data from the U.S. Census Bureau's March Current Population Surveys and analyses by E.R. Brown, R.B. Valdez, H. Morgenstern, P. Nourjah, and C. Hafner in a study undertaken for the California Legislature and funded by the California Policy Seminar.

[2] Under "experience rating," the insurer bases the premium in part on the costs of health benefits used by that covered group. This is distinguished from "community rating," in "risk group," rather than considering the experience of particular subgroups

[3] A joint federal-state NHI proposal is being introduced as a bill by Senator Robert Kerrey (D-Neb.).

[4] This is the strategy of the bill being introduced by Senator Robert Kerrey and incorporated into a legislative proposal of Health Access, a large California coalition.

REFERENCES

Blendon, R.J., and H. Taylor. "Views on Health Care: Public Opinion in Three Nations." *Health Affairs.* 8:149–57, Spring, 1989.

Blendon, R.J., et al. "Satisfaction with Health Systems in Ten Nations." *Health Affairs.* 9:185–92, Summer, 1990.

Braveman, P., et al. "Adverse Outcomes and Lack of Health Insurance Among Newborns in an Eight-County Area of California, 1982 to 1986." *New England Journal of Medicine.* 321:508–13, 1989.

Brown, E.R. "Principles for a National Health Program: A Framework for Analysis and Development." *Milbank Quarterly.* 66(4):573–617, 1988.

Brown, E.R., and G. Dallek. "State Approaches to Financing Health Care for the Poor." *Annual Review of Public Health.* 11:377–400, 1990.

Brown, E.R., R.B. Valdez, H. Morgenstern, T. Bradley, and C. Hafner. *Californians Without Health Insurance: A Report to the California Legislature.* Berkeley, California: California Policy Seminar, University of California, September, 1987.

Congressional Research Service, Library of Congress. *Health Insurance and the Uninsured: Background Data and Analysis.* Washington, D.C.: U.S. Government Printing Office, May, 1988.

Davis, K., and D. Rowland. "Uninsured and Underserved: Inequities in Health Care in the United States." *Milbank Memorial*

Fund Quarterly. 61:149–76, 1983.

DiCarlo, S., and J. Gabel. "Convention Health Insurance: A Decade Later." *Health Care Financing Review.* 10(3):77–89, 1989.

Enthoven, A., and R. Kronick. "A Consumer-Choice Health Plan for the 1990s." *New England Journal of Medicine.* 320:29–37; 94–101, 1989.

Evans, R.G., et al. "Controlling Health Expenditures—The Canadian Reality." *New England Journal of Medicine.* 320:571–77, 1989.

Freeman, H.E. *Americans Report on Their Access to Health Care: The 1986 Robert Wood Johnson Foundation Survey.* Institute for Social Science Research, University of California, Los Angeles, May, 1987.

Freeman, H.E., et al. "Americans Report on Their Access to Health Care." *Health Affairs.* 6:6–18, 1987.

Gabel, J., S. DiCarlo, S. Fink, and G. de Lissovoy. *Employer-Sponsored Health Insurance in America: Preliminary Results from the 1988 Survey.* Washington, D.C.: Health Insurance Association of America, January, 1989.

———. "Health Care Benefits Survey, 1988." *Medical Benefits.* 1–2, February 28, 1989.

Himmelstein, D.U., and S. Woolhandler. "A National Health Program for the United States: A Physicians' Proposal." *New England Journal of Medicine.* 320:102–8, 1989.

Holzman, D. "Rising Cost of Insuring Workers." *Insight.* 5(3):54–5, January, 16, 1989.

Jensen, G.A., M.A. Morrisey, and J.W. Marcus. "Cost Sharing and the Changing Pattern of Employer-sponsored Health Benefits." *Milbank Quarterly.* 65:521–50, 1987.

Lurie, N., N.B. Ward, M.F. Shapiro, and R.H. Brook. "Termination from Medi-Cal: Does It Affect Health?" *New England Journal of Medicine.* 311:480–4, 1984.

Lurie, N., N.B. Ward, M.F. Shapiro, C. Gallego, R. Vaghaiwalla, and R.H. Brook. "Termination of Medi-Cal Benefits: A Follow-up Study One Year Later." *New England Journal of Medicine.* 314:1266–8, 1986.

Parachini, A. "AIDS Is No. 1 Health Issue in State Poll." *Los Angeles Times.* March 29, 1988.

———. "Health Care Debate: Who Will Pay the Way?" *Los Angeles Times.* Aug. 30, 1987.

Pokorny, G. "Report Card on Health Care." *Health Management Quarterly.* 10:3–7, 1988.

Reich, K. "Allstate's Dropping of Small Group Health Coverage Stings Many." *Los Angeles Times.* Part II:1, 4, July 15, 1989.

Roan, S. "Californians Willing to Pay to Overhaul Health System." *Los Angeles Times.* May 3, 1990, A1, A36.

Schieber, G.J., and J.P. Poullier. "International Health Care Expenditure Trends: 1987." *Health Affairs.* 8(3):169–77, 1989.

Service Employees International Union. *The Hidden Story of Taxpayer Subsidies for Low-Wage Employers.* Washington, D.C.: Service Employees International Union, 1988.

Short, P.F. "Trends in Employee Health Insurance Benefits." *Health Affairs.* 7:186–96, 1988.

Short, P.F., A. Monheit, and K. Beauregard. *A Profile of Uninsured Americans.* National Medical Expenditure Survey research findings, Rockville, Maryland, National Center for Health Services Research and Health Care Technology Assessment, September, 1989.

Small Business Administration (SBA). *The State of Small Business: A Report of the President.* Washington, D.C.: U.S. Government Printing Office, 1987, 145–148.

Sofaer, S., T.G. Rundall, and W.L. Zeller. "Restrictive Reimbursement Policies and Uncompensated Care in California Hospitals, 1981 to 1986." Paper presented at American Public Health Association annual meeting, Boston, November 1988.

White, G. "The Uninsured: Health Gamble Affects 1 in 5." *Los Angeles Times.* 29 January, 1990, A1, A16.

Health Care: Lessons From Canada

DAVID D. SCHRECK
Economic Consultant Specializing in Health Care Issues, Vancouver, B.C.;

PAUL PETRIE
Director, Labour Program, Simon Fraser University

Despite proclamations by the American Medical Association, public health insurance has worked and is working in Canada. Canadians have eliminated the inefficiency of the private insurance industry and have replaced it with public health insurance among the best in Western industrialized countries. We have our controversies, and our problems to overcome, but they serve to reinforce the lesson that yesterday's victories cannot be taken for granted. This paper reviews the development of Medicare in Canada, discusses some of the controversies within our system, and makes comparisons relative to the U.S. system of health insurance.

Canadians did not introduce Medicare for the primary purpose of controlling cost. Canadian Medicare came into being in order to provide a basic element of a social safety net, freedom from financial hardship due to illness. It just happened to be a logical consequence that costs were reduced when the benefits of a natural monopoly were exploited. The Canadian story would have worked out much differently if, like the U.S., private health insurance had been allowed to cream the good risks, while public health insurance picked up the "uninsurable" cases.

There are always those who would like to turn back the clock, but few in Canada would publicly propose to reopen the debate on national health insurance. Many Canadians would like to take the next step to reduce the inequality of health status. Equal access to health care is a necessary, but not a sufficient condition for equality of health status. Public health insurance has resolved many of the financial problems associated with disease treatment, but the level of health status is still related to income level, housing, job hazards, and environmental pollution.

PRINCIPLES OF THE CANADIAN SYSTEM

The term "Medicare" is used in both the U.S. and Canada and has different meanings in each country. In Canada, "Medicare" refers to a system of provincially operated insurance covering hospitals and physicians. It is a monopoly. By contrast, in the U.S., the term "Medicare" refers to a federal system of limited coverage for seniors. Together with "Medicaid," a state-operated welfare system, it provides part of an elaborate patchwork system which, combined with private health insurance, still leaves more than thirty million Americans without any form of health insurance.

Canadian Medicare is founded on five basic principles:

Universitality: covers all legal residents after they meet residency requirement (usually three months).

Comprehensiveness: covers all medically required services rendered by or referred by medical practitioners.

Accessibilty: there must be equal access to health services for all who are covered. There are no deductibles.

Portability: coverage includes services while temporarily out of the province.

Public Administration: designed by and responsible to the provincial government.

An unstated, but sixth principle, is **Choice**. In the Canadian system, people are free to choose their own physician and change physicians when they want. U.S. health insurance, public and private, still involves discussion of the insurance principles of co-insurance, deductibles, maximums, exclusions, limitations, and limited choice of practitioner. These concepts are foreign to the Canadian version of Medicare in which virtually all services are covered with 100 percent first dollar payment by each provincial plan.

Canada's constitution puts health in the jurisdiction of the provinces. Medicare originated in the province of Saskatchewan where a provincial hospital program was started in 1947. In 1957, the federal government used its spending authority to encourage a national plan of public hospital insurance. Provinces that introduced hospital insurance based on a set of common principles were offered 50 percent federal cost sharing.

In 1962, under a New Democratic Government, Saskatchewan again showed leadership by introducing public health insurance to cover the services of physicians. Saskatchewan's doctors responded by withdrawing services. The twenty-three-day dispute was concluded in favor of the provincial plan but with an agreement that allowed physicians to extra bill, to charge more than the amount allowed by the provincial plan.

Following a Royal Commission, the federal government responded in 1966 with legislation to provide 50 percent cost sharing to other provinces if they would introduce provincial plans to cover physician services consistent with federally determined principles. In 1971, the system of Canadian Medicare was complete with all ten provinces providing public health insurance covering both hospital and physician services. Most provinces have also added coverage for prescription drugs, and a few have included coverage for chiropractors, naturopaths, ambulance services, and massage therapists.

ISSUES AND CONTROVERSIES

Controversies surrounding Canadian Medicare have focused on:

- federal cost sharing;
- extra billing and user fees;
- waiting lists; and
- health care incomes and fees.

Federal Cost Sharing

No sooner was the basic system of Medicare in Canada complete than alarms were sounded over rising costs. From 1960 to 1971, health care spending rose from 5.5 percent to 7.5 percent of GNP. For the same period, without comprehensive, universal public health insurance, health spending in the U.S. rose from 5.2 percent to 7.6 percent of GNP. Differences in the growth of health spending between the U.S. and Canada were more pronounced after 1971. By 1981, health spending had reached 7.7 percent in Canada but 8.6 percent in the U.S. In 1990, health spending is estimated at under 9 percent of GNP in Canada, but is close to 12 percent in the U.S. National health insurance has saved Canadians billions of dollars.

Canada's federal government has steadily changed the original cost-sharing rules for health care. In 1977, funding was changed from a percentage basis, roughly 50-50, to what was called block funding. It established a base year and provided that federal per capita funding for health would increase from that base at the same rate as a three-year moving average of per capita GNP. Some saw the change as a way to give provinces greater freedom in how to allocate health dollars; others saw it as a way to make provinces responsible for any escalation in health costs. The deal was sweetened to get provincial agreement through the federal offering of two additional pots of money: (1) money for extended care, and (2) a revenue guarantee that the new formula would not yield less money. Successive federal budgets have unilaterally changed the 1977 block funding arrangement. First, the revenue guarantee was removed. Next a cap was put on the indexing of health transfers. In the 1990 federal budget, the cap was changed to GNP growth less 3 percent.

It depends on one's point of view whether the changes in federal cost sharing with the provinces is a matter of public policy for health care or public policy in federal/provincial fiscal arrangements. Perhaps the two cannot be separated, but it is useful to remember that Saskatchewan started with both public hospital insurance and public medical insurance without any offer of federal cost sharing.

Within two years of the implementation of block funding, there were complaints that provinces were diverting health care dollars to highways and turning a blind eye to extra billing by doctors. Thanks to the Canadian Labour Congress, national attention was focused on these problems. In 1979, the Canadian Labour Congress organized a conference titled "SOS Medicare." The conference led to the formation of the Canadian Health Coalition and various provincial health coalitions. Lobbying efforts helped contribute to the passage in 1984 of the Canada Health Act, which provided financial penalties against any province that tolerated extra billing or user fees.

By 1987, all provinces negotiated or legislated an end to extra billing and British Columbia eliminated its $8.50 per day hospital user fee. The reaction against these threats to accessibility occurred long before extra billing or user fees were significant financial threats. However, the mere possibility that the principles of Medicare might be eroded was sufficient to rally public opinion and gain all party support for the Canada Health Act. Not surprisingly, medical associations opposed the act, but all political parties voted for it.

Trial balloons are still floated about the introduction of user fees. In British Columbia, the finance minister muses aloud about the need to escape federal standards, and in Alberta, a report to the premier has suggested a form of limited coverage. Everyone understands that it is political suicide to attack the principles of Medicare.

Waiting Lists

But there are problems within the Canadian system. Waiting lists for treatment are often raised by critics. The referral of heart patients to the United States has no doubt served as a powerful propaganda tool in the hands of those who would question the accomplishments of Canadian Medicare. We may never fully know why the government of British Columbia entered into agreements with some Washington state hospitals for the treatment of up to 700 heart patients from B.C. There are several possible explanations. The B.C. government lays the blame on a shortage of nurses and perfusionists who assist with surgery. Some health economists lay the blame on a few queue jumpers who would suffer no ill effect if they were to wait their turn. The provincial Auditor General's report indicates a possible reason in its reference to limiting heart surgeries as a method of cost control. Whatever the real reason, it is clear that the political pressure was too much to bear. When the government of British Columbia was perceived as restricting access to heart surgery, it found a convenient immediate escape valve in the form of funding referrals to U.S. hospitals. It did not attack doctors and say that the patients were nonemergent and could wait. It did not go the route of the U.K. and say that private health insurance could fund those who wanted quicker treatment. It responded to political pressure by providing coverage through alternate services.

Canadian politicians may attempt to divert priorities from excellence in health care delivery, but so far the public has always supported health care as a right. It is politically unacceptable for waiting lists to become so long that patients seek alternative sources of care outside the medical insurance system.

Health Care Incomes and Fees

It is relatively rare that patients complain of problems of access in the Canadian health care system, although there are certainly some well publicized instances. Where there are delays in surgery, they are often due to shortages of skilled staff. We have a major nursing shortage in Canada. Unfortunately, our Medicare system is more responsive to the funding demands of doctors and hospital administrators and not nearly responsive enough to the legitimate demands for improved wages and working conditions of health workers.

While health worker demands interact with issues concerning quality of care, they are frequently not recognized in their own right. Many health care occupations are underpaid, in predominantly female job ghettos. Improving conditions for these workers has more to do with issues of pay equity than it does with issues of health care. Concerns over health costs should not be used as an excuse for frustrating efforts to achieve pay equity.

Canadian hospitals are union hospitals. Nurses, technicians, housekeepers, and other hospital workers are all members of their respective health sector unions. The American Medical Association would have you believe that Canadians have socialized medicine. That is simply not true. Ninety-five percent of doctors in Canada work for themselves, not for the state. And 90 percent of our hospitals are private, nonprofit corporations. Each province negotiates a fee schedule with its respective medical association. With the end of extra billing in 1987, no physician bills any fee that is different than that provided for in the negotiated fee schedule. It is important to appreciate that Canadians have the right to choose our own doctors and hospitals.

Physicians took job action in Saskatchewan and Quebec in their initial opposition to Medicare, and they recently took job action in Ontario in their fight to keep the privilege to extra bill. However, doctors have not taken job action over their contract negotiations. Fee disputes are more likely to involve battles for public opinion with physicians pointing to an erosion of quality health care if they don't get more money. That battle for public opinion, part of negotiations, can be misinterpreted by outside observers as indicating basic problems with the system rather than internal struggles. The low number of emigrating physicians and complaints from some health economists and politicians that Canada has too many physicians suggest that the doctors have been reasonably satisfied with the Canadian system.

Few objective measures exist for determining the quality of health care in Canada. Crude measures such as age-specific life expectancies show that Canada performs slightly better than the U.S. If any evidence existed to objectively show a lower standard of health or health care in Canada, we would expect opponents of public health insurance in the U.S. to trumpet the evidence.

CONCLUSIONS

Medicare is credited with controlling health care expenditures when compared to the U.S. On the basis of an OECD survey, Canadians spent $1,580 (U.S. dollars) per person for health care in 1988, while Americans spent $2,268 per person, about 44 percent more.

One of the more obvious reasons for the difference in health care costs between the U.S. and Canada is the high cost of administering private insurance in America. Administrative costs of U.S. private insurance represents 10 percent of all health care expenditures. In Canada, public insurance administrative costs are only 2.5 percent of health care expenditures. Research indicates that if the United States were to adopt a Canadian-style system, they could save more than 8 percent of their total health care spending through public administration.

A ten-nation survey conducted by Lou Harris in 1988–1990 of Western industrial nations found that Canadians had the highest level of satisfaction in our health care system, while the U.S. had the lowest.

The most important lesson to learn from the Canadian experience is that health insurance is better run as a public monopoly.

Canadian unions representing health care workers and Canadian community groups have expressed strong concerns that the U.S.-Canada free trade agreement will have a negative impact on the Canadian health care system. The agreement gives American for-profit companies the right to manage Canadian health care facilities and the right to be treated as if they were Canadian (national treatment). Management of hospitals, clinics, rehabilitation services, nursing homes, and laboratories, along with other health and social services, are included in the agreement. Our quality of care may be adversely affected because such American management practices bring with them a different set of values that are not consistent with Canadian values and practices such as universality.

It is tempting to suggest that U.S. labor mount a concerted campaign to "harmonize up" to the Canadian standard of universal health care; or perhaps it would be more accurate to suggest that the U.S. "harmonize down" to the lower costs of the Canadian health care system.

At the beginning of this paper, we said that many Canadians would like to take the next step to reduce inequalities in health status. It is regrettable that in all systems, poor people die sooner. At least in the Canadian system, people aren't made poor by the cost of medical care.

The Role of the States in Health Care Reform

JOHN A. KITZHABER, M.D.

President, Oregon State Senate

Although the U.S. and Canadian health care systems evolved in significantly different ways, both face some common problems in the years ahead. It is possible, I believe, for us to learn from one another and to develop a joint strategy to guide us into the twenty-first century.

In this paper I will discuss the health care crisis from the standpoint of the states, identify the problems common to the U.S. and Canada, and demonstrate that action by individual states offers the best hope toward a solution—at least in this country.

Let me begin by saying that the crisis in U.S. health care is real. It is a crisis in both the cost and the availability of health care and is the result of a system that evolved in the absence of any clear and comprehensive national policy. Ironically, the Canadian system, which did evolve along clear policy lines, and which has been suggested as an alternative to the U.S. system, is suffering from some of the same problems: the reality of fiscal limits, the implicit assumption that health care is synonymous with health, and the belief that all medical services are of equal value and efficacy.

Given that the U.S. and Canada face a common crisis with common root causes, let us look more closely at the problem as it manifests itself in this country. If one were to stand back and look at the U.S. health care system as it is today—and then to outline the policy it represents—one would be shocked to discover the following: a system insensitive to both need and ability to pay; a system in which the poor have no entitlement to care, yet which offers subsidized care to all those over sixty-five regardless of their wealth; a system that considers neither the effectiveness nor the appropriateness of care and assumes that all services are of equal value; a system which systematically excludes from coverage over 20 percent of the population; which specifically excludes poor men and poor women without children; and which makes arbitrary distinctions between sick children merely on the basis of their age. If someone set out to design the worst system possible they could hardly have met with greater success.

As costs continue to escalate, more and more people are squeezed out of the system—ineligible for any public program, not offered workplace-based coverage, and yet unable to afford the price of a private policy. They are losing access to health care either because a provider refuses to see them (due to reimbursement or liability concerns) or because they delay or avoid seeking treatment out of concern over how they will pay for it.

This situation has resulted in a number of very serious consequences from the standpoint of health—both in the traditional sense of the word and in terms of the social and economic health of the nation. Not only is the physical health of the nation suffering, but we also are crippling our ability to increase domestic productivity relative to our major competitors who invest far more than we do in education and in civilian research and development, while investing far less in health care—yet maintain significantly better national health statistics. It should be obvious that health is one of the critical factors needed to increase productivity, yet we are denying health care and health to a large percentage of our current and future work force, because most of those with restricted access today are workers and their dependents. What they are losing access to is not, by and large, transplants, MRIs, and other technological wonders,

John Kitzhaber is an emergency room physician in Roseburg, Oregon.

but rather the management of hypertension, respiratory infections, diabetes, and minor trauma. These are conditions that are both easy and inexpensive to treat if attended to promptly. Treating such conditions effectively can keep people healthy and productive members of the work force, but the current system ignores this reality.

The growing cost of health care is also restricting our ability to make investments in civilian research and development, education, and the infrastructure that underpins our economy. Without significantly increasing our national productivity, we will be unable to provide adequate support for essential social institutions and services, or to provide for the needs of the rapidly growing retired population.

To compound the problem, enormous costs are being shifted to American businesses, which are no longer competing just among themselves, as the auto industry once did, but rather are competing with a host of other countries including Japan, West Germany and, indeed, Canada. The result is that many American goods and services are fast becoming noncompetitive on the world market. American automakers, for example, must sell their cars at prices that include five times more health care than do their major competitors who are able to keep their workers healthier at a fraction of what we spend. And as the cost shift intensifies, pressure increases for workers to shoulder more of the costs or give up wages to balance benefits. This situation is going to grow worse with each passing year.

THREE REALITIES

To arrive at a solution to this problem—both in the United States and, I believe, in Canada—we must recognize and be guided by three fundamental realities: (1) the reality of fiscal limits; (2) the reality that health care is not necessarily synonymous with health; and (3) the reality that all medical services are not of equal value and efficacy.

The Reality of Fiscal Limits

While definitive systemwide federal action is ultimately required, it is clear that the states are in a far better position than is the federal government to initiate the process necessary to develop a solution. In the first place, the federal government, for a variety of reasons, is increasingly impotent to respond effectively to this crisis. Although it is beyond the scope of this paper to discuss the structural and political factors responsible for this paralysis, it is fair to say that the growing budget deficit is a central component.

Beyond the inability of the federal government to act, however, the states are in a better position to recognize and to act on the three realities necessary to craft a solution. While legislators at all levels are acutely aware that there is a limit to the amount of taxation the public will tolerate, the reality of fiscal limits is easier to recognize at the state level than at the federal level because states, unlike the federal government, must operate within the constraints of balanced budgets. They do not have the option of pushing things into a deficit, and thus it is very clear that there is a finite budget from which to fund the activities of state government. And while health care is unquestionably a governmental responsibility, it is not the only responsibility. States also need to pay for law enforcement, the correctional system, infrastructure, public schools, higher education, and for an enormous variety of other essential social programs. Health care must compete with all the other legitimate services state government must provide.

Health Care Versus Health

Because of their appreciation of fiscal limits, states are also more aware than is the federal government that health care is not always synonymous with health and that increased spending on health care does not necessarily result in improved health. The classic example of this contrast can be found in federal Medicaid mandates. The federal government, aware of the tremendous problems in the current Medicaid program, has attempted to remedy them primarily by mandating coverage for specific benefits and for specific populations. But merely mandating health services does not in itself necessarily produce any more money and can have a devastating effect on state budgets, in which health care dollars must compete with dollars to fund a variety of other legitimate services. In other words, the United States Congress, itself unwilling to raise taxes or cut entitlements to deal with the deficit, has required the states to come up with substantial amounts of new revenue for Medicaid, either by raising taxes or by cutting other state programs.

Last year, while the federal government spent $152 billion more than it took in, states balanced their budgets by raising taxes, cutting expenditures, or both. This year the deficit is approaching $320 billion, while the states continue to make the difficult choices necessary to keep their budgets in balance. Let's assume, for argument's sake, however, that the states are unable to raise new revenue and do not wish or cannot afford to cut other budgets. The only alternative left is to find the money for the new mandates within the existing health care budget. This can be accomplished in two ways: either by changing Medicaid eligibility standards for those not affected by the mandate, or by cutting provider reimbursement rates.

Cutting eligibility amounts to nothing more than "redefining the poor" for accounting purposes, throwing people off the program in order to balance the budget—complying with the new mandates by reducing the number of people eligible for the services. If the states choose not to change eligibility, the only other option within the health care budget is to cut provider reimbursement rates. This action creates yet another barrier to access: many providers refuse to participate in the Medicaid program, and the objective of the mandates has not been realized.

The actual result of federal mandates, then, is to improve a benefit package for one group of poor Americans at the expense of denying access to another group of poor Americans. The federal government as an institution refuses to recognize that this is happening. States, on the other hand, are acutely aware of this reality.

In addition, federal Medicaid mandates assume that providing health care is the most important way to improve health. Yet even a casual observation of the current health care system reveals that the enormous and increasing expenditure for health care has not in fact made us healthier as a nation. In 1990 the U.S. spent over $650 billion on health care, yet nineteen countries had lower infant mortality rates and twenty-six had better cardiovascular statistics. An American female is seventh worldwide in life expectancy while an American male is tenth. The reality is that these statistics do not reflect so much a problem of access as they do a failure to allocate sufficient resources to a variety of other social conditions which have an important bearing on health.

Women fail to get prenatal care, for example, not just because they lack health insurance coverage, but also because of transportation barriers, communication barriers, and a lack of day care. Infant mortality reflects not just the lack of prenatal care, but also housing problems, environmental problems, teenage pregnancies, and the enormous problem of substance abuse. We cannot improve the health of our nation if, for example, we continue to spend money only on the medical complications of substance abuse, yet ignore the social conditions that lead to addiction in the first place. We cannot achieve the goal of health, in other words, unless we recognize that the condition of health represents more than health care alone.

Federal Medicaid mandates ignore this reality, which is abundantly clear to the states. Since states must balance their budgets, it is easy to grasp the fact that increases in health care spending are often accomplished at the expense of other programs that clearly affect health. For example, whether a public transportation system is adequate to meet the needs of low-income citizens is not a health care issue, but could certainly be a health issue. The best insurance coverage in the world will not help the child who cannot get to the health clinic or to the hospital.

Medical Services Are Not of Equal Value

Finally, Medicaid mandates assume that all medical services and procedures are of equal value and effectiveness by requiring states to provide all "medically necessary" services while failing to provide any way to determine what in fact, is "medically necessary." In fairness, this is a problem not unique to the Medicaid program, but one which permeates not only U.S. medicine but Canadian medicine as well. Dr. Robert Evans (1989), in his article "Controlling Health Care Costs in Canada," which appeared in last year's New England Journal of Medicine, wrote: "What is disturbing is that the aggregate approach to control the use of services, leave unexplored the cost-effectiveness, and even the efficacy, of the actual services provided." One of the fundamental principles of the Canadian system, of course, is "completeness," which is defined as "all medically required services." Yet there is no mechanism to ascertain what, in fact, is "medically required."

If we are willing to recognize fiscal limits and the distinction between health care and health, the next question we must ask, then, is whether all medical services and procedures are of equal value and effectiveness and whether all medical interventions are appropriate. In short, we must begin to evaluate what we are buying for our health care dollars in terms of the health produced from the investment. The classic study by Dr. John Wennberg on variations in hospital use between Boston and New Haven— populations that are similar demographically—illuminates the need for this kind of scrutiny. Wennberg demonstrated that physicians in Boston admitted patients nearly twice as often as did physicians in New Haven—yet health statistics in the two cities are not significantly different. As a result, in 1982 Bostonians spent $300 million more on health care and used 739 more beds than they would have if the hospital use rates of New Haven applied to Boston. Wennberg further demonstrated that bed supply was the major determinant of hospital utilization.

Dr. Wennberg's work, along with a growing body of information concerning medical outcomes, should make us aware of a very important point: that the efforts to resolve the crisis in health care cost and access need not precipitate a major confrontation between labor and management. While labor is legitimately concerned that "cost containment" will result in a reduction in benefits, we have never really considered what a "benefit" is. It is increasingly clear that health care is not necessarily synonymous with health; that the condition of health represents more than health care alone; that many of the elements of a "benefit" are not beneficial at all. If we can develop a solution to our crisis that is predicated on these facts, then it is entirely possible to reduce cost without jeopardizing health.

REFORMS NEEDED

Thus, the issues that must be addressed in crafting a solution to the health care crisis—in Canada or in the U.S.—include: (1) the reality of fiscal limits; (2) the crucial distinction between health and health care; and (3) the fact that all medical interventions are not of equal value and efficacy. To these I would add the need for a major restructuring of the insurance industry. Canada has much to teach us about this last point. I believe that the states can offer some enlightenment on the first three. Because the states are acutely aware of fiscal limits, because they recognize the difference between health and health care, and because they understand the need to develop a health policy as opposed to simply purchasing health care, they are uniquely positioned to serve as a catalyst for resolving this problem.

This is beginning to occur. Both Massachusetts and Oregon have passed legislation aimed at providing universal access to the health care system. Oregon has gone a step further by attempting to develop a health policy that recognizes that the policy objective is not to guarantee access to health care but rather to keep people healthy and that this can only be accomplished if expenditures for health care are responsibly balanced with expenditures in other important areas. In addition, Oregon has developed a public process by which to define the basic level of care that will be universally accessible—a process that reflects a consensus of public values and considers the effectiveness and the appropriateness the medical services provided. Washington state has introduced and debated a bill to establish a single-payer system. Next year Oregon will also consider legislation to restructure the insurance system so that competition will be based on cost as opposed to risk avoidance.

These are all worthwhile initiatives and all of us, both in the United States and Canada, can benefit from them. States should be encouraged to serve as laboratories for both nations. That is not to say that we should abandon efforts to craft a national solution. Ultimately, comprehensive federal action is required. But in the absence of such action, leadership has fallen to the states. In assuming that leadership we cannot allow our thinking to be constrained by the narrow and contradictory parameters of the current federal system. Rather, we must question that system at every turn, force those who refuse to act to justify their inaction, and offer creative alternatives based on clear policy objectives.

Let me conclude with one final thought. As we create a vision for future action, we must recognize that health care itself is not an end, but rather a means to an end. What our people deserve is not just access to health care, but an equal opportunity for health. While a system that guarantees universal access to health care is a part of the solution, we will not achieve our goal until we begin to critically evaluate health care "benefits" from the standpoint of the health produced for the dollars invested. And we will not improve the health of the population until we begin to balance expenditures in health care with expenditures in education, housing, infrastructure and a variety of other areas that also affect health.

The challenge posed by this problem is not a labor issue or a management issue. It is a common issue faced by the citizens of our countries—regardless of their age, income, sex, race or party affiliation. It is a challenge which we must face together because none of us goes into the future alone.

REFERENCES

Evans, Robert G., et al. "Controlling Health Expenditures—The Canadian Reality." *New England Journal of Medicine*. 320(9):571–7, 1989.